914,563
N277
2020

NATIONAL GEOGRAPHIC

JUN 11 2020

T R A V E L E R

ROME

Sari Gilbert & Michael Brouse
photography by Tino Soriano

Bibliothèaue - Library

BEA......FIELD

303 b.....

Beac....

D1279884

National Geographic
Washington, D.C.

CONTENTS

Pages 2–3: The Scalinata della Trinità dei Monti (better known as the Spanish Steps), one of Rome's great set pieces.
Opposite: Salon (with ceiling fresco by Pietro da Cortona, begun 1633), Palazzo Barberini

TRAVELING WITH EYES OPEN

Alert travelers go with a purpose and leave with a benefit. If you travel responsibly, you can help support wildlife conservation, historic preservation, and cultural enrichment in the places you visit. You can enrich your own travel experience as well.

To be a geo-savvy traveler:

- Recognize that your presence has an impact on the places you visit.

- Spend your time and money in ways that sustain local character. (Besides, it's more interesting that way.)

- Value the destination's natural and cultural heritage.

- Respect the local customs and traditions.

- Express appreciation to local people about things you find interesting and unique to the place: its nature, scenery, music or food, historic villages, and buildings.

- Vote with your wallet: Support the people who support the place, patronizing businesses that make an effort to celebrate and protect what's special about the place. Seek out shops, local restaurants, inns, and tour operators who love the place—who love taking care of it and showing it off. Avoid businesses that detract from the character of the place.

- Enrich yourself, taking home more memories and stories to tell, knowing that you have contributed to the preservation and en-hancement of the destination.

That is the type of travel now called geotourism, defined as "tourism that sustains or enhances the geographical character of a place—its environment, culture, aesthetics, heritage, and the well-being of its residents." To learn more, visit National Geographic's Center for Sustainable Destinations at *nationalgeographic.com/maps/geotourism.*

T R A V E L E R

ROME

ABOUT THE AUTHORS & PHOTOGRAPHER

■ **Sari Gilbert** was born in New York City and became interested in things Mediterranean while still attending Hunter High School there. She spent part of her junior year in Italy, at Syracuse University's semester abroad program in Florence. After receiving her B.A. in political science from Syracuse, Gilbert returned to Italy to attend the Johns Hopkins Bologna Center, and subsequently received an M.A. and a Ph.D. in international relations from the School of Advanced International Studies in Washington, D.C. Her doctoral dissertation was on Italian foreign policy. After concluding her studies, Gilbert returned again to Rome, where she lives in the oh-so-"in" Trastevere district. For the past 40 years she has worked as a journalist for U.S. and Italian news organizations.

■ **Michael Brouse** is a native San Franciscan who spent much of his childhood in Hawaii. After graduating from high school in Marin County, Brouse received a B.A. in history from the University of Santa Clara, but only after spending his junior year abroad at the Loyola Rome Center. Brouse returned to the Eternal City in 1972, where he has lived since. His ongoing passion for history and art history found an outlet in popular walking tours he conducts for visitors to the city. A licensed Rome guide, Brouse is fluent in Italian, French, and German and is also an accomplished translator. He has been a history teacher at St. Stephen's School, an American international high school, for many years.

■ Born and raised in Barcelona, Spain, **Tino Soriano** divides his work between photojournalism and travel photography. He has received a First Prize from the World Press Photo Foundation as well as awards from UNESCO, Fujifilm, and FotoPres. In addition to Rome, since 1988 Soriano has photographed in Spain, France, Portugal, Sicily, Scotland, and South Africa on assignments for National Geographic. His work has also appeared in *Geo, Merian, Der Spiegel, Paris Match, La Vanguardia, El Pais,* and other major magazines. Soriano likes to write, and he has published *El Futuro Existe* (a story about children with cancer), *Travel Photography* and *Beats From a Hospital* (both in Spanish), and *Dalí, 1904–2004.*

CHARTING YOUR TRIP

Lucian, the second-century Greek rhetorician, described Rome as "a bit of Paradise." The 15th-century Tuscan scholar Gian Francesco Poggio Bracciolini praised the city as "the most beautiful and magnificent of all those that either have been or shall be."

Opinions such as these still prevail and may have helped convince you to visit what has long been described as the Eternal City. And you can't go wrong. Almost 3,000 years of history, layer upon layer of it, testify not only to the genius, perseverance, and adaptability of the peoples who founded Rome and helped transform it into a major power of the ancient world, but also to that of those who followed.

Getting Around

Like many other great cities, there's no better way to explore Rome than by using your own feet. (A car in central Rome is more of a hindrance than a help.) The city also has three subway lines (A, B, and C), although they service only limited parts of the city. The A line can be useful to reach the Basilica di San Pietro in the Vatican (Ottaviano station), Piazza di Spagna, Piazza Barberini, and the Musei Vaticani (Cipro station). The southern terminus is Anagnina. The B line, which intersects with the A line at Termini station, enables you to visit the Colosseo, the Circo Massimo, the Basilica di San Giovanni in Laterano, and the Basilica di San Paolo fuori le Mura (St. Paul Outside the Walls). The new C line, under construction since 2007 and not yet complete, only operates on the section linking the San Giovanni district to the eastern limits of the capital. The project envisions extending the line as far as the Colosseo by 2022. Also, the integrated network of trams, buses, and urban rail is very convenient and useful.

Ancient Rome: Fortunately for tourists, the visible remains of the Roman Empire are for the most part located in a fairly manageable area in the city center. The first thing you should see is the **Colosseo** (Colosseum), also known in English as the Flavian Amphitheater, after the family of first-century emperors who sponsored its construction. It took ten years to build and could house 50,000 spectators, and it has survived miraculously through the centuries. A block or so away from this impressive structure sprawl the ruins of the **Foro Romano** (Roman Forum), where you can see what's left of the Roman Senate, the most important temples and basilicas of the ancient city, and the imposing arches erected by its emperors. Along one side of the Roman Forum lie the remains of the **Fori**

■ Lancellotti "Discobolus," first century A.D., Palazzo Massimo alle Terme

Imperiali, built by a variety of emperors. The most important of these imperial forums is that of Trajan, positioned at the foot of the Mercati di Traiano (these markets are now a museum dedicated to the forums). On the other side of the Roman Forum looms the imposing **Palatino** (Palatine Hill), where Augustus and other emperors and dignitaries lived. It was here the city's legendary founders, twins Romulus and Remus, are said to have been raised. From here you can see the broad expanse of the **Circo Massimo,** where chariots once raced before massive, cheering crowds.

If you leave Palatine's archaeological trove from the Palatine exit, it is only an easy half-mile (0.8 km) walk to the **Terme di Caracalla** (Baths of Caracalla), which once served as a health club and spa for the citizens of Rome. Other important monuments in this area include the **Case Romane del Celio,** an ancient villa and apartment block under the church of Santi Giovanni e Paolo; and the mysterious **Basilica di San Clemente,** a short walk away where intriguing first- to fourth-century structures co-exist in underground layers.

The Vatican: A bus, taxi, or subway ride from the ancient sites brings you across the Tiber River to the walled **Città del Vaticano** (Vatican City), the smallest city-state in the world. The **Basilica di San Pietro** (St. Peter's Basilica) supposedly stands on the spot where the Apostle Peter was buried after his crucifixion by the Romans. But the basilica you see today was built centuries later, its foundation stone laid in 1506. The church and square, designed by Michelangelo, Bernini, and a host of others, may well be one of the most imposing landmarks in the world as well as an inspiring place of worship. No one, except perhaps die-hard claustrophobes, should come to Rome without going to the top of the magnificent dome.

Info Made Easy

There is a dedicated tourism information phone number, 060608, where English-speaking operators can provide details about museums, monuments, places of worship, libraries, sports facilities, parks, hotels and restaurants, and theater, concert, and dance performances. They can help you buy tickets and give you the best city transportation from one point to another. Visit their website at *www.060608.it.*

There are also Tourist Infopoints located in various parts of the city (open 9:30 a.m. to 7 p.m. unless otherwise indicated):

Fiumicino APT *(Aeroporto Leonardo da Vinci, International Arrivals, Terminal 3, 8 a.m.–8:45 p.m.)*
Stazione Termini *(Via Giovanni Giolitti 34, Inside Building F–Platform 24, 8 a.m.–6:45 p.m.)*
Fori Imperiali *(Via dei Fori Imperiali)*
San Pietro–Info Point ORP *(Largo del Colonnato 1, Piazza San Pietro)*
Navona *(Piazza delle Cinque Lune)*
Castel S. Angelo *(Piazza Pia, by the gardens, Nov.–Mar., 8:30 a.m.–6 p.m.)*
Via Minghetti *(corner Via del Corso)*

But there is much more to the Vatican. A walk around Vatican City's perimeter brings you to the **Musei Vaticani** (Vatican Museums), one of the finest museum complexes anywhere. You don't want to miss the **Cappella Sistina,** built in the late 1400s and once the private chapel of the popes. Here, for centuries, the cardinals of the Roman Catholic Church have met to elect the next pontiff. And here you will find Michelangelo's masterpiece ceiling and his glorious "Last Judgement" on the wall behind the altar.

If You Have More Time

What next after the sites of ancient Rome, St. Peter's, and the Vatican Museums? Only about another thousand years of history. Rome is teeming with medieval, Renaissance, and baroque riches, as well as some new, contemporary sites.

Since time immemorial, the **Campidoglio** on the Capitoline Hill has been the center of the city. All the roads that led to Rome led here. The design for the piazza has been attributed to Michelangelo, who decided to place the second-century equestrian statue of Marcus Aurelius center square (the original is now inside one of the Musei Capitolini museums) and renovate the existing buildings that framed it. The three are Rome's City Hall, in the center, and the two wings of the **Musei Capitolini** on the right and left.

A mile (1.6 km) northwest of the Musei Capitolini, and another must-see, is the elliptically shaped **Piazza Navona.** Originally the site of the first-century emperor Domitian's stadium, the piazza is ringed by Renaissance and baroque buildings built on the ancient structure's foundations. By day, Piazza Navona buzzes with activity: The throngs include street artists, patrons of outdoor cafés, and art students and tourists studying the details of Bernini's beautiful fountain or of Borromini's imposing facade on the church of **Sant'Agnese in Agone.** From here you can easily walk to the **Pantheon,** one of the world's most sublime examples of Roman classical architecture, and to the nearby lovely church of **Santa Maria sopra Minerva.**

Rome's cafés, such as this one on central Via del Tritone, attract locals and visitors alike.

Roma Pass

Visiting Rome has now become easier with the city's Roma Pass, a two- or three-day tourist card offering discounts for museums combined with full free access to the public transportation system. For €28 or €38.50, you get free admission to the first or first two museums or archaeological sites visited, discounts on other participating sites and museums, and a pass for in-city public transportation. Also included is a city map and guidebook detailing the complete list of eligible museums and sites. You can buy the pass at any participating museum or at a tourist information kiosk (see sidebar p. 9). For further information, visit *www.romapass.it*. Important events, news, and suggested itineraries can be found at *www.turismoroma.it*.

And if baroque is what you crave, the **Galleria Borghese** (1.5 miles/2.5 km northeast of Piazza Navona) in the beautiful Villa Borghese park is the place to visit. This former *casino*, or suburban estate, was built to house the family's magnificent sculpture collection and has several magnificent Berninis and Canovas on display. It also boasts masterpieces by the likes of Raphael, Caravaggio, Rubens, Titian, and more. The building alone, with its sumptuous inch-by-inch decor, is well worth the visit. *(While you are advised to buy tickets in advance for many of Rome's museums, it is compulsory for the Galleria Borghese.)*

Not far away is the **Piazza di Spagna,** Rome's dining and shopping center, with the famous **Scalinata,** the steps that are a magnet for visitors from all over.

Roman Neighborhoods: Several *rioni* (neighborhoods) in Rome still maintain their colorful local character and can allow you to savor the city in a less touristy environment. The *rione* **Monti,** region number one in Augustus' first-century A.D. city reorganization, lies northeast of the Colosseum and Piazza Venezia. It includes two of Rome's patriarchal basilicas, **San Giovanni in Laterano** and **Santa Maria Maggiore,** as well as the churches of two sister saints, **Santa Prassede** and **Santa Pudenziana,** in which you will find some of the most beautiful mosaics in the city.

Two thousand years ago, foreigners (including thousands of Jews) settled in **Trastevere,** on the west side of the Tiber to the south of Vatican City. Today's Trasteverini proudly bill themselves as the *veraci* (true) Romans. By day, the neighborhood's warren of picturesque alleys and lanes provide the perfect setting for wandering while making your way to the **Villa Farnesina** (decorated by Raphael and other top Renaissance artists) or churches such as **Santa Cecilia** or **Santa Maria in Trastevere.** The area swarms with restaurants, pubs, and wine bars.

Of late, **Campo de' Fiori** has grown to rival Trastevere as the hot spot for nightlife, at least for the under-25 set. Here, too, there is much to see during the day. **Via Giulia** is perhaps the most beautiful street in town, and the **Palazzo Farnese** (designed by Antonio Sangallo, Michelangelo, and others) is considered to be the epitome of high Renaissance architecture. Both lie between Piazza Navona and the Tiber. ∎

When to Visit

The peak tourist seasons in Rome are May to June and September to October, when temperatures are perfect for sightseeing. Easter is also busy, with pilgrims flocking to the city for Holy Week. Christmas, on the other hand, attracts fewer visitors. January and February are the quietest months for tourists. (See also Travelwise p. 236.)

HISTORY & CULTURE

■ Bronze coins minted during the ancient Roman republican period Opposite: Construction of the Colosseum began under Emperor Vespasian (A.D. 69–79).

ROME TODAY

Known since ancient times as *caput mundi,* the center of the world, Rome was a crossroads of power, wealth, and culture for centuries—far beyond the decline of the Roman Empire. Today the city wields less international influence, but the beauty and fascination of its attractions and allure survive, despite the difficulties of modern life.

You can visit this city countless times, or live here for years, and its magnificent light, its colors (soft reds, ochers, and oranges mixed with the off-white and gray of marble and travertine), its harmonies of marble bridges across a winding river, its tree-shaded Renaissance villas and parks, its skyline of domes and campaniles, will still take your breath away. The Pantheon, the Colosseum, the Campidoglio at sunset, the Roman Forum in the flattening afternoon light—

> **You can visit this city countless times, or live here for years, and its magnificent light, its colors . . . its harmonies . . . its skyline . . . will still take your breath away.**

these are timeless wonders that over past centuries have made this city a destination for anyone who loves history and admires the artistic capacities of man. While the rampant building speculation that took place after World War II has turned the city's outskirts into prosaic concrete canyons, the area within the still resistant Aurelian Walls, particularly the *centro storico* (historic center), has lost little of its magic.

Rome, of course, has always had its critics. Scan the centuries for the reports of travelers, or talk to some of today's inhabitants, and words such as decay, dirt, noise, and traffic jump off the page. Even Poggio Bracciolini, writing in the early 1400s, told in dismay of a city "stripped of beauty, lying prostrate like a giant corpse, decayed and everywhere eaten away." At that time the popes had recently returned to Rome from self-imposed exile in Avignon, France, to find a city that plague and factional strife had reduced to severe filth and disarray. Other low points in Rome's history include the Visigoth invasion in 410; the bloody aftermath of the sack of Rome in 1527 by the French and German troops of the Holy Roman Emperor, Charles V; and, centuries later, the brutal German occupation, which ended with the Allied liberation in 1944.

Italy's capital since 1870, Rome gradually recovered after World War II, thanks largely to the Marshall Plan and to the Italians' natural resilience. The new, democratic party system that was grafted onto the roots of pre-fascist liberalism, grew quickly, if chaotically. And despite all the problems that have ensued—government instability, strikes, terrorism, and corruption—Rome remains the flourishing capital of a major, and wealthy, European power.

Largely a service and administrative center as well as a tourist destination, Rome has elegant stores and boutiques, and busy restaurants and *trattorie*. Its lovely parks provide strollers and families with some 9,800 acres (4,000 ha) of green within the urban fabric. The Parco Regionale dell'Appia Antica, the largest public park in Rome, stands out among the open spaces. It is located in the south of the city and includes a section of the ancient via Appia; it represents the most important remains, for archaeology and landscape, of the vast rural area surrounding the capital. Among the villas most loved by the Romans, we should mention Villa Doria Pamphilj, the seventh-century residence which includes the second-largest park in the city. It is situated to the west of the Gianicolo, close to the Trastevere district. There is an unforgettable walk along the Lungotevere; you can also bike.

An artist shows off his talent in Piazza Navona, one of Rome's most beautiful squares.

Cross the center of the city along the main north-south road–from the Testaccio district as far as Castel Sant'Angelo and beyond–following the meanders in the river. As you go, you can admire the island of Tiberina, on which the Basilica di San Bartolomeo is placed: It was built on the ruins of the temple of Aesculapius.

A City in Transition

Rome today is a city of almost three million people, most of whom have come from the surrounding Lazio region or from southern Italy. Drawn to the capital by the possibility of work and useful political contacts, they have helped the city to expand far beyond its original perimeters. Although it has never been an industrial capital, Rome is the seat of government of the Italian Republic: It has about twenty ministries. The headquarters of many major banks are located here, as are those of airlines, labor unions, and the plethora of Italian political parties. Many young Italians have poured into Rome to attend its three open-admission public universities and some newer private ones. And, of course, Rome is also an important center of Italian high fashion *(alta moda),* not to mention the home of the Vatican and the pope.

> **Rome appears to be on the brink of recapturing the multiethnic and polyglot atmosphere it surely had during the imperial period.**

In March 2013, more than 150,000 people, including dignitaries from around the world, packed St. Peter's Square to hear Pope Francis give his inaugural Mass. In 2017, the annual tourism report for the hotel sector recorded more than 12 million tourists, mostly foreign. The highest number in this group was from the United States, followed by tourists from the United Kingdom, Germany, Japan, France, Russia, China, Canada, and Brazil.

Despite this constant influx, for decades Rome strongly resisted most foreign influences, boasting a society that was almost stiflingly homogeneous: Almost everyone was white and Catholic (at least nominally). As recently as the mid-1970s, you could count the number of foreign restaurants on two hands. Now all this has changed, and Rome appears to be on the brink of recapturing the multiethnic and polyglot atmosphere it surely had during the imperial period, when people from all corners of the Roman Empire came here, albeit–especially in the case of slaves–not always voluntarily.

The arrival of tens of thousands of immigrants from Africa, Asia, and the Middle East has set in motion an ethnic revolution that is bound to have profound social and cultural implications.

La Dolce Vita, Roman Style

Most of the new arrivals have come to Rome for very clear, work-related reasons. They are part of a huge south-north, east-west migration toward Europe that reflects the sharp differences in living standards that afflict our world. In contrast, foreigners who have come to Rome from developed countries such as the United States and the United Kingdom are generally motivated by different considerations. First, they know that this city is an open-air museum where the ruins of the near and more distant past can be found at almost every turn in the road and under nearly every step.

Furthermore, Rome would also appear to have an inside track on sensuality, relaxation, and overall hedonism. And how could it be otherwise in a society that puts beauty and

■ **Newlyweds are feted outside the church of Santi Giovanni e Paolo.**

pleasure first and foremost? Although they frequently lose their tempers in traffic, Romans have turned being laid-back into an art form. More than 2,000 years of history, with all its vagaries, have left the average Roman with one major conviction: Nothing is more important than the here and now. And Romans do their best to live up to that conviction.

How do you know when it's spring in Rome? Because at the first warming of the sun's rays, everyone is outdoors, chatting on street corners, filling sidewalk cafés, or taking prolonged coffee breaks. How do you know when it's summer? Because everyone has left the city for the nearby beaches of Ostia, Fregene, and Fiumicino to soak up the sun, hoping to become even more beautiful in the process. In the other seasons, the climate is mild enough for you to go on a trip out of town to the Castelli Romani, the group of 17 towns in the area of the Colli Albani (Alban Hills), 18.6 miles (30 km) south of Rome. These places are the favorite destination of Romans fleeing from the stress of the metropolis because of their villas with Italian gardens, clean air, and typical Lazio wine and gastronomic products, like Frascati wine and Ariccia Porchetta (porkmeat). The districts of Trastevere, Testaccio, and the area around the Pantheon are the most popular parts in the evening for those forced to remain in the city. ■

HISTORY OF ROME

Rome is one of the few cities in the world to have been continuously inhabited for the past 2,700 years, which is why so few traces of early settlement have been found. Although centuries may have passed, the influence of Rome's ancient heritage remains paramount and holds the key to understanding its later development.

The Founding of Rome

From a literary point of view it sounds great: Aeneas flees Troy by boat, carrying his aged father Anchises on his back and leading his small son Ascanius by the hand. He lands in Italy and founds the city of Lavinium on the coast. When Ascanius grows up, he founds Alba Longa in the Alban Hills, but because of family squabbles over the throne in a succeeding generation, Romulus and Remus (distant relatives of Ascanius') are thrown into the Tiber River and wash up on the slopes of the

■ Eight massive columns are all that remain of the Temple of Saturn in the Roman Forum.

Palatine Hill where they are, in short order, suckled by a she-wolf and rescued by a shepherd. The boys grow up and set about founding their own city. In the process they quarrel; Romulus kills Remus and becomes the first king of Rome.

Unfortunately, very little of this may be true. The Romans, in fact, were just one of the many various peoples to inhabit the central portion of the peninsula in the late Iron Age, sharing the land with Etruscans, Latins, and Samnites. The original population of the area occupied by the future city of Rome was therefore probably composed of an aggregation of local tribes. In this context, the legend of the Sabine women makes perfect sense. The women were probably kidnapped by Romulus' men because of a real shortage of females.

The traces of Rome's early Iron Age dwellings found on the Palatine Hill indicate that whoever settled this area had good instincts. Easy to defend and close to a major river with natural port facilities, the Palatine was, after all, the most strategic location for a primitive settlement. Furthermore, the hill was not too distant from the most fordable spot on the river, where the existence of Tiber Island made crossing considerably easier.

> **The traces of Rome's early Iron Age dwellings found on the Palatine Hill indicate that whoever settled this area had good instincts.**

Royal & Republican Rome

Legend tells us that Romulus was the first of seven kings, the others being Numa Pompilius, Tullus Hostilius, Ancus Marcius, Tarquinius Priscus, Servius Tullius, and Tarquinius Superbus ("the proud"). The existence of the first four cannot be proved, but indications are that the last three did exist. Their Etruscan names testify to possible tribal intermingling. Another clue is that the Etruscans had highly developed engineering skills—and it was precisely then, in the sixth century B.C., that the marshy area between the Palatine and Capitoline Hills, the future Roman Forum, was drained.

After Tarquinius Superbus was deposed in 509 B.C., the monarchy was replaced by a republic with two consuls elected annually by the men of the city. The consuls appointed the members of an advisory council that eventually became known as the Senate. Formally at least, this system lasted until the advent of imperial rule under Octavius, or Augustus, as he preferred to be called after 27 B.C. But over the centuries it evolved and changed. At first, the republican government was dominated by a patrician elite whose influence derived largely from the wealth that allowed them to lead the republic's armies and, later, to dominate the Senate. During the fourth century B.C., after years of conflict and skillful manipulation of public opinion in the Forum's open-air assemblies, the dispossessed finally won the right to equal representation. In fact, say historians, Rome's first expansionist forays may have been designed to acquire territory for the newly enfranchised.

The Roman Empire, Its Rise & Its Decline

Rome had an empire long before it had an emperor. In fact, despite the ongoing conflict between plebeians and patricians (or perhaps because of it!), the Roman Republic gradually gained control of the city's hinterland. According to Roman mythology, the twin deities, Castor and Pollux, lent a hand during the Battle of Lake Regillus in 496 B.C., when the Romans defeated the Latin League. Be that as it may, the victory proved to be the start of an almost unbroken series of military successes, ending with the complete conquest of Latium, the area surrounding Rome. And if the invasion of central Italy by the Gauls in 390 B.C. looked like it was about to become a major setback, it didn't. The young republic was saved when the Veneti attacked the Gauls on their northern flank, forcing them to head back home.

By the middle of the third century B.C., Rome's armies had conquered most of southern Italy. During this period the Romans built the major consular roads, beginning with the Via Appia to the south and the Via Aurelia and Via Flaminia to the north, to facilitate troop movement and trade. Expansion almost to the shores of Sicily brought Rome into open conflict with the North African stronghold Carthage. The three Punic wars, lasting on and off for 118 years (264–146 B.C.), ended with the destruction of what was then Rome's only major rival for power in the western Mediterranean and witnessed the first Roman expansion outside the Italian peninsula. Sardinia, Corsica, and Illyria (today's Dalmatian coast) then fell, soon followed by Macedonia, Greece, and parts of Asia Minor.

When Julius Caesar appeared on the scene in the first century B.C., Rome's attention had for almost a century been focused on political and social problems at home rather than on further expansion. During his reign, however, Caesar did manage to defeat and annex Gaul. The social unrest of the era allowed him increasingly to concentrate power in his own hands, a trend that continued and was further reinforced by Augustus. Under Augustus, who defeated Mark Antony and Cleopatra, Egypt became a Roman province, Spain was completely subjugated, and the empire's borders were extended as far as the Rhine and the Danube. The next hundred years saw more of the same. The Romans conquered Britain and annexed Palestine. Under Trajan (A.D. 98–117), the empire reached its maximum limits, stretching from the British Isles to Asia Minor.

The Empire's Legacy

Despite its unhappy end, the achievements of the Roman Empire cannot be minimized. Military prowess, combined with an ability to incorporate conquered peoples into its social and political system, brought unparalleled success. The proof? Five Latin-based Romance languages (Italian, French, Spanish, Portuguese, and Romanian), the 26-letter Western alphabet, the continued use of Roman numerals, and a Rome-inspired calendar of 12 months and 365 days.

By the late second century A.D., however, barbarian tribes had begun to pose a real threat. Hadrian's decision to build his famous defensive wall in England, completed in A.D. 136, was significant. As Roman competence on the battlefield declined, partly attributable to the empire's overextension, barbarian encroachments increased. In A.D. 330, Constantine inaugurated Constantinople, which soon became the administrative capital of the empire. Almost sixty years after Constantine's death in A.D. 337, the empire was divided in half.

Governed from Constantinople, the Eastern Empire was strong enough to survive for another thousand years. Disaster loomed in the west, however, where repeated barbarian invasions took place. In 410, the Visigoths, led by Alaric, descended on Rome, pillaging for three days and putting an end to the city's reputation of invincibility. In 476, the Germanic warrior Odovacar deposed the last emperor, Romulus Augustulus, then but a teenager. The western Roman Empire had come to an end.

Christianity & the Papacy

The history of Christianity is inextricably intertwined with that of the Roman Empire. Indeed, in the Middle Ages many believed that the Roman Empire had been part of a divine plan to provide a stable geographical area and a fertile terrain for the spread of Christianity. Having achieved its purpose, the pagan Roman Empire could decline and disappear, to be replaced by the new universal, but Christian, empire. Unfortunately, things were not quite so cut-and-dried.

■ An illustration depicts second-century A.D. Roman soldiers leading captives into Rome.

Peter and Paul both died in Rome, probably during Nero's persecutions between A.D. 64 and 67. For centuries, however, Christianity remained only one of many cults exported to Rome from the East. And even after it had become the favored sect of the imperial family under Constantine, there were problems. Much of the Roman elite remained fiercely pagan. It was only in the fifth century that Christianity became strong enough to step, definitively, out of the closet. It was in this period that the first grandiose churches, such as Santa Sabina (see pp. 210–211), were built.

As the papacy began to reign supreme in spiritual matters it also gradually assumed responsibility for the temporal welfare of Rome's population, filling in increasingly for the absentee rulers in Constantinople. In the aftermath of the disastrous sixth-century Gothic wars, Pope St. Gregory the Great (590–604) had to provide food and shelter for a population swollen with impoverished refugees. Newly created *diaconates* supervised the distribution of food, and in the ninth century, Leo IV had defensive structures erected around the Vatican to protect it from marauding Saracens. Greater power meant a larger bureaucracy and, particularly after the reign of Pope Gregory VII (1073–1085), an increased determination to remain independent of any temporal authority, be it king or emperor. This led to the conflict over who had the authority to appoint (or invest) bishops, the so-called Investiture Controversy, between the Holy Roman Emperor Henry IV and Gregory VII, which continued to rankle even after the compromise solution of the Concordat of Worms (1122).

If the 12th and 13th centuries witnessed the papacy's transformation into a first-rate European political power, a gradual decline in status and effective political clout was inevitable. By the beginning of the 1300s, other European nations, as well as the increasingly prosperous Italian city-states, were emerging as independent power brokers. In Rome, rampant factionalism and bitter rivalries among the city's noble families led the popes to move the Holy See to Avignon in France (the so-called Babylonian Captivity), where they were to remain for much of the 14th century. During this period a vast reorganization of church agencies and administration was begun, as were reform measures for the clergy. The close connection to the French court, and the consequent tensions with England and Germany, ended by damaging the papacy's prestige.

Designed by Gian Lorenzo Bernini in the mid-1600s, St. Peter's Square is a baroque masterpiece.

Renaissance

Historians have been discussing the true significance of the Renaissance (literally "rebirth") almost since its inception. What is not questioned, however, is its outcome (the birth of modern Europe) and its place of origin (Italy). The upsurge of renewed interest in the learning and values of classicism was probably inevitable in Italy with its abundance of classical ruins. The result was humanism, a philosophy propounded by secular men of letters as well as church scholars whose primary emphasis was on the intellectual and artistic capacities of man. This period of heightened artistic expression really took off when the prosperous and ambitious princes of the burgeoning Italian city-states, such as the Medici in Florence, summoned to their courts some of the era's most prestigious painters, sculptors, architects, and draftsmen.

The papacy, always resilient, reached new heights in the rarefied atmosphere of the Renaissance, and again in the 1500s, in response to the birth of Protestantism, becoming an incomparable patron of the arts. By the middle of the 15th century, the pontiffs had reasserted their authority over the Eternal City and, applying their vast resources to the city's embellishment, shifted the center of the Renaissance from Florence to Rome.

Starting about 1450, a series of ambitious, wily, and, occasionally, erudite popes dedicated much of their attention to beautifying their city. They brought to Rome Tuscan and Umbrian artists such as Fra Angelico, Pinturicchio, and Michelangelo to decorate Vatican interiors such as Nicholas V's chapel, the Borgia apartments, and, of course, the Sistine Chapel, which for close to 60 years kept many famous artists occupied. In architecture, too, the Renaissance left its mark on Rome and here, as well, the church proved a major patron. An eloquent example, Donato Bramante—considered the creator of High Renaissance architecture—designed the classically inspired Tempietto at San Pietro in Montorio and then, appointed Papal Architect by Julius II (1503–1513), produced the first designs for the new, gigantic St. Peter's.

Counter-Reformation & the Baroque

The religious movement identified as the Counter-Reformation had a profound effect on its capital, Rome, as well as on the psychology of its governing elite. At its inception, it was a reaction to the Protestant Reformation begun by Martin Luther in the early part of the 16th century. The reaction and reforms set off by the challenge of that breakaway movement (see also sidebar this page) stimulated an era of intense religious fervor, bringing to the fore zealot saints such as St. Philip Neri, St. Theresa of Ávila, and St. Ignatius of Loyola. The latter's soldier mentality (he was once quoted as declaring that he had "never left the army") left its mark on the quasi-military structure of his newly created order, the Society of Jesus (the Jesuits), who were often referred to as the "pope's legions."

Il Risorgimento & National Unification

Il Risorgimento (from the Italian verb *risorgere*, to rise again) was the prime force in 19th-century Italy. The ideological and bureaucratic groundwork laid by the French Revolution and the Napoleonic Wars had set in motion a desire for national unification. Three great men were on hand to make it happen: Giuseppe Mazzini,

The Counter-Reformation & the Council of Trent

The Counter-Reformation lasted from the mid-16th to the 17th century and represented a period of serious self-analysis on the part of the Roman Catholic Church. The three-part Council of Trent (1545–1563) established the doctrinal foundations and institutional structures that helped the church survive the Protestant challenge. It also outlined the basic tenets that governed the life of ordinary Catholics until the Second Vatican Council (1962–1965). Primarily conservative in nature, it confirmed that the church alone could interpret Scripture, reformed monastic and religious orders, created a new catechism, and adopted the Tridentine Latin Mass.

The renewed vigor brought to the papacy by the Counter-Reformation and the Council of Trent also gave it a new lease on political life and two more centuries as a truly important player on the European stage. The emergence of a new world of young nation-states changed things, however, gradually pushing a reluctant Holy See to the political sidelines.

a democratic nationalist; Giuseppe Garibaldi, a firebrand general; and Count Camillo Cavour, a Piedmontese aristocrat and skilled politician-diplomat. Their combined efforts resulted in the proclamation of the Kingdom of Italy in March 1861. Only two pieces were missing: Venice (to be conquered from Austria in 1866) and Rome, which, thanks to French acquiescence, was taken from the pope by Italian armies on September 20, 1870.

Papal rule and the overweening influence of the fractious Roman nobility had not done much for the city. At the end of the 18th century, Rome, with a population of under 200,000, was still a backwater provincial capital. But intellectual currents were running swift. Occupation by Napoleon's armies had infected many with the virus of liberalism and republicanism, and in 1848 Pope Pius IX was forced to grant a constitution. This didn't satisfy Mazzini and his supporters, who, in 1849, proclaimed the short-lived Roman Republic. Despite a valiant defense by the "Garibaldini" and others, the French, acting for the pope, retook the city. But time was running out for the papacy.

Before 1859, as Austria's Metternich had put it, Italy was only "a geographical expression." Divided into eight separate states, it was subject to the domination of foreign powers, mainly France, Spain, and Austria, while the popes still controlled a broad swath of central Italy. The desire for unification snowballed, however, particularly after Cavour became prime minister of Piedmont in 1852. Allied with the French, in 1859 the Piedmontese took Lombardy from the Austrians and the next year annexed Umbria and the Marches. In the south, Garibaldi and his Thousand defeated the Bourbon armies, conquering Sicily and then Naples. The remaining Italian states chose union with Piedmont. Rome remained in papal hands, although attempts by Garibaldi to capture the city in 1862 and 1867 were unsuccessful. In 1870, with France weakened by its war with Prussia, Italy had its chance. On September 20, Italian troops opened a breach in the city walls (at Porta Pia) and entered Rome. After a plebiscite, Rome became Italy's capital.

> " At the end of the 18th century, Rome, with a population of under 200,000, was still a backwater provincial capital. "

Fascism, War, & Democracy

Rome's population grew rapidly after 1870. By the onset of World War I it had hit 500,000. Neutral when the war began, Italy joined up in hopes of territorial gains. The war was unpopular, however, and the loss of 600,000 men made it particularly hard to swallow the Triple Entente's refusal to give Italy Dalmatia and Fiume, now part of Croatia, leading nationalists to bemoan a "mutilated victory." Serious postwar economic problems increased the social unrest. Fascist Benito Mussolini's October 1922 march on Rome won him the government, but within two years he had already eliminated democracy, disbanding most of Italy's constitutional system, banning free speech and association, bridling the press, and, in the late 1930s, introducing anti-Semitic laws. Nevertheless, many aspects of the regime were genuinely popular.

At this point, the city had expanded well beyond the old Roman walls built by Emperor Aurelian (by 1930 there were more than one million inhabitants). Given the imperial ambitions of Mussolini, it is not surprising that the fascist regime undertook important archaeological excavations that brought to light or restored many of the monuments of ancient Rome. It was then, too, that a major impetus was given to the transformation of the city into a modern capital. The then avant-garde EUR section was built, as were new, grandiose avenues such as Fori Imperiali and Conciliazione, although these renovations cost the city two important medieval neighborhoods.

Following Italy's censure by the League of Nations for invading Ethiopia, Mussolini moved closer to Hitler. The military alliance with Germany had disastrous economic and military consequences. In July 1943, following the Allied invasion of Sicily, Mussolini was dismissed and arrested and an armistice signed. The Germans immediately occupied Rome and the Italian army disintegrated. Despite the valiant efforts of the Resistance, more active farther north, the Allies were not able to liberate Rome until June 1944. After World War II, which had left the country devastated and Rome demoralized,

■ Benito Mussolini, leader of Italy 1922–1943

the foundations were laid for a democratic system. In 1946 Italians voted to end the monarchy and found a republic. The new 1948 constitution established a multiparty, parliamentary system which has allowed Italy to regain a place of respect within the family of nations.

To the Present

The Marshall Plan provided the catalyst for a postwar economic boom and a remarkable national transformation. The country's emergence into the European mainstream was symbolized by the 1957 Treaty of Rome, laying the foundations of the European Union (EU), of which Italy was a founding member. But Italy's transformation was not without problems. By the 1960s, coalition governments became weaker, and the economy faltered, leading to violent social tensions. Unrest exploded in the *autunno caldo* (literally, "hot fall") of 1969, when worker and student demonstrations swept Rome and the country. And then during the next couple of decades, Italy was ravaged by political terrorism, left-wing and right-wing alike.

No sooner had the terrorist menace abated than a massive corruption scandal wracked the country in the early 1990s, causing the demise of two major political parties, the Socialists and the Christian Democrats. The appearance on the scene at that time of Silvio Berlusconi and the final transformation into a bona fide social democratic party of the once "mainline" communists brought about a bipolar political system. Italian socio-economic policy and political choices have been increasingly formed with reference to agreements with the EU. Although the recent financial crisis and the recession are threatening the prosperity achieved in the last few decades, we are confident that Italy will succeed in overcoming this moment in history in the same inspired way that has marked it, in good and bad times, for most of its history. ■

THE ARTS

The beauty of the Eternal City is not contemporary. The two major influences on Rome's artistic heritage were, without a doubt, the Roman Empire and the papacy, both of which have left their indelible marks on the city.

Architecture & Art

The emperor Augustus reportedly claimed that he had found a city made of brick and left one made of marble. In a sense this is true. Like his adoptive father, Julius Caesar, Augustus learned early on that public works constituted an effective way not just to embellish an imperial city and heighten its prestige, but to gain the good will, or at least the tolerance, of the public. From the Colosseum and the Arch of Titus to the refurbished Temple of Vesta and the Baths of Caracalla, the political significance of monumental architecture was fundamental. We all

■ Raphael's frescoes in the Vatican's Stanza della Segnatura are Renaissance masterpieces.

know that "art is the handmaiden of politics." But perhaps no other country has so benefited from the ambitions and, yes, megalomania of its rulers, be they emperors, popes, or princes. The final result is layer upon layer of artistic and architectural glory. Look around you at the ruins of so many past regimes. The stratification is such that if you observe carefully, you can usually identify the successive layers of Rome's past majesty, often in the very same structure.

Architecture had its first real boom with the advent of imperial Rome. Some emperors built for their own enjoyment alone: Nero and his Domus Aurea come to mind. But in most instances, their major building projects were destined for public use. The architects remain largely unknown, but some of their constructions—the Pantheon, the Colosseum, Trajan's Markets, and the Arches of Titus, Septimius Severus, and Constantine— still stand, mute witnesses of past glories, silent embellishments even today of humankind's all too brief existence.

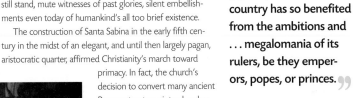

[P]erhaps no other country has so benefited from the ambitions and . . . megalomania of its rulers, be they emperors, popes, or princes.

The construction of Santa Sabina in the early fifth century in the midst of an elegant, and until then largely pagan, aristocratic quarter, affirmed Christianity's march toward primacy. In fact, the church's decision to convert many ancient Roman structures into churches was hardly made on practical grounds alone. The symbolic and psychological significance of certain gestures, for example moving the doors of Julius Caesar's Senate to the Basilica of San Giovanni in Laterano, appears obvious.

Naturally, some Christian buildings were largely idealistic in inspiration. In some of the earliest churches, built near or over the shrines of early martyrs, or like Santa Maria in Cosmedin, on the site of an early *diaconate,* you can almost sense the aura of Christian faith. Later, vigorous building campaigns by the papacy, especially in the 9th and 13th centuries, served a dual purpose. New structures were needed not only to welcome the faithful but also to glorify the mother institution. The building of St. Peter's Basilica in the 16th and 17th centuries may have been the most blatant example of architectural self-glorification.

The papacy also used interior decoration to effectively reaffirm its precepts, and the examples of decorative work with an explicit political quality are numerous. One of the most eloquent examples from the Middle Ages is the series of 13th-century frescoes in the Chapel of St. Sylvester in the church of the Santi Quattro Coronati near the Colosseum. The decision to depict events in the life of the emperor Constantine in such a way as to make him appear subservient to Pope Sylvester is propaganda at its best. How else to explain the final scene, in which Constantine, on foot, humbly holds the reins of the pope's donkey!

Renaissance: Starting in the Renaissance, mosaic work—for centuries the most widely used decorative medium in the classical world—was replaced gradually by sculpture and painting, perfect tools for the expression of political concepts and conceits. For centuries, most statues represented gods and rulers. One thinks, for example, of the equestrian statue of Marcus Aurelius (long believed to be Constantine) or the statue of Augustus from Livia's villa at Prima Porta. In the 13th century, the popes, too, began to commission statues of themselves—as rulers rather than religious leaders—to be displayed in public. So only a few feet away from Arnolfo di Cambio's statue of Charles of Anjou (dressed as a Roman senator) in the Capitoline Museums are Bernini's statue of Pope Urban VIII, a Barberini, and Algardi's statue of Innocent X, a Pamphilj. And you can't miss the political overtones of Raphael's paintings in the so-called Rooms of Raphael in the Vatican Museums. The "Expulsion of Heliodorus," for example, was a clear allusion to Pope Julius II's military campaign to expel usurpers from church lands.

Baroque: Gian Lorenzo Bernini, "sovereign of the arts, to whom popes, princes and peoples reverently bowed" (see the plaque on his house on Via della Mercede), was undoubtedly a genius. The baroque style, of which Bernini is indisputably one of the major creative protagonists, is perhaps the maximum example of art used to convey concepts—primarily faith in the church and in its doctrines—that transcend the purely ornamental. Designed to combat the rapidly spreading Protestant Reformation and, at the same time, to emphasize the importance of Catholicism, the baroque was blatantly propagandistic. All the plastic arts (architecture, painting, sculpture) were used to make an appeal to the faithful that was both sensory and emotional. The magnificence of Rome's baroque churches, such as Il Gesù (the mother Jesuit church) or Santa Maria della Vittoria, intended to underscore the splendor and importance of the papacy, to convince the viewer that the Roman Catholic Church was the only institution qualified to decipher divine will and scripture, a sharp contrast to Martin Luther's reforms, which stressed the necessity for individual interpretation of scripture.

Great Baroque Artists

The three great baroque geniuses—Gian Lorenzo Bernini, Francesco Borromini, and Pietro da Cortona—were contemporaries and spent most of their creative lives in Rome. Utilized in complex compositions, their extravagant styles were characterized by rich colors, gold decoration, unlimited movement, endless depth, diagonal lines, dramatic lighting, and theatricality. Impressive and dramatic, their works stimulated piety and devotion in viewers, and helped underline the importance of the clergy and the church as an institution. The overall effect—marked by dynamism and movement in sharp contrast to the stability and unambiguous definition of Renaissance painting and sculpture—is often overwhelming.

The church also encouraged and utilized musicians. Palestrina, from the nearby town of the same name, was a major innovator of contrapuntal composition. He composed at least 105 Masses while in Rome, many of which he dedicated to Pope Julius III, for a while his patron.

In the 17th century, secular rulers elsewhere adopted the Italian baroque. The situations may have been different, but the message was the same: I am powerful, I am to be admired, feared, and—above all—respected.

■ Designed by Bernini, a baroque master, this elephant statue stands in Piazza della Minerva.

20th Century: In the 20th century, the fascist government continued (albeit less successfully) to use art and architecture to reinforce its own power and prestige. In the 1920s and 1930s, Mussolini's regime fostered a style that used many ancient Roman motifs in modern guise in order to bolster its legitimacy as the true heir to the grandeur of Rome. At its inauguration, the present-day Via dei Fori Imperiali was called the Via dell'Impero (Avenue of the Empire). No doubt a reference to the empire that Italy sought to create with the annexation of territory in North Africa, the name also evokes the "Impero" that, with far greater success, had existed 2,000 years before.

Literature

Although Greek was initially popular, by the first century B.C. Latin had asserted itself as the written language of choice. Plautus, a comic poet, used colloquial Latin for his plays, as did Ennius in his epics and tragedies. By the second half of the first century B.C., there were many Roman writers of distinction, including Julius Caesar, but it was the complex, abstract thought of Cicero—philosopher, orator, and poet—that stood out. Although Virgil, the author of the *Aeneid,* was not a Roman, he became part of an elite circle of poets close to the emperor Augustus. The poet Horace was lauded for the perfection of form of his *Odes* and

Epistles. Ovid wrote witty and elegiac poetry. Whereas Livy and Tacitus excelled in history, Seneca chose tragedy, and Juvenal, satire. The post-Augustan period, while subject to political repression, still produced writers as skillful as Petronius, Statius, Martial, and Suetonius. Later, some scholars again wrote in Greek; the greatest work by a Roman, Marcus Aurelius' *Meditations*, was composed in Greek.

Subsequently, most writing in Latin was done by prelates or people trained in church schools. The 13th century, however, brought the first examples of literature in the vernacular and the emergence of major Italian writers such as Dante, Petrarch, and Boccaccio, none of whom were Roman, although Petrarch was crowned with laurel at the Campidoglio in 1341. Torquato Tasso was also supposed to be made poet laureate of Rome but died shortly after arriving (1595) and is buried in the Church of Sant'Onofrio. Papal rule was probably not conducive to the development of secular literature and poetry. It was not until the 19th century, in fact, that a major Roman poet appeared. Composed for the most part around 1830, Giovanni Gioacchino Belli's 2,000 sonnets in Roman dialect present a vivid and satirical picture of contemporary Rome.

By the late Renaissance, however, Rome had become a magnet for many foreign writers. Well-known early visitors include the French essayist Montaigne and the English poet John Milton. In the 18th and 19th centuries, inspired visitors included the German poet Goethe, the French writer Stendhal, the American writers Nathaniel Hawthorne, Mark Twain, and later Theodore Dreiser, and the English poets Percy Bysshe Shelley, George Gordon Byron, and John Keats as well as Robert and Elizabeth Browning. George Eliot sent her *Middlemarch* protagonist, Dorothea Brooke, on an eye-opening trip to Rome with her parson husband, and much of Henry James's *Daisy Miller* is set here.

In the 20th century, several major writers emerged in Rome. Alberto Moravia, who died in 1990, started out as a journalist and wrote of alienation in modern society. His first novel, *Gli Indifferenti (Time of Indifference),* was published when he was only 21. Other major works, most of which have been translated into English, include *Agostino (Two Adolescents,* 1944*), La Romana (The Woman of Rome,* 1947*), Il Conformista (The Conformist,* 1951*),* and *La Ciociara (Two Women,* 1957*),* which became a prize-winning movie with Sophia Loren. Moravia was married

The Palazzo Braschi now houses the Museo di Roma.

for a while to the writer Elsa Morante, who died in 1985. Her best known work, remark-able for its epic quality, is the 1974 *La Storia,* published in English as *History: A Novel.*

Born in northern Italy in 1922, Pier Paolo Pasolini, a well-known writer, poet, and movie director, came to Rome after World War II and used the material from his contacts among the city's down-and-outs for two novels: *Ragazzi di Vita (The Ragazzi,* 1955) and *Una Vita Violenta (A Violent Life,* 1959). Like his first film, *Accattone,* the novels deal with the lives of thieves, prostitutes, and other denizens of the Roman underworld. Other major postwar writers include Italo Calvino, Primo Levi, and Umberto Eco *(The Name of the Rose, Foucault's Pendulum).* More recently, Susana Tamaro, Alessandro Baricco, and Sicilian detective writer Andrea Camilleri have been translated and pub-lished abroad.

An Open-air Museum & More

Rome has incomparable riches to offer any art lover.

Itself an open-air museum full of temples, palaces, and fountains designed by master sculptors, Rome also has a large number of well-endowed museums. Many of them have been renovated, reorganized, and reopened to become far more user-friendly. A case in point is the Galleria Borghese. Now on everyone's A list (and justly so), it can be considered unique in the world for the number and quality of works by Bernini and Caravaggio, not forgetting those by Raphael, Titian, Lotto, and Bellini. The visit also enables you to discover the beauty of the parco di Villa Borghese.

The Museo Nazionale Romano (National Museum of Rome), originally housed in the Baths of Diocletian, has been drastically reor-ganized; its works, long hidden from view in storerooms and cellars, have been brilliantly distributed among four separate sites. The baths now house the excellently reorganized Epigraphic Museum, while other sections are

> ## A Few Smaller Museums
>
> Rome also has a series of lesser known museums that are also worth a visit. The Museo di Roma, housed in the Palazzo Braschi, has artifacts and art related to Rome's history from the Middle Ages on. Across the street is the Museo Barracco, with its collec-tion of ancient sculpture. A museum in the Rome synagogue tells (in English) the history of the Jews of Rome. The Museo dei Fori Imperiali, in the Mercati di Traiano, covers the Imperial Forums in-depth. And itinerant exhibitions are housed in the Palazzo Ruspoli and the Museo del Corso, on different ends of Via del Corso; in the popular Complesso del Vittoriano, around the back of the Vittoriano, the monument to Vittorio Emanuele II, a king of Italy; in the Mer-cati di Traiano on Via IV Novembre; and in the magnificently restored Scuderie, or stables, across the piazza from the Palazzo del Quirinale.

devoted to pre-Roman history; Palazzo Massimo alle Terme, a former high school right across Piazza della Repubblica, harbors magnificent Greek and Roman statuary, mosaics, and frescoes; treasures such as the Ludovisi throne are on display at a former Renais-sance cardinal's palace, Palazzo Altemps, near Piazza Navona; and the Crypta Balbi, just a short walk from Largo Argentina, presents relics of the city's history from the end of the ancient Roman period through the later Middle Ages up to modern times.

Located in a former power plant in the Ostiense neighborhood, and originally established to host many artworks from the Capitoline Museums (then under restora-tion), the Montemartini has become a permanent structure that displays alternating parts of the Capitoline's overflow collection. The Villa Giulia (the Etruscan Museum) has been refurbished, with its magnificent collection that boasts among its most famous works the Sarcofago degli Sposi (Sarcophagus of the Spouses). The National Gallery in the Palazzo Barberini has finally been able to expand into the space relinquished by the Army Officers' Club: Recently the museum has presented a new layout and it is continuously evolving. There is a lively movement of loans and exchanges of works of art: Currently the Museo Jacquemart-André Museum of Paris is involved.

The cultural ferment of recent times has contributed to the creation of new spaces that welcome the community by involving it in the world of art and by re-creating a contact with society. Among these are the new buildings of the Fondazione Alda Fendi Silos and Rhinoceros: the first at the Foro di Traiano (Trajan's Forum), and the second–which will become the principal one–in the heart of the Foro Boario (Forum Boarium). These spaces give free access and present performances and installations, while also displaying important artworks on loan from the most important museums in the world. In addition, the contemporary art museum MACRO is part of this context with the new social inclusion project MACRO ASILO, which entirely opens its spaces to citizens and visitors. In fact, the new situation in Palazzo Merulana is certainly an interesting encounter between the municipality's need to develop urban spaces and private collectors' passion for works of art.

> **As early as the 1950s, neorealism and post-neorealism had put the Italian film industry on the map, and the names of the best directors and actors were known throughout the intellectual world.**

"Hollywood on the Tiber"

Determined to make Italian film production into a source of national prestige, Mussolini founded the giant studio Cinecittà in 1937. Ironically, his project bore its best fruit only after the fascist regime had been soundly defeated in World War II and superseded by a young democratic republic. As early as the 1950s, neorealism and post-neorealism had put the Italian film industry on the map, and the names of the best directors and actors were known throughout the intellectual world. The success of Cinecittà was brought home to all in 1963 on the set of Cleopatra, which also became the setting for a love story between the film's two principal stars, Elizabeth Taylor and Richard Burton. By the end of the 1960s, "Hollywood on the Tiber" was churning out between 200 and 250 films a year, some of which, over 40 years later, are still considered masterpieces.

The link formed between the city of Rome and Italian cinema has always been extremely strong: just think of directors such as Roberto Rossellini (Roma Città Aperta), Lucchino Visconti (Obsession, Senso, The Earth Trembles), Vittorio De Sica (The Bicycle Thief and Sciuscià), Pietro Germi (Divorce Italian Style, Seduced and Abandoned), Federico Fellini (La Strada, La Dolce Vita, Roma, Amarcord, etc.), Michelangelo Antonioni (L'Avventura, L'Eclisse, Blow-Up), Mario Monicelli (Big Deal on Madonna Street, Il Marchese del Grillo, Il sorpasso), Gillo Pontecorvo (The Battle of Algiers), Pier Paolo Pasolini (Accattone, Mamma Roma, The Hawks and the Sparrows), and Stefano Vanzina (An American in Rome). Not to mention the icons of Italian cinema, such as Marcello Mastroianni, Ugo Tognazzi, and Sophia Loren. Among films of international significance shot recently in Cinecittà are Oceans 12 and Martin Scorsese's 2002 hit, Gangs of New York.

Today, Cinecittà Holding rents out the once bustling studios primarily to RAI (Italian

■ Federico Fellini's critically acclaimed 1960 film, *La Dolce Vita,* turned a spotlight on Rome.

state television) and Mediaset (Silvio Berlusconi's film production company).

Decidedly, American films are today among the most popular in Italy, although Roman intellectuals prefer other genres. In March 1999, the Tuscan comedian Roberto Benigni won three Oscars for *Life Is Beautiful,* about an Italian Jew in a German concentration camp who convinces his young son to believe it is all a game. There are, moreover, other native bright stars: Giuseppe Tornatore *(Cinema Paradiso, The Best Offer, The Correspondence),* Marco Bellocchio *(Vincere, The Traitor),* and iconoclast Nanni Moretti *(Habemus Papam)* are popular with many. And younger directors such as Gabriele Muccino *(The Last Kiss),* Matteo Garrone *(Gomorra, Tale of Tales, Dogman),* Paolo Sorrentino *(Il Divo, This Must Be the Place, The Great Beauty),* Luca Guadagnino *(I Am Love, Call Me by Your Name, Suspiria),* and Cristina Comencini *(The Beast in the Heart)* have won international nominations and prizes.

L'Estate Romana (The Roman Summer)

The concept of *L'Estate Romana* was first set in motion in the mid-1970s, when city culture commissioner Renato Nicolini turned the city into an outdoor festival with a something-for-everyone flavor. Every summer, piazzas are turned into concert halls, basilicas into auditoriums, and riverbanks into bookstalls. Film showings are held at intriguing venues such as the Circus Maximus and Tiber Island, as well as the area facing the Arch of Constantine where, in a groundbreaking September 1981 event, thousands turned up for the screening of Abel Gance's *Napoleon.*

Parks are co-opted, too, with ballet in Villa Ada, concerts in Villa Pamphilj, jazz at Villa Celimontana and in the Testaccio neighborhood, and prose near what remains of Tasso's Oak. Concerts, classical to rock, are also held in different downtown sites, while mimes, poets, Sicilian puppet troupes, majorettes, and other performers fan out through less central neighborhoods. In recent summers, events have attracted as many as five million spectators. There is no doubt that the Roman "Kulturmarket" is alive and well, making sure that tourists and non-vacationers alike have no excuse to be bored (see Travelwise pp. 261–263). ■

FOOD

The ancients may have liked honey-glazed dormouse (a favorite of Trimalchio, Petronius' intemperate gourmet in *Satyricon*), crushed boiled brains, fish sauce made from fermented fish intestines, and roast pig stuffed with live quail, but don't worry. Although food is as important today, some things have changed, and happily dormice and fish sauce are off the menu.

Other things, too, have changed for the better. In fact, if you look through Apicius' *De Re Coquinaria,* the first thing you'll realize is that many of the staple products that we associate with Italian cuisine today were unknown in ancient Rome. Tomatoes, eggplant, and zucchini to name just a few, arrived later from the New World. Instead of durum wheat—not used to make pasta in Naples until the 17th century—the

Rome's bakeries offer a variety of local pastries and desserts in addition to breads.

Romans imported a type of grain called *faro adoreum,* and this was used to make *puls,* a boiled cereal that may have been similar to polenta. The unleavened bread of those days was sometimes cut into strips, but it was far different from ours. What the two eras have in common, however, is gastronomic enthusiasm. Although the crowded sandwich bars and the proliferation of fast-food outlets confirm that the three-hour lunch has more or less disappeared (and multicourse dinners are, also, increasingly infrequent), food is still a top priority. In fact, if there is anything a Roman likes to do more than eat, it is to regale his dinner companions with tales of what he ate yesterday, or on some more remote occasion.

> **[I]f there is anything a Roman likes to do more than eat, it is to regale his dinner companions with tales of what he ate yesterday.**

Rome has never been cited for the delicacy or the refinement of its cuisine, which is instead hearty and robust, a collection of dishes, often washed down with a bottle of Castelli white, that represent real comfort food but which the wise will ingest only infrequently. Among the best vegetable dishes are artichokes, either Roman style *(carciofi alla romana)* or fried, Jewish style *(carciofi alla giudia).* Also typical are *puntarelle in salsa d'alici* (raw chicory with anchovy sauce), *peperoni alla romana* (red and green peppers sautéed with onion), lima beans with pancetta, or wild chicory with oil and lemon.

Another favorite is fried zucchini flowers, often part of a *fritto misto* (mixed fry) of mozzarella, artichokes, olives, and sometimes brains. As far as meat goes, the most characteristic dishes are roast pork *(maialino arrosto),* baby lamb *(abbacchio),* and tripe. In fact, innards are an important part of the city's traditional *cucina povera,* roughly translated as "poor man's cuisine." Once *rigatoni alla pajata* (pasta with lamb's intestine) was popular, and some people still swear by lamb heart *(coratella),* served with artichokes, and *coda alla vaccinara* (oxtail stew).

Pizza & Pasta

No discussion of Italian food is complete without a few paragraphs about pizza and pasta.

In contrast to the Neapolitan pizza, the Roman pizza is very thin and crisp. When it is sliced, it is sold by weight and for this reason there are many heavy toppings, often in innovative and strange combinations. In the restaurant the pizza is usually accompanied or preceded by a dish of fried food, usually *fiori di zucca* (zucchini flowers), *baccalà* (salted cod), *supplì* (rice croquette) filled with meat sauce, vegetables, and olives.

But most of all, like everyone, you will adore pasta, and the only question is, How much of it are you going to eat while you are here? For Romans, *pastaciutta* traditionally was a first course of a longer meal. But things change and if you order just pasta and a salad or antipasto, no one will mind.

Romans love pasta just as much as other Italians do and, indeed, in the city's thousands of restaurants you can certainly find pasta dishes of every type. But Romans do put their own spin on it. They generally don't go in for using butter or cream sauces as in some parts of the Italian north. Nor do they specialize in serving pasta made with vegetables, as in much of the Italian south. Rome's pastas reflect the area's general culinary background of *cucina povera*, in which primary importance is given to simple ingredients within everyone's reach, like oil, garlic, pancetta or *guanciale* (which to use is a long-smoldering dispute), eggs, and one of the Lazio region's best known products, pecorino cheese. So it's important that you know what to order when you go out to eat while you are here. Here are the main "Roman" choices.

> Said to have originated in Amatrice, in the Rieti province of Lazio, bucatini *all'amatriciana,* or *la matriciana* . . . is now considered a typical Roman pasta dish.

1. The very basic *aglio, olio, peperoncino,* which the true Romans refer to as spaghetti *ajo e ojo,* is simply spaghetti that has been seasoned with oil in which garlic and hot red pepper (some add parsley) have been fried.

2. For spaghetti *alla carbonara* (the origins of the name are unclear), the spaghetti is "dressed" with fried guanciale or pancetta and then raw egg yolk mixed with Roman pecorino cheese.

3. Spaghetti *cacio e pepe* has nearly cooked spaghetti tossed in a pan with olive oil and a cream made from pecorino cheese and some of the pasta water. The dish is then amply sprinkled with black pepper and, if one likes, more pecorino.

4. Said to have originated in Amatrice, in the Rieti province of Lazio, bucatini *all'amatriciana,* or *la matriciana* as some call it, is now considered a typical Roman pasta dish. Never mind that there are bitter arguments between those who add onion to the sauce of guanciale, tomato, and red chili pepper and those who shudder at the thought. At the end it is amply dusted with pecorino, or pecorino and parmigiano mixed. It is a real favorite.

5. Spaghetti or pasta *alla gricia* is basically the matriciana without tomato sauce.

6. Penne *all'arrabbiata* is a spicier pasta dish, with the same basic ingredients—tomato, garlic, red chili pepper, parsley, and pecorino. Here, too, some use onion rather than garlic.

7. Fettuccine *alla romana* are fresh noodles served with a tomato sauce with mushrooms and bits of ham.

8. Spaghetti *alla carrettiera* includes lard, tuna, mushrooms, garlic, and tomato sauce.

. . . and, for the truly courageous, there is

9. Rigatoni *alla pajata,* in which the pasta sauce is made from the intestines of a milk-fed or unweaned calf, along with tomato sauce, celery, garlic and onion, pancetta, parsley, white wine, and a touch of vinegar.

Of course, if you are staying in an apartment, you can also make these dishes for yourself. If you want to learn how while you are here, you can even take a one-day cooking class (see sidebar p. 185). ■

The heart of ancient Rome, where splendid ruins testify loudly to when the city was the *caput mundi,* center of the world

ANCIENT ROME

◼ A statue of Romulus and Remus, the mythological founders of Rome

ANCIENT ROME

From the back of the Capitoline Hill, the Foro Romano (Roman Forum) stretches for almost half a mile (0.8 km). Alongside it lie excavated portions of the later imperial *fora*, built to enlarge and beautify an increasingly cramped downtown area. This small valley, tucked among several hills, is the heart of ancient Rome, in effect its birthplace.

The first settlements on Rome's hilltops date to the ninth and eighth centuries B.C. Below them, in a somewhat marshy enclave, lay an open space that was soon used for everything from town meetings to commerce. As the city grew, this space, known as the Forum, gradually transformed into a bona fide civic and religious center, a site for everything from protests and funerals to gladiatorial fights and theatrical presentations.

The Forum's first monuments were erected during the monarchy. The Comitium, the circular open space in front of the Senate building, quickly became institutionalized as a place for discussion and debate. As Rome's wealth and power grew, and as conquering rulers returned victorious from their first encounters with the more advanced Hellenistic world, the Forum was further transformed, and increasingly embellished, to represent the grandeur of what was rapidly becoming a far-flung empire. The importance of the Forum began to decline in the fifth century A.D. Until the excavations of the 1800s, it held little interest for most Romans, who called the area Campo Vaccino, the cow pasture.

From atop the Capitoline Hill, the smallest of the city's seven hills, you can easily identify the Forum's major sites. In the foreground stands the Arco di Settimio Severo and, to the arch's left, Diocletian's massive brick Curia, or Senate building. The large open space in front of the arch is the original Roman Forum, for centuries kept cleared of anything but Rome's three traditional food staples: the olive, the fig, and the grape. Farther to the right are the eight large columns that belonged to the portico of the Tempio di Saturno. The long rectangle beyond is all that remains of the Basilica Giulia courthouse. Winding its way toward the Arco di Tito is the famous Via Sacra, once a major thoroughfare. Opposite you, toward the right, is the Palatino (Palatine Hill), and farther away, to the left, you can just make out the top of the Colosseum.

Atop Capitoline Hill

Crowning the Capitoline Hill, just to your right, you can see the gray blocks of peperino marble that were once part of the Tabularium, the archives of ancient Rome. Nearby, atop a column, is a copy of the Capitoline wolf suckling Romulus and Remus. In front of the Palazzo Senatorio is the Campidoglio, the Renaissance complex designed by Michelangelo to bring renewed glory to a site that for kings, tribunes, tyrants, and emperors was the heart of political and religious Rome. The Musei Capitolini are also here. ∎

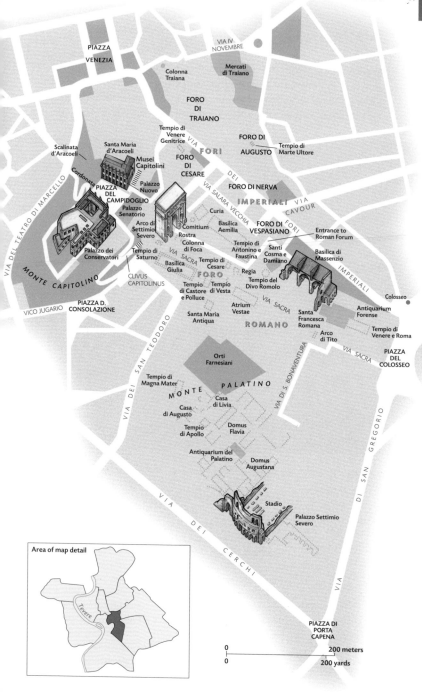

PIAZZA VENEZIA

VIA IV NOVEMBRE

Colonna Traiana

Mercati di Traiano

FORO DI TRAIANO

Tempio di Venere Genitrice

FORO DI AUGUSTO

Tempio di Marte Ultore

Scalinata d'Aracoeli

Santa Maria d'Aracoeli

Musei Capitolini

FORO DI CESARE

FORI

Cordonata

Palazzo Nuovo

VIA DEI

PIAZZA DEL CAMPIDOGLIO

Palazzo Senatorio

FORO DI NERVA

VIA SALARA VECCHIA

IMPERIALI

VIA CAVOUR

Curia

Basilica Aemilia

FORO DI VESPASIANO

Entrance to Roman Forum

Arco di Settimio Severo

Comitium

Rostra

Palazzo dei Conservatori

Tempio di Saturno

Colonna di Foca

Tempio di Antonino e Faustina

Santi Cosma e Damiano

Basilica di Massenzio

VIA DEL TEATRO DI MARCELLO

VIA SACRA

Tempio di Cesare

Basilica Giulia

Regia

MONTE CAPITOLINO

CLIVUS CAPITOLINUS

FORO

Tempio del Divo Romolo

IMPERIALI

Tempio di Castore e Polluce

Tempio di Vesta

Colosseo

VICO JUGARIO

PIAZZA D. CONSOLAZIONE

Santa Maria Antiqua

Atrium Vestae

VIA SACRA

Santa Francesca Romana

Antiquarium Forense

ROMANO

Arco di Tito

Tempio di Venere e Roma

VIA DEI SAN TEODORO

PIAZZA DEL COLOSSEO

Orti Farnesiani

VIA SACRA

VIA DI S. BONAVENTURA

Tempio di Magna Mater

MONTE

PALATINO

Casa di Augusto

Casa di Livia

Tempio di Apollo

Domus Flavia

Antiquarium del Palatino

Domus Augustana

VIA DI SAN GREGORIO

VIA DEI CERCHI

Stadio

Palazzo Settimio Severo

Tevere

VIA

PIAZZA DI PORTA CAPENA

Area of map detail

0   200 meters
0   200 yards

CAMPIDOGLIO

Its architecture and history make the Campidoglio, or Capitolino (Capitoline Hill), an absolute must for every visitor. Come during the day, preferably in the late afternoon, for an astonishing view of the sun-kissed Roman Forum below, and again at night, when marvelous lighting turns the piazza, designed by Michelangelo, and the Roman ruins beneath into pure magic.

A statue of Emperor Marcus Aurelius stands center stage in front of the Palazzo Senatorio.

Piazza del Campidoglio

The best way to reach the Piazza del Campidoglio is from the gradually ascending flight of stairs, called the **Cordonata,** designed by Michelangelo in 1536 and flanked at the bottom by two black, basalt Egyptian lions. At the top of the staircase stand giant, ancient marble statues of Castor and Pollux. Before you lies the piazza, set in a hollow between two hill crests.

Commissioned by Pope Paul III for a visit by the Holy Roman Emperor Charles V, the piazza features statues of Emperor Constantine and his son, Constantius, as well as two milestones from the Via Appia. The modern statue halfway up the hill, to the left of the Cordonata, marks the spot where Cola di Rienzo, the 14th-century tribune who dreamed of restoring the Roman republic, was executed.

The two identical buildings on your left and right are, respectively, the **Palazzo Nuovo** (built from scratch in 1655 to Michelangelo's design) and the older **Palazzo dei Conservatori,** the facade of which was redesigned by the Florentine sculptor and further modified by later Renaissance and baroque architects. Today, the two buildings house different sections of the Musei Capitolini (see p. 43).

The back portion of the Palazzo dei Conservatori (originally called Palazzo Caffarelli) stands on the site of what in ancient times was the **Temple of Jupiter Maximus Capitolinus,** built in the sixth century B.C. and reputed to be the largest of its kind ever constructed. The areas that can be seen from the Tempio di Giove (podium and cell) are located inside and in the gardens of the Palazzo dei Conservatori, which also houses the original bronze equestrian statue of Marcus Aurelius. Recently architectural decorations and other terra-cotta objects from the fourth and third century have been discovered.

Palazzo Senatorio: Facing you from the bottom of the Cordonata is the Palazzo Senatorio. Built in the 13th and 14th centuries on the remains of the Roman Tabularium, it is today the seat of Rome's municipal government.

Michelangelo designed the double ramp of stairs at the front, which is embellished by a fountain sporting two enormous reclining river gods, the Tiber on the right and the Nile on the left. In the niche in between is the "Dea Roma," a red-and-white stone composite of two earlier statues of Minerva, the goddess of wisdom and war. The bell tower, designed by Martino Longhi the Elder, was built between 1578 and 1582. The rest of the facade was added a bit later by architects Giacomo della Porta and Girolamo Rainaldi.

The Palazzo Senatorio rests on the ancient Tabularium and, if you take the road to the left of the building—which leads to a lovely lookout point over the Roman Forum—you will see the blocks of peperino marble from the Tabularium that have been incorporated into the sides of the newer building, as well as the medieval corner towers added later.

INSIDER TIP:

The Campidoglio is one of Rome's original seven hills. Walk to the top at dawn for an unprecedented view of the sunrise over the ancient city.

—MERVYN CHIMES
National Geographic contributor

Statue of Marcus Aurelius:
At this point, you'll probably only have eyes for the equestrian statue of the emperor Marcus Aurelius that stands in the center of the Piazza del Campidoglio. Actually, what you are looking at is a copy (the original, removed in 1981 for restoration, is now in the Palazzo dei Conservatori), but it manages to convey the same sense of history and drama.

The original sculpture is one of the rare surviving equestrian statues from classical Rome,

Campidoglio

 Map p. 39

Bus: C3, H, 40, 44, 60, 63, 81, 83, 87, 130, 160, 170, 190, 628, 715, 716, 780, 781, 810

possibly because for centuries it was believed to be a statue of Constantine, the emperor who converted to Christianity. It was brought to the Campidoglio in 1538 on the recommendation of Michelangelo, who created the pedestal.

The statue shows the bearded emperor with his right hand raised in a gesture of clemency. But don't be fooled! Historians tell us that the horse's raised hoof originally rested on the head of a vanquished barbarian. The bronze statue was once covered in gold, and Romans used to say that if the gilt coating ever reappeared it would signal that the day of judgment had arrived.

Stairs to Santa Maria d'Aracoeli: As you walked up the Cordonata, you will have noticed a second, much steeper flight of stairs on the left,

leading to the church of **Santa Maria in Aracoeli** (pronounced a-ra-CHEY-li; see p. 139), which translates into "St. Mary of the Altar of Heaven." Don't miss the partly concealed remains of a multistory, second-century *insula*, or apartment building, on the far side of this staircase.

Said to have been built in 1348 in gratitude for God's deliverance from the plague, the 124 steps up to the church (not to worry, you can also get in from Piazza del Campidoglio) provide a telling contrast to the Cordonata and reflect the medieval view that to achieve salvation life must be painful and arduous. Michelangelo's design, conceived 200 years later, embodied the concepts of Renaissance humanism; life's final destination is the same—death and salvation—but why not make the intervening voyage more enjoyable? ∎

EXPERIENCE: The Panoramic Views of Rome

Rome has many panoramic vantage points, each one of which is particular and in its own way unforgettable. In these places the Eternal City allows us to see all its beauty and splendor, and the fortunate visitors are entranced.

You can admire it in all all-around view from the Vittoriano, in Piazza Venezia, by taking the elevator Roma dal Cielo, which goes to the top of the white marble building. Or you can lean out from the Terrazza del Gianicolo to enjoy a panoramic view of the city from Trastevere and take part unintendedly in the customs from the Roman tradition. Those who need to communicate with relatives or friends held in Regina

Coeli prison, right at the foot of the hill, come up here and shout. This practice has gone on since the end of the nineteenth century. You might hear long-distance conversations between lovers separated by the misfortunes of life or families who express their closeness to the prisoners.

Another vantage point is on the colle Aventino (Aventine Hill), near the Giardino degli Aranci (Orange Tree Garden), close to the Tiber. Peeping through the keyhole in the gate in the nearby Priorato dei Cavalieri di Malta, you will receive a pleasant surprise: You will see the Basilica di San Pietro framed by the hedges of the villa.

MUSEI CAPITOLINI

Together, the two palazzos on either side of the Piazza del Campidoglio constitute the Musei Capitolini (Capitoline Museums)—the city's sculpture and painting gallery and one of the world's oldest public museums. A passageway linking the two buildings runs under the Palazzo Senatorio and through the ancient Tabularium, affording a splendid view of the Forum.

Start in the delightful courtyard of the **Palazzo dei Conservatori.** The marble body parts on view here come from the colossal statue of Constantine that originally stood in the huge Basilica di Massenzio (or di Costantino) in the Forum. The marble fragments embedded on the upper portion of the opposite wall are also interesting. Look for the word "brit" on one of the larger pieces, a relic of the triumphal arch celebrating the emperor Claudius' military campaigns in Britain. The large marble reliefs below probably come from Hadrian's temple in the Piazza di Pietra (see p. 136).

The first floor of the palazzo contains magnificent statuary, including such celebrated pieces as the "Boy with a Thorn," the Capitoline wolf, and Bernini's statue of Pope Urban VIII. The latter is in the Horatii and Curatii room, which contains frescoes depicting episodes from the days of the earliest Roman kings. You'll also find on this floor the equestrian statue of Marcus Aurelius (see pp. 41–42) and a few other giant bronzes next to the extant remains of Jupiter's temple.

The **Pinacoteca** (Painting Gallery) on the second floor includes works by Titian, Rubens, Guido Reni, Annibale Caracci, Caravaggio, Velázquez, and Dosso Dossi.

■ "Marforio," in the courtyard of Palazzo Nuovo

On the staircase landings you will find reliefs showing Marcus Aurelius making sacrifices to the gods. They may be part of the same series that Constantine "borrowed" to decorate the upper portion of the Arch of Constantine.

Built in 1655, and opened to the public in 1734, the **Palazzo Nuovo** includes much of the city's best-known statuary. "Marforio," one of Rome's famous "talking" statues (see sidebar p. 147), reclines in the courtyard. The **Sala dei Filosofi** (Philosophers' Room) and the **Sala degli Imperatori** (Emperors' Room) contain innumerable Roman busts and heads. Upstairs is the poignant "Dying Gaul," a marble Roman copy of the bronze Hellenistic original and a superb example of classical sculpture. ■

Musei Capitolini

🅰 Map p. 39

✉ Piazza del Campidoglio 1

☎ 060608. For disabled access: 06 6710 2071

🕐 Closed Mon.

💲 $$. Audio guide: $

🚌 Bus: C3, H, 40, 44, 60, 63, 81, 83, 87, 130, 160, 170, 190, 628, 715, 716, 780, 781, 810

www.musei capitolini.org

FORO ROMANO

For almost a thousand years, the Foro Romano (Roman Forum) was the heart of ancient Rome and the nerve center of an empire. Altered and rebuilt over many centuries, its monuments—one superimposed on another—are often confusing. Today, all that remains is a jumble of romantic ruins, although its wistful, gentle beauty and myriad historical echoes still make the Forum the most important archaeological site in Europe.

Foro Romano

- 🅰 Map p. 39
- ✉ Entrances: Largo della Salara Vecchia 5–6 (off Via dei Fori Imperiali); Via di S. Gregorio 30; Via Sacra (near the Arco di Tito)
- ☎ 06 3996 7700. Online tickets: www.coopculture.it
- 💲 $$ (valid 2 days; includes entry to Colosseum & Palatine). Guided tours in English can be booked: $$
- 🚌 Bus: 75, 81, 175, 204, 673. Tram: 3. Metro: Linea B (Colosseo)

colosseo. beniculturali.it

Enter the Forum from Via dei Fori Imperiali, and when you get to the end of the ramp, turn right. To your left lies the Forum proper, a rectangular open space surrounded by a low iron railing. The remains of basilicas flank the Forum's long sides. On its short west side, you will see the high Rostra, which faces the Tempio di Cesare on the east. In front of you stands the Arco di Settimio Severo and, to its right, the surviving columns of the portico of the Tempio di Saturno.

Western Section

Originally built in 179 B.C., the **Basilica Aemilia** once stood to the right of the Forum proper. Like all basilicas—which the Romans used primarily as tribunals or meeting halls, not churches—it had one wide central nave and two narrower side aisles.

At the far end of the basilica you'll find the **Curia** (Senate). Built by Julius Caesar, and reconstructed by Diocletian after a fire in A.D. 283, the building was converted into a church in the seventh century. The original doors are now an entrance to San Giovanni in Laterano.

The Curia's marble pavement is a stunning example of *opus sectile,* a repetitive geometric

pattern of different colors. The wide, marble-faced steps on the right and left sides are the platforms where the senators sat in their portable *curile* chairs, moving to the "aye" or "nay" side as necessity dictated. The two marble reliefs, or *plutei* (note the Roman buildings in the background), probably came from the **Rostra,** or speakers' platform, outside. The holes on the base of the Rostra once held the iron "beaks" of captured warships.

The triple **Arco di Settimio Severo** (Arch of Septimius Severus) was erected in A.D. 203 to mark the tenth anniversary of Septimius' reign and to honor his and his sons' military victories. The "barbarians" carved on the column pedestals appear to support the weight of the entire arch. Nearby, the **Lapis Niger** (literally "black stone") marked the location of an important early grave, possibly that of Romulus himself.

On the other side of the Forum, and just across the Via Sacra, stood the **Basilica Giulia,**

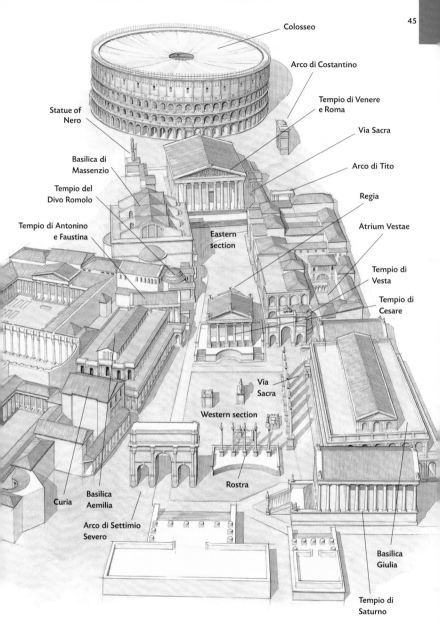

Colosseo

Arco di Costantino

Tempio di Venere e Roma

Statue of Nero

Via Sacra

Basilica di Massenzio

Arco di Tito

Tempio del Divo Romolo

Regia

Tempio di Antonino e Faustina

Atrium Vestae

Eastern section

Tempio di Vesta

Tempio di Cesare

Via Sacra

Western section

Rostra

Curia

Basilica Aemilia

Arco di Settimio Severo

Basilica Giulia

Tempio di Saturno

Foro Romano Reconstruction

another courthouse. On the steps leading up to the ground floor you can still see some stone game boards that may have provided diversion to those waiting patiently outside.

Farther ahead, toward the Capitoline, only eight towering Ionic columns remain of the portico of the **Tempio di Saturno** (Temple of Saturn). Saturnus was originally the god of seed or sowing, and

Built in A.D. 81, the Arco di Tito spans the Via Sacra, the main street of the Forum.

the Saturnalia festival was the Romans' favorite holiday. A mix of Christmas and Mardi Gras, it lasted seven days. The temple also served as the state treasury. The top line of the inscription on the architrave reads "Senatus Populusque Romanus" ("the Senate and People of Rome"). Today you can see the famous acronym, SPQR, mainly on manhole covers and buses.

The **Forum** measures 394 feet by 164 feet (120 m by 50 m). Paved in travertine under Augustus, this area was deliberately left clear and unencumbered to symbolize the openness of democracy. For centuries its only "occupants" were the three Mediterranean plants par excellence, the fig, the olive, and the grape. Only under later emperors were commemorative columns erected.

Julius Caesar rebuilt the Rostra and the Basilica Giulia, and after his death the Romans erected a monument over the site of his funeral pyre, effectively closing off the Forum on the eastern side. From then on, the Forum grew increasingly crowded, with commemorative columns and triumphal arches springing up everywhere. The **Colonna di Foca** (Column of Phocas), put up in 608 to honor the Byzantine emperor of the same name, was the last monument erected here.

Looking eastward toward the Palatine, you will see three lovely Corinthian columns on the right that once belonged to the **Tempio di Castore e Polluce** (Temple of Castor and Pollux), twin brothers and semi-gods. Legend has it that, in the early fifth century B.C., the brothers helped the Romans defeat the Latins in the battle of Lake Regillus.

After his assassination in 44 B.C., Julius Caesar's body lay in state in a gilded shrine on the Rostra. Mark Antony's funeral oration so moved the crowd that the Romans decided to forgo the traditional funeral on the Campus Martius and cremate Julius Caesar in front of the **Regia** instead. Little more than a pile of rubble today, the Regia was the headquarters of the chief priest, or Pontifex Maximus, a title still used by the Roman Catholic Church for the pope.

Although controversial, Caesar's deification soon followed his funeral, initiating a practice adopted by many later emperors, some of whom actually became divine even before death! The **Tempio di Cesare** (Temple of Julius Caesar) was built in 29 B.C. on the spot where he was cremated. Sadly, the remains of the temple are rather insignificant. But stand in front of it for a nice view of the western Forum. Note, too, the imposing size of the **Tabularium,** which forms the base of the Campidoglio's Palazzo Senatorio.

Eastern Section

Return to where you entered the Forum, and walk up the Via Sacra in the direction of the Arch of Titus. On your left stands the

Tempio di Antonino e Faustina (Temple of Antoninus and Faustina). Erected by Emperor Antoninus in A.D. 141 upon the death of his beloved wife, Faustina, the temple was rededicated to both after the emperor died 20 years later. On the entablature above the columns, you can see "Divo Antonino" ("Divine Antoninus"), which was added above the original inscription. The temple was later converted into a church.

On your right, on the other side of the Regia, you'll find the intriguing complex of the Vestal Virgins. Composed of the circular **Tempio di Vesta** (Temple of Vesta, goddess of the sacred fire) and the **Atrium Vestae,** the complex housed the Vestal Virgins (see sidebar below), six priestesses who lived in isolation and safeguarded the sacred fire. The size of this second-century residence gives you an idea of the vital role the Vestal Virgins played in Roman life. In fact, they were probably the most important women after members of the royal family. A cornerstone of Roman life, the cult survived until the end of the fourth century,

Vestal Virgins

Chosen from Rome's grandest patrician families when they were between the ages of six and ten, the Vestal Virgins tended the city's sacred flame for 30 years. Housed in the Tempio di Vesta, the flame burned perpetually, a symbol of Rome's eternal nature.

In return for their services, the Vestals enjoyed high esteem and special rights, among them the power of mercy over condemned criminals, permission to drive in carriages (a right usually granted only to empresses), and the safekeeping of wills, including that of the emperor.

Once the 30 years had expired, those who had successfully performed their duties received a pension and could finally marry. However, any Vestal who lost her virginity before then was buried alive since the Vestals could not be killed. If a virgin allowed the flame to die out, she was whipped by Rome's highest priest and forced to rekindle the fire with sacred pieces of wood.

Santi Cosma e Damiano

⛰ Map p. 39

☎ 06 699 0808

🕐 Closed 1–3 p.m.

Santa Francesca Romana

⛰ Map p. 39

☎ 06 679 5528

🕐 Closed noon–3 p.m.

when Christianity had practically become the state religion.

Located on the left, a short way up the Via Sacra, the small, round **Tempio del Divo Romolo** (Temple of Deified Romulus)—whose original bronze doors still operate perfectly—may have served as a vestibule to Vespasian's Forum of Peace. Today the temple is occupied in part by the church of **Santi Cosma e Damiano** (Sts. Cosmas and Damian), whose entrance lies outside the Forum on Via dei Fori Imperiali.

INSIDER TIP:

The Foro Romano has little shade and no cafés or concession stands, so take a sun hat and something to drink—and avoid the heat of midsummer afternoons.

—TIM JEPSON
National Geographic author

In its apse, the church boasts a magnificent sixth-century mosaic, whose stylized design shows Jesus raising his arm in benediction with saints flanking him. Below, 12 sheep, representing the Apostles, stand between the holy cities of Bethlehem and Jerusalem. One of few surviving mosaics in the late classical Roman style, it was used as a model for later mosaics in many Roman churches.

Continue along the road to the huge **Basilica di Massenzio** (or di Costantino; Basilica of Maxentius, or Constantine). The building

was begun by Maxentius (A.D. 306–312), who was killed by his brother-in-law, Constantine, in the Battle of the Milvian Bridge before he could finish it. The giant statue of Constantine, now on display in pieces in the Palazzo dei Conservatori, once stood here.

Follow the Via Sacra uphill to a wide flight of steps leading to a large open space. The steps are all that remain of the western entrance to the enormous double temple complex designed by the emperor Hadrian in the second century A.D. and rebuilt later, after a fire, by Maxentius. Joined at their apses, the **Tempio di Roma** (Temple of Rome) faced the Forum and the **Tempio di Venere** (Temple of Venus) faced the Colosseum. Built on the site of the Tempio di Roma, **Santa Francesca Romana,** also called Santa Maria Nova, is also accessible from Via dei Fori Imperiali.

Arco di Tito: Farther up the Via Sacra, you'll find yourself at the Arco di Tito (Arch of Titus). Completed in A.D. 81, this triumphal arch commemorated a victory against the Jews and the destruction of the Jerusalem Temple in A.D. 70. The reliefs inside the archway are particularly interesting. The one on the south side, closest to the Palatine, depicts the triumphal procession on its return from the campaign. Jewish slaves, money, and the trumpets and menorah from the Temple are depicted as campaign booty—one reason why, until the foundation of Israel in 1948, no Roman Jew would walk under the arch. ■

PALATINO

One of the loveliest spots in the city, the Palatino (Palatine Hill) was the site of Rome's original Paleolithic settlements and, later, of many of its ancient imperial palaces. Lush and green, often breezy, and featuring a reasonable number of park benches, this hill, one of Rome's seven, is a place tailor-made for dreaming and contemplation.

■ The Palatino was turned into a cardinal's private park during the Renaissance period.

None of the structures erected atop the Palatine are intact today, and the average visitor will find most of the ruins hard to identify. Nevertheless, because of their extent and intricacy (there are massive substructures beneath these buildings, many of which housed workshops, warehouses, and underground passages), the ruins are still imposing. So arm yourself with imagination, and keep in mind that this is where it all started!

This area has always been associated with Rome's founder, Romulus, and his twin, Remus.

Supposedly, the two brothers were brought up somewhere on this hill by Faustulus, the shepherd who had found them after they washed up onto the river bank.

Paradoxically, then, this area was the site of both humble, early Iron Age settlements and—as time went by—a residential neighborhood reserved for the elite. During the late republican period (the second and first centuries B.C.), notables such as Cicero, the politicians Crassus and Catullus, and the orator Hortensius lived here. Once Octavius (later Augustus) chose to forsake his residence near the

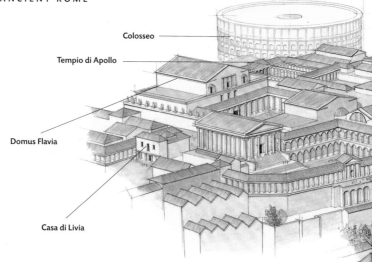

Colosseo

Tempio di Apollo

Domus Flavia

Casa di Livia

Palatino

🅰 Map p. 39

✉ Entrances: Via
di S. Gregorio
30 & Largo della
Salara Vecchia
5–6 (off Via dei
Fori Imperiali)

☎ 06 3996
7700. Online
tickets: www.
coopculture.it

💲 $$ (valid 2 days;
includes entry
to Colosseum &
Roman Forum).
Guided tours in
English can be
booked: $$

🚌 Bus: 75, 81, 175,
204, 673. Tram:
3. Metro: Linea
B (Colosseo)

**colosseo.
beniculturali.it**

Forum for the Palatine house he
had bought (from Hortensius),
it became the "in" place to live,
especially if you were a Roman
emperor. It remained the site of
the imperial residences until Constantine moved to his new capital
in the fourth century in what is
today Turkey. But if Octavius' lifestyle was fairly austere, he found
few imitators among his successors (in particular Nero, Domitian,
and Septimius Severus), whose
unchecked taste for opulence
made the Palatine synonymous
with luxury. No wonder it is the
root of our word "palace."

What Remains Today

Although much of it remains to
be excavated today, the Palatine
can be divided into three sections. The first includes the ruins
from the imperial residences,
particularly that of the emperor
Domitian (A.D. 81–96), which
includes a private area (Domus
Augustana) and a public, or ceremonial, area (Domus Flavia).

From the Arch of Titus, walk
up the hill following the path

(Via di San Bonaventura) to the
left, skirting the ruins of the
Domus Flavia on your right.
Dedicated to official business,
this part of Domitian's palace
includes the audience hall, or
aula regia, a basilica for court
cases that required the emperor's
personal attention, and the enormous *triclinium* for state dining.
This last structure—decorated
in different colored marbles
and flanked by courtyards, each
containing a fountain—must have
been impressive.

Domitian and his architect,
Rabirius, erected the Domus Flavia
over earlier buildings constructed
by the emperors Tiberius and
Nero, among others. Furthermore, despite all the greenery, the
ground level has been artificially
pumped up (some scholars say
by as much as 50 feet/15 m) by
layers and layers of used and dis-
carded building materials. Located
in an ex-convent between the
Domus Flavia and the Domus
Augustana, the **Antiquarium del
Palatino** displays archaeological
finds from the area.

Palatino

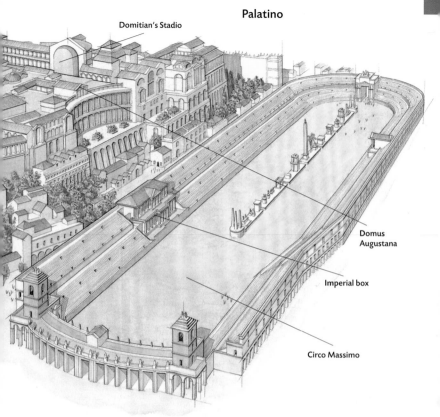

Domitian's Stadio

Domus Augustana

Imperial box

Circo Massimo

Keep walking until you reach **Domitian's Stadio** (or hippodrome), an impressive, large sunken area generally assumed to have been a racecourse or stadium. The ruins directly to the right of the stadium once comprised the **Domus Augustana,** a sprawling complex of archways, sunken rooms, some of which may have been pools or fountains, and courtyards that you can explore, even if they are not easily identifiable. Gradually work your way toward the terrace, where there is a fantastic view of the **Circo Massimo** (see p. 209) below.

At the southwestern end of the hill lie the sites of those Iron Age settlements from the time of Romulus and Remus. There is also a temple to Apollo and another to a goddess known as Magna Mater. There are also two houses from the late republican period, the so-called **Casa di Livia** and **Casa di Augusto.** Visits can be booked at certain times.

The **Orti Farnesiani,** a Renaissance garden once full of rare botanical species, was created in the 16th century. Two pavilions afford a fine view of the Forum below. Steps to the right and the left lead down to another landing with a stupendous, fern-draped nymphaeum, or monument dedicated to the nymphs. ■

THE CONDUCT OF THE ROMAN EMPERORS

The Roman emperors personified the best and the worst of Roman culture. One of the best was Octavius (27 B.C.–A.D. 14), who assumed the title of Augustus in 27 B.C. and is generally considered to be the first true emperor in the Julio-Claudian dynasty started by Julius Caesar. One of the worst was Caligula, also a Julio-Claudian.

Emperor Hadrian inspects a fort along the German frontier in this illustration for *National Geographic* magazine. Hadrian visited nearly all of the Roman Empire's provinces during his reign.

Augustus

Born in 63 B.C. to Julius Caesar's niece, and later adopted by his great-uncle, Octavius was only 19 when Caesar was assassinated in 44 B.C. He joined with Mark Antony to punish the assassins then divided the empire with him. The alliance ended in 31 B.C., when Octavius trounced Antony and the Egyptian queen, Cleopatra, at the naval Battle of Actium (Greece). Although he always made sure to maintain a facade of republicanism, Octavius dedicated the rest of his life to the process, begun by his uncle, of concentrating power in the hands of one person: himself.

Shrewd, astute, and an able administrator, Octavius (soon to become Augustus)

reformed the Roman bureaucracy, overhauled the fiscal system, and reorganized the military. Above all, he extended and secured the empire's borders, giving rise to what was known as the Pax Romana, a 200-year period of stability and security. Under this same stable and secure regime the new Christian religion was born. Furthermore, the solidity of Augustan Rome proved conducive to the new cult's rapid expansion.

Hadrian & Other Virtuous Emperors

Several other emperors left important legacies. Vespasian (A.D. 69–79) restored stability after the Neronian chaos, and Trajan (A.D.

98–117) extended the empire to its greatest limits. His successor, Hadrian (A.D. 117–138), is often referred to as the philosopher-emperor because of his devotion to the arts, literature, and architecture. Hadrian enormously embellished the city of Rome. He built a magnificent mausoleum that today we call Castel Sant'Angelo (see pp. 179–180), the sprawling villa in Tivoli that bears his name (see p. 233), and he rebuilt the Pantheon (see pp. 128–131).

Hadrian also put into effect a policy of containment that had far-reaching impact. Military contingents became fixed rather than mobile. Civilian settlements near military installations thus grew in size, and commerce exploded. Fortification became increasingly important, with defensive architecture reaching new heights with the construction of Hadrian's Wall in Britain. Hadrian traveled widely during his reign, both for pleasure and because of his unusual view of the Roman Empire as a single political entity rather than a series of subject states.

Nero & Other Bloodthirsty Emperors

This category of emperors includes: Caligula, tall, pale, ungainly, with a wide but sinister forehead and clearly mentally unstable, and Caracalla, who had his younger brother, Geta, killed. But it is Nero who most frequently personifies the worst in Roman imperial rule.

Born into the imperial family in A.D. 37, Nero was adopted by Claudius after the emperor had married Nero's mother, Agrippina the Younger (Caligula's sister). He became emperor in A.D. 54. During the first ten years of his reign, Nero had a good record. He promoted legal and bureaucratic reform and demonstrated interest

in the well-being of his population. All of this changed with the raging, nine-day fire of A.D. 64 during which the emperor did not actually fiddle, as the story goes, but did take his time in leaving his villa to come to Rome. Later, he blamed the new Christian religious sect, setting off a series of persecutions during which both Peter and Paul were probably martyred.

Although Nero rebuilt much of the city after the fire, he gave precedence to his own personal interests, expropriating large tracts of terrain to build the vast and sumptuous Domus Aurea. The populace seethed in response and threatened rebellion. In A.D. 68, Nero committed suicide, thus bringing the Julio-Claudian dynasty to a premature and inglorious end.

■ Statue of Emperor Augustus, Palazzo Massimo alle Terme

FORI IMPERIALI

Rome's highest leaders built the Fori Imperiali (Imperial Forums) between the first century B.C. and the start of the second century A.D., in order to glorify themselves and to create additional space for the political, religious, and institutional needs of the expanding Roman Empire. Although they appear to be separate today, the forums of Augustus, Nerva, Vespasian, and Trajan once were an integral part of the Roman Forum.

■ Trajan's Column, built to honor the emperor's military glory, also serves as his memorial. Trajan's remains were placed in the column's hollow base after his death in A.D. 117.

You may find it difficult to comprehend the layout of the five forums because the Via dei Fori Imperiali, built for military parades by the fascist regime in the early 1930s, cuts through them and over much of the area. The long-term plan is to narrow the avenue significantly.

Earlier Imperial Forums

Begun in 54 B.C. by Julius Caesar, the **Foro di Cesare**— the first forum built by an emperor—stands between the Curia, or Senate building, and Via dei Fori Imperiali. Measuring 147 by 406 feet (45 by 124 m), it was surrounded by a double portico, a small portion of which is still visible, as is the base of the Tempio di Venere Genitrice, the goddess from whom the Julio-Claudian dynasty traced its descent.

Augustus, Caesar's political heir, followed suit. The **Foro di Augusto,** near that of his

adoptive father, ends at the high
fire wall he erected to protect the
civic center from the frequent fires
in the densely populated residential Suburra area on the other side.
The forum took 20 years to complete and was dominated by the
Tempio di Marte Ultore, which
the young emperor built after kill-
ing Caesar's assassins at the battle
of Philippi in 42 B.C. Three of its 24
tall Corinthian marble columns are
more or less all that remain, but
try to imagine it as it was. Statuary
dotted the porticoes; floors and
walls were constructed in colored
marbles; there was even a separate
room for a colossus in precious
metal, possibly Caesar or Augustus
himself, presumably some 33 feet
(10 m) tall.

Most of the **Foro di Vespasiano** (built between A.D. 71 and
75 to mark the defeat of the
Jews) lies hidden beneath the
intersection of Via dei Fori Imperiali and Via Cavour. What remains
of the Temple of Peace, as it was
called, is incorporated into the
monastery and church of **Santi
Cosma e Damiano** (see p. 48).

In between Augustus' and
Vespasian's forums is the **Foro di
Nerva,** which actually was built
by Domitian, Nerva's predecessor.
Long and narrow, and flanked by
colonnades, it was often called
the Forum Transitorium, as it
transformed the Argiletum, the
route from the Suburra to the
Roman Forum, into a decorated
passageway. All that remains are
two massive Corinthian columns
in the corner near Via dei Fori
Imperiali and the podium of a
temple dedicated to Minerva.
The entablature between the

columns has a lovely frieze depicting the myth of Arachne and
other scenes linked to the figure
of Minerva, while the relief in the
attic above probably represents
the personification of one of the
Roman provinces.

Foro di Traiano

The major attraction of the
Imperial Forums is the magnifi-
cent forum and markets built by
Trajan and dedicated in A.D. 112.

Colonna Traiana

**The Colonna Traiana
(Trajan's Column) stands
in a small courtyard
beyond the Basilica Ulpia.
Made of 29 cylindrical
blocks, and spiraling up for
about 100 feet (30 m), the
column features magnifi-
cent carved reliefs—2,600
figures in all—that tell the
story of the emperor's
military campaigns against
the Dacians. Forty small
windows light the staircase
inside. In the 16th century,
the statue of St. Peter
replaced the original one
of Trajan.**

This was the last of the forums
to be built and undoubtedly
was the grandest and the
most splendid.

The entrance to Trajan's
Forum is a large, rectangular
courtyard flanked by two porticoes, 367 feet (112 m) in length,
and closed off at the northern
end by the gigantic two-story
Basilica Ulpia. The latter, richly
decorated in sumptuous colors,

Fori Imperiali
- Map p. 39
- Visitor Center, Via dei Fori Imperiali
- 060608
- Only pre-booked visits for groups of at most 30 people
- $
- Bus: 75, 81, 175, 204, 673. Tram: 3. Metro: Linea B (Colosseo)

Palazzo Valentini

- ✉ Via Foro Traiano 85
- ☎ 06 22761280 for bookings
- 🕐 Closed Tues., Dec. 25, Jan. 1, & May 1
- 💲 $$

www.palazzo valentini.it

Mercati di Traiano & Museo dei Fori Imperiali

- 🅰 Map p. 39
- ✉ Via IV Novembre 94
- ☎ 060608
- 💲 $$. Audio guide: $
- 🚌 Bus: H, 40, 60, 64, 70, 117, 170

www.mercatidi traiano.it

marble work, and precious metals, had five aisles separated by columns, with a semicircular apse at each end.

Near the Basilica Ulpia is the **Colonna Traiana** (Trajan's Column; see sidebar p. 55). To better appreciate the column, visit the exhibition of the *domus romanae* (Roman houses) of **Palazzo Valentini.** An underground area just feet from the column's base, it contains the remains of travertine walls and colossal columns of Egyptian granite. Projections and a video show how the area around the column originally looked and provide close-ups of its magnificent bas-reliefs. The main part of the exhibit focuses on the remains of two fourth-century villas where mosaics, wall decorations, polychrome floors, baths, and kitchens are brought back to life by a wonderful sound-and-light show.

Mercati di Traiano: Don't miss the Mercati di Traiano (Trajan's Markets). This three- or four-story semicircular structure was essentially a reconstruction of the neighborhood removed by the forum's construction.

An ancient Roman street runs through it, and wandering from shop to shop (there are about 150) will give you an idea of what life was like in the second century A.D. The alcove-like shops on the ground floor probably sold dry goods, flowers, and vegetables. Those off the gallery were probably storehouses for wine and oil. There were also fishponds as well as special shops for Eastern spices. The world's first mall, with its impressive vaulting, now hosts the **Museo dei Fori Imperiali,** where each room is dedicated to one of the imperial forums. ■

EXPERIENCE: Bike Around Town

When in Rome, why not get around the way the Romans do, on two wheels? Motorbikes abound but, increasingly, Romans who live in the flatter parts of the *centro storico* are discovering that biking is healthy, fun, and a time-efficient means of transportation. They use bikes to go to work, run errands, and even transport their children from place to place.

Visitors unused to the vagaries of Roman drivers should not attempt to ride a bike through Rome's traffic. However, the city has created some bike paths, including a long, picturesque stretch along the lower banks of the Tiber River.

On Sundays you can enjoy all of Via dei Fori Imperiali, which is entirely closed to motorized traffic. If you go past the Foro and the Colosseo, and then the Terme

di Caracalla, you will reach the Via Appia Antica and you will be able to join scores of bikers pedaling past ancient monuments. The initial stretch, outside Porta San Sebastiano, is now a bike-friendly park (*www. parcoappiaantica.it*), offering various guided visits according to the season (*Centro Servizi Appia Antica, Via Appia Antica 58-60, tel 06 513 5316, email: infopointappia@gmail.com, bike rental and guided visits*).

Conveniently located bike-rental shops include: **Bici & Baci** (*Via del Viminale 5, tel 06 482 8443, www.bicibaci.com*), near the Stazione Termini; **Vittoria Rent** (*Via Vittoria 20, tel 338 294 9084, www.vittoria rent.it*), in Piazza di Spagna; and **Ascol Bike** (*Via dell'Uccelliera, tel 339 602 0423*), in the Borghese Gardens. Prices range from €4 an hour to €12 a day.

The massive **Colosseum**, imperial monuments, and the glorious frescoes and mosaics of early Christian churches

COLOSSEO TO SAN CLEMENTE

■ Detail of a ceiling fresco in the church of Santi Giovanni e Paolo

COLOSSEO TO SAN CLEMENTE

Set in a valley between the Palatine, Esquiline, and Caelian Hills, the Colosseo (Colosseum) is the Roman world's largest surviving structure, its majestic impact undimmed either by the passage of time or the blight of encircling traffic. It is also, undoubtedly, the landmark most closely identified with the city itself.

Two thousand years after it was built by the emperor Vespasian, on the site of the artificial lake that Nero had built for his magnificent Domus Aurea, the Colosseum still stands. It looms over one of the most extensive archaeological areas in the world, a reminder of man's achievements and his cruelty. It cannot be forgotten, after all, that while this was a place of celebration it was also a site of unchecked slaughter, both human and animal.

Nearby is the Arco di Costantino, built in A.D. 315 to celebrate Emperor Constantine's victory at Ponte Milvio over his brother-in-law and predecessor, Maxentius. But for all its size (it is the largest surviving triumphal arch) and apparent splendor, the arch is generally considered to be a sign of Rome's incipient decline.

On the other side of the Colosseum are the remains of the first-century Domus Aurea (Golden House), which, with the exception of Diocletian's Palace in Split (Croatia), is the only floor-to-ceiling Roman imperial structure to have survived. Nero's extensive pleasure palace, which reflects the vast wealth and architectural prowess of imperial Rome, was built in the aftermath of the fire of A.D. 64 that totally destroyed 3 of Rome's 14 neighborhoods. Its exact dimensions are as yet unknown. It is possible to visit the Domus Aurea restoration site in virtual reality.

The surrounding area has many important early churches. San Pietro in Vincoli, the location of Michelangelo's imposing "Moses," was originally named the Basilica Eudoxiana, after the empress who built it to hold St. Peter's chains. The multilevel San Clemente, which lies between the Colosseum and San Giovanni in Laterano, was built in the fourth century to commemorate Clement, martyred in the Crimea sometime during the reign of Trajan (A.D. 98–117). In the 11th century, invading Norman armies destroyed the original church, but important treasures from the new church survive, such as the wonderful 12th-century apse mosaic. San Clemente is also a prime example of Rome's architectural stratification, concealing the remains of a fourth-century church as well as older, first-century structures.

Celio

The quiet Celio (Caelian Hill), facing the Palatine on the opposite side of Via di San Gregorio, offers other jewels of both early Christian culture and Renaissance design. St. Gregory (San Gregorio Magno) built his church and monastery here in the sixth century, although the church and the three frescoed chapels near it were rebuilt in the

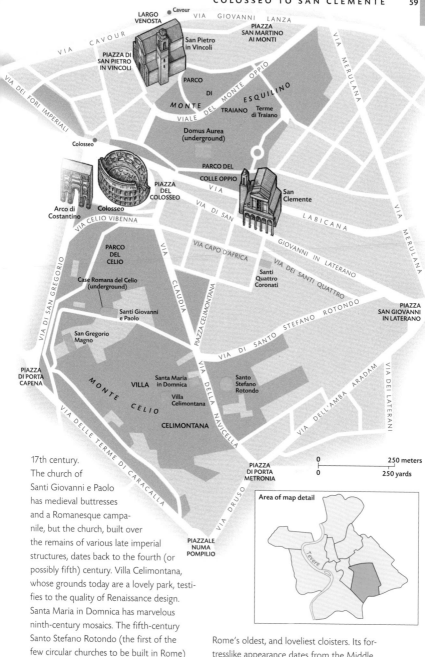

17th century.
The church of
Santi Giovanni e Paolo
has medieval buttresses
and a Romanesque campa-
nile, but the church, built over
the remains of various late imperial
structures, dates back to the fourth (or
possibly fifth) century. Villa Celimontana,
whose grounds today are a lovely park, testifies to the quality of Renaissance design.
Santa Maria in Domnica has marvelous
ninth-century mosaics. The fifth-century
Santo Stefano Rotondo (the first of the
few circular churches to be built in Rome)
retains its aura of mystery, and Santi Quattro
Coronati has interesting frescoes and one of

Rome's oldest, and loveliest cloisters. Its for-
tresslike appearance dates from the Middle
Ages when the monastery was fortified to
serve as a refuge for the popes. ■

COLOSSEO

Properly called the Flavian Amphitheater, the Colosseo, or Colosseum, was built by the three Flavian emperors to promote a good public image. Construction began under Vespasian (A.D. 69–79), who drained the artificial lake that had formed part of Nero's extravagant Domus Aurea complex to transform the site into a place for public entertainment.

■ Participants—humans and animals alike—in the Colosseum's spectacles entered via the warren of corridors and tunnels beneath the arena's wooden floor.

Inaugurated in A.D. 80, the Colosseum was probably built with the spoils brought back from the Temple of Jerusalem at the end of the so-called Jewish campaign, a war waged and won by Vespasian's son Titus in A.D. 70. It was made from travertine hewn from quarries near Tivoli and hauled to Rome along a specially built road. The largest amphitheater in the Roman world, this stone oval measures 620 feet (189 m) long, 512 feet (156 m) wide, and 157 feet (48 m) high. Some 300 tons of iron are believed to have been used for the grapples that held the stones together.

Many historians believe that the name, Colosseum, derives not from the structure's super size but from the giant, or colossal, bronze statue that stood nearby. You can still see its base, today planted with five trees, between the arena and the Temple of Venus and Rome. The original statue depicted Nero, but later the Flavians very pragmatically added sunbeams around the statue's head, changed the inscription, and dedicated the image to the sun god instead. The statue remained standing until sometime in the early Middle Ages, when it was removed and probably melted down.

The Colosseum itself is composed of a series of three **arcades,** topped by a fourth story, or attic. The columns are disposed on three levels—from the ground up, Doric, Ionic, and Corinthian—according to classical canons. Running below the fourth-story cornice, 240 small ledges once held the long wooden poles that supported the velarium, the canvas awning that sailors from the imperial fleet raised to protect spectators from the heat, rain, and winter cold.

Inside the Arena

Estimates of crowd capacity in the Colosseum range from 50,000 to almost 90,000. There were three tiers of seats: the *ima* (lowest), the *media,* and the *summa,* each arranged according to social status and profession. Members of the imperial family and the Vestal Virgins had special boxes. The senators, in their red-bordered white togas, sat on the same level, in the "orchestra" section. Then came the knights *(equites)* followed by the *plebs* (ordinary citizens). Other sections were set aside for soldiers, scribes, students with tutors, and foreign dignitaries. A standing-room-only balcony

at the top of the arena was reserved for the least important members of society: women, slaves, and the poor.

Spectators poured into the Colosseum through the 80 arched entrances on the ground level. They poured in and out through the 160 exits, called vomitoria, distributed throughout the tiers on various levels and allowing for quick exit by often unruly and rambunctious crowds. Some say the Colosseum could empty in as few as ten minutes.

INSIDER TIP:

In order to avoid waiting in line for tickets to the Colosseum, first visit the much less crowded Roman Forum, where you can purchase a combination ticket for both sites.

—BRIDGET A. ENGLISH
National Geographic Books editor

Animal Hunts & Gladiator Games: The Colosseum's program included animal hunts *(venationes)* in the morning, public executions at noon, and gladiatorial contests in the afternoon. The arena's wood floor, which has been partially reconstructed, was covered with sand to absorb the blood and stench of the spectacles. Today, the uncovered portion reveals the **corridors and tunnels** underneath that animals

Colosseo

Map p. 59

Piazza del Colosseo

06 3996 7700. Online tickets: www. coopculture.it

$$ (valid 2 days; includes entry to Roman Forum & Palatine). Guided tours in English can be booked: $$

Bus: 75, 81, 175, 204, 673. Tram: 3. Metro: Linea B (Colosseo)

colosseo. beniculturali.it

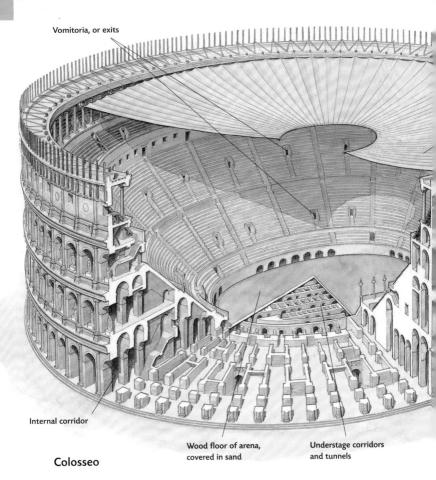

Vomitoria, or exits

Internal corridor

Wood floor of arena,
covered in sand

Understage corridors
and tunnels

Colosseo

and gladiators used to enter the arena. Vertical shafts held caged animals, which were brought up to the arena level in pulley-system elevators. Guided tours to the underground areas were introduced in the last few years.

A tunnel connected the understage section with the Ludus Magnus, the gladiatorial barracks and training area located between the Colosseum and San Clemente. The gladiators—who were chosen from among condemned criminals, slaves, and prisoners of war—were divided into three categories: those who fought heavily armed, with swords and shields; those lightly armed with daggers and arm bucklers; and those armed only with nets and tridents as can be seen in the Roman floor mosaics in the Galleria Borghese.

"Ave, Caesar, morituri te salutant" ("Hail, Emperor, we who are about to die, salute you"), the gladiators scheduled to fight that day would intone during the pre-games

Velarium, a canvas awning for all-weather protection

gladiatorial games were held in the early fifth century; animal hunts lasted another hundred years.

After the Heyday

After the decline of Rome, the Colosseum was utilized for a variety of purposes. However, time, natural calamities, and the Romans themselves led to its deterioration. The southern side of the arena collapsed in a major earthquake in 1349. Afterward, for about 400 years, it served as a quarry for marble and travertine building blocks used in other city structures, such as the Palazzo Venezia and even the new St. Peter's.

INSIDER TIP:

Many Roman sights merit a late-night visit when they are floodlit. St. Peter's, the Colosseum, the Piazza del Campidoglio, and the Trevi Fountain are four of the best.

—TIM JEPSON
National Geographic author

---

parade. Naturally, they all hoped to survive and enjoy the booty that came with victory. Except in rare cases, however, survival (or the thumbs-up sign from the crowd) generally meant only having to fight again. The lucky few were awarded the laurel crown and allowed to retire.

The thousands of animals killed in the festivities, which on special occasions could last for three to four months, included lions, tigers, hyenas, elephants, hippopotamuses, giraffes, and zebras.

As Christian influence grew, the importance of the Colosseum declined. The last recorded

This practice ended when Pope Benedict XIV (1740–1758) declared the Colosseum a sacred place because of the Christian martyrs' blood that reportedly had been shed there. Since the 19th century, a Way of the Cross ceremony involving the direct participation of the pope has been held in the Colosseum every year on the evening of Good Friday before Easter. ∎

ARCO DI COSTANTINO

Constantine is often referred to as the first Christian emperor, but you won't find any Christian images on the arch built in his honor in A.D. 315. His baptism, such as it was, only took place on his deathbed 22 years later. And, impressive as it seems, the Arco di Costantino (Arch of Constantine) is atypical.

Arco di Costantino

🅰 Map p. 59

✉ Between Via di San Gregorio & Piazza del Colosseo

🚌 Bus: 75, 81, 175, 204, 673. Tram: 3. Metro: Linea B (Colosseo)

Most of the arch's decorative work was, in fact, taken from structures built by previous emperors, suggesting that Roman art had entered a phase of decline. Thus, the eight **rectangular reliefs** on both sides of the upper portion (the attic) originally adorned a structure dedicated to Marcus Aurelius (A.D. 161–180) and the portrait of the emperor was recut with Constantine's likeness. (The

■ Constantine built this arch to mark his tenth year in power.

narrative content of three other reliefs from the same series, now in the Musei Capitolini, clearly shows the emperor Marcus Aurelius.)

Also plundered from other monuments were the **round medallions** over the lateral arches (four on each side). These hunting and sacrificial scenes date from the first half of the second century, a period coinciding not with the reign of Constantine but with that of Hadrian. Eight **statues of barbarians** (the ones wearing trousers, of course!) on top of the columns were also derivative. Naturally, some of the work was original but, even to the untrained eye, it appears to be clearly inferior workmanship.

By way of example, the four **panel friezes** below the above-mentioned medallions, on both sides, were sculpted specifically for the arch. Note the one on the south side (toward the Circus Maximus), over the leftmost arch, showing Constantine and his army besieging the city of Verona: The figure of the centurion who is scaling the walls appears dwarfish, and there is a general lack of perspective. Compare the body proportions in this relief with the ones directly above, sculpted about 180 years earlier, and the difference in artistic skill becomes quite apparent. ■

SAN PIETRO IN VINCOLI

Schedule your visit to San Pietro in Vincoli (also known as the Basilica Eudoxiana) early in the day, in order to beat the crush of tourists coming to see Michelangelo's "Moses." Situated at the end of the right transept, this is the pièce de résistance of the unfinished tomb of Pope Julius II (1503–1513), the pontiff who ordered Michelangelo to paint the Sistine Chapel.

A gash on Moses' knee is said to have been caused when Michelangelo threw a tool at it.

The empress Eudoxia built San Pietro in Vincoli to house the chains worn by St. Peter during his imprisonments in Jerusalem and Rome. According to the story, when the chains were placed side by side they miraculously fused. Today they are displayed under the church's altar.

Michelangelo's incredibly powerful **statue of Moses** shows Moses returning from Mount Sinai carrying God's Commandments under his arm and scowling, clearly annoyed with his idolatrous brethren for flirting with the Golden Calf. The striking statues of Jacob's two wives, Leah and Rachel—symbols of the active

and the contemplative life—were probably finished by one of Michelangelo's pupils, Raffaello da Montelupo.

Ignore the baroque ceiling to get a good idea of the stark and simple basilica structure that so appealed to the ancient Romans and which was later adopted by many churches. Despite repeated reconstruction, the brickwork above the windows of the Renaissance facade, best seen inside, still reveals the outline of the five arches of the church's original fifth-century entrances.

The lovely 15th-century fresco to the left of the main entrance depicts a 1476 procession against the plague. ■

San Pietro in Vincoli

Map p. 59

Piazza di San Pietro in Vincoli 4a

06 9784 4950

Closed 12:30–3 p.m.

Bus: 51, 75, 85, 87, 117, 118. Metro: Linea B (Cavour)

MONKS, MOSAICS, & MARTYRS WALK

Only a short distance from the hue and cry of the Colosseum, the Celio (Caelian Hill) has always been one of the quieter and less populated areas of Rome. Right from the earliest centuries of Christian Rome it was therefore a perfect setting for monastic life and spiritual contemplation.

Interior detail of Santi Giovanni e Paolo

NOT TO BE MISSED:

Chapel of Santa Barbara • Santa Maria in Domnica • Case Romane del Celio • Santi Quattro Coronati

From the Colosseum, follow Via di San Gregorio on the left-hand sidewalk. The brick arch across the street once formed part of an aqueduct built by the emperor Nero to supply water to the imperial residences on the Palatine. Just past the arch, the steps on your left lead up to the imposing facade of **San Gregorio Magno ❶.** (Be careful crossing the tram tracks!) Pope Gregory the Great (A.D. 590–604)—later St. Gregory—built the church *(tel 06 700 8227, closed 1–3:30 p.m. & when celebrating Mass)* on the grounds of his family home.

The church's baroque facade was added in the 17th century, but its atrium is typical of Rome's early churches, especially those built in sparsely inhabited areas like the Celio (see p. 72). The fresco in the right-most lunette shows Gregory at the head of a procession to St. Peter's in 590 to pray for deliverance from the plague afflicting

Rome. Along the way he sees the archangel Michael above Hadrian's mausoleum. The angel is sheathing his sword, a clear sign that the plague has ended (and the reason a statue of the archangel stands atop Castel Sant'Angelo). To see the interior, ring the bell on the wall of the atrium's right portico.

By the way, it was from here that Pope Gregory, himself a monk, dispatched St. Augustine of Canterbury and 40 Benedictine monks to the British Isles to convert the Angles and Saxons to Christianity and bring that distant land back into contact with the classical world. All ties with Rome had been cut in the early fifth century, when the last Roman garrisons were withdrawn.

Leaving the church, an iron gate on the left leads to three small chapels *(tel 06 7049 4966, open 9:30 a.m.–12:30 p.m. Tues., Thurs., & Sat.–Sun.).* The chapel of **Santa Barbara,** farthest to the left, is frescoed with scenes from the life of St. Gregory, including one showing him sending Augustine off on his mission. In it is the stone table at which Gregory usually served meals to 12 paupers. Once, an unexpected 13th diner arrived and turned out to be an angel.

The other two chapels, dedicated to St. Andrew and St. Sylvia (Gregory's mother), contain frescoes by Domenichino and Guido

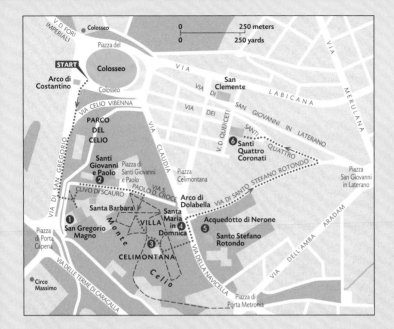

Reni. Behind the chapels stands the so-called **Library of Agapetus,** originally part of a late Roman mansion.

Beyond San Gregorio Magno

From San Gregorio, walk up the steep Clivo di Scauro on the left, from where you will have a fine view of the apse of the church of **Santi Giovanni e Paolo** 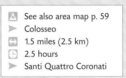, dedicated to John and Paul, two Roman soldiers who suffered martyrdom after refusing to worship pagan idols. To enter the church, walk under the church's medieval flying buttresses, unusual for this city, up to **Piazza di Santi Giovanni e Paolo.** The entrance to the fine small museum **Case Romane del Celio** (see p. 72), showcasing the ruins, is located beneath the flying buttresses.

Directly ahead, you will see the back entrance to the **Villa Celimontana** ❸, once the gardens to the Renaissance Villa Mattei. After a pleasant stroll past the fountains and ferns, leave the park from its main entrance. You'll find yourself on **Via della Navicella,** named

> 🗺 See also area map p. 59
> ▶ Colosseo
> ↔ 1.5 miles (2.5 km)
> ⏱ 2.5 hours
> ▶ Santi Quattro Coronati

for a Roman votive boat now placed atop a fountain in the middle of the street to your left as you exit. The fountain stands in front of the church of **Santa Maria in Domnica** ❹, with its superb ninth-century apse mosaic of the "Virgin Enthroned with the Christ Child."

Across the street (beyond more remnants of Nero's aqueduct) begins Via di Santo Stefano Rotondo. At No. 7 is the round church of **Santo Stefano Rotondo** ❺ (see p. 73). Continue along Via di Santo Stefano Rotondo to a Romanesque portico made with recycled Roman columns.

Turn left onto Via dei Santi Quattro, which leads to the medieval fortress that encloses the church of **Santi Quattro Coronati** ❻ (see p. 74) and its monastery.

SAN CLEMENTE

This multilevel church, founded in the fourth century atop earlier first-century structures to commemorate the martyr Clement, the Roman Catholic Church's fourth pope, is one of the most fascinating in the city. Destroyed by the invading Norman armies in 1084, the church was ordered rebuilt by Pope Paschal II in the early 12th century.

■ Much of San Clemente is baroque in style, but this has not altered its 12th-century essence.

San Clemente

- Map p. 59
- Via di San Giovanni in Laterano 108
- 06 774 0021
- Underground: $
- Church: closed 12:30–3 p.m. Underground: closed 12:30–3 p.m. & Sun. a.m.
- Bus: C3,51, 85, 87, 117. Tram: 3. Metro: Linea B (Colosseo)

San Clemente may have a baroque veneer—primarily the out-of-place gilded ceiling and the pilasters that encase several of the original columns—but fortunately it does not overwhelm the church's older treasures, such as the reconstructed sixth-century *schola cantorum*, the marble barrier defining the monks' choir stall, the colorful pre-cosmatesque (see sidebar p. 208) pavement, and the porticoed atrium, which is conceptually part of the main entrance from Piazza San Clemente.

The wonderful 12th-century **apse mosaic** has a triumphal

cross in the center (with 12 doves symbolizing the Twelve Apostles) between Mary and St. John. From the base of the cross, a luxuriant Tree of Life sends out spirals of foliage, each of which encloses images of the learned Doctors of the Church, exotic birds, flowers, and other Christian symbols.

The waters of life flow at the base of the mosaic, and if you've brought your binoculars, be sure to note the tiny figures performing daily farmyard activities, a return to the classical style that, by the fifth century, had largely disappeared. Farther below is the Lamb of God, *Agnus Dei,* standing in the center with six sheep on either side.

The external arch around the apse is just as interestingly decorated. Jesus is center top, flanked by symbols of the four Evangelists. Just below, Paul and St. Lawrence are shown on the left while Peter and Clement are shown in the corresponding spot on the right.

Chapel of St. Catherine of Alexandria

Located immediately to the right of the Via di San Giovanni in Laterano entrance, the Chapel of St. Catherine of Alexandria contains a series of celebrated frescoes dating from about 1430 and painted by Masolino

frescoes, however, are on the side walls. Those on the right depict scenes from the life of St. Ambrose. Those on the left are scenes from the life of St. Catherine, including, in the middle scene in the lower order, the unsuccessful attempt to murder her on a spiked wheel.

Note the 15th-century St. Christopher painted on the outside left wall of the chapel (protected by a glass panel) with some ancient graffiti etched into its lower right-hand section.

An Odyssey Through Time

San Clemente is a microcosm of the architectural stratification that is a prime characteristic of Rome. You enter the

Saints & Their Symbols

In Roman Catholic iconography, many saints—especially those who were martyred—have a symbol that represents them, often the instrument of their death. Thus Bartholomew is represented by a knife because he was skinned alive. Cecilia's symbol is a musical instrument because she sang while her persecutors tried to steam her to death. And Jerome—who was not martyred, but exiled himself in the desert to resist temptation and translate the holy scriptures—is shown as a scantily clad old man with a lion.

The church of San Clemente is notable because you can find the symbols of three saints here. First, of course, is Clement himself, whose symbol, the anchor, appears on the canopy over the main altar in both the upper and lower church.

The frescoes in the Chapel of St. Catherine of Alexandria show the torture wheel on which she was martyred. And on the arch outside the apse, St. Lawrence is shown with his foot over a flame and grill, his symbol because he was slowly roasted to death.

da Panicale, who was probably helped by his assistant, Masaccio. A Crucifixion scene completely covers the far wall, while the ceiling vaults show the four Evangelists and their symbols, as well as the Doctors of the Church. The most interesting

12th-century church at street level, descend to the excavated fourth-century church below, and eventually go down a further level to the remains of several first-century structures, including a temple to Mithras, one of the many mystery cults

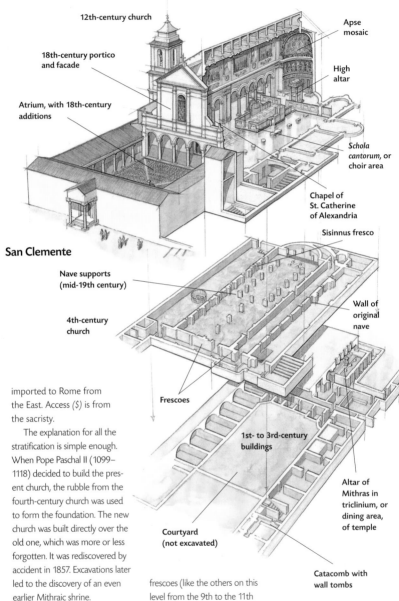

12th-century church

Apse mosaic

18th-century portico and facade

High altar

Atrium, with 18th-century additions

Schola cantorum, or choir area

Chapel of St. Catherine of Alexandria

Sisinnus fresco

San Clemente

Nave supports (mid-19th century)

Wall of original nave

4th-century church

Frescoes

1st- to 3rd-century buildings

Altar of Mithras in triclinium, or dining area, of temple

Courtyard (not excavated)

Catacomb with wall tombs

imported to Rome from the East. Access ($) is from the sacristy.

The explanation for all the stratification is simple enough. When Pope Paschal II (1099–1118) decided to build the present church, the rubble from the fourth-century church was used to form the foundation. The new church was built directly over the old one, which was more or less forgotten. It was rediscovered by accident in 1857. Excavations later led to the discovery of an even earlier Mithraic shrine.

From the sacristy, descend a staircase to what was once the entrance portico. The three doorways in front of you correspond to the standard three aisles. Two

frescoes (like the others on this level from the 9th to the 11th century) flank the middle door. The one on the right narrates one of Clement's miracles. Allegedly, every year the waters of the Black Sea would part to allow the faithful to pray at the spot where Clement drowned. One year an apparently absentminded mother forgot her child and he was submerged. But when she returned the next year, she found him safe and sound; the fish painted around the border represent the encroaching sea.

Step through the doorway and walk until you are almost parallel with a door leading off to the right aisle. To get an idea of the dimensions of this church, look through the door at a column embedded in a retaining wall. Now look, to your left, at the wall where other columns are embedded. The distance between the columns indicates the width of the central nave of the fourth-century church (which was bigger than the present one), laid out in a typical basilica plan.

■ **Detail of San Clemente's apse fresco**

INSIDER TIP:

San Clemente is a lesser known gem with literally layers of history. Deep below the current basilica is a second-century temple dedicated to the Persian god Mithras.

—NATASHA SCRIPTURE
National Geographic contributor

There are other interesting frescoes here. One (on the left wall of the nave, just before the altar) tells the story of a Roman prefect named Sisinnus. Scholars believe that the inscription on the bottom half is one of the earliest written examples of the vernacular, the language that eventually evolved into Italian.

Mithraeum: Reach the third and lowest level of the site by descending another staircase at the far end of the left aisle. At the bottom, you'll hear the gurgling of an underground spring. Follow the path until you reach the ancient Mithraeum, a temple to the eastern god Mithras. Dating from around the end of the second century, or the beginning of the third, it has an altar and a ceiling decorated to simulate a grotto (Mithras was reportedly born in one). The barrel-vaulted room opposite, with traces of stucco work on the ceiling, was probably a vestibule of the temple. The Mithraeum stood opposite the original first-century Christian place of worship, possibly Clement's own house.

The labyrinthine way to the exit takes you through a series of first-century rooms and is truly amazing. ■

CELIO

The least known of the seven hills of Rome, the Celio (Caelian Hill) sits between the Palatine Hill and the Roman basilica of San Giovanni in Laterano (St. John Lateran). Due to its proximity to the latter, it was here that many of the oldest churches in Rome were built soon after Constantine legalized Christianity in A.D. 313.

Celio

- Map p. 59

Case Romane del Celio

- Map p. 59
- Clivo di Scauro
- 06 7045 4544
- Closed Tues.– Wed. p.m.
- $$
- Bus: 60, 75, 81, 175, 673. Tram: 3. Metro: Linea B (Circo Massimo)

www.caseromane.it

Some were built *ex novo* while others were erected over the remains of preexisting pagan structures. The church of **Santi Giovanni e Paolo** (Sts. John and Paul) falls into the second category. It is dedicated to two soldier saints who converted to Christianity under the reign of Constantine only to die at the hands of Julian the Apostate (A.D. 361–363); they had refused to worship the pagan gods which that emperor had decided to rehabilitate at Chris-

---

INSIDER TIP:

The Virgin Mary icons you see everywhere in Rome are not displays of art; they're crime deterrents. The hope is that robbers avoid plying their trade in front of them.

—RAFAEL SANDOR
National Geographic International Channel

---

tianity's expense. The church was built over several edifices dating variously from the first to fourth centuries A.D. These included a Roman domus (private home) and several *insulae* (apartment blocks).

The entrance to the church can be reached by walking up the evocative Roman road called the Clivo di Scauro, which passes underneath the flying buttresses supporting the church. As you walk up, look at the walls on your left (above the flying buttresses); here, outlines of the walled-in windows of the ancient flats are still visible.

Case Romane del Celio

From below one of these flying buttresses you can enter into the small but extremely interesting Case Romane del Celio. There are about 20 rooms in this museum, distributed on different levels belonging to the original structures (the Roman domus and insulae, and a paleo-Christian basilica) upon which the foundations of the church were laid. Some of the rooms are decorated with frescoes and each room has explanatory panels in both Italian and English.

In the small, futuristic **Antiquarium,** you can see artifacts found during the various excavations plus a collection of Muslim ceramics. On certain dates the museum offers a guided tour in English followed by an aperitif with hors d'oeuvres based on recipes from 2,000 years ago. Consult the events page on the website. Reservations are necessary. ■

SANTO STEFANO ROTONDO

Modeled on the Church of the Holy Sepulchre in Jerusalem, and unusual because of its spherical shape, this extremely picturesque building is the oldest circular church in Rome. Extremely realistic 16th-century frescoes depicting the various methods of persecution and torture suffered by early Christian martyrs adorn the interior.

Enter the church grounds through the sustaining wall of Nero's aqueduct. The church itself, which probably dates to the fifth century, is dedicated to St. Stephen, the first Christian martyr, whose feast day, December 26, is an official holiday in most Catholic countries.

The original structure consisted of a circular center space surrounded by two concentric rings, or ambulatories, which in turn were intersected by the four "arms" of a virtual Greek cross (one with arms that are all the same length). Two circles of granite columns, 22 in all, still stand between the central space and the first ambulatory. The 34 marble columns embedded in the frescoed walls once divided the second ambulatory from a third, which is no longer extant. This outer ambulatory, and the walls of three of the cross's four arms, were eliminated in the 1450s. Today a single portico encircles the central space, which includes the main altar.

Three arches, supported by two giant Corinthian columns added in the 12th century, dissect the central space. To enter the church, you must walk from an external portico, also added in the 12th century, through the vestibule, or entrance hall, and past the remains of the fourth arm of the cross.

■ **An inscription below each fresco explains the pictured scene.**

Visit in midmorning, when sunlight streams in through the church's 22 clerestory windows. Once inside, however, you may find your reverent serenity disrupted by more than 30 extremely realistic frescoes that depict the various torture methods used by Rome's authorities on the empire's early Christians.

To the left of the entrance, the marble bishop's throne may have belonged to Pope St. Gregory the Great (A.D. 590–604). The chapel to the left of the throne, dedicated to Sts. Primus and Felician, features a magnificent seventh-century mosaic of Christ and a jeweled cross. Archaeologists have also discovered a Mithraic temple *(not usually open to the public)* beneath this church. ■

Santo Stefano Rotondo

◪ Map p. 59

✉ Via di Santo Stefano Rotondo 7

☎ 06 421199

🕐 Closed Mon. & 1–2 p.m. in winter, 1–3:30 p.m. in summer

🚌 Bus: 81, 117 (from downtown & Circo Massimo). Metro: Linea B (Colosseo)

More Places to Visit

Santi Quattro Coronati

The Church of the Four Crowned Saints commemorates nine martyred saints. The four soldiers and five sculptors were killed for refusing either to pray to the Greek god Aesculapius or to sculpt his image. The early 17th-century apse fresco shows the story of their demise.

Partially damaged during the 1084 Norman invasion, the church was rebuilt by Pope Paschal II (1099–1118); the second of the two outdoor courtyards was once part of the interior. Ring the bell near the door in the left aisle and a nun will admit you to the beautiful, tiny 13th-century cloister *(donation),* one of the first in Rome.

To see the frescoes in the **Chapel of St. Sylvester** *(closed 11:45 a.m.–4 p.m. Mon.–Sat. & Sun., $),* head for the vestibule marked "Suore Agostiniane," ring the bell, and get the key from the nun who answers. The chapel's frescoes seek to explain

Constantine's supposed "donation" to Sylvester of the western Roman Empire.

Map p. 59 ⊠ Via dei Santi Quattro 20 ☎ 06 7047 5427 Bus: C3, 51, 85, 87, 117. Tram: 3. Metro: Linea B (Colosseo)

Villa Celimontana

In the mid-sixteenth century, the villa's estate, which in medieval and early Renaissance times was taken up with vegetable gardens and vineyards, was purchased by the Mattei family. The villa is situated on the western peak of the Celio, and today houses the Società Geografica Italiana; it preserves some of the most important maps in Italy. The garden, which is filled with statues and Renaissance fountains, has become a public park hosting important jazz events from June to September. *villagecelimontana.it* Map p. 59 ⊠ Via della Navicella 12 ☎ 349 0709 468 Bus: 81, 673. Metro: Linea B (Colosseo)

EXPERIENCE: Go Underneath & See It All

Over the past 3,000 years, Romans have continued to use old buildings as the foundations for new. This means that there is another, older city underground, one that includes not only the catacombs but also other early Christian structures, pagan temples dedicated to Roman gods and pre-Roman deities such as Mithras and Dionysius, secular Roman structures such as *insulae*—apartment houses—sewers, and aqueducts, and even more exotic remains, like the vestiges of Augustus' huge *Horologium solarium,* or sundial.

You can see many of these places on your own by visiting sights like San Clemente (see pp. 68–71) with its layers of civilization, the Roman houses underneath the church of Santi Giovanni e Paolo (see p. 72), and the excavations

under San Nicola in Carcere, not to mention the excavations of the two Roman houses beneath the Palazzo Valentini (see p. 56), off of Piazza Venezia. The Vatican allows tourists to visit the excavation of the necropolis under the basilica, which holds the Tomb of Saint Peter (see pp. 164–170), but you must book in advance using the form on the website *www.scavi.va,* and then wait for authorization. Each group is accompanied by a specialist guide and the visit lasts an hour and a half.

Another option, should you speak or understand Italian, is to visit the websites *www.romasotterranea.it* and *www.sotterraneidiroma.it* to check whether they have organized interesting visits to take part in while you are in the city.

Byzantine mosaics, relics from the Holy Land, and a treasure
trove of antiquities in a major museum complex

LATERANO TO TERME DI DIOCLEZIANO

■ Detail of a second-century A.D.
mosaic pavement, Palazzo Massimo
alle Terme

LATERANO TO TERME DI DIOCLEZIANO

After St. Peter's, San Giovanni in Laterano is the most important Roman Catholic church in the world; it was one of few Christian structures built by the emperor Constantine inside Rome's walls. Today it is the episcopal seat of the bishop of Rome, the pope.

The term "in Laterano" means that the basilica is part of a loosely knit complex of structures that includes some of Christianity's most important monuments: the Scala Santa, the Sancta Sanctorum, the Battistero, and the Palazzo Lateranense. The area takes its name from the Laterani, a Roman family whose paterfamilias, Plautius, participated in a plot against Nero, thus losing both his life and the family estate. The land was confiscated by the emperor, and later

Constantine chose the location for the cathedral of San Giovanni.

For centuries, the original Palazzo Lateranense was the official residence of the popes, who moved to St. Peter's only after their return from self-imposed exile in Avignon in 1377. Today the area is traditionally the site of the annual May Day rally organized by Italy's unions and of demonstrations by left-wing political parties.

The area that lies between the Lateran and the Esquiline and Viminale Hills contains other important Christian churches, most notably Santa Pudenziana and Santa Prassede, both known for their mosaics. Here, too, you will find the imposing Santa Maria Maggiore, one of Rome's seven pilgrim churches, dedicated to the Virgin Mary and filled with mosaics celebrating her life. Several popes lie buried in this church, which, unusually, has two impressive domes. Also buried here, is the baroque sculptor and architect Gian Lorenzo Bernini. The most famous of Bernini's three "Ecstasies," the "Ecstasy of St. Theresa," is nearby in the church of Santa Maria della Vittoria.

Beyond the Churches

About a century after its creation in the Terme di Diocleziano (1889), the Museo Nazionale Romano (National Museum of Rome) was reorganized in four different sites: Palazzo Massimo, Palazzo Altemps, and la Crypta Balbi were

added to Terme. The Palazzo Massimo is located in front of the baths a few meters from the frenetic Stazione Termini. It houses one of the best organized museums in the city, with a unique exhibition of ancient Roman frescoes and mosaics. The museum's collection of Greek and Roman statues is equally magnificent.

Facing the Terme di Diocleziano (Baths of Diocletian), Piazza della Repubblica also illustrates the architectural stratification of Rome. Built shortly before World War I, the piazza's design follows the outlines of the external perimeter and the exedra (a hemicycle enclosure) of the ancient baths.

The modern fountain in the center of the piazza raised eyebrows when it was unveiled at the beginning of the 20th century because of the generously endowed female statues.

This busy traffic circle, which the Romans call Piazza Esedra, coincides with what was once the open-air palaestra, or gym, of Diocletian's complex. At the break in the exedra is the onset of Via Nazionale, a major thoroughfare and shopping street that passes by the Palazzo delle Esposizioni, a giant exhibition space, as well as Trajan's Markets, to end in Piazza Venezia. ■

Stazione Centrale Roma-Termini

VIA MARSALA

VIA GIOVANNI

C. ALBERTO

PIAZZA VITTORIO EMANUELE II

● Vittorio Emanuele

VIA PR. EUGENIO

VIA CONTE VERDE

VIA EMANUELE

MERULANA

VIALE

FILIBERTO

VIA MANZONI

VIA S. CROCE

● Manzoni

GIOLITTI

VIA PORTA MAGGIORE

PIAZZA DI PORTA MAGGIORE

STATILIA

IN GERUSALEMME

VIA

VIA ELENIANA

VIA CASILINA

Santa Croce in Gerusalemme

PIAZZA DI S. CROCE IN GERUSALEMME

VIALE CASTRENSE

PIAZZA S. GIOVANNI IN LATERANO

Palazzo Lateranense

Scala Santa e Sancta Sanctorum

VIALE CARLO FELICE

Obelisco Lateranense

Battistero

PIAZZA DI PORTA SAN GIOVANNI

VIA LA SPEZIA

San Giovanni in Laterano

VIA SANNIO

● San Giovanni

0 ___ 400 meters
0 ___ 400 yards

Area of map detail

Tevere

SAN GIOVANNI IN LATERANO & AROUND

Founded by Constantine in the fourth century A.D., San Giovanni in Laterano (St. John Lateran) has been rebuilt several times. In fact, the pope's church only assumed its modern appearance in the 17th century, after major overhauls of the interior and the facade.

Huge statues of the Apostles, including St. Philip with his symbol, the Latin cross, line San Giovanni in Laterano's nave.

Alessandro Galilei designed the church's travertine **facade** in 1735. Divided into a ground-floor portico with a loggia above, it is crowned by 15 statues, each about 23 feet (7 m) tall and visible from miles away. The three central statues—Jesus, St. John the Baptist, and St. John the Evangelist—are flanked, six on each side, by 12 Doctors of the Church, men and women recognized for the profundity of their theological thinking.

Five doors lead into the barrel-vaulted portico, one for each of the aisles within. The central bronze doors open onto the wide central nave. Brought here in 1600, the doors originally stood in the Curia (or Senate) in the Roman Forum. Like in St. Peter's, the door farthest to the right—the Holy Door—is only opened during the Holy Years, generally every 25 years.

The Church Interior

The interior, in some ways rather cold and unwelcoming (although this is less true of the warmly hued transept), betrays nothing of the church's ancient past. But there is significant grandeur, not surprising since the popes were crowned here until 1870, the year pontifical Rome—until then an independent state—fell to the armies of the Savoy monarchy. But the basilica's monumental magnificence reflects, above all, the creative genius of Francesco Borromini, commissioned by Pope Innocent X in 1646 to do a total renovation for the 1650 Holy Year.

Borromini created the 12 niches flanking the central nave, later transformed into a parade of giant baroque **statues of the Apostles.** If you are not well versed in Apostolic lore, not to worry, the statues are labeled. If you are, you'll be able to identify them by their trademarks: for example, St. Matthew's bag of money (he had been a tax collector) or St. Bartholomew's knife, the symbol of his martyrdom. Artistically, however, the most interesting are the four statues sculpted by Camillo Rusconi: Matthew, James the Elder, Andrew, and John.

To preserve something of the church's former style, Borromini selected pieces of medieval monuments or artworks housed in the church, enclosed them in elaborate baroque frames, and created the **funerary monuments** against the pilasters in the outer aisles. The cosmatesque-style pavement (see sidebar p. 208) in the central aisle was made during the reign of Pope Martin V (1417–1431), whose floor tomb is in the sunken *confessio.*

Transept: The transept of the church was renovated in the late 16th century by Giacomo della Porta, and the frescoes ("Baptism of Constantine" and "Foundation of the Basilica") were painted under the direction of Cavalier d'Arpino, who was responsible for the "Ascension" over the altar at the end of the left transept. The beautiful frescoed Gothic canopy over the main altar dates from 1367. Above the frescoes, a grill safeguards two silver bust-shaped reliquaries that contain the **heads of St. Peter and St. Paul,** the two founders of the Church of Rome.

Although reconstructed, the **apse mosaic,** portions of which may date from the original fourth-century basilica, is striking. It depicts a panoply of figures

---

INSIDER TIP:

See the church of San Giovanni in Laterano in the morning. That way you can also visit the morning market in nearby Via Sannio, one of Rome's best.

—TIM JEPSON
National Geographic author

---

of varying sizes depending on their importance. The tiny figure kneeling at the feet of the Virgin is Pope Nicholas IV (1288–1292), who commissioned the mosaic's restoration. The even smaller kneeling figures inserted into the row of Apostles on the bottom are the mosaicists, Jacopo Torriti and Jacopo da Camerino.

A door in the left-hand wall, just before the transept, leads to the **cloister** and its mini-museum. Fashioned between 1215 and 1223 by cosmati maestro Pietro Vassalletto and his son, the cloister has a lovely mosaic frieze running around the garden side of the portico and a number of attractive

---

San Giovanni in Laterano

🗺 Map p. 77

✉ Piazza di Porta San Giovanni in Laterano 4

☎ 06 9886 433

💲 Basilica: Free. Cloister: $. Audio guide: $

🚌 Bus: 16, 81, 85, 87, 117, 218, 360, 590, 650, 665. Tram: 3. Metro: Linea A (San Giovanni)

Museo Storico Vaticano

✉ Palazzo Lateranense, Piazza San Giovanni in Laterano

☎ 06 6988 4019

🕐 Only with a booking

💲 $$

Battistero

🗺 Map p. 77

✉ Piazza San Giovanni in Laterano 4

☎ 06 6988 6452

🕐 Closed 12:30–4 p.m.

cosmatesque colonettes. Monuments from the original basilica decorate the walls, including what may be one of the oldest surviving papal thrones.

Piazza San Giovanni in Laterano

Leaving the church by the side door (in the right transept), you will be in Piazza San Giovanni in Laterano, with the tallest and oldest obelisk in Rome facing you (see p. 86), the Battistero on your left and, to the right, the **Palazzo Lateranense** (Lateran Palace). Built by Domenico Fontana, the Lateran Palace replaced the original papal residence, which after a thousand years had been reduced to a pitiful state. It houses the **Museo Storico Vaticano,** the frescoed papal apartments with furniture, tapestries, and sculpture. On the other side of the piazza, note the double brick arch. It was part of the Claudian aqueduct lengthened by Nero to furnish his Domus Aurea with

water. If you cross the street, you get an excellent look at the Lateran complex. The basilica's side facade has a portico, surmounted by a loggia designed by Fontana in 1586. The twin, triangle-topped bell towers of an older 13th-century version of the church are visible above it.

Battistero: The Battistero (Baptistery) also dates back to Constantine and was built into a previous structure that formed part of an imperial residence. In the earliest days of Christianity, only the pope could baptize new converts, usually on Easter, and this was where it was done. With the spread of the new religion, however, this became impractical and parish priests were authorized to perform baptisms.

Restored many times, the Baptistery has retained its fourth-century octagonal shape. The circular center space is surrounded by eight porphyry columns surmounted by an architrave

EXPERIENCE: Learning Italian

You can get through and around this city with just a couple of phrases, a map, and a lot of finger-pointing. But you'll enjoy your stay in Rome so much more if you know a bit of Italian. Romans are very patient and don't mind if you make mistakes, although they may answer in English if they know any.

So why not choose to combine sightseeing with an Italian language course? If this is the route you choose to follow, you may find yourself pleasantly surprised by the number of choices available. A quick search on the Internet for *"scuole di italiano roma"* or "Italian

language schools in Rome" will yield a remarkably long list.

If you are looking to learn something specific, however, a few schools do offer a bit more. The **Torre di Babele** school *(www.torredibabele.com),* for example, features cultural classes and cooking courses. **Percorsi d'Italiano** *(www.percorsi ditaliano.it)* combines language classes with discovery walks through the city. It also offers Sunday guided tours. And the program at the **Dilit** school *(www.dilit.it)* also includes courses in art history, cooking, and archaeology. A more extensive list can be found at *www.inromenow.com.*

San Giovanni in Laterano's main facade, on Piazza di Porta San Giovanni

with eight smaller white marble columns above. A green basalt urn (for baptisms) stands in the center. The 17th-century frescoes on the outer walls depict scenes from the life of Constantine, and the medallions encompass views of Roman churches somehow connected to him. The chapel to St. Venantius, on the left, has magnificent seventh-century Byzantine-style mosaics, although the altar partially obstructs them.

Perhaps the most interesting mosaics are in the chapel opposite the door, which until the 12th century was the narthex (entrance) into the Baptistery. Their classical motifs—acanthus or vine leaves on a blue background—confirm that in the fifth century a real Christian iconography had not yet emerged.

Sancta Sanctorum & Scala Santa:

Fontana salvaged the **Sancta Sanctorum,** the private chapel of the early pontiffs in the original papal residence, and moved it to an uninspiring structure across the street. Because of the many relics accumulated there, this chapel was known in the Middle Ages as the holiest site on Earth. Renovated in the 13th century, it, too, is a cosmatesque marvel. Above the altar is an *acheiropoieton* image of the Redeemer, meaning it was (supposedly) not painted by human hands.

Leading up to the Sancta Sanctorum is the **Scala Santa,** the

Sancta Sanctorum & Scala Santa

🏛 Map p. 77

✉ Piazza San Giovanni in Laterano 14

☎ 06 7726 641 or 329 7511 111

🕐 Sancta Sanctorum: open 9:30–12:40 a.m. & 3–5:10 p.m.; closed Sun. Scala Santa: closed 2–3 p.m.

💲 Sancta Sanctorum: $

Santa Croce in Gerusalemme

- Map p. 77
- Piazza di Santa Croce in Gerusalemme 12
- 06 7061 3053
- Closed 12:45–3:30 p.m.
- Bus: 649. Tram: 3. Metro: Linea A (San Giovanni), Linea C (Lodi)

ceremonial staircase believed to have been the one ascended by Jesus in Pontius Pilate's Jerusalem palace. Even today the highly religious climb its 28 marble steps—restored in 2019 and sheltered by a wooden covering—on their knees. A lateral staircases are available for nonbelievers and the less energetic.

Santa Croce in Gerusalemme

Santa Croce, a short walk from San Giovanni down Viale Carlo Felice, was originally part of the palace of St. Helena, Constantine's mother. Its baroque appearance belies its classical origins. Redecorated in the 18th century, the facade's concave and convex movement reveals a strong Borromini influence.

It is topped by an array of statues, including St. Helen on the left and her son, Constantine, on the right. The name (Holy Cross in Jerusalem) derives from the church's foundation as a home for the important relics Helen brought back from the Holy Land. Around the back of the church to the right, just through the arches in the Aurelian Wall you can see the outlines of the Castrense amphitheater, used for court performances.

It's hard to discern the original

INSIDER TIP:

The San Lorenzo district around Piazza dei Sanniti (north of Santa Croce in Gerusalemme) is a lively new hot spot for cafés, restaurants, and music clubs.

—RUTH ELLEN GRUBER
National Geographic author

basilica's layout. Only eight of the original granite columns remain; the others are encased in concrete piers. Fortunately, the cosmatesque pavement has survived, as has the wonderful fresco in the apse, sometimes attributed to Antoniazzo Romano (circa 1492), showing Jesus and scenes relating to the discovery of the cross.

Downstairs, the **Chapel of St. Helen** is built over soil that she brought back from the Holy Land. From the left aisle in the church, stairs lead up to the **Chapel of the Relics.** Here you'll find what are said to be parts of the True Cross, parts of its inscription, two thorns from the Crown of Thorns, a nail from the Cross, and the finger of (the Doubting) St. Thomas. ■

Rome's Seven Pilgrim Churches

The relics of Santa Croce, all of which relate to Jesus' Passion, made it one of Rome's seven pilgrim churches, Christian places of worship notable because of their association with important saints or their relics. In medieval and Renaissance times, pilgrims who managed to visit all seven were granted a special indulgence known as a plenary indulgence. A formal itinerary helped them better navigate the distances. The grand tour included the four patriarchal basilicas (St. Peter's, San Giovanni in Laterano, Santa Maria Maggiore, and San Paolo fuori le Mura), plus San Lorenzo fuori le Mura, Santa Croce in Gerusalemme, and San Sebastiano on the Via Appia.

SANTA MARIA MAGGIORE
& AROUND

Legend has it that in A.D. 352 Pope Liberius had a vision: The Virgin Mary commanded him to build a church dedicated to her on a snow-covered spot. It hardly ever snows in Rome, much less in the summer. Nonetheless, on August 5 it supposedly snowed on the Esquiline Hill, the place where Liberius built what was to become one of the four major basilicas of Rome.

Santa Maria Maggiore's sumptuous Borghese Chapel, designed by Flaminio Ponzio in the early 1600s

Every August a ceremony is held inside Santa Maria Maggiore to reenact that miracle, with thousands of white flower petals (the snow) fluttering down from the ceiling. Naturally, the church you see is a later version, built by Pope Sixtus III in the early fifth century, at the tail end of a raging battle among Christian dogmatists over Mary's status: Was she only the mother of Christ the human being (Christotokos)? Or was she the mother of Christ in both his human and divine natures (Theotokos)?

The second view prevailed at the Council of Ephesus in 431, so it shouldn't surprise you that Jacopo Torriti's 13th-century **mosaic** in the apse depicts Mary as a Byzantine princess being crowned by Jesus. By the way, if you have binoculars, you will need them here. The 36 **fifth-century mosaic panels** in the nave, illustrating scenes from the Old and New Testaments, have recently been cleaned, but they are high up and hard to see.

Santa Maria Maggiore

Map p. 76

Piazza Santa Maria Maggiore

06 6988 6800 (sacristy), 06 6988 6802 (museum)

Museum: $. Audio guide: $

Bus: C3, 16, 50, 75, 105, 150, 360, 590, 649, 714, 717. Tram: 5, 14. Metro: Linea A (Repubblica), Linea B (Cavour)

Many additions have been made to this church throughout the centuries, but its basic form—a basilica with three wide aisles divided by 40 massive Ionic columns—faithfully reflects fifth-century canons. The beautiful coffered ceiling was gilded with gold from the New World donated by Ferdinand and Isabella of Spain. The sunken *confessio* holds an 1802 gold and silver relic case said to contain pieces of Jesus' cradle. The giant statue is of Pope Pius IX (1846–1878), who enlarged the confessio.

The two richly decorated, domed chapels on the ends of the transept were added in the 16th and 17th centuries. The one on the left was built by Pope Paul V, who is buried in the Borghese family crypt below. The other, commissioned by Pope Sixtus V, is, like its cousin in the Vatican, called the **Sistine Chapel.** It is decorated with colored marbles from the Septizodium (a pagan structure which stood below the Palatino) and contains Sixtus's tomb. Near the chapel entrance, in front of the side presbytery banister, a marble slab on the floor marks the **grave of sculptor Gian Lorenzo Bernini** and his ancestors. How peculiar so lavishly baroque an artist should have such a simple, nondescript tomb!

In the small museum, the most precious objects from the Basilica apartments are displayed; among them a nearly complete set of magnificent manger figures from the 13th century, some by Arnolfo di Cambio, as well as sketches of the basilica's facade before renovation in the 18th century.

The 18th-century front facade partially covers the early 14th-century mosaics in the loggia.

EXPERIENCE: *Archeo-stazione* of the Metro Line C

The metro station San Giovanni on the new C Line (*metrocspa.it/stazione/san-giovanni*), which was opened in May 2018, is effectively a museum. You'll find on two levels displays of archaeological remains unearthed during the excavation to build the new subway.

The difference between street level and the subway lines is 88.5 feet (27 m). The visitor can find explanatory panels with a stratigrapher accompanying him/her along the stairs from and toward the station platform through the Atrium and the Corrispondenze floor. On the first floor, there are fragments of statues and marble remains from the Roman era reused in the modern and contemporary era. In the level below (Corrispondenze) we go backward in time with vases, amphorae, low-relief antefixes, and drainage systems from the first to second century A.D., before reaching the organic remains—seeds, peach stones, and mollusk shells from the first century A.D.

The stratigrapher employs two narrative registers: The first matches the progressive stratification of terrain from the modern era at ground level to the Paleolithic, 88.5 feet (27 m) belowground—and the infrastructural and sociopolitical changes, while the second relates the transformation of the area with particular reference to the theme of water. A third narrative register interprets the archaeological remains displayed along the horizontal floors through interpretations linked to the relation between present and past that mark the identity of contemporary Rome.

INSIDER TIP:

The inscription SPQR
(a Latin abbreviation
of "the Senate and Peo-
ple of Rome") on many
road grates is a quick
reminder of Rome's
enduring past.

—ADAM THEILER
*National Geographic
International Channel*

These are worth a visit anyway
since they tell the story of that
miraculous August snowfall. Stop
by the piazza at night when,
thanks to the Italian genius for
artificial lighting, the mosaics
glow much as they must have
by candlelight. The 14th-century
bell tower is the tallest in Rome.
The giant marble column in front
of the church comes from the
Roman Forum.

Santa Prassede

The present church was built by
Pope Paschal I (817–824) and
later restored several times, most
recently in the 19th century. A
typical basilica structure with
a restored cosmatesque pavement (see sidebar p. 208), this
church dedicated to St. Praxedes
is known for the ninth-century
Byzantine mosaics in its apse.

The Redeemer is flanked on
the right by St. Peter, St. Pudentiana, and St. Zeno, and on the
left by St. Paul, St. Praxedes,
and Pope Paschal, who holds a
model of the church and whose
square halo shows he was alive
at the time. These mosaics are
Byzantine in character (the
two sisters are dressed like
Byzantine princesses). A second mosaic, one of the most
important Byzantine monu-
ments in Rome, is the decoration in the **Chapel of St. Zeno.**
The figures are placed against
a gold background, which in
Eastern iconography symbolized heaven.

Santa Pudenziana

It is unclear whether St. Pudentiana, supposedly St. Praxedes'
sister, really existed. The name
may stem from a semantic
error. Her father was a senator and early Christian named
Pudens who had welcomed
St. Peter into the family home.
Centuries later, the church
built on the site was referred
to as Ecclesia Pudenziana. In
any event, this is believed to
be one of the oldest churches
in Rome, although frequent
restorations have undermined
much of its charm.

A notable exception is the
fourth-century **apse mosaic.**
Classical in style, it shows Jesus
seated on a jeweled throne surrounded by ten Apostles; the
two others were cut off during
a 16th-century restoration. The
women standing behind the
Apostles hold crowns in their
hands and have been variously
identified as Praxedes and
Pudentiana, or as symbols of
the early church. What is significant is that they are all dressed
as Romans. Furthermore, the
architectural background, with
temples and basilicas, is unmis-
takably classical in nature. ∎

Santa Prassede

- Map p. 76
- Via S. Prassede 9a
- 06 4882 456
- Closed noon–
  4 p.m. (Sun.
  12:30–4 p.m.)
- Bus: C3, 16, 70,
  71, 360, 590,
  649, 714, 717.
  Metro: Linea B
  (Cavour)

Santa Pudenziana

- Map p. 76
- Via Urbana 160
- 06 4817 292
- Closed noon–
  3 p.m.
- Bus: C3, 16, 70
  71, 75, 105, 360,
  590, 649, 714.
  Metro: Linea B
  (Cavour)

OBELISKS

One of the most popular trophies for a victorious Roman leader from an Egyptian campaign was an authentic obelisk *(obelisco)*. Symbols of divinity and immortality for the pharaohs, obelisks were brought to Rome and used to decorate temples, circuses, and mausoleums. After the fall of Rome they lay buried for centuries until the Renaissance, when they were unearthed and given over to the glory of the popes.

Part of the Landscape

Today, you can find 13 of these stone giants in modern Rome. They embellish some of the city's most beautiful squares and are now as much a part of the Romans' cultural heritage as triumphal columns or arches.

In fact, obelisks have been so well integrated into Rome's decor that you may almost miss them. Bernini incorporated the Agonale Obelisk into his imposing baroque Fontana dei Quattro Fiumi (see pp. 98–99 & 147) in Piazza Navona, and the Minerva Obelisk, a relative dwarf at only 17 feet (5 m), rides on the back of the whimsical marble elephant in front of Santa Maria sopra Minerva (see pp. 134–135). Renaissance nobleman Ciriaco Mattei placed his in the gardens of Villa Celimontana. And the Macuteo Obelisk stands atop Giacomo della Porta's fountain in Piazza della Rotonda.

Converting Pagan Monuments to Christian Use

Pope Sixtus V (1585–1590), known for his urban planning schemes, obviously had a thing about obelisks: He converted four of them to Christian usage. The Vatican Obelisk in St. Peter's Square was brought to Rome by either Caligula or Nero, and from A.D. 40 on it beautified a nearby circus. It was, amazingly, still standing in 1585, when Sixtus ordered architect Domenico Fontana to move it to its current location, a feat requiring 900 men and 140 horses.

The pontiff's campaign to Christianize Rome's pagan monuments proceeded with the installation on the Esquiline Hill (behind Santa Maria Maggiore and, incidentally, in front of Sixtus's private villa) of the almost 50-foot (15 m) Esquiline Obelisk. Once, it had graced the entrance to the mausoleum of Emperor Augustus but now, says the inscription, it is "serving the Lord Christ."

The Lateran Obelisk (see p. 80) was retrieved from the Circo Massimo, along with another now in Piazza del Popolo, and the Flaminio Obelisk was now "prouder and happier" to be dedicated to Mary.

Sixtus V was not the only obelisk-minded pontiff. Two centuries later, Pope Pius VI (1775–1799) also had a go at relocating a few. He put the red granite Quirinal Obelisk in between Castor and Pollux in front of the Palazzo del Quirinale. A similar monument was erected at the top of the Spanish Steps. And in 1792, the obelisk Augustus had used as the needle for his giant Campus Martius sundial was raised in Piazza Montecitorio.

Two other obelisks were repositioned in the 19th century. The Antinous Obelisk, originally erected by Emperor Hadrian to honor the memory of his dazzlingly handsome friend and lover, Antinous, was put on the Pincian Hill by Pius VII in 1822. The Termini Obelisk dates from the reign of Rameses II. Excavated in 1883, it has been relegated to a small, somewhat neglected park near the Termini train station.

Rome's only modern obelisk was erected during Mussolini's rule. The 118-foot (36 m) monument stands on the grounds of the Foro Italico sports complex and still reads "Mussolini Dux." After his demise, any and all references to "Il Duce" were ordered deleted, but the inscription on the obelisk was too large to be removed and now stands as testament to the man's ego.

■ Bernini incorporated the Agonale Obelisk, originally built for Emperor Domitian's villa at Albano, into the Fontana dei Quattro Fiumi he designed for Piazza Navona.

PALAZZO MASSIMO ALLE TERME

Linchpin of the National Museum of Rome's four sites scattered around the city, the Palazzo Massimo alle Terme plays host to some of the museum's finest pieces of Greek and Roman sculpture. Here you'll also find mosaics, frescoes, paintings, and jewelry, as well as the world's premier coin collection. The building, constructed in 1883–1887 to house a Jesuit college, copies the style of early Roman baroque noble residences.

■ The "Reclining Hermaphrodite," a popular statue found in the ruins of a private garden in Pompeii

The collection of Palazzo Massimo is displayed on four floors. The basement houses the Medagliere, a coin collection which derives from private donations from the Collezione Gnecchi and the collection of Vittorio Emanuele III di Savoia. We can see the evolution of the art of money and commerce of the pre-Roman Italic peoples of ancient Rome to the Roman-barbaric; the section continues with the various eras until the coining of the Euro. For every three displays you will find an iPad presenting useful information and photographic details of the exhibits.

Ground & First Floors

Whichever way you organize your visit, you won't want to miss the ground and first floors, dedicated to the sculpture and statuary that make up the bulk of the Museo Nazionale Romano's ancient art section. The museum has sought, quite successfully, to organize the sculptures thematically and by historical periods: You can follow the Roman portrait of the late Republican era up to the beginning of the empire on the ground floor and the beginning of the Flavian period to the late antique period on the first floor.

The building is located opposite Termini. At the autobus terminus in Piazza dei Cinquecento cross the road in the direction of Piazza della Repubblica. It is worth considering a combined visit with the Terme di Diocleziano, one of the sites of the Museo Nazionale Romano, a short distance away. You'll find the entrance to the Terme within the park skirting Viale Enrico de Nicola, on the opposite side from the statue of John Paul II, which stands in the large square in front of stazione Termini.

Ground Floor: It is impossible to mention all the pieces, but the ground floor, which deals primarily with the images and accoutrements of power, mainly from the second and first centuries B.C., contains a variety of treasures, some of which are Greek or bear clear Hellenistic influences. Near the entrance you will find the multicolored giant cult **statue of Minerva** (the head is a modern plaster cast of the statue of Athena from the Villa Carpegna); and in Room V you will find the statue of **Via Labicana Augustus,** which represents the Emperor Augustus solemnly intent on celebrating the sacrifice of the gods. This sculpture was probably created between 12 B.C., the year in which Augustus assumed the role of Pontifex Maximus, and the beginning of the first century A.D. In the same room, you can admire the beautiful **Ostia altar,** dedicated to Mars and the **frescoes** from the Esquiline colombarium.

Also the massive pavement of a suburban villa is particularly worthy of note (Gallery I). **Room VII** holds a masterpiece of the late Hellenic age: The **"Boxer"** depicts an exhausted athlete seated after having just fought (and won?) his match; note the wounds on face, nose and ears.

First Floor: One flight up, on the first floor, there's more . . . much more. Here the emphasis is on the iconographic trends in official Roman art, again many with considerable Greek influence. The collection is extremely rich and varied.

Room V, for example, contains marvelous pieces from suburban imperial villas (Anzio, Tivoli, Subiaco) and includes the "Anzio Apollo" and the magnificent "Crouching Aphrodite." The Lancellotti "Discobolus" **(Room VI),** the bronze "Dionysus," the "Wounded Niobid," and the amazingly beautiful "Reclining Hermaphrodite" (all in **Room VII**), and the not-to-be-missed Portonaccio Sarcophagus **(Room XII),** with its battle scenes between Roman and barbarian soldiers, are all simply thrilling.

You'll be amused to note the juxtaposition of the statues

INSIDER TIP:

One of Rome's newer museums, Palazzo Massimo is a hidden treasure. Don't miss Empress Livia's magic frescoed garden.

—DENNIS CIGLER
Tour coordinator & guide,
In Italy's Companions

---

in **Room II.** The busts of the emperor Hadrian, his wife Sabina, and Hadrian's lover, Antinous (the one to whom he dedicated an obelisk), are grouped together. The busts of the emperors will give you a good idea of what these men looked like. Another gallery is dedicated to women's head portraits.

The art in **Room XIV** is also memorable. Grouped under the title "Iconography and

---

Palazzo Massimo alle Terme

🗺 Map p. 76

✉ Largo di Villa Peretti 1

☎ 06 480201 or 06 3996 7700. Online tickets: www.coopculture .it

🕐 Closed Mon.

💲 $$ (You can buy a combined ticket to visit the other sites of the Museo Nazionale Romano: It is valid for three days). Audio guide: $. Guided tours in Italian: Sun.; for groups in English on request: $$$

🚌 Bus: C2, C3, H, 16, 38, 40, 50, 64, 66, 75, 82, 85, 90, 92, 170, 223, 310, 360, 649, 714, 910. Metro: Linea A (Termini), Linea B (Termini)

www.museonazionale romano.beniculturali.it

Celebration from the Severi to the Constantine," the pieces here include several commemorative sarcophagi. The artwork on some of the sarcophagi—for example that of Marcus Claudianus, with its scenes from the Old and New Testaments—indicates that influential Romans were beginning to forsake paganism for Christianity. In general, however, there is only one word for the carved reliefs on these stone coffins: breathtaking.

Top Floor

Whether you've been to Pompeii or not, you probably won't be prepared for the beauty of the summer triclinium (dining room) with the garden wall frescoes from the **House of Livia.** Married to Augustus and the mother of a future emperor, Tiberius, Livia also had taste. The walls of this room, transported here from a site on the Via Flaminia outside Rome, were frescoed to create an imaginary walled garden with trees, plants, flowers, exotic birds and animals, and fruits of all types. Incredibly, experts were able to remove the frescoes from each of the long side walls in a single piece. Take notice of the stucco work on the ceiling, as well as the grotesques, smallish painted decorations on walls and ceilings in which leaves, spirals, and mythological figures generally alternate.

Another set of staggeringly beautiful **frescoes** comes from a first-century villa discovered in 1879 on the grounds of the Villa Farnesina in Trastevere (see pp. 188–189). These frescoes have black backgrounds with friezes and decorative motifs.

The **mosaics** are equally enthralling. The four charioteers from a third-century villa belonging to the imperial Severi family show the delicacy of pictorial design. The marble inlay decorations from the Basilica of Junius Bassus are disturbingly modern. ∎

EXPERIENCE: A Pause Among the Sculptures

A short distance from the Basilica di San Giovanni, the former Rome health department, which for 50 years was the sore in Via Merulana, reopened in 2018 following a faithful reconstruction of the original 1929 building. It is now a dynamic and welcoming civic space that organizes meetings, workshops, and educational visits (*Via Merulana 121, tel 06 3996 7800, www.palazzomerulana.it, closed Tues.*).

The site hosts the Collezione Cerasi and about 100 pieces concentrating on figurative work of the Roman school from the 1920s to the 1940s, with some exceptions. Among the most interesting works are Giorgio De Chirico's "Mysterious Baths" and the great "Genesi n. 4" by Antonietta Raphaël, as well as works by Balla, Depero, Sironi, Donghi, and Capograssi.

The first room, Sala delle Sculture, is accessible at no cost. There is an entrance portico with a cafeteria, a bookshop, and garden, a place of refreshment, where you can sip a coffee and enjoy the gourmet dishes surrounded by the sculptures of Fontana, Raphaël, and Pericle Fazzini. On the other floors, you'll find the rest of the permanent collection, the temporary exhibits, a conference hall, and a splendid terrace for events.

TERME DI DIOCLEZIANO

The Terme di Diocleziano (Baths of Diocletian), inaugurated in A.D. 306, could accommodate about 3,000 bathers. They were built so well that much of the complex's outer structure is still standing. As in Trajan's and Caracalla's baths, the *natatio* (swimming pool), frigidarium, tepidarium, and *calidarium* were laid out along a central axis.

The Great Cloister of Santa Maria degli Angeli was built into a portion of the Baths of Diocletian.

In 1561, Pope Pius IV (1559–1565) commissioned Michelangelo (age 86) to design a church utilizing part of the baths. The result was **Santa Maria degli Angeli** *(Piazza della Repubblica, tel 06 488 0812, Bus: 60, 61, 62, 64, 115, 492, 640, Metro: Linea A/ Repubblica)*, the imposing entrance to which was built into an apse of the calidarium (hot room), while the vestibule corresponded to the ancient tepidarium (warm room).

In the 18th century, architect Luigi Vanvitelli changed the axis of the church by creating a new main altar opposite the entryway and transforming Michelangelo's nave into a somewhat oversize transept. The proportions are awe inspiring. The eight massive granite columns are 45 feet (14 m) high. The overwhelming transept is 298 feet (90 m) long, 88 feet (26 m) wide, and more than 90 feet (27 m) high.

In 1889, another portion of the baths was transformed into the **Museo Nazionale Romano** (National Museum of Rome), which has since been decentralized into four different sites (see p. 31). This branch, recently renovated, now holds the **Epigraphic Museum,** where 10,000 inscriptions and funerary monuments, along with mosaics and frescoes, illustrate aspects of ancient Roman daily life such as religion, education, and professions.

And don't miss the **Great Cloister,** built in 1565 and attributed to Michelangelo. ∎

Terme di Diocleziano

- 🗺 Map p. 76
- ✉ Viale E. De Nicola 78
- ☎ 06 4521 0411 or 06 3996 7700. Online tickets: www.coopculture.it
- 🕐 Closed Mon.
- 💲 $$. Audio guide: $. Guided tours in Italian: Sun.; in English on request: $$$
- 🚌 Bus: C2, C3, H, 16, 38, 40, 50, 64, 66, 75, 82, 85, 90, 92, 170, 223, 310, 360, 649, 714, 910. Metro: Linea A (Repubblica, Termini), Linea B (Termini)

www.museonazionale romano.beniculturali.it

More Places to Visit

■ Santa Maria della Vittoria's baroque decor reflects the style in fashion at the time of its completion.

Santa Maria della Vittoria

Built between 1608 and 1620, this church designed by Carlo Maderno was originally dedicated to St. Paul. But in 1622, in commemoration of a victory over Protestant forces in the Battle of the White Mountain, near Prague, it was renamed Santa Maria della Vittoria (St. Mary of Victory). The image of the Madonna displayed in the giant sunburst over the altar is a copy of one found near the scene of the battle and to which the victory was attributed.

The church's decoration is the epitome of baroque opulence. Marble, gilded stucco work, sculptures, and paintings abound. Despite the works of artists such as Guercino and Domenichino, the main attraction is Gian Lorenzo Bernini's **"Ecstasy of St. Theresa"** in the **Cornaro Chapel** at the left end of the transept. St. Theresa, enveloped in folds of marble drapery, wounded by an arrow shot by the cherubic angel to her left, lies in the throes of a mystical ecstasy. Members of the Cornaro family are sculpted into what appear to be theater boxes on the right and left walls of the chapel. This emphasizes the dramatic, theatrical effect so often achieved by Bernini and is enhanced by the indirect lighting, in

this case from above, favored by the artist.
🔼 Map p. 76 ✉ Via XX Settembre 17
☎ 06 4274 0571 🕐 Closed noon–3:30 p.m.
🚌 Bus: 16, 60, 61, 62, 85, 150, 492, 590.
Metro: Linea A (Repubblica)

Santa Susanna

It is no coincidence that the church of Santa Susanna is located just outside the perimeter (marked by the round church across the street) of the Baths of Diocletian. Susanna was martyred during Diocletian's reign after refusing to worship a pagan god and to marry (supposedly) the emperor's son. The original church, founded in the sixth century, has been rebuilt many times since then. The facade by Carlo Maderno, who also designed St. Peter's facade, is an excellent example of late Renaissance/Mannerist architecture and the interior is richly decorated. Santa Susanna was the national church for the American community of Rome until 2017, when the community acquired a new site in the church of San Patrizio a Villa Ludovisi.
🔼 Map p. 76 ✉ Via XX Settembre 15 ☎ 06 4201 3734 🕐 Temporarily closed for restoration 🚌 Bus: 16, 60, 61, 62, 85, 150, 492, 590. Metro: Linea A (Repubblica)

The Trevi Fountain, other Renaissance and baroque masterpieces, a major museum, and Via Veneto with its luxurious hotels and cafés

FONTANA DI TREVI TO VIA VENETO

Passersby admire a vehicle parked along luxury-laden Via Veneto.

FONTANA DI TREVI TO VIA VENETO

Instantly recognizable, the giant Fontana di Trevi (Trevi Fountain) lies tucked away among narrow side streets. Even in a city like Rome, where fountains abound, you will find it hard not to be impressed by Nicola Salvi's dramatic, late baroque masterpiece, cunningly built into the side of a contemporary princely palace.

Even though it is right downtown, the area around the Trevi Fountain—where simple artisans' shops and boutiques mix with baroque masterpieces—has retained much of its traditional character. Nearby is the Palazzo Colonna, with its private art gallery. Walk uphill along Via della Dataria to reach the Quirinal Hill and, atop it, the Palazzo del Quirinale. Once the summer residence of the popes, the palace is now the home of the president of the Italian Republic, where most afternoons you can see the changing of the guard.

After the late Renaissance popes made this their summer getaway (today's pontiffs head instead to Castel Gandolfo on Lake Albano),

the surrounding neighborhood became more desirable and several important churches, such as the Jesuit Sant'Andrea al Quirinale and San Carlo alle Quattro Fontane, were built here by architects such as Bernini and Borromini.

These two masters of Italian architecture were thrown together repeatedly; in fact, at the outset Borromini worked for the older Bernini as a draftsman. They had already collaborated on Palazzo Barberini, the huge baroque palace that Maffeo Barberini, recently elected Urban VIII, had decided to refurbish and expand to make worthy of the Barberini family's newly exalted status. Decorated by some of the major artists of the 17th century, it is now one of the two sites of the National Gallery (the other is Palazzo Corsini). Its collection includes a series of masterpiece paintings ranging from a Fra Filippo Lippi "Annunciation" to Caravaggio's "Judith Beheading Holofernes."

Piazza Barberini & Via Veneto

Near the palace lies Piazza Barberini, which is today both a busy traffic circle and the center of a major shopping area. Because of all the activity, and despite the repaved traffic island, most passersby probably don't even notice Bernini's charming Fontana del Tritone, one of the first fountains he designed.

The Fontana delle Api (Fountain of the Bees), which enshrines the Barberini family's bee symbol, is now located across the street. Today's Romans don't pay much attention to this monument either, but when it was erected in the 17th century things were different. An inscription stated that the fountain had been put up in the 22nd year of the

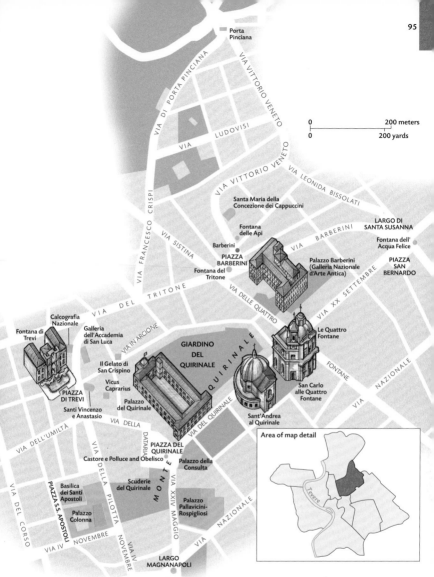

Porta Pinciana

VIA DI PORTA PINCIANA

VIA VITTORIO VENETO

LUDOVISI

VIA

200 meters
200 yards

VIA VITTORIO VENETO

VIA LEONIDA BISSOLATI

FRANCESCO CRISPI

VIA SISTINA

Santa Maria della Concezione dei Cappuccini

LARGO DI SANTA SUSANNA

Fontana delle Api

VIA BARBERINI

Fontana dell' Acqua Felice

Barberini

PIAZZA BARBERINI

VIA

Palazzo Barberini (Galleria Nazionale d'Arte Antica)

PIAZZA SAN BERNARDO

Fontana del Tritone

VIA DELLE QUATTRO

VIA XX SETTEMBRE

VIA DEL TRITONE

VIA IN ARCIONE

Calcografia Nazionale

Galleria dell'Accademia di San Luca

GIARDINO DEL QUIRINALE

Le Quattro Fontane

FONTANE

Fontana di Trevi

Il Gelato di San Crispino

NAZIONALE

Vicus Caprarius

QUIRINALE

San Carlo alle Quattro Fontane

VIA

PIAZZA DI TREVI

Palazzo del Quirinale

Santi Vincenzo e Anastasio

VIA DEL QUIRINALE

Sant'Andrea al Quirinale

VIA DELLA

DATARIA

Area of map detail

VIA DELL'UMILTÀ

MONTE

PIAZZA DEL QUIRINALE

VIA DELLA PILOTTA

Castore e Polluce and Obelisco

Palazzo della Consulta

Basilica dei Santi Apostoli

Scuderie del Quirinale

VIA XXIV MAGGIO

Palazzo Pallavicini-Rospigliosi

Tevere

VIA DEL CORSO

PIAZZA SS. APOSTOLI

Palazzo Colonna

VIA NAZIONALE

VIA IV NOVEMBRE

VIA IV NOVEMBRE

VIA

LARGO MAGNANAPOLI

papacy of the Barberini pope, Urban VIII. Unfortunately, it was unveiled a few weeks before the anniversary, making the superstitious Romans nervous. Rightly so, it would seem. Urban died eight days before his 22nd year would have begun.

The Fountain of the Bees sits at the start of Via Veneto, the long winding avenue that for decades was this city's "great white way" as well as the location of the most elegant hotels and cafés. Once (both in Roman times as well as much later, in the 16th and 17th centuries) a neighborhood of sprawling residential villas, after 1870 this area was wantonly subdivided in a frenzy of real estate speculation. Following World War II, the Via Veneto became known for the dolce vita, an era of now vanished glamour and glitter that was depicted in many movies of the time, in particular, Federico Fellini's *La Dolce Vita* (1960). ∎

FONTANA DI TREVI

By Roman standards the Fontana di Trevi, or Trevi Fountain, is almost new; it was, after all, built only some 240 years ago. However, the water that flows through it was brought to Rome by the Aqua Virgo, a largely underground aqueduct originally built by Marcus Agrippa (Augustus' right-hand man) in 19 B.C. to supply water to baths in the Campus Martius.

■ **The Fontana di Trevi is a masterpiece of baroque allegory.**

The Aqua Virgo got its name because the spring from which it comes was reputedly revealed to Agrippa's soldiers by a young virgin. You can see her in the relief on the right side of the fountain's upper portion (the attic) as she points to the spring.

A succession of popes thought about building a monumental fountain on this spot, and various projects, including one by Bernini, were presented. In 1732, Pope Clement XII—whose papal crest you can see at the top of the fountain—approved a design submitted by Nicola Salvi.

The project, which took 30 years to complete, emphasizes the central portion of the fountain, dominated by Neptune. Below, among the rocks, two Tritons struggle with two horses (one calm, one bucking to represent the sea in its various moods), while the bubbling and gushing water re-creates the ocean's power and turbulence. These central figures were begun by little-known Giovanbattista Maini but were finished by Pietro Bracci. Created by Filippo Valle, the figures in the niches represent Abundance (left) and Health (right). The four figures set against the attic, all by different sculptors, represent the beneficial and fertilizing effects of water in the different seasons.

As the terminus of the Aqua Virgo aqueduct, the Trevi Fountain is also one of Rome's several *mostre d'acqua*, a term meant to denote a monumental fountain with enough pressure to push water on to other outlets.

INSIDER TIP:

Near the Trevi is Vicus Caprarius, where you can see ancient Roman dwellings. Listen closely to hear water from Aqua Virgo, the last functioning aqueduct in Rome.

—PAUL BENNETT
*National Geographic writer &
founder of Context Travel*

Where and when the custom began of throwing a coin (over your shoulder, if you please!) into the Trevi Fountain in order to guarantee a return trip to Rome is not really known. But to judge from the amount and type of coins pitched in here daily, the practice has become generally accepted by tourists and was, of course, immortalized in the 1954 film *Three Coins in the Fountain*.

Don't miss the beautiful late 18th-century aedicula (niche) on the building at the corner of the piazza with Via del Lavatore. Facing it is the high baroque church of **Santi Vincenzo e Anastasio**, parish church for the popes while they lived on the Quirinal. In the crypt are the hearts of almost all the popes of the 17th, 18th, and 19th centuries. The surrounding streets, Via del Lavatore (where there is a morning food market), Via della Panetteria, and Via in Arcione, have grocery and artisans' shops. ∎

Fontana di Trevi

- 🅰 Map p. 95
- ✉ Piazza di Trevi
- 🚌 Bus: C3, 51, 53, 62, 63, 71, 80, 83, 85, 117, 160, 492, 628. Metro: Linea A (Barberini)

Vicus Caprarius

- 🅰 Map p. 95
- ✉ Vicolo del Puttarello 25
- ☎ 339 778 6192
- 💲 $
- 🕐 Closed Mon.; opens at 11 a.m.

www.vicuscaprarius
.com

EXPERIENCE: Doin' the Gelato Crawl

What is it that makes gelato so special and different from the ice cream you eat at home? One reason: Gelato is kept frozen at a lower temperature for a shorter period of time than ice cream. It also has less butterfat, which intensifies the flavor.

And flavor you will find. Varieties of fresh fruit gelato include melon, raspberry, strawberry, kiwi, banana, watermelon, lemon, and orange. The amazing array of cream gelatos runs from vanilla (*crema*) and *fior di latte* (cream) to yogurt, hazelnut, walnut, almond, pistachio, and nougat. And then there's chocolate, a remarkable range of tastes from *stracciatella* (vanilla with chocolate stripes) and milk chocolate to dark chocolate, darker chocolate, *bacio*, *gianduia*, and many more.

You will find *gelaterie* everywhere in Rome. It's hard to go wrong, but there is a difference between those that sell *gelato artigianale*, made on the premises, and those offering *gelato industriale*, which only looks like it's made on the premises. Some of the best are the tried-and-true like **Alberto Pica** (*Via della Seggiola 12*), near Campo dei Fiori; **Giolitti** (*Via degli Uffici del Vicario 40*) and **Il Gelato di San Crispino** (*Piazza della Maddalena 3*), both near the Pantheon; **Gelateria Fassi** (*Via Principe Eugenio 65/67*), near Termini Station; and **Al Settimo Gelo** (*Via Vodice 21a*) and **Gelateria dei Gracchi** (*Via dei Gracchi 272*), both in the Prati area. The **Gelateria del Teatro** (*Via di San Simone 70*), off Via dei Coronari, has a mouthwatering range of out-of-the-ordinary flavors. In Trastevere try **La Fonte della Salute** (*Via Cardinale Marmaggi 2*) and **Fiordiluna** (*Via della Lungaretta 96*).

For something different there is *cremolata*, like sherbet but made only with fresh, seasonal fruit. **Umberto** at Bar Orchidea, in front of the Gesù church, has the best.

FOUNTAINS & AQUEDUCTS

Immortalized in two films, Jean Negulesco's *Three Coins in the Fountain* (1954) and Fellini's *La Dolce Vita* (1960), the Trevi Fountain is certainly the best known fountain in Rome. But it is hardly alone. Water spouts from fountains *(fontane)*—small and large, sculpted and plain—everywhere in the Eternal City. It trickles, too, from the small neighborhood *fontanelle* from which many Romans once drew their drinking water.

Rome's many neighborhood *fontanelle* offer thirst-relief on hot summer days.

Romans swear by their fontanelle, learning early that a finger placed over the spigot opening turns a small hole in the top into a drinking spout. It gushes from the *mostre d'acqua* (monumental fonts) that help circulate water throughout the fountain network.

"Nothing can be more agreeable to the eyes of a stranger, especially in the heats of summer, than the great number of public fountains that appear in every part of Rome, embellished with all the ornaments of sculpture, and pouring forth prodigious quantities of cool, delicious water," wrote British writer Tobias Smollett in 1765. In fact, the fountains are omnipresent, testifying both to the grandiosity of the city's former

ruling class, and to the special relationship that Romans have always had with this life-giving liquid. Historically, Rome had few nearby sources of water, and its engineers built aqueducts *(acquedotti)* to bring enough of it into the urban area, from as far as 31 miles (50 km) away.

Spectacular Works of Art

For a fountain lover, Rome is a dream. In the Trident area, on the same aqueduct line as the Trevi, are the **Barcaccia** (at the foot of the Spanish Steps; see pp. 110–111), the **Pantheon Fountain,** and the magnificent 16th-century **fountains of Piazza Navona,** designed by Gian Lorenzo Bernini. The star attraction

INSIDER TIP:

The best water you could ever taste comes from the little metal fountains you see everywhere in Rome. It's direct from the aqueduct source.

—RAFAEL SANDOR
National Geographic International Channel

■ **Detail of fountain, Piazza della Rotonda**

in Piazza Navona is Bernini's **Fontana dei Quattro Fiumi** (Fountain of the Four Rivers), inaugurated in 1651 and financed to the tune of 29,000 scudi by a highly unpopular bread tax. Its four stone giants represent the great rivers of the then known world: the Ganges, the Plate, the Danube, and the Nile, whose veiled countenance stood for the mystery of its (then) uncharted source.

Bernini also designed the **Fontana del Tritone** (Triton Fountain) and the **Fontana delle Api** (Fountain of the Bees) in Piazza Barberini. These fountains are fed by another mostra d'acqua, the oversize fountain in Piazza San Bernardo near the Grand Hotel. Commonly called the **Moses Fountain** because of its large central figure, its real name is the Fontana dell'Acqua Felice, after the modern aqueduct built in 1586 by Pope Sixtus V to bring running water to that area. It also sends water to the four charming **corner fountains on the intersection of Via delle Quattro Fontane with Via XX Settembre,** and to another beautiful Bernini **Triton Fountain** in the courtyard at Via della Panetteria 15 (near the Trevi).

A third mostra d'acqua is **Fontana dell'Acqua Paola** (see p. 191) on the Janiculum Hill, which marks the reopening in 1612 of Trajan's aqueduct, built in A.D. 109 to bring water from Lake Bracciano. Probably one of the city's most beautiful fountains is the **Fontana delle Tartarughe** (Fountain of the Tortoises; see pp. 204–205) in Piazza Mattei, a tiny square tucked away behind the Ghetto. In 1581 Giacomo della Porta's design was executed by Taddeo Landini, who sculpted the four boys and dolphins that make up this bronze composition. The tortoises, by an unknown artist, were added a century later.

EXPERIENCE: Tours of the Fountains

Enjoying the beauty of Rome's celebrated fountains is one of the best parts of visiting the Eternal City. A guided tour will give you an opportunity to learn how the aqueduct system has served the city practically and aesthetically for centuries.

Argiletum Tour Operators *(tel 06 4782 5706, www.argiletumtour.com)* organizes a three-hour walk that includes some of the city's most important fountains,

such as Trevi and Piazza Navona.

Fragrance Tour *(tel 06 3260 0636, www.fragrancetour.com)* offers a private walking tour in different languages that highlights Rome's most famous fountains, as well as other notable feats of architecture. It also allows you to extend or modify the itinerary.

Storiavivaviaggi *(tel 06 6502 9853, www.storiavivaviaggi.it)* offers evening tours from Piazza di Spagna to Piazza Navona.

QUIRINALE & AROUND

The Monte Quirinale (Quirinal Hill), the highest of Rome's seven famous hills, is just up the street from the Trevi Fountain and offers a magnificent view over the city. Probably named after the ancient Temple of Quirinus, which once stood here, it boasts a fine piazza as well as two outstanding churches, of contrasting design, created by rivals Bernini and Borromini.

As far back as the first century B.C., this area had a particular residential cachet. The writer Martial lived here, as did Cicero's good friend, Pomponius Atticus. In the late 1500s, Pope Gregory XIII decided to build a summer residence here, where it was somewhat cooler than at the Vatican. Over the decades many important artists—Ponzio, Fontana, Bernini, Maderno, Fuga—worked on the **Palazzo del Quirinale,** which has a Renaissance facade facing onto the piazza and a secondary entrance on the wing known as the *manica lunga* (long sleeve) on the Via del Quirinale. After Italian unification in 1870, Italy's Savoy kings moved into the palazzo. Since 1947, it has been the residence of the Italian president.

Other Quirinale Palazzi

Several other important palazzi front the piazza. The **Consulta,** looking toward St. Peter's, was built by Pope Clement XII in the 1730s to house a papal tribunal. Today it is the site of Italy's Constitutional Court.

Next door to it is the **Palazzo Pallavicini-Rospigliosi,** constructed in 1603 for the Borghese family. And directly facing across from the Quirinale is the renovated **Scuderie del**

■ At the center of Piazza del Quirinale, statues of Castor and Pollux flank one of Rome's ancient obelisks.

Quirinale, or stables, now used as a venue for world-class art shows; unlike most of Rome's museums, it is open every day.

Sant'Andrea al Quirinale

In 1658, the Jesuits decided to build a new church to serve their novices. They chose the "Strada Pia" (today's XX Settembre), the road designed a century earlier by Michelangelo to connect the Palazzo del Quirinale—then the summer residence of the popes—to the Porta Pia gate. The man in charge was Cardinal Camillo Pamphilj, and his choice of designer fell on Gian Lorenzo Bernini, who had already created the Piazza Navona fountains for the Pamphilj family.

Oval in shape, the church is generally considered Bernini's masterpiece in ecclesiastical architecture. The interior embodies his theory that the visual arts, combined with effective lighting and color, should aim at the creation of an intensely emotional, even theatrical, experience. For Bernini lovers, this is a site not to be missed. Note the colored marbles, the gilded ceiling, and the stucco cherubs tumbling down from the small, elliptical dome in a swirl of frenetic activity.

San Carlo alle Quattro Fontane

How fitting that the architect of San Carlo alle Quattro Fontane, down the street from Sant'Andrea, should be none other than Bernini's archrival, Francesco Borromini. In his first solo commission, Borromini seems to have knowingly created an antithesis to Bernini's opulence. Take note especially of the church's monochromatic off-white interior. Completed in 1667, the church is so small that it could fit into one of the four supporting pilasters of St. Peter's.

INSIDER TIP:

Try the gelato at Il Gelato di San Crispino (*Via della Panetteria 42, www.ilgelatodisancrispino.com*). Favorites include the wild honey and *crema al whisky* flavors; the latter features a 32-year-old Highland malt.

—IAN D'AGATA
National Geographic contributor & director of the International Wine Academy of Roma

---

Borromini's genius is exemplified by his sublimely beautiful dome, as well as a beehive of geometric design—crosses, octagons, and hexagons in relief. Stucco decorations ingeniously hide the church's windows.

Outside, note the four late 16th-century fountains (two river gods and two virtues, Fidelity and Strength) at the intersection with **Via delle Quattro Fontane.** From the intersection's center you can see three of Rome's obelisks—but watch out for Roman drivers! ∎

Palazzo del Quirinale

🗺 Map p. 95

✉ Piazza del Quirinale

☎ 06 3996 7557

🕐 Only with a booking. Closed Mon. & Tues. Changing of the guard: Sun. at 6 p.m. from June to Sept.; at 4 p.m. rest of year

💲 $$

🚌 Bus: 40, 60, 64, 70, 71, 117, 170. Metro: Linea A (Repubblica), Linea B (Cavour)

Sant'Andrea al Quirinale

🗺 Map p. 95

✉ Via del Quirinale 30

☎ 06 4819 399

🕐 Closed noon–3 p.m. & Mon.

🚌 Bus: H, 40, 60, 64, 70, 71, 170. Metro: Linea A (Barberini)

San Carlo alle Quattro Fontane

🗺 Map p. 95

✉ Via del Quirinale 23

☎ 06 4883 261

🕐 Closed p.m. & Sun.

🚌 Bus: C3, H, 40, 52, 53, 60, 62, 63, 64, 66, 70, 80, 82, 83, 85, 160, 170, 492. Metro: Linea A (Barberini)

PALAZZO BARBERINI & GALLERIA NAZIONALE D'ARTE ANTICA

An architectural wonder, the Palazzo Barberini was the home of the powerful, aristocratic Barberini family. It was purchased after Maffeo Barberini was elected Pope Urban VIII in 1623. A wealthy art patron, the pope hired some of the major artists of the 17th century—Gian Lorenzo Bernini, Francesco Borromini, and Pietro da Cortona among them—to build and decorate the palazzo, today the seat of the National Gallery and its masterpieces.

The supreme symbol of the baroque era, the *reggia* of the Barberini family, has an area of 130,000 square feet (12,000 sq m), 187 rooms, and 11 staircases. The building is located a short distance from Piazza Barberini, halfway along the road ascending to the Incrocio delle Quattro Fontane.

Gian Lorenzo Bernini (1598-1680) and Francesco Borromini (1599-1667) both contributed greatly to the palazzo's design, although the original is attributed to Carlo Maderno, Borromini's uncle, who died a year after construction began. Commissioned in 1625, it provides a good idea of how the nobility lived in 17th-century Rome. Borromini is believed to be the architect of the helical stairway in the southern wing of the building. It can be seen from Via delle Quattro Fontane and originally led to the Pope's library. Bernini designed the square staircase that allows access to the north wing and the central hall on two stories of the building.

■ Italian rococo artist Antonio Corradini sculpted this "Vestal Tuccia" in the 1740s.

Visiting the Museum

Be sure to use the map distributed at the ticket office, as it will facilitate navigation through the museum's many rooms. And remember to always look up: Like others of his time, Pope Urban VIII considered ceiling art an essential part of a palace's decor (the

Sala del Mappamondo on the first floor is particularly admirable).

The permanent collection of the gallery has been reorganized and is currently found on two floors. On the ground floor and in the north wing of the *piano nobile* there are displayed some lovely wooden crucifixes and selected paintings from the 13th to the 16th centuries, while the south wing of the first floor, to which you accede by crossing the Sala Ovale and the Sala Marmi, presents Neapolitan painting from the 17th-century, an 18th-century collection preserving important works by Maratti, Batoni, Canaletto, Subleyras, Mengs, and van Wittel, and paintings from the donazione Lemme.

The gallery contains paintings from various parts of Italy and Europe. You can admire works by Fra Filippo Lippi like "Annunciation with two Kneeling Donors" and "Madonna and Child Enthroned" (1437) with a late Gothic frame; as well as those of il Perugino, Antoniazzo Romano, and Pedro Fernandez. It also shows Andrea del Sarto's "Sacred Family" and "Madonna and Child," as well as Piero del Cosimo's "Mary Maddalena." Particularly notable are the two paintings by Giovanni Bellini ("Christ Blessing" and "Portrait of a Man") and the "Rape of the Sabine Women" by Giovan Antonio Bazzi, known (for obvious reasons) as "Il Sodoma."

You also won't want to miss Raphael's portrait of his mistress,

"La Fornarina" ("The Baker's Daughter"). Although some art historians attribute it to his pupil, Giulio Romano, it is probably significant that Raphael's name is lettered on her bracelet.

The 16th and 18th centuries are the best represented: In the rooms you will find works

---

INSIDER TIP:

Choose a hotel that is close to the attractions. You need to walk Rome to best explore it.

—ANTONIO BARBIERI
National Geographic contributor & co-founder of Concierge in Rome

---

like Lorenzo Lotto's "Sacred Conversation," Titian's "Venus and Adonis," Tintoretto's "St. Jerome," and exceptional Caravaggios ("Judith Beheading Holofernes," "Narcissus," and "St. Francis in Meditation").

And farther on are paintings by Guido Reni (including his "Beatrice Cenci"), Domenichino ("The Virgin and Child with Saints John the Baptist and Petronius"), Guercino ("Flagellation of Christ"), and the Carracci brothers. We should remember, among the most interesting spaces in the building, the first floor, the splendid **Sala delle Colonne,** with a Renaissance Fontana di Bacco, and, on the *piano nobile*, Pietro da Cortona's magnificent ceiling in the **Salone,** the "Allegory of Divine Providence." ∎

Palazzo Barberini & Galleria Nazionale d'Arte Antica

🗺 Map p. 95

✉ Via delle Quattro Fontane 13

☎ 06 4814 591 or 06 32810 (reservations for groups)

🕐 Closed Mon.

💲 \$\$ (the ticket is valid for ten days). Audio guide: \$. Visitors must leave the following in the lockers at the entrance: helmets, bags, backpacks, and objects considered unsuitable.

🚌 Bus: 53, 61, 62, 63, 80, 81, 83, 160, 492, 590. Metro: Linea A (Barberini)

www. barberinicorsini.org

VIA VENETO

In ancient times, this area was a residential suburb where the wealthy had their landscaped villas. Today, there are next to no traces of those first-century buildings or of the extensive gardens that surrounded most of them.

Crowds still flock to the cafés that line Via Veneto, the hub of *la dolce vita* in the 1950s and '60s.

Via Veneto

 Map p. 95

Bus: 53, 61, 63, 80, 83, 150, 160, 590. Metro: Linea A (Barberini)

The best known of the first-century gardens were the Horti Sallustiani. They surrounded the magnificent home of Sallust, a Roman general and scholar who was a contemporary of Julius Caesar. After the turmoil of the fifth and sixth centuries A.D., a period marked by barbarian invasions and a series of wars that interrupted the water supply into the city, the area was abandoned in favor of more central zones.

The suburban tradition was reborn in the 17th century, when the Ludovisi family built its sprawling villa here. Its sale in the late 19th century was part of the real estate speculation that opened the way for modern urban development.

The Sweet Life

By the early 20th century, the Via Veneto (officially the Via Vittorio Veneto) had become Rome's most elegant street, the site of the city's best hotels and restaurants. In the 1950s, its upper portion became the undisputed hub of *la dolce vita* (the sweet life), a term used during Italy's economic boom of the 1950s and '60s to describe the gossip and glitter of Roman night life, the comings and goings of the Eternal City's international galaxy of stars, and the unrelenting assault of its tabloid photographers on the city's beautiful people.

The era was depicted in many movies of the time, in particular *La Dolce Vita* (1960), one of the finest works of Federico Fellini. The movie includes the unforgettable scene of a voluptuous Anita Ekberg, the prey of the cynical reporter Marcello Rubini (Marcello Mastroianni), immersing herself in the waters of the Trevi Fountain (see pp. 96–97). The most memorable character was Paparazzo, Rubini's photographer sidekick.

By then the street's most famous bars and cafés—Doney's, Café de Paris, and Harry's Bar—had become hangouts for actors and directors such as Sophia Loren, Gina Lollobrigida, Vittorio De Sica, Roberto Rossellini, Ingrid Bergman, Liz Taylor, Richard Burton, Burt Lancaster, and many more who went there to see and to be seen.

Today, however, Via Veneto is simply one of Rome's broader avenues, pleasingly lined with charming (and very expensive) sidewalk cafés, elegant shops, and luxury hotels such as the Excelsior and the Marriott Grand Hotel Flora. At the upper end is **Porta Pinciana,** the fortified gateway built into the Aurelian Wall in 403 by the emperor Honorius, leading to Villa Borghese and the Galleria Borghese.

Its lower end, where you'll find banks, ministries, and more hotels, ends in **Piazza Barberini,** one of downtown Rome's major traffic junctions and the site of two famous Bernini statues (see pp. 94–95). ■

Thwarting Pickpockets & Other Thieves

The crime rate in Italy is lower than in many other countries. But, as in any big city, Rome has its share of extremely talented pickpockets and purse snatchers.

As a result, it is a good idea to learn how to protect yourself from thieves and also how to file a police report, should the worst happen. Ensure a smooth trip by following a few simple rules, many of which you probably follow at home.

- Leave your passport, valuables, money, and credit cards you don't need right away in a hotel safe—but keep a photocopy of your passport with you.
- Try not to bring out tempting wads of cash when you're paying for anything.
- Cameras and purses should be worn across the chest.
- If you wear a backpack, take it off when you are on the metro or bus.
- Do not keep your wallet in an outside jacket or pants pocket.

- If you are sitting at an outdoor café, do not hang your purse or backpack on a chair near the street or leave it sitting on the ground.
- Do not wear expensive watches or jewelry while touring.
- If you are surrounded by a small group of children carrying pieces of cardboard or newspaper, don't be intimidated. Yell "*Via, via!*" and, if you're comfortable doing so, swat the cardboard away.
- Be especially alert on crowded public transportation, especially bus No. 64.

In the unfortunate event you are the victim of a robbery, head for the nearest police station (*commissariato*) or Carabinieri post (*stazione dei Carabinieri*). The stations most used to dealing with foreigners downtown are those at Piazza Collegio Romano (police) and Piazza Venezia (Carabinieri), and, in Trastevere, Via Francesco a Ripa (police) and Via Garibaldi 43 (Carabinieri).

More Places to Visit

Galleria Colonna

Although only open on Saturday mornings, the art gallery of the magnificent 15th-century **Palazzo Colonna** is well worth a visit. Built between 1650 and 1700 to house the Colonna family's art collection, the gallery is a masterpiece of baroque architecture with colored marbles, ornate mirrors, and frescoed ceilings. You'll find works by such masters as Bronzino, Ghirlandaio, Jacopo and Domenico Tintoretto, and Rubens. Walk around the corner to Piazza S.S. Apostoli 66 to look at the facade. Beside it is the **Basilica dei Santi Apostoli** with its 15th-century portico and an 18th-century facade designed by Carlo Fontana.

🗺 Map p. 95 ✉ Via della Pilotta 17 ☎ 06 6784 350 🕐 Only open 9 a.m.–1:15 p.m. Sat.; closed Aug. 💲 $$ (includes guided tour in English at noon) 🚌 Bus: 30, 40, 46, 62, 64, 70, 81, 87, 130, 190, 492, 628, 916. Tram: 8

Galleria dell'Accademia di San Luca

Since the 1930s, when the neighborhood near the Roman Forum, where it was formerly located, was razed by Mussolini, the Academy of St. Luke has been housed in Palazzo Carpegna near the Trevi Fountain. The late 16th-century building, originally designed by Giacomo della Porta, was later modified by Borromini, who built its spiral staircase. This was one of the little optical diversions that Borromini and his rival Bernini liked to create to trick the eye of the beholder. The staircase is beyond the tiny open garden on the right, which is decorated with 19th- and 20th-century sculptures.

The academy was founded in the late 16th century by a group of artists whose gifts, along with bequests by nonmembers, make up the interesting collection. It was named for St. Luke because the Apostle was supposed to have had artistic inclinations. The collection includes works by such masters as Raphael, Titian,

Bronzino, Rubens, Van Dyck, and Canova, as well as some of the few female artists of the time, including Lavinia Fontana, Angelika Kauffmann, and Élisabeth Vigée-Lebrun.

Nearby, at Via della Stamperia 6, is the **Calcografia Nazionale,** with what may be the largest collection of copperplate engravings in the world. It has more than 20,000 plates, including more than 1,400 by G. B. Piranesi, and is generally open to the public.

🗺 Map p. 95 ✉ Piazza dell'Accademia di San Luca 77 ☎ 06 6798 850 🕐 Closed Sun. & after 12:30 p.m. 🚌 Bus: C3, 51, 53, 62, 63, 71, 80, 83, 85, 117, 160, 492, 628. Metro: Linea A (Barberini)

Santa Maria della Concezione dei Cappuccini

From an architectural point of view, Our Lady of the Conception of the Capuchins, named after the hooded Franciscan monks that run it, is simple and unprepossessing, an attempt by its founder, Cardinal Antonio Barberini (the younger brother of Pope Urban VIII—he is buried there), to run counter to the then (1626) baroque tide. Inside, however, there is rich decoration. The first chapel on the right has Guido Reni's "St. Michael Trampling on the Devil" and was decorated by Pietro da Cortona; the second has works by Lanfranco; the third by Domenichino; and the fifth by Andrea Sacchi. Most visitors, however, head to the **museum** in the old convent—which boasts a purported Caravaggio—and to the unique **crypt** below, where several somewhat macabre but nonetheless fascinating underground burial chapels are artistically decorated with the skeletons and loose bones of some 4,000 Capuchins. Take a sweater.

🗺 Map p. 95 ✉ Via Veneto 27 ☎ 06 8880 3695 🕐 Church & crypt: closed 1–3 p.m. 💲 Museum: $$ 🚌 Bus: C3, 52, 53, 61, 63, 80, 83, 150, 160, 590. Metro: Linea A (Barberini)

The magnificent Spanish Steps, elegant shops, the impressive Piazza del Popolo, and shady Villa Borghese park

PIAZZA DI SPAGNA TO VILLA BORGHESE

■ Caravaggio's "Youth With a Fruit Basket" (ca 1594), Galleria Borghese

PIAZZA DI SPAGNA TO VILLA BORGHESE

The Italian word *salotto,* living room, describes an area that is both central and
welcoming. In that sense the Tridente, and in particular Piazza di Spagna, is the salotto
of Rome, the neighborhood that best plays host to the city's myriad visitors, who
come to dine, shop, and revisit Rome's architectural, artistic, and archaeological past.

The area begins just inside the Porta del
Popolo (once called Porta Flaminia), the
gateway in the Aurelian Wall that was the
terminus of the Via Flaminia, the Roman
road built to connect the capital to Rimini
on the Adriatic Sea. It includes important
archaeological monuments such as Augustus' mausoleum and his Ara Pacis, Renaissance palaces such as Villa Medici, and
innumerable churches, including Trinità dei
Monti, with its splendid view of the city.

The name, "il Tridente," literally something with three teeth, takes its cue from
the street plan developed by the popes
of the 1500s, who were then the city's
temporal rulers. Three major streets fan
out from Piazza del Popolo: Via di Ripetta,
which ran to the ancient river port; Via del
Babuino, which reaches Piazza di Spagna;
and Via del Corso, which cuts straight
through downtown Rome before ending at
Piazza Venezia. The side streets in the Tridente, such as the evocative Via
Margutta, are interesting
and much quieter than
the big three.

For centuries, the area
stretching from the Pincio
to the Tiber River had been
uninhabited. Rumored to be
haunted by evil spirits, this was a
weak point in the city's defenses.
With the construction of Santa Maria
del Popolo and the other churches of
Piazza del Popolo all this was to change.
The area was transformed into the most
famous fashion district in the city. The
Salita del Pincio leads from Piazza del
Popolo to Villa Borghese, a wonderful park in which there is the
lovely Galleria Borghese.
On the northwestern
edge of the park, you will
also find the Museo di
Valle Giulia and the Gal-
leria Nazionale d'Arte Moderna. Piazza di Spagna, on
the other hand, is home to the
Spanish Steps leading to the Chiesa
della Trinità dei Monti. ∎

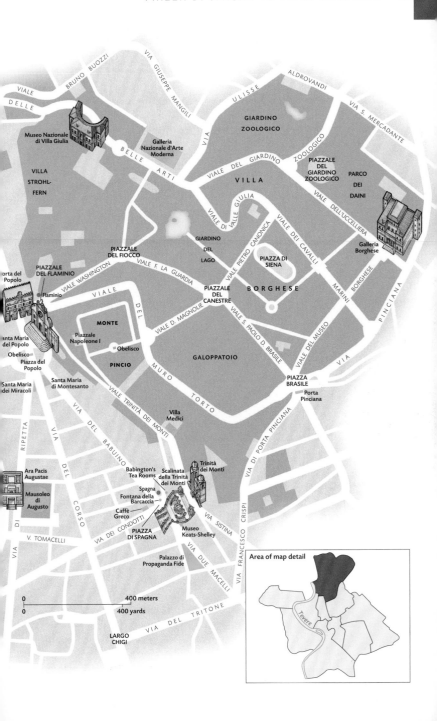

VIALE
DELLE

BRUNO BUOZZI

VIA GIUSEPPE MANGILI

ULISSE ALDROVANDI

VIA S. MERCADANTE

Museo Nazionale
di Villa Giulia

Galleria
Nazionale d'Arte
Moderna

BELLE

ARTI

VIA

GIARDINO
ZOOLOGICO

VIALE DEL GIARDINO

ZOOLOGICO

PIAZZALE
DEL
GIARDINO
ZOOLOGICO

PARCO
DEI
DAINI

VILLA
STROHL-
FERN

VIALE DI VILLA GIULIA

VILLA

VIALE DELL'UCCELLIERA

Galleria
Borghese

PIAZZALE
DEL FIOCCO

GIARDINO
DEL
LAGO

VIALE PIETRO CANONICA

VIALE DEI CAVALLI

PIAZZA DI
SIENA

rta del
Popolo

PIAZZALE
DEL FLAMINIO

VIALE F. LA GUARDIA

VIALE WASHINGTON

VIALE DEL

B O R G H E S E

MARINI

BORGHESE

PINCIANA

VIA

VIALE
Flaminio

PIAZZALE
DEL
CANESTRE

anta Maria
del Popolo

MONTE

Piazzale
Napoleone I

Obelisco
Piazza del
Popolo

Obelisco

Santa Maria
dei Miracoli

PINCIO

Santa Maria
di Montesanto

VIALE TRINITÀ DEI MONTI

MURO

VIALE D. MAGNOLIE

TORTO

VIALE S. PAOLO D. BRASILE

GALOPPATOIO

VIALE DEL MUSEO

PIAZZA
BRASILE

Porta
Pinciana

RIPETTA

VIA

VIA DEL

BABUINO

Villa
Medici

VIA DI PORTA PINCIANA

VIA

DEL

Ara Pacis
Augustae

Mausoleo
di
Augusto

CORSO

Babington's
Tea Rooms

Spagna

Caffè
Greco

PIAZZA
DI SPAGNA

VIA DEI CONDOTTI

Scalinata
della Trinità
dei Monti

Fontana della
Barcaccia

Trinità
dei Monti

VIA SISTINA

Museo
Keats-Shelley

VIA DUE MACELLI

VIA FRANCESCO CRISPI

VIA

V. TOMACELLI

DI

Palazzo di
Propaganda Fide

| 0 | | 400 meters |
| 0 | | 400 yards |

VIA DEL TRITONE

LARGO
CHIGI

Area of map detail

Tevere

PIAZZA DI SPAGNA

For at least four centuries, this sprawling, irregularly shaped piazza with its un-Italian palm trees has been the heart of nonarchaeological Rome. The elongated square boasts two of the city's major monumental attractions, the Scalinata (Spanish Steps) and the Fontana della Barcaccia.

In the 18th century, the Spanish Steps were crowded with artists' models looking for work.

Piazza di Spagna

 Map p. 109

 Bus: 117, 301, 913, or any bus going to Via del Tritone. Metro: Linea A (Spagna)

Scalinata della Trinità dei Monti

Designed by Francesco de Sanctis, the Scalinata della Trinità dei Monti, or Spanish Steps, were built in the 1720s to replace the footpath linking the piazza to the lovely French church of **Trinità dei Monti,** with its double bell towers and a double flight of front stairs. The money to build the 138 travertine steps (24,000 scudi) was bequeathed by a 17th-century French diplomat in his will and then augmented by a

contribution from the then king of France, Louis XV.

The steps, today a popular meeting place for young tourists, are particularly lovely in the spring, when they are adorned with a magnificent display of flowering azaleas. At Christmastime, a life-size nativity scene is erected there, and every December 8 the pope pays a visit to the narrower, southern end of the piazza where a wreath is placed on the statue of the Virgin Mary atop a Roman column, erected in the 19th century to mark the 1854 dogma of the Immaculate Conception.

Fontana della Barcaccia

Attributed to Pietro Bernini (Gian Lorenzo's father), the Fontana della Barcaccia at the foot of the Spanish Steps was commissioned by Pope Urban VIII in the 1620s, almost a century before the staircase was built. The pope was a Barberini, and his family's symbol, the bee, adorns the fountain.

Because of low pressure, the water does not spout forcefully from the top of the fountain but rather trickles from nozzles located on the prow, stern, and sides of this marble version of an old, leaky boat (*barcaccia* means "old boat"). Was this a reference to St. Peter's role as a fisher of men? Or a commemoration of the 1598 flood? It's not clear.

Other Piazza Attractions

The street directly facing the steps is **Via dei Condotti,** *the* shopping street in Rome. It is named for the underground conduits that Pope Gregory XIII (1572–1585) had

INSIDER TIP:

Visit the top of the Spanish Steps at the end of the day to catch a spectacular sunset over the city.

—RUTH ELLEN GRUBER
National Geographic author

built to supply the neighborhood with running water.

Beyond the Roman column you'll see, wedged between two streets, the 17th-century **Palazzo di Propaganda Fide,** which houses the Vatican's Congregation for the Propagation of the Faith. Considered an architectural masterpiece, the building combines the work of the two rival geniuses of the era, Gian Lorenzo Bernini and Francesco Borromini. Bernini designed the facade facing the piazza. Note that it features yet more bees, like those found on the fountain. His artistic nemesis, Borromini, was commissioned to create the side facade fronting Via Propaganda Fide. ■

The English Quarter

In the 18th century, the foreign presence in the Piazza di Spagna area escalated, with intellectuals and artists of many nationalities taking up residence in the surrounding streets. But there were so many English visitors that Italians began using the word *inglesi* to mean foreigners in general. The major hotels had names like Hotel de Londres and the Hotel des Anglais (even today, a favorite in the area is the Hotel d'Inghilterra).

Tennyson and Thackeray had lodgings on Via dei Condotti across the street from the Caffè Greco, a famed meeting place for intellectuals. The young English poet John Keats was living at Piazza di Spagna 26 (the rose-colored building to the right of the steps) when he died in 1821, and his apartment now houses the small but interesting Museo Keats-Shelley (Keats and Shelley Museum and library). Babington's Tea Rooms, on the other side of the Steps (great scones!), is an expensive but charming Victorian institution opened to cater to Rome's English-speaking community.

SHOPPING & FASHION

Piazza di Spagna and adjoining Via dei Condotti are at the heart of Rome's major shopping district and the city's fashion world. Armani, Fendi, Ferragamo, Gucci, Max Mara, Prada, Valentino, Versace—all the signature stores are here, as are countless other shops that sell elegant clothing, jewelry, housewares, and objets d'art.

Fashionable Via dei Condotti attracts window-shoppers with its glamorous streetfront offerings.

The prices are not low, bargaining is rare, *saldi* (sales) are very often misleading, and tax rebates, while enticing, generally require enormous patience at the airport on your day of departure. Nevertheless, the clothes are beautiful, eye-catching, and well made and, with some products, particularly leather goods—clothing, shoes, and bags—you may find a real bargain, a trophy to show off at home.

Naturally, there are also apparel stores with lower prices. On tiny **Via del Gambero** you can find bargain blouses and sweaters. On **Via del Corso,** the long street running between

Piazza del Popolo and Piazza Venezia (adored by writers such as Stendhal for its now vanished 18th-century elegance), there are many shoe stores and casual wear outlets. And the same goes for **Via della Croce,** which in addition has some nice food stores.

Department Stores

Zara, the Spanish-owned department store located at Largo Chigi, does a brisk trade in attractive clothing and accessories for men, women, and children. Rinascente, the Italian department store that occupied these

INSIDER TIP:

For men, there is nothing more Roman than Battistoni, a historic shop at Via dei Condotti 61a, just down from Piazza di Spagna. Their tailoring provides the typical Roman look you can take home with you.

—BARBARA LESSONA
National Geographic Traveler
magazine contributor & personal shopper

One alternative is **Via Nazionale,** the broad cobblestoned avenue that runs from Largo Magnanapoli to Piazza della Repubblica (or Esedra), where lower-priced clothing and leather goods stores abound. Another is **Via Cola di Rienzo,** across the river in Prati, which offers similar prices. If you are in this neighborhood, check out Franchi (pronounced FRANCK-ee), known for its expensive-but-worth-it takeout food. If you have a craving for something from home, Castroni, the specialty food shop next door, may well have it. In addition, the area around Campo de' Fiori and Piazza Navona is filled with interesting boutiques and specialty shops.

premises until a few years ago, has now moved across Via del Tritone, opening two new sites: one within the Galleria Alberto Sordi, recently renewed, and one at No. 61, the new flagship store with 150,695 square feet (14,000 sq m) of floor space, opened in 2017. Both stores are open every day, including Sunday, when many other clothing stores are closed.

Specialty Shops

Some of the many specialty shops that once filled the center still survive, often carrying items for a specific clientele. The shops clustered in the streets behind the Pantheon, for example, satisfy the haberdashery needs of ecclesiastics. Others make articles requiring a great deal of time and qualified workmanship, such as handmade knotted silk fringes, the tassels for keys to antique armoires, and drapery pull ropes. You can find one of these *passamanerie* shops on the **Via d'Aracoeli,** up the street from Il Gesù; another is in Piazza del Parlamento.

Despite the overflow of clothing stores, **Via del Babuino** retains something of its former character as a center for antiques. Shops along here sell everything from silver spoons to marble-topped tables and credenzas.

Other Districts

The streets around the Spanish Steps are not the only important shopping district.

■ Shoes displayed much like works of art

PINCIO

Historians disagree about the origins of the Pincio (pronounced pin-CHO). Was this hill the location of an imperial residence? The site of Emperor Nero's tomb? Or simply a suburban residential area inhabited by ancient Rome's patrician families, including the Pinci, to whom the hill owes its name? Whatever. At the beginning of the 19th century, the area was transformed into a charming park and promenade often called the Bois de Boulogne of Rome.

Pincio

- Map p. 109
- Bus: 61, 117, 120, 150, 160, 490, 495, 590. Tram: 2. Metro: Linea A (Flaminio)

The French influence in the Pincio's layout was inevitable since it was landscaped during a brief period of French administration (1800–1815). Architect Giuseppe Valadier designed circular ramps and terraced landings that climb from the Piazza del Popolo to a lookout with a magnificent view.

The paths of the park are decorated with the busts of Italian patriots added several decades later at the instigation of Giuseppe Mazzini, the 19th-century Italian nationalist. The Egyptian **obelisk** (see p. 86), brought to Rome by the emperor Hadrian, was placed on the Pincio in 1822 by Pope Pius VII.

A Magnificent View

The view from the lookout is spectacular, especially at sunset. The cupolas of Rome, including that of St. Peter's, loom up through the gathering dusk, as does the impressive dome of the Pantheon and the starkly white Vittoriano, the monument to Vittorio Emanuele II.

Like the **Piazza del Popolo** below, a century ago the Pincio was considered to be the "in" place for a stroll. Today, however, on weekends there are far more children than lords and ladies, but the view is certainly worth a visit. For those in the mood for a long walk, you can walk from the Pincio to the Villa Medici, Trinità dei Monti, and Spanish Steps, or, in another direction, to the Villa Borghese park (see pp. 120–121). ∎

The Pincio is a leafy, tranquil neighborhood.

PIAZZA & PORTA DEL POPOLO

This large, open space echoes the monumental architectonic style of Paris and is probably one of the most impressive piazzas in Rome, especially now that the municipal government has banned all traffic. Piazza del Popolo takes its name from the church of Santa Maria del Popolo (see pp. 116–117), but it has always been a major landmark. Since Roman times, the Porta del Popolo, once the Porta Flaminia, has been one of the principal entrances into the city.

■ Blood once ran in Piazza del Popolo, used for public executions in the 18th and early 19th centuries.

In 1589, Pope Sixtus V moved the Egyptian **obelisk** that stood in the Circo Massimo (see p. 209) to the center of the piazza. The foundations for the two churches, whose presence dramatically enhances the theatrical effect of the square for those entering via the Porta del Popolo, were laid in the 17th century. Although apparently identical, **Santa Maria di Montesanto,** on the left, has an oval dome, whereas **Santa Maria dei Miracoli**'s dome is round.

In 1655, Pope Alexander VII commissioned Bernini to redecorate the inside facade of the *porta* (gate) to honor the arrival of Queen Christina of Sweden, whose conversion to Catholicism was regarded as a great propaganda coup for the Counter-Reformation. *"Felici faustoque ingressui"* reads the inscription, "For a happy and blessed entrance."

Credit for the piazza's final neoclassical layout, however, goes to Valadier, who created the semicircular structures that enclose the piazza, as well as the fountains and the lions. Since the early 19th century, Piazza del Popolo has been considered a chic place to enjoy a coffee or an *aperitivo*. ■

Piazza & Porta del Popolo
- Map p. 109
- Bus: C3, 61, 117, 120, 150, 160, 628. Tram: 2. Metro: Linea A (Flaminio)

SANTA MARIA DEL POPOLO

The remains of the emperor Nero were said to have been buried on the site of this church, and as part of the medieval penchant for exorcising the remnants of paganism, Pope Paschal II (1099–1118) dug up the supposed grave site, burned the remains he found there, and threw them into the Tiber. He then built a chapel and dedicated it to the Virgin Mary.

Santa Maria del Popolo

- 🗺 Map p. 109
- ✉ Piazza del Popolo 12
- ☎ 06 3610 836
- 🕐 Closed noon–4 p.m. Mon.–Fri. & 1:30–4:30 p.m. Sun.
- 🚍 Bus: C3, 61, 117, 120, 150, 160, 628. Tram: 2. Metro: Linea A (Flaminio)

Santa Maria del Popolo has been rebuilt several times, and what we see today—a church with three aisles and many side chapels—is basically the 15th-century Renaissance version. Subsequently, there were some other modifications. Donato Bramante enlarged the apse, and Gian Lorenzo Bernini redecorated the interior and added some baroque touches to the facade.

They Knew Him When . . .

In the early 1500s, Martin Luther boarded in the monastery that adjoined Santa Maria del Popolo. It was only a few years later that the Augustinian monk triggered the Protestant Reformation when he posted his 95 Theses on the church door in Wittenberg (in today's Germany). The monastery no longer exists.

Interior Adornments

The enormous artistic value of the church lies in its interior decoration, to which some of the most talented artists of the 1500s and 1600s contributed. The Della Rovere Chapel, the first on the right, has frescoes by Pinturicchio, who also painted the "Adoration of the Child" located above the altar and the magnificent biblical scenes that adorn the vaulted ceiling of the presbytery.

The painting of the "Madonna del Popolo," set into the main altar, which is baroque in style, for centuries was believed to have been painted by St. Luke. The latest restoration revealed the signature of Filippo Rusuti, a painter and musician of the thirteenth-century Roman School.

The original marble altar designed by Andrea Bregno in 1473 now stands in the sacristy. To see it, go through the door at the end of the right transept and down the corridor within.

The magnificent tombs of Cardinal Ascanio Sforza and Cardinal Girolamo Basso della Rovere, both by Andrea Sansovino, lie behind the main altar.

Cerasi & Chigi Chapels

The star attraction of the church is the **Cerasi Chapel,** which lies to the left of the main altar. Here you will find two of Caravaggio's paintings, the "Conversion of St. Paul" and the "Crucifixion of St. Peter."

Also not to be missed is the **Chigi Chapel** by Raphael. The chapel's unusual pyramid-shaped marble tombs of the banker Agostino Chigi and his brother,

■ **The faithful sit in prayer, facing Santa Maria del Popolo's glorious baroque altar.**

on the left and right walls of the chapel, may have been inspired by the Roman pyramid of Cestius.

The mosaic decoration in the dome of the chapel is based on designs (generally known as cartoons) of Raphael. Two of the four corner statues, "Habakkuk" (who in the Old Testament brought food to Daniel in the lion's den) and "Daniel and the Lion," are by Bernini. The "Birth of the Virgin," above the altar, was created by Sebastiano del Piombo. Unusual in Rome to begin with, the two stained-glass windows in the apse (behind the main altar) were surely among the first in the city.

Before you leave the church, note the Gisleni tomb to the left of the main door with its somewhat gruesome skeleton in a cage with a nearby butterfly (symbolizing rebirth or resurrection). ■

ARA PACIS AUGUSTAE

One of the most famous monuments in ancient Rome, the Ara Pacis was a ceremonial altar inaugurated in 9 B.C. to commemorate the Pax Romana that followed Augustus' conquest of Spain and Gaul (as France was then known). Recovered in 1568 near Piazza San Lorenzo in Lucina, the altar was reassembled (with missing segments reconstructed) in the 1930s.

Ara Pacis Augustae

- Map p. 109
- Lungotevere in Augusta
- 060608
- Closed Mon.
- $$ (extra for special exhibits). Audio guide: $
- Bus: C3, 30, 70, 81, 87, 301, 628, 913

www.arapacis.it

Made of white Italian (Luna) marble, the altar is set on a rectangular platform and surrounded by four walls with entrances on two sides. The reliefs are a stunning example of the highest quality classical sculpture and are also of great historical interest. The procession represented on the outside of the longer, lateral walls actually took place (on July 4, 13 B.C.). The half figure on the side facing the nearby mausoleum is Augustus. He is followed by several priests (*flavins*) and family members, including his son-in-law Agrippa, whose place as the second nobleman in the procession indicates he is the heir apparent. An inscription on the outer modern structure reads "*Res gestae Divi Augusti*," the title of the emperor's own account of his accomplishments.

The Ara Pacis has been the focal point of the grandiose renovation project directed by well-known American architect Richard Meier. The show "L'Ara Com'era" ("The Ara As It Was") is an immersive evening visit presenting the Campo Marzio and the Ara Pacis in its original colors by means of 3-D reconstructions, virtual reality, and augmented reality. The area also houses a conference center, a bookshop, libraries, offices, and new exhibition spaces. The **Mausoleo di Augusto** next door was once a major monument of ancient Rome, the first of the city's two large circular tombs. The masterpiece honoring the first emperor of the Roman Empire is currently under restoration. ■

EXPERIENCE: Learn More About Wine

Archaeologists tell us that wine has been with us in some form since almost the beginning of civilized life, and that it has been produced on a large scale since about 3000 B.C. The ancient Romans drank wine daily, although theirs was a syrupy brew that they diluted with water. They then added honey and spices to improve the taste. Today, wine continues to be an essential part of Italian life.

In Rome's smaller *trattorie*, you may want to save money and try the house white or red, asking simply for *il vino della casa*. Elsewhere, you'll want bottled wine. But how will you know what to ask for?

To taste Lazio and high-quality Italian wines, try: **VyTA Enoteca Regionale del Lazio** (*Via Frattina 94, tel 06 8771 6018, open 9 a.m.–11 p.m., www.vytaenotecalazio.it);* **Il Pentagrappolo** (*Via Celimonata 21b, tel 06 7096 301, open L Mon.–Fri., D Tues.– Sun., www.ilpentagrappolo.com);* or the historic **Trimani** (*Via Goito 20, tel 06 4469 661, open 9 a.m.–8:30 p.m., www.trimani.com).*

VILLA GIULIA

Since 1889, the 16th-century Villa Giulia—a superb example of Renaissance architecture—has housed one of the most important collections of Etruscan and pre-Roman antiquities in the world. The building is a consummate expression of the Renaissance architectural concept of exterior–interior "interpenetration" that began with the Villa Farnesina 40 years earlier.

The Villa Giulia was built between 1551 and 1553 by Pope Julius III (1550–1555), who commissioned some of the most important architects of the time, including Michelangelo, to enlarge and ennoble an earlier structure.

Once past the entrance vestibule, you find yourself in a semicircular portico, its ceiling frescoed to create a pergola effect that is in perfect harmony with the courtyard and gardens. At the other end of the courtyard follow the loggia down to a shady, sunken nymphaeum.

The two-floor museum **(Museo Nazionale di Villa Giulia)** is housed in the villa's right and left wings, access to which is from the far left-hand side of the portico. The first six rooms display artifacts primarily from the necropolis of Vulci and other sites. There is even a reconstruction of a tomb from Cerveteri, a town in the heart of what was once Etruria.

Not all of these artifacts will have general appeal, but no one will want to miss **Room 40** with its compelling, life-size terra-cotta polychrome statues of Hercules, Apollo, and Leto holding young Apollo, all dating from the late sixth century B.C. They were probably created by a pupil of Vulca, sculptor of Veio, who may also have decorated the giant temple to Jupiter that stood on the Capitoline Hill.

The Etruscan "Spouses" sarcophagus was once brightly painted.

Room 12 on the left-hand side of the ground floor houses the magnificent world-famous sarcophagus (also sixth century B.C.) of a young husband and wife reclining on a couch. Upstairs are countless objects—domestic implements, bronze utensils, armor, jewelry, and ceramics.

The other wing of the museum exhibits additional material from tombs or temples. The partially reconstructed pediment of the Temple of Apollo dello Scasato is intriguing, and the bust of Apollo is superb. His face, in deep concentration, is turned slightly to the right as if he were listening to a prophetic phrase. ∎

Villa Giulia

🗺 Map p. 109

✉ Piazzale di Villa Giulia 9

☎ 06 3226 571. Online tickets: www.ticketone.it

🕐 Closed Mon.

💲 $$. Audio guide: $

🚌 Bus: 52, 982. Tram: 2, 3, 19. Metro: Linea A (Flaminio)

VILLAS & PARKS

One of Europe's greenest cities, Rome has vast areas of rolling parkland, normally open from dawn to dusk and ideal for joggers, pensioners, and idlers of all types. The city owes its unusual number of parks to the aristocracy and—it must be said— to the financial difficulties that forced them, in modern times, to sell their suburban villas to the state. The word "villa" indicates that a park was once a private estate.

Villa Borghese's Tempio di Esculapio was built in the 19th century merely as a landscape feature.

The first villas were called *casinas* or *casinos*, literally little houses, but the word "little" should be used advisedly. Starting in the Renaissance and continuing into the baroque era, as the nobility rushed to build elegant pleasure palaces steeped in verdant and contemplative surroundings, the houses grew ever greater and grander. They used these buildings as refuge from the summer heat, a place to picnic or party, or, as in the case of Villa Borghese, to house and display a magnificent art collection.

Not all have survived. Villa Ludovisi, which once occupied much of the Via Veneto area, has totally disappeared. The gardens of Villa Giulia, today the Etruscan Museum, have been swallowed up by urban encroachment, as have those of Villa Giustiniani near the Lateran. But

fortunately for today's Romans, dozens remain. **Villa Ada, Villa Torlonia,** and **Villa Sciarra** are only some of the parks providing a fresh-air outlet for families, lovers, and fitness freaks.

Naturally, there are other parks, including those built around ancient monuments, such as the **Parco di Traiano** (the Colle Oppio) around Trajan's Baths and the **Parco degli Scipioni,** near the Via Appia, extending around the remains of the tomb of the Cornelii Scipiones, built by that powerful family around the third or second century B.C.

Villa Borghese

Villa Borghese (pronounced bor-GAY-zi) is the Roman equivalent of Central Park in New York or St. James's Park in London. Its 198 acres (80 ha) offer the city's residents a downtown escape for strolling, biking, horseback riding, and jogging among extensive greenery, statuary, neoclassical temples, and fountains. There is an artificial lake, a zoo, and a grassy amphitheater (Piazza di Siena) shaded by graceful umbrella pines where a horse show is held every May.

You can access the Villa Borghese from various points, including Porta Pinciana, at the top end of Via Veneto; Piazzale Flaminio, just beyond Piazza del Popolo; and from the Galleria Borghese. Several major museums (Galleria Borghese, see pp. 122–124; Galleria Nazionale d'Arte Moderna; and Villa Giulia, see p. 119) are located within the park.

Other Villas, Casinos, & Gardens

Heading south from Villa Borghese, between the Pincio and the Spanish Steps, is **Villa Medici.** Built for a Tuscan cardinal on the site of the gardens of Lucullus, the famed Roman gourmet and high liver, this late Renaissance building's gardens were described by Henry James as "a fabled, haunted place." Today it houses the French Academy, which is used for temporary art exhibitions (tel 06 676311). In summer, outdoor concerts and film festivals offer a rare chance to see the spectacular gardens.

Among the city's other parks, **Villa Doria Pamphilj** on the Janiculum Hill was laid out in the 17th century for Prince Camillo Pamphilj and has a beautiful casino, unfortunately not generally open to the public. With 445 acres (180 ha) and a 5.5-mile (9 km) perimeter, it is the city's largest park, a haven for joggers and fresh-air enthusiasts. **Villa Celimontana** (see p. 74), originally Villa Mattei after the family that built it in the 16th century, is on the Caelian Hill. It is a lovely place for a stroll amid pieces of ancient sculpture and one of Rome's 13 obelisks (see pp. 86–87). A popular jazz festival is often held here in summer.

EXPERIENCE: Sunday in the Park

Find yourself in Rome on a lazy Sunday? Why not relax like the Romans do and head for **Villa Doria Pamphilj,** a public park located in the Monteverde neighborhood on the Janiculum Hill above Trastevere. It certainly offers something for everyone.

Here you will find joggers and cyclists enjoying the paths that wind through the park, whole families crowded around the pond throwing bread to the ducks and swans, and kids of all ages scrambling up the steps of the 17th-century villa, Il Casino del Bel Respiro. You may even run across a yoga class in full swing or a group of amateur artists sketching the 18th-century Palazzo Corsini. Sit back and enjoy the activity, but be sure not to miss the museum, which draws lines of people. Located in the Villa Vecchia, it traces the history of the park, much of which was once a farm.

You can also have lunch or get a picnic basket at the ViVi Bistrot (tel 06 582 7540, www.vivibistrot.com) near the Via Vitellia entrance. Or bring your own and eat lunch at one of the picnic tables or even spread your tablecloth out on the grass.

Depending on where in Rome you are staying, there are other open-air choices. **Villa Sciarra,** also in the Monteverde area, **Villa Ada** between the Parioli and Salario neighborhoods, and of course, **Villa Borghese,** where, if you can walk far enough, you also have the option of visiting major museums like the Villa Giulia, Galleria Nazionale d'Arte Moderna, and Galleria Borghese (reservations required), as well as the children's movie house, the Cinema dei Piccoli, and the newer Casa del Cinema.

GALLERIA BORGHESE

The building housing the Galleria Borghese was originally built in the early 1600s as a *casino* (a suburban estate or summerhouse) on the vast estate of Cardinal Scipione Borghese in what was then the outskirts of the city. Today it is owned by the state but still exhibits the Borghese painting collection as well as many pieces from the family's amazing array of sculpture.

Among the gallery's treasures is Barocci's "Aeneas Fleeing the Burning Troy" (center, far wall).

Modified in the 18th century and restored again in recent years, the gleaming white, three-story building today has a facade composed of twin towers flanking a recessed central core or portico. A double ramped staircase (that deliberately imitates Michelangelo's entrance to the Palazzo del Senatore in the Campidoglio) leads up to the main entrance, a mezzanine which is nevertheless considered the ground floor. Stuccowork and decorative niches embellish parts of the facade.

Inside the Villa

The remarkable interior decoration of the villa also dates from the 18th century. On both floors, frescoed ceilings, sumptuous wall coverings, faux marble wall decoration, porphyry mantelpieces, gilded moldings, and marble inlay all vie for attention. Remember that every room has a theme, that the ceiling decorations (you mustn't forget to look up) and sculptures are displayed in tandem, and that wherever possible an attempt has been made to extend this thematic link to the paintings on the walls. You'll want to buy a book in the basement bookshop or rent an audio guide.

Sculptures & Mosaics: The fourth-century Roman floor mosaics in the entrance room on what passes for the ground floor, or *pianterreno*, depict gladiatorial combat scenes. Excavated from a family estate, they are portraits of real gladiators, whose names appear near them in the mosaic. Those marked with a θ, the first letter in the Greek word *thanatos* (death), got the thumbs-down sign and were no more. The frescoed vault depicts a Roman victory over the invading Gauls.

The sculpture collection contains some of the most famous pieces in the world. In **Room I** is Canova's marble **statue of Paolina Borghese,** also known as Pauline Bonaparte, Napoleon's sister. She is reclining, seminude, on a sort of chaise longue, and legend has it that the sculpture was kept under lock and key for years by her husband, Prince Camillo, who was scandalized by her lack of modesty.

There are also extraordinary **sculptures by Bernini,** all completed while he was still in his mid-20s. In **Room II** you'll find his "David" (ca 1624), in which the young hero is preparing to hurl a stone at his adversary. The face, with its intense and concentrated expression, is a self-portrait of the sculptor. In **Room III, "Apollo and Daphne"** (1622–1625) depicts the young nymph's vain attempts to escape the god (the same scene is painted on the ceiling). Daphne's hands and feet are in the process of being transformed into a laurel tree. The swirling and sensual movement of the two intertwined bodies shows Bernini's amazing ability to capture in bronze the surface texture of skin and hair, as does his other work, in the next

Galleria Borghese

🅰 Map p. 109

✉ Piazzale Scipione Borghese 5

☎ 06 32810 (for reservations)

🕒 Closed Mon. Advanced booking required

💲 $$$. Audio guide: $. Guided tours in English can be booked: $$$

🚌 Bus: 52, 53, 60, 61, 63, 83, 89, 92, 160, 490, 495, 910. Metro: Linea A (Spagna) then walk, following signs

**www.galleriaborghese.
beniculturali.it**

Galleria Borghese Access

Usually a compulsory booking is necessary (2 euros more for every type of ticket) but a limited number of last-minute tickets is available: You can purchase them directly from the ticket office 30 minutes after the starting time of each visit. It is forbidden to bring in food and drinks, and animals (except for guide dogs). Use of the cloakroom is compulsory for objects like: bags, backpacks, strollers, and other objects whose bulk and dangerousness is determined by security staff. The cloakroom is located in the basement of the Museo.

room, the **"Rape of Proserpine"** (ca 1622). Notice the way Pluto's fingers sink into Proserpine's thigh.

The last room **(Room VIII)** on this floor is exceptional more for its paintings than its sculptures. There are six incredible **Caravaggios** here, including "St. Jerome" (1605), "David With the Head

---

INSIDER TIP:

The Galleria Borghese is not to be missed, but advance reservations are compulsory. You'll either have to pick up your tickets ahead of time or arrive at least 30 minutes early and wait in line to collect them.

—ANTONIO BARBIERI
*National Geographic contributor
& co-founder of Concierge in Rome*

---

of Goliath" (1609–1610), and the "Madonna dei Palafrenieri," sometimes called the "Madonna del Serpente," which was removed from an important altar in St. Peter's almost immediately as sacrilegious. The "Bacchino Malato" ("Sick Bacchus") from 1593 is a self-portrait.

Pinacoteca: Upstairs (a good place to peek out at the gardens in the back) is the painting gallery, or Pinacoteca, where one marvelous painting succeeds another and where astounding works by some of the best known painters in Western

history—Bellini, Bronzino, Correggio, Cranach, Domenichino, Fra Bartolomeo, Lanfranco, Lorenzo Lotto, Pinturicchio, Raphael, Reni, Rubens, Titian, and Veronese—are represented.

Room IX is particularly thrilling, with Botticelli's richly colored "Madonna col Bambino, S. Giovannino e Angeli" (ca 1488) and Raphael's "Ritratto di Giovane Donna con Unicorno" ("Young Woman With a Unicorn"), dated 1506, as well as his very well-known "Deposition" (1507) and many other treasures. Next door in **Room X** is Bronzino's intriguing "Young San Giovanni Battista" (1525). Note the ceiling. Its theme is Hercules but along with the mythological scenes is a sumptuous prune-colored geometric design. The gilded eagles and dragons are the two symbols of the Borghese family.

You might want to pay special attention to **Room XIV,** where there are several more works by Bernini, including two self-portraits, the busts of his patron, Scipione Borghese, and the majestic terra-cotta model of a statue of Louis XV of France, which was never made. **Room XIX** contains Domenichino's famous painting of the "Cumana Sibyl," in all her turbaned glory, as well as his "Diana" (1616–1617). Federico Barocci's painting of "Aeneas Fleeing the Burning Troy" (1598) inspired Scipione Borghese to commission Bernini to produce the large marble group you saw on the ground floor **(Room VI).** The gloriously beautiful "Sacred and Profane Love" is among several Titians in **Room XX.** ∎

The heart of modern Rome, where massive monuments of yesterday brush against major modern political institutions

PANTHEON TO PIAZZA VENEZIA

A statue of the Virgin Mary and Child, Santa Maria sopra Minerva

PANTHEON TO PIAZZA VENEZIA

The downtown area stretching from the Pantheon to Piazza Venezia is an unusual mélange of ancient, medieval, and Renaissance history. Along the Via del Corso and on Piazza Venezia, major Italian banks and insurance companies are ensconced in magnificent stone palaces once owned by Roman princes and noblemen.

In Piazza Colonna, the Italian prime minister's office (16th-century Palazzo Chigi) looks out on the Marcus Aurelius column, which dates to A.D. 193. In nearby Palazzo di Montecitorio, the view from the Chamber of Deputies, with a facade by Bernini, includes one of the city's 13 Egyptian obelisks. And only in this neighborhood can you sip a cappuccino against the thrilling backdrop of the Pantheon. Built 1,900 years ago, this pagan temple subsequently became a church and is today a national monument and the burial place of kings, a queen, and several painters.

The rulers of Rome have always found it difficult to keep order in Piazza della Rotonda. Today lined with cafés, it is now closed to traffic. But the trying task of keeping out the mopeds

resembles the problems of the 19th century, when authorities tried desperately to close down the fish market and other food stands that continued to spring up here. On one of the buildings looking onto the square you can read the plaque erected by Pope Pius VII to commemorate the demolition and reclamation of the area.

Only a short distance away stands Santa Maria sopra Minerva. Steeped in history, the church belongs to the prestigious Dominican religious order, a major protagonist of both the Inquisition and the Counter-Reformation. The charming small stone elephant in the piazza, designed (but not sculpted) by Gian Lorenzo Bernini, symbolized intelligence. The overhead bridge spanning Via di Sant'Ignazio (behind the Minerva church) gave 16th-century Dominican prelates access to their Jesuit counterparts and to the Jesuit church of Sant'Ignazio.

Across the street from the Collegio Romano—once a Jesuit college—is Palazzo Doria Pamphilj. That noble Roman family, which boasts both popes and princes among its ancestors, has now turned its imposing block-wide palace, with its magnificent private art collection, into a very modern museum with masterpieces by Caravaggio, Titian, Raphael, and the Flemish masters of the baroque era. A short distance away at the Jesuit mother church, Il Gesù, baroque opulence has been unstintingly employed to the glory of God.

Piazza Venezia

The Via del Corso terminates at Piazza Venezia, which, since several major streets

---

NOT TO BE MISSED:

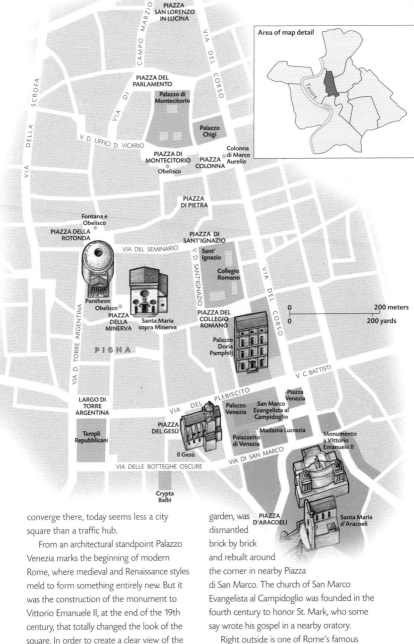

converge there, today seems less a city square than a traffic hub.

From an architectural standpoint Palazzo Venezia marks the beginning of modern Rome, where medieval and Renaissance styles meld to form something entirely new. But it was the construction of the monument to Vittorio Emanuele II, at the end of the 19th century, that totally changed the look of the square. In order to create a clear view of the monument from Via del Corso, the Palazzetto di Venezia, with its lovely courtyard and garden, was dismantled brick by brick and rebuilt around the corner in nearby Piazza di San Marco. The church of San Marco Evangelista al Campidoglio was founded in the fourth century to honor St. Mark, who some say wrote his gospel in a nearby oratory.

Right outside is one of Rome's famous "talking" statues (see sidebar p. 147), the bosomy Madama Lucrezia. ■

PANTHEON

Originally a pagan temple and later a Christian church, the Pantheon is a perfect example of classical architectural harmony. Gracefully combining a variety of shapes and forms, this circular building, or rotunda, features a massive dome—an architectural and engineering feat so important that it became a prototype in much of the world.

■ The Pantheon's large oculus lets in rain as well as light. There are drainage holes below, in the center of the pavement.

Wider than that of St. Peter's, the **cupola,** which was cast by pouring concrete over a temporary wooden frame, has a diameter of 142 feet (43 m). At the base, the dome measures almost 20 feet (6 m), but the thickness gradually diminishes with height, as do the widths of the five rows of coffers lining it. The architectonic function of these was to reduce the weight of the vault, but they also create an optical effect that draws attention toward the center.

The opening or "eye" in the ceiling is 30 feet (9 m) in diameter. Apart from any allusion to an eye looking at the cosmos, the *oculus,* as it is called in Latin, is the only source of light and air in the building, the walls of which are too thick (about 20 feet/6 m) to have made windows an option.

Built between A.D. 118 and 125 by the philosopher-emperor Hadrian to replace an earlier edifice, the Pantheon—it is important to remember—was also used as an astronomical instrument. The ancients gave great significance to the two equinoxes (March 21 and September 22), the dates when day and night are of equal length, and to the summer and winter solstices (June 21 and December 21 or 22), all of which had a particular significance for agriculture and for checking the accuracy of the calendar. It also had ceremonial

INSIDER TIP:

If it's raining, head for the Pantheon. The sight of rain pouring through the oculus, the hole in the vast dome, is one of Rome's most remarkable.

—TIM JEPSON
National Geographic author

possibilities. If every June 21 at noon the beam of light streaming through the oculus hit the floor right in front of the main door, it'd be a good time, wouldn't you think, for an appearance-conscious emperor in full regalia to make a sun-kissed entrance?

The Building's Exterior

The outside **portico**, once preceded by a short staircase, consists of 16 columns of red or gray granite, each 41 feet (12 m) tall and 15 feet (4 m) in circumference and only three of which (on the left side) are replacements. The inscription running below the pediment, *"M. Agrippa L. F .Cos. Tertium Fecit"* ("Marcus Agrippa, son of Lucius, in his third consulate, built this"), refers to the earlier structure erected in 27 B.C. by Agrippa to honor his friend and father-in-law, the emperor Augustus. The bronze letters are new—19th-century fittings made for the original letter holes.

Other changes have been made to the Pantheon through-out the centuries. During his visit to Rome in 663, the Byzantine emperor Constans II plundered the gilded bronze sheeting that originally covered the dome; it was replaced with lead in the eighth century. The central bell tower added in the Middle Ages was replaced in the 17th century by twin turrets. Nicknamed "the donkey's ears," they were removed in 1883. The enormous **bronze doors** are ancient but may in fact have been taken from another structure.

Pantheon

⬛ Map p. 127
✉ Piazza della Rotonda 12
☎ 06 6830 0230
🚌 Bus: C3, 30, 40, 46, 62, 64, 70, 81, 87, 130, 190, 492, 628, 916. Tram: 8

From Paganism to Christianity

As early as the sixth century, pagan structures in Rome were converted into Christian places of worship. However, the original buildings had all been con-structed for secular, not religious, pur-poses—take, for example, Santi Cosma e Damiano in the Roman Forum, and Santa Maria in Cosmedin near the Forum Boar-ium. Furthermore, many of the early Christian churches, such as San Giovanni in Laterano, Santa Croce, and indeed St. Peter's, were built on what were then the outskirts of the city. This made things easier for incoming pilgrims and also avoided offending Rome's pagan population. After all, the spread of Chris-tianity did not take place overnight nor without considerable conflict and resistance.

In the seventh century, the Pantheon became the first pagan temple in Rome to be converted into a church. It was also the first temple-to-church conversion to take place at the very center of the city, a development of great consequence that demonstrated to everyone that Chris-tianity had by then become the most important religion in Rome.

In the mid-1600s, Pope Urban VIII of the Barberini family ordered that the bronze covering of the portico beams be stripped away to make the cannon for Castel Sant'Angelo. For this act of vandalism came the famous Latin quip, *"Quod non fecerunt barbari, fecerunt Barberini"* ("What the barbarians did not do, the Barberini did").

The Interior

The Pantheon is the best preserved ancient monument in Rome, largely thanks to its conversion to a Christian church after the Byzantine emperor Phocas gave the building to Pope Boniface IV in 608 or 609. And its interior is awe inspiring.

Unlike other pagan temples, the Pantheon's cavernous **central body,** or *cella,* was accessible to ordinary worshippers and not reserved for priests or notables alone. It is divided into three distinct segments. The lower part has six niches (not including the apse), which originally contained

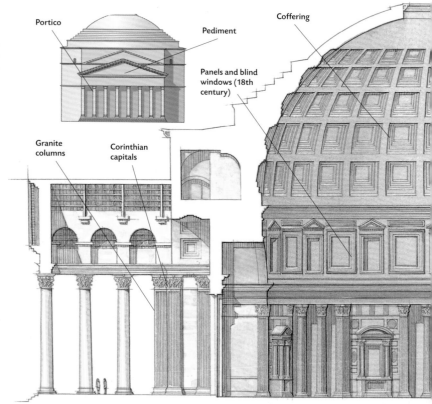

Portico

Pediment

Coffering

Panels and blind windows (18th century)

Granite columns

Corinthian capitals

Interior

states of the principal gods. In between are eight aediculae (shrines) flanked by marble columns. The floor, restored in 1872, repeats the colored, geometric patterns of antiquity. Except for a small area, the original marble decoration of the attic, the segment that runs around the base of the dome, no longer exists.

The current decor, begun in the 15th century but added to over the following 400 years, contains few major artworks.

One exception is Lorenzetto's "Madonna del Sasso" ("Madonna of the Stone"), which stands on the altar in the third aedicula to the left, above the **tomb of the painter Raphael,** who died in 1520.

Two Italian kings and a queen are also buried here, as well as several other painters. This is not surprising since for centuries the Pantheon has been associated with the arts, and one of the most famous artists' groups in Rome, the Accademia dei Virtuosi, had its headquarters here.

The **fountain** outside, built in 1578, was designed by Giacomo della Porta. The Egyptian **obelisk** was placed on the fountain trough in 1711 by Pope Clement XI. ■

Pantheon

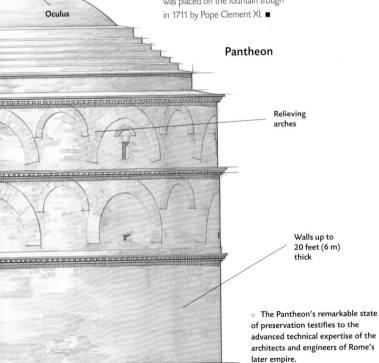

Oculus

Relieving arches

Walls up to 20 feet (6 m) thick

Exterior

■ The Pantheon's remarkable state of preservation testifies to the advanced technical expertise of the architects and engineers of Rome's later empire.

PALAZZO DORIA PAMPHILJ

The fifteenth-century palace hides the richest and most important art collections in the capital. It has been owned by the Doria Pamphilj family since the seventeenth century, and its descendants still live there today. The Galleria, which is part of it, boasts many masterpieces and offers an atmosphere similar to the one guests could enjoy in the second half of the eighteenth century.

The Galleria degli Specchi with frescoes by A. Milani (1733) depicting the stories of Hercules on the ceiling

The palace is a short distance from Piazza Venezia, right at the beginning of Via del Corso. This enormous block-long building, which today houses the Doria Pamphilj Museum, dates back to 1435, when it belonged to Cardinal Santorio. The rococo facade on Via del Corso, considered notable, was added later.

The Pamphiljs moved here in the 1700s, bringing with them the collection begun a century earlier by Donna (or Lady) Olimpia, when the family still lived at Piazza Navona. It is the largest and most important patrician collection still in private Roman hands.

The Galleria comprises four sections–Galleria Aldobrandini, Galleria degli Specchi, Galleria Pamphilj, and Galleria Doria–facing the internal courtyard, with splendid Renaissance arches–and four adjacent rooms. Among the numerous masterworks are "Salomè with the head of John the Baptist" by Titian, and two Caravaggios (the "Maddalena" and the "Riposo Durante la Fuga in Egitto") in the Sala Aldobrandini. The star attraction of the collection is probably the Velázquez portrait of Pope Innocent X (1644–1655), a seventeenth-century masterpiece in this genre. The facial features and expression of the pontiff, seated on the throne, are depicted very realistically and the work's excellent state of preservation enables one to appreciate them to the utmost. The portrait is located in a small chamber built by the architect Andrea Busiri Vici in the mid-19th century at the end of the Galleria Aldobrandini (first section). In the same room you will also find Bernini's bust of the same pontiff. You will be able to note evident differences in stylistic approach.

In the Galleria there are also works by Annibale Carracci, Guido Reni, Guercino, and Tintoretto. You can also admire many other works by Flemish masters like Pieter Brueghel the Elder: His work "Battle in the Bay of Naples," an early example of marine painting from the mid-16th century, is displayed in the Galleria Pamphilj (third section).

The private apartments, with sumptuous decorations and works of art, are open to the public. The audio-guides are included in the ticket. For students of the Accademia di Belle Arti or those who wish to, it is possible to draw in the gallery, if possessing prior authorization from the administration with at least two days' notice. ■

Palazzo Doria Pamphilj

🗺 Map p. 127

✉ Via del Corso 305

☎ 06 6797 323 or 331 1641 490 (for visit to the private apartments)

💲 $$. Audio guides: free while available

🚌 Bus: 62, 85, 95, 175, 492, 630, 850. Metro: Linea A (Barberini), Linea B (Colosseo)

www.doriapamphilj.it/roma

EXPERIENCE: Finding the Best Espresso

The **Casa del Caffè Tazza d'Oro** on the Piazza della Rotonda sells excellent fresh-ground coffee for home use in a mocha or Neapolitan coffeepot. A couple of blocks away, **Bar Sant'Eustachio** (Piazza di Sant'Eustachio 82) uses a closely guarded procedure to make its particularly strong *ristretto* brew.

Rome boasts a selection of cafés where the city's denizens go to chat and people-watch, another national sport. Along with the cafés at Piazza della Rotonda, two others in this area offer ample indoor seating: **Giolitti** (Via degli Uffici del Vicario 40), also known for its gelato, and **La Caffettiera** on Piazza di Pietra.

For decades, the best known café in Rome was the **Caffè Greco** on the fashionable Via dei Condotti, almost facing the Spanish Steps. This was the place where writers and artists gathered to discuss cultural trends and to gossip, and it is still a charming place (indoors only, however) for a rendezvous. But many prefer **Rosati** and **Canova** with their outdoor tables on opposite sides of the now car-free Piazza del Popolo. **Ciampini** on the repaved Piazza San Lorenzo in Lucina (off the Corso) is an "in" place. And if you happen to be on Viale Trinità dei Monti, above the Spanish Steps, try Ciampini's outdoor café, immersed in greenery and overlooking the rooftops of Piazza di Spagna.

The weatherproofed sidewalk cafés that line the Via Veneto are pricey but make a nice change. If you're over on the Trastevere side of the river, **De Marzio** on Piazza Santa Maria in Trastevere, facing the facade of the basilica, isn't fancy, but it is patronized but many residents, and also foreigners.

SANTA MARIA SOPRA MINERVA

This lovely church, with its three aisles and vaulted ceilings, is said to be the one true Gothic church in Rome, although the facade is early Renaissance and the interior, complete with rose windows, has been changed all too often. The structure dates to the 13th century, when two monks began its construction as the religious center of the Dominican order.

■ The Minerva's nave ceiling, redecorated in the 19th century

This being Rome, however, the monks did not have to break new ground. An earlier church had already been erected on this site in the eighth century amid the remains of a pagan temple perhaps dedicated to the Roman goddess of war, Minerva. Note the wall plaques on the right side of the facade, which show the waterline from the frequent floods that inundated the area until the 19th-century Tiber embankments were built.

Because of the power and influence of the Dominicans—the order that would later spearhead the Inquisition and, together with the Jesuits, act as standard-bearers to the popes during the Counter-Reformation—Santa Maria sopra Minerva became a very prestigious church. Four popes are buried here, as are the Tuscan painter Fra Angelico, and St. Catherine of Siena, one of Italy's two patron saints (the other is St. Francis).

Notable Artwork

Many noble Roman families hired the most famous artists and architects to decorate their chapel inside the church. The **Carafa family chapel** at the end of the right transept boasts a splendid "Assumption" and an "Annunciation," as well as a cycle of glorious frescoes by Filippino Lippi illustrating

INSIDER TIP:

Be sure to visit the cloister through the first door to the immediate left of Santa Maria sopra Minerva. Join the Dominicans in silent reverence, stopping for a moment to view the room where Galileo was tried.

—DENNIS CIGLER
Tour coordinator & guide,
In Italy's Companions

the life of the Dominican saint Thomas Aquinas.

In the "Triumph of St. Thomas" on the right wall, the two small boys represent the future Medici popes, Clement VII and Leo X, who are buried in the church. On the left wall is the tomb of Pope Paul IV, who bears the blame for shutting Rome's Jews into their 16th-century ghetto.

To the left of the chapel, note the cosmatesque funeral monument, a mosaic **"Virgin and Child Enthroned,"** flanked by two saints on a gold background. To the left of the main altar stands Michelangelo's **"Christ Bearing the Cross."**

In the fifth chapel on the right see the interesting detail in Antoniazzo Romano's **"Annunciation,"** with the Madonna handing money bags (for dowries) to three girls. The seventh has the marvelous Renaissance tomb by Andrea Bregno. The sarcophagus

under the main altar holds the remains of St. Catherine, who convinced the popes to return from exile in Avignon.

Behind the altar are the wall tombs of Clement VII and Leo X, created by Antonio Sangallo the Younger. On the left, in a poorly lit passageway near the rear door, is **Fra Angelico's** strikingly simple floor **tomb.**

Sacristy & More

Ask to see the *sacrestia* (sacristy), where two papal conclaves were held in the 15th century, and the room where Catherine died, now a chapel. In the 1566 *chiostro* (cloister), the vaulted ceiling of the fourth arch on the right side of the portico bears the headless images of four inquisitors, who were themselves tried and executed.

In the piazza outside is the delightful **stone elephant** designed by Bernini in 1667. Pope Alexander VII composed the inscription, which speaks of the elephant's wisdom and intelligence. ■

Santa Maria sopra Minerva

- Map p. 127
- Piazza della Minerva 42
- 06 6992 0384
- Closed 12:30–3:30 p.m. Sat.–Sun.
- Bus: C3, 30, 40, 46, 51, 62, 63, 64, 70, 80, 81, 83, 85, 87, 117, 130, 160, 190, 492, 628, 916. Tram: 8

Galileo's Trial

In the monastery adjoining Santa Maria sopra Minerva, Galileo Galilei was tried for heresy in 1633 and forced to repudiate his belief that the Earth moved around the sun. Supposedly, after the guilty verdict had been read, as he was getting off his knees, he whispered under his breath *"Eppur si muove"* ("But it does move").

A WALK THROUGH THE HEART OF ROME

As it has throughout the centuries, this area—really the heart of contemporary Rome—includes some of the city's major political institutions. The walk will take you from Piazza di Montecitorio to Piazza di San Marco, enabling you to bear witness to the city's intricate mix of old and even older.

Start at Piazza di Montecitorio, where one of the Egyptian obelisks (see pp. 86–87) that Augustus brought back to Rome stands in front of the massive Palazzo di Montecitorio, now the Chamber of Deputies, the lower house of Parliament. From this piazza, where protesters sometimes gather, walk east to the Piazza Colonna, named for the **Colonna di Marco Aurelio ❶** (Marcus Aurelius' triumphal column), erected in A.D. 193 to celebrate that emperor's victory over the Marcomanni, one of the barbarian tribes that was beginning to threaten Rome. The column stands in front of **Palazzo Chigi** (built in the 16th and 17th centuries), today the prime minister's office and the seat of the Italian government. The column may seem out of place, but it reminds us that this area was also very important in Roman times.

Leaving Piazza Colonna by Via dei Bergamaschi, you'll see 11 massive Corinthian columns in **Piazza di Pietra ❷**, now closed to traffic. Embedded in the wall of the **Borsa,** or Rome Stock Exchange, these columns were once part of a temple inaugurated in A.D. 145 in honor of Hadrian by his successor, Antoninus Pius.

Continue in the same direction along Via del Burro for another treat. **Piazza di Sant'Ignazio ❸** (see p. 142) is a rococo jewel, constructed by an 18th-century architect to resemble a theatrical stage. View it from the central door of **Sant'Ignazio,** a major Jesuit church. Walk along the side of the church on Via di Sant'Ignazio, noting the arch that connected the Jesuits to their Counter-Reformation allies, the Dominicans, masters of the Minerva church around the corner (see pp. 134–135). Via di Sant'Ignazio ends at

NOT TO BE MISSED:

Column of Marcus Aurelius • Piazza di Pietra • Sant'Ignazio • Il Gesù

Piazza del Collegio Romano ❹, where you will see **Palazzo Doria Pamphilj,** home to the Galleria Doria Pamphilj (see pp. 132–133); its entrance is on Via del Corso.

Turn right on Via di Pie' di Marmo, being sure to note the huge marble foot (from which this street gets its name) at the intersection with Via Santo Stefano del Cacco. Like the obelisk in front of the Minerva church, it probably came from a nearby Temple of Isis and Serapis. Facing it at No. 21 is a marvelous chocolate shop.

Il Gesù & Beyond

The next cross street, just before you get to the Minerva church, is Via del Gesù. Turn left, making sure you peek into the courtyards, most of which have fountains (observe the beautiful water clock at No. 62). At the intersection with Corso Vittorio Emanuele II, you'll see the Jesuit mother church, **Il Gesù ❺** (see p. 141).

Turn right and walk a block to **Largo di Torre Argentina ❻**, more commonly known as Largo Argentina, to see the remains of four republican-era Roman temples (**Templi Repubblicani**). On the other side of the Largo, cross Via delle Botteghe Oscure (Street of the Dark Shops) and walk back along it in the direction from which you just came. At No. 31 you'll spot the entrance to the **Crypta Balbi** (see pp. 139-140), the section of the

Museo Nazionale Romano (see p. 31) dedicated to medieval Rome. It's built over the
ruins of an imperial-era theater.

Farther on, turn right on Via dei Polacchi and walk to lovely **Piazza Margana 7**.
Turn left here and take Via Margana to Via
d'Aracoeli. On the right stand Santa Maria
d'Aracoeli and the Campidoglio.

Turn left and return to the Botteghe
Oscure, which becomes Via di San Marco.

Cross and walk right along Via di San Marco to
Piazza di San Marco 8, where you'll see the
basilica (see p. 142) and the Madama Lucrezia
"talking" statue (see sidebar p. 147).

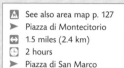

- See also area map p. 127
- Piazza di Montecitorio
- 1.5 miles (2.4 km)
- 2 hours
- Piazza di San Marco

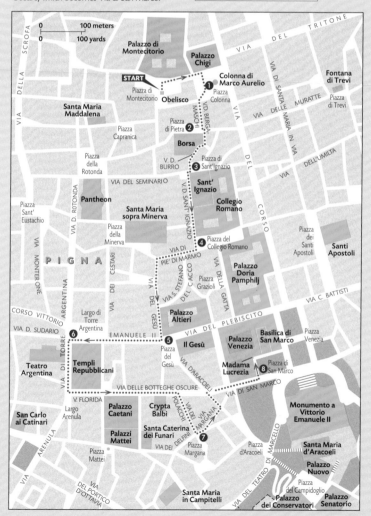

PIAZZA VENEZIA & AROUND

Begun in 1885 and inaugurated in 1911, Il Vittoriano—the stark white marble monument to Vittorio Emanuele II, the Savoy monarch associated with the Risorgimento and the first king of united Italy—dominates the piazza. Today it is home to Italy's Tomb of the Unknown Soldier and has acquired status as a patriotic symbol and cultural center. Nearby are two important churches, Santa Maria in Aracoeli and Il Gesù, and the Crypta Balbi.

Tourists walking in Via del Corso; in the background, the Vittoriano of Piazza Venezia

Piazza Venezia

🗺 Map p. 127

🚌 Bus: C3, H, 30,
44, 46, 60, 63,
80, 81, 83, 118,
130, 160, 170,
190, 628, 715,
716, 780, 781,
916

**Il Vittoriano
(Monumento
a Vittorio
Emanuele II)**

🗺 Map p. 127

✉ Piazza Venezia

☎ 06 6783 587

The **Vittoriano** is also the site of the new Museo Centrale del Risorgimento as well as a venue, through an entrance on Via dei Fori Imperiali, for important exhibitions.

Built in the late 15th century by Venetian cardinal Pietro Barbo (the future Pope Paul II), **Palazzo Venezia** was Rome's first important Renaissance palace, although by incorporating a preexisting medieval tower and some battlements, it can be seen as a transition. The palace was built at a time of significant architectural

change in Rome. Until the early 14th century, when the popes fled to Avignon in France, urban development was centered around the Lateran Palace, then the papal residence. On their return from exile, the Lateran having fallen into disrepair, the popes moved to the Vatican, spurring growth in the area in between.

Over the centuries the palace has served as a papal residence, as the embassy of the Venetian Republic, and, from 1797 to 1916, as the residence of the Austrian ambassador to the Holy See.

Under fascism it was the headquarters of Benito Mussolini, whose major speeches were declaimed from its balcony. The building now houses the **Museo del Palazzo Venezia,** with a vast collection of artworks and objets d'art, which often hosts special exhibitions.

Santa Maria in Aracoeli

Few other churches in Rome better embody the stratified nature of Rome's architectural development, and this is not just because its 22 columns were recycled from some important Roman structures. Santa Maria d'Aracoeli (St. Mary of the Altar of Heaven) was built over the ruins of an ancient Roman temple to Juno.

The early Christian church marks the site where, in the first century B.C., Octavius, the future emperor Augustus, is said to have experienced a vision foretelling the birth of Jesus. He built an altar here, and for this reason, in a break with tradition, he is depicted in the fresco on the arch of the apse—quite a place of honor for a ruler of Rome. Rebuilt in the 13th century by the Franciscans, the church has retained the rather austere Romanesque style of that era, intensified by the fact that the facade was never completed.

An Aura of Mystery: Inside, despite the chandeliers and considerable restoration, the church retains its aura of mystery. The cosmatesque pavement (see p. 208) is interspersed with floor tombs (Donatello designed that of Archdeacon Crivelli). The ceiling decoration commemorates the European naval victory at Lepanto in 1571.

Don't miss the **Bufalini Chapel** (the first on the right) with Pinturicchio's magnificently colored rendition of scenes from the "Life of San Bernardino" (1485). Note how the Renaissance realism of this painting contrasts with the stylized Byzantine icon of the "Madonna" on the main altar. Other works are by Benozzo Gozzoli, Arnolfo di Cambio, Andrea Sansovino, and Pietro Cavallini.

The Climb to Santa Maria in Aracoeli

You'll surely notice the 124 wide steps that visitors need to climb to reach the entrance of Santa Maria in Aracoeli. The painfully steep staircase—a reflection of the medieval view that salvation can only be obtained by sacrifice—was built in 1348, probably as a physical symbol of thanksgiving for the end of the Black Death.

Nearby is the chapel of the **Santissimo Bambino** (Holy Infant). Romans were outraged when, in February 1994, thieves "abducted" its occupant, a gem-studded statue of an infant Jesus said to be carved out of olive wood from the garden of Gethsemane and reputed to have miraculous healing powers. It was replaced by a copy.

Crypta Balbi

We are halfway between Largo di Torre Argentina and Piazza Venezia. What originally was a vast colonnade attached to the

Museo del Palazzo Venezia
- Map p. 127
- Palazzo Venezia, Via del Plebiscito 118
- 06 32810
- Closed Mon.
- $

Santa Maria in Aracoeli
- Map p. 127
- Piazza del Campidoglio 4
- 06 6976 3837
- Closed 12:30–3 p.m. May–Sep., 12:30–2 p.m. Oct.–Apr. Cannot be visited during religious services
- Bus: C3, H, 30, 44, 63, 81, 83, 118, 130, 160, 170, 628, 715, 716, 780, 781

Crypta Balbi
- Map p. 127
- Via delle Botteghe Oscure 31
- 06 3996 7700
- Closed Mon.
- $$ (You can buy a combined ticket to visit the other sites of the Museo Nazionale Romano: It is valid for three days)
- Bus: 70, 81, 87, 116, 116T, 186, 492, 628. Tram: 8

www.museonazionale romano.beniculturali.it

The monument to Vittorio Emanuele II provides spectacular views of the city from the top terrace.

Theater of Balbus, built at the end of the first century B.C., is today a museum of urban archaeology that relates the evolutions, the settlements, and the changes of use over the centuries of an entire block in the historic center of Rome between via delle Botteghe Oscure, Via Caetani, Via dei Delfini, and Via dei Polacchi. The area of the Crypta Balbi was purchased by the Italian state in 1981 for it to become the fourth site of the Museo Nazionale Romano. The museum fundamentally comprises three sections: the museum proper, where the designers have placed a system of panels that accompany the visitor in discovery of the site, skillfully constructed as a chronological progress in the rooms of the museum; the basement, which can be visited by means of a steel gangway showing the remains of the Porticus Minucia–an ancient quadrangular structure that enclosed the sacred complex of the temples in Largo Argentina–as well as the Roman, medieval, and Renaissance street stratifications; and finally, the exterior, which leads to the ancient exedra of the Teatro di Balbo and to the Mithraeum: Also in this case, access is by means of a gangway over the rest of the Chiesa di Santa Maria Domine Rosae, dating from the 12th and 13th centuries. The site is extraordinary evidence of the evolution of Roman society and of the urban landscape from ancient times until the 20th century.

Il Gesù

The mother church of the Jesuit order, this is a pre-baroque structure that, in ecclesiastical terms, fully embodies the Counter-Reformation spirit. Begun by St. Ignatius Loyola (1491–1556) to complement the new Jesuit headquarters at Collegio Romano, it was consecrated in 1584, although the decoration of the interior continued, to be completed in the 19th century.

This church, like many, is built in the form of a Latin cross, meaning that there is a long central nave, making one of the four arms that radiate from the center under the dome longer than all the others. The decoration is extremely opulent. These things were done deliberately. To counter the influence of Protestantism (which stressed simplicity and personal responsibility), the Jesuits sought to emphasize the importance of the church and the clergy.

Designed for Effect

Il Gesù's long nave made processions more dramatic, while darkness encouraged the faithful to focus on the priest, who stood on a raised main altar. The ample use of marble, gilded bronze, lapis lazuli, and silver in the decoration of the chapels, especially the two at the opposite ends of the main transept, was another way to stress the magnificence of God.

INSIDER TIP:

Since the 1700s, a brief ceremony has occurred at the Gesù church every day at 5:30 p.m.: The painting over the St. Ignatius altar gradually descends to dramatically reveal a silver-plated statue of the saint hidden behind it.

—STEFANO CIAMEI
Archaeologist

The chapel in the right transept, by Pietro da Cortona, is dedicated to St. Francis Xavier; the relic case is said to contain the saint's arm. The chapel directly opposite belongs to St. Ignatius, whose remains are buried here. The silver statue of the saint is attributed to the sculptor Canova. It replaced a more valuable effigy, melted down by Pope Pius VI to pay a tribute to Napoleon. The ceiling fresco and the cupola, decorated with prophets, Evangelists, and Doctors of the Church, are from the end of the 17th century. The ornate bronze banister in front of the chapel is decorated with cherubs and with candelabra set on elaborate marble bases. Note the cherub at the top holding up a lapis lazuli globe.

Next door at Piazza del Gesù 45 are the **rooms where St. Ignatius lived.** There are paintings in a magnificent trompe l'oeil style by Padre Andrea Pozzo; some memorabilia are also displayed. ∎

Il Gesù

⚠ Map p. 127

✉ Piazza del Gesù 1

☎ 06 697001

🕐 Church: closed 12:30–4 p.m. St. Ignatius's rooms: only open 4–6 p.m. Mon.–Sat. & 10 a.m.–noon Sun.

🚌 Bus: C3, H, 30, 44, 46, 60, 63, 80, 81, 83, 118, 130, 160, 170, 190, 628, 715, 716, 780, 781, 916

More Places to Visit

Piazza di Sant'Ignazio

Designed by architect Filippo Raguzzini, this piazza (1727–1728) resembles a theatrical stage set, especially when viewed from the central door of the church of **Sant'Ignazio** (tel 06 6794 560). Historically the official place of worship for the nearby Jesuit Collegio Romano, the church, completed in 1650, was built to celebrate St. Ignatius Loyola, the founder of the Jesuit order. Funds ran out before the cupola could be built, so ingenious artists painted a 56-foot-wide (17 m) circular trompe l'oeil canvas that simulates the interior of a dome. The best view is from the yellow marble disk set in the floor of the central nave.

Built in the form of a Latin cross, the church is heavily and ornately decorated with an abundance of stucco, gilt, and colored marbles. The most notable artwork is Padre Andrea Pozzo's ceiling fresco depicting "St. Ignatius' Entrance Into Paradise" and, along the sides, his frescoes commemorating the order's missionary activities around the world. Note the four large female figures representing the continents on which the Jesuits were active. Guess which one is meant to personify the Americas.

🅰 Map p. 127 🚌 Bus: 30, 51, 62, 63, 70, 80, 81, 83, 85, 87, 117, 130, 160, 429, 628

San Marco Evangelista al Campidoglio

One of Rome's 25 titular churches (nonparish churches founded in early Christian times), the basilica of San Marco was established by Pope St. Mark in A.D. 336 and dedicated to his namesake, St. Mark the Evangelist. It has been rebuilt and restored several times since. The ninth-century apse mosaic shows Jesus flanked by saints, his arm lifted in a blessing. Note that his fingers are positioned in the Greek style, with the index and middle fingers raised while the thumb is crossed over. This is said to mimic the first letters, in Greek, of "Jesus Christ," while the Western blessing style—the thumb plus the first two fingers—signifies the Trinity. Pope Gregory IV, on the far left, holds a model of the church.

A fine example of Renaissance architecture, the facade, and its two-story portico, may be the work of Leon Battista Alberti. From the Palazzo Venezia (see pp. 138–139) next door you can get a good look at the courtyard with its charming 18th-century fountain and its beautiful, if incomplete, two-story Renaissance loggia.

🅰 Map p. 127 ✉ Piazza San Marco 48 ☎ 06 6795 205 🕐 Closed 1–4 p.m. & Mon. 🚌 Bus: C3, H, 30, 44, 46, 60, 63, 80, 81, 83, 118, 130, 160, 170, 190, 628, 715, 716, 780, 781, 916

Family & Papal Heraldic Crests

Bears, bulls, castles, bees, fleurs-de-lis, doves, and dragons are everywhere in Rome, gracing facades, fountains, occasionally a pavement, and often a ceiling (especially in churches). In case you've wondered about these ubiquitous symbols, they are the heraldic crests of Rome's noble families.

These coats of arms may be carved in marble or wood, molded in bronze, and in one case (in the Aracoeli church) represented in stained glass. If the symbol is topped by a papal tiara (a large beehive-shaped crown) and two crisscrossed keys, then there is a pope somewhere on the family tree. (A broad brimmed hat with tassels means a cardinal.) As the city's rulers over centuries, the pontiffs left more traces than most. Some, like Urban VIII Barberini, went on real building binges; in fact, the Barberini bee is probably more frequent than the Chigi star, the Farnese fleur-de-lis, the Pamphilj dove, or the Borghese dragon and eagle.

A buried imperial stadium, Renaissance palaces, baroque churches, medieval passageways, and other intriguing traces of the past

CAMPO MARZIO

■ Detail of the Grande Ludovisi
Sarcophagus, Palazzo Altemps

CAMPO MARZIO

Originally separated from the Roman Forum by a land ridge, the Campo Marzio or Campus Martius (Field of Mars) was a broad expanse of flat land that stretched from the Quirinal Hill to the Tiber River. From about the fourth century B.C. on, the Romans used it first for military exercises and later for games and athletic competitions.

At first, Campo Marzio included most of what is today downtown Rome, with numerous porticoes built among the trees for the citizens' enjoyment and relaxation. Subsequently it shrank in size and came to be identified primarily with the area tucked into the curve of the Tiber that faces Castel Sant'Angelo and St. Peter's, enclosing more or less everything from Via del Corso to the river. Only in 1377, when the popes returned from Avignon and took up residence across the river in the Vatican, did this area become a focus for residential construction.

In fact, this is one of the oldest parts of modern Rome, and in vast areas much has remained more or less as it was before broad avenues like Corso Vittorio Emanuele II had even been imagined. Then, as now, there was a warren of narrow streets interrupted only by spacious squares such as Piazza Navona with its grand baroque fountains, Piazza Campo de' Fiori (a food and flower market), and Piazza Farnese, a study in Renaissance elegance.

Exploring Campo Marzio

There are traces of the past everywhere in Campo Marzio. Beneath Piazza Navona lie the remains of Emperor Domitian's stadium, parts of which are visible several yards below modern ground level. To see them exit the square at its north end and turn left at the end of Via Agonale. Buildings here bear flood marks from the pre-embankment days, while medieval arches and passageways evoke images of tradesmen in leather jerkins and soldiers in suits of clanking armor.

It is in this neighborhood, too, that the Renaissance and baroque best meet. Renaissance palaces such as Palazzo Altemps and the

Cancelleria alternate with baroque baronies and churches such as Palazzo Pamphilj's Sant'Agnese in Agone, or Sant'Andrea della Valle.

Elegant high-rent streets such as Via Giulia, Via di Monserrato, and Via dei Coronari—with their churches, art galleries, and exquisite antiques shops—give way to humbler crossways. On Via dei Giubbonari and the streets that surround Teatro di Pompeo or, in the other direction, on Via del Governo Vecchio, you will find countless small *botteghe* (shops of craftsmen and artisans), the descendants of the guilds of an earlier era that more often than not gave their names to the streets. ■

PONTE VITTORIO EMANUELE II

PONTE PR. AMEDEO SAVOIA AOSTA

LUNGOTEVERE

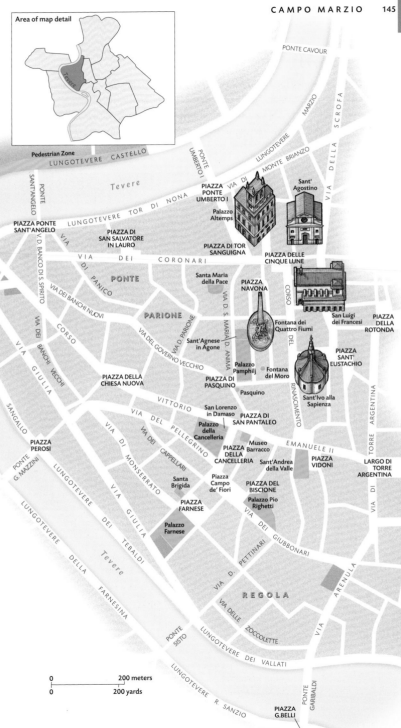

Area of map detail

Pedestrian Zone

LUNGOTEVERE CASTELLO

Tevere

PONTE SANT'ANGELO

PONTE SANT'ANGELO

PIAZZA PONTE SANT'ANGELO

V. D. BANCO DI S. SPIRITO

LUNGOTEVERE TOR DI NONA

PIAZZA DI SAN SALVATORE IN LAURO

VIA DEI CORONARI

PONTE UMBERTO I

VIA DI MONTE BRIANZO

LUNGOTEVERE

VIA DELLA SCROFA

VIA MARZIO

PONTE CAVOUR

PIAZZA PONTE UMBERTO I

Palazzo Altemps

Sant' Agostino

VIA DI

PIAZZA DI TOR SANGUIGNA

PIAZZA DELLE CINQUE LUNE

VIA DI PANICO

PONTE

PARIONE

VIA DEI BANCHI NUOVI

VIA DEL GOVERNO VECCHIO

Santa Maria della Pace

VIA D. S. MARIA D. ANIMA

PIAZZA NAVONA

CORSO

VIA D. PARIONE

Sant'Agnese in Agone

Fontana dei Quattro Fiumi

San Luigi dei Francesi

PIAZZA DELLA ROTONDA

CORSO

VIA DEI BANCHI VECCHI

SANGALLO

CORSO

VIA GIULIA

Palazzo Pamphilj

Fontana del Moro

PIAZZA DI PASQUINO

PIAZZA SANT' EUSTACHIO

Sant'Ivo alla Sapienza

DEL RINASCIMENTO

VITTORIO

Pasquino

PIAZZA PEROSI

PONTE G. MAZZINI

VIA DEL PELLEGRINO

VIA DEI CAPPELLARI

San Lorenzo in Damaso

Palazzo della Cancelleria

PIAZZA DI SAN PANTALEO

PIAZZA DELLA CHIESA NUOVA

PIAZZA DELLA CANCELLERIA

Museo Barracco

EMANUELE II

Sant'Andrea della Valle

PIAZZA VIDONI

LARGO DI TORRE ARGENTINA

VIA DI TORRE ARGENTINA

LUNGOTEVERE DEI TEBALDI

VIA DI MONSERRATO

Santa Brigida

Piazza Campo de' Fiori

PIAZZA DEL BISCIONE

PIAZZA FARNESE

Palazzo Farnese

Palazzo Pio Righetti

VIA DEI GIUBBONARI

VIA DI ARENULA

VIA GIULIA

Tevere

LUNGOTEVERE DELLA FARNESINA

VIA D. PETTINARI

REGOLA

VIA ARENULA

VIA DELLE ZOCCOLETTE

PONTE SISTO

LUNGOTEVERE DEI VALLATI

PONTE GARIBALDI

LUNGOTEVERE R. SANZIO

PIAZZA G.BELLI

| 0 | 200 meters |
| 0 | 200 yards |

PIAZZA NAVONA

One of the world's most beautiful squares, Piazza Navona gives the visitor an opportunity to grasp the complexity of 2,000 years of Roman history. A spectacular baroque composition, the piazza lies within the contours of an ancient Roman stadium. Today it plays host to those who flock here for a moment of relaxation—a chat, an *aperitivo*, a meal—against a backdrop of magnificent man-made beauty.

 Artists peddle their skill and artwork on Piazza Navona.

Piazza Navona

Map p. 145

Bus: C3, 30, 40, 46, 62, 64, 70, 81, 87, 130, 190, 492, 628, 916

In A.D. 86, the emperor Domitian constructed a stadium, the Circus Agonalis, on this site. But urban development did not begin in earnest in this area until 1377, when the popes returned from Avignon and chose the Vatican as their new residence.

In 1477, Pope Sixtus IV moved the city's central market here from its historic location at the Capitol (Campidoglio). It remained here for 390 years and survives today in the traditional Christmas stalls set up by merchants every December to sell toys and decorations.

The modern Piazza Navona dates from the 1640s, when Pope Innocent X, a Pamphilj, chose the square as the site of the new family residence. His plan included

INSIDER TIP:

The Piazza Navona is best experienced at dawn, before the crowds descend upon the place.

—SHEILA BUCKMASTER
National Geographic Traveler
magazine editor at large

elaborate fountains and a church. The Palazzo Pamphilj, completed in 1650, and Sant'Agnese in Agone, completed 20 years later, were done by Francesco Borromini, Girolomo Rainaldi, and Rainaldi's son Carlo.

Palazzo Pamphilj & Sant'Agnese in Agone

Now the Brazilian Embassy, Palazzo Pamphilj boasts frescoes by Pietro da Cortona telling the story of Aeneas. Sant'Agnese in Agone was built where 13-year-old Agnes, a fourth-century Christian maiden who rejected the advances of a Roman official's son, was reportedly stripped naked in public. Legend has it the girl's hair grew so long and so fast that it quickly covered her body.

Agnes was nevertheless martyred, beheaded in A.D. 304 during Diocletian's anti-Christian persecutions. The church's facade was begun by Borromini, who worked on it until his falling out with the family in 1657.

Fountains

The piazza's magnificent baroque fountains conceal yet another chapter in the legendary rivalry between Bernini and Borromini. Borromini lost his commission for the central **Fontana dei Quattro Fiumi** (Fountain of the Four Rivers; see pp. 98–99) because of the savvier, more diplomatic Bernini's successful flattery of Donna Olimpia, the pope's sister-in-law. The story goes that Bernini gave the statue representing the Plate River a raised arm to ward off the imminent collapse of Sant'Agnese; while Borromini's statue of the saint on the church, her hand on her heart, replies, "I will not fall." But it is not true; the fountain was completed in 1651, years earlier than Borromini's facade.

The **Fontana del Moro** (Fountain of the Moor) is by Giacomo della Porta, but Bernini designed the central figure. ■

Pasquino, the Talking Statue

In the 16th century, a church official placed an ancient Roman statue near Piazza Navona in what is today known as Piazza di Pasquino. Hoping to incite the populace against the popes, dissidents and those opposed to the clerics began affixing radical messages to the torso of the statue, which was soon named Pasquino in honor of an outspoken neighborhood tailor. Later, several other "talking" statues popped up around Rome, including Marforio, the river god, now in the Capitoline Museums; the Facchino (the porter), on Via Lata off the Corso; Abbot Luigi, on Piazza Vidoni near Corso Vittorio Emanuele II; and buxom Madama Lucrezia, who today stands outside the Palazzetto di Venezia.

PALAZZO ALTEMPS

After a long period of decline and abandon, Palazzo Altemps—once the residence of 16th- and 17th-century noblemen and cardinals—has been superbly restored by the Italian government. Part of the Museo Nazionale Romano complex, it contains many priceless pieces of classical statuary, although the building's structure and decor compete for the visitor's attention.

A detail of the Palazzo Altemps's elegant central courtyard, designed by Martino Longhi the Elder

Palazzo Altemps belonged to Cardinal Marco Sittico Altemps, who bought the building in 1568. In it he housed his magnificent collection of books and ancient sculptures. Today most of the original pieces are scattered among the world's major museums, although some of them have now been returned. The family sold the palace to the Holy See, which turned it into a seminary. In a dismal state, it was purchased by the Italian government in 1982 and transformed into a museum.

The Collection

The museum's inventory includes artworks from several major Roman art collections, in particular the Boncompagni Ludovisi collection that for years was accessible only to scholars. Now, world-famous pieces such as the magnificent **Ludovisi throne** depicting the birth of Aphrodite, the breathtaking **Grande Ludovisi Sarcophagus** with its violent battles between Roman and barbarian soldiers, the tragically moving "Gaul Committing Suicide," and the inspiring, noble "Ares" are all displayed here. The Painted Loggia on the first floor (one flight up) is now the setting for the Ludovisi **busts of the Caesars.**

In the 16th and 17th centuries, restoring sculpture meant

reconstructing their missing parts. The Altemps Museum is one of a very few that explains this. Panels near the statues use shading to indicate the parts that were added. There are also ample explanations in English.

Sant'Aniceto

Inaugurated in 1617, this beautiful but tiny church may have been the only private church to house the remains of a saint. Anicetus was one of Rome's early popes and martyrs. The frescoes tell the story of his death by decapitation. In reality, however, the story of Anicetus was altered to resemble that of Roberto Altemps, who was sentenced to death by decapitation (for adultery) by Pope Sixtus V. Richly decorated in high baroque style, the church features striking examples of marble and mother-of-pearl inlay.

The Palazzo as Art

The palace's original wall and ceiling decorations have been restored so that the decor of this patrician palace embodies the gradual transition from Renaissance to baroque. The breathtaking **courtyard** features a nymphaeum: a curved wall-fountain decorated with mosaic, paste shells, and colored gravel of the type found in ancient Roman villas. Four of the statues in the courtyard come from the original Altemps collection.

And don't miss the **Fireplace Room,** with Cardinal Altemps's monumental fireplace, and the **Room of the Painted Landscapes.** The wall fresco in the **Cupboard Room,** once the 15th-century reception room, displays wedding gifts and greeting cards received by Girolamo Riario and Caterina Sforza, the palace's first occupants. ∎

Palazzo Altemps

- ⬛ Map p. 145
- ✉ Piazza Sant'Apollinare 44
- ☎ 06 684851 or 06 3996 7700. Online tickets: www. coopculture.it
- 🕐 Closed Mon.
- 💲 $$ (You can buy a combined ticket to visit the other sites of the Museo Nazionale Romano: It is valid for three days). Audio guide: $. Guided tours in Italian on Sun.; for groups in English on request: $$$
- 🚌 Bus: C3, 30, 70, 81, 87, 130, 280, 492, 628

www.museonazionale romano.beniculturali.it

EXPERIENCE: Attend a Concert in a Roman Church

There is something special about listening to music in a church. The lights are dim, a slight perfume of candles floats through the air, statuary and frescoed ceilings complete the solemn atmosphere as the strains of sacred choral music filter through the air. Whether in Sant'Ignazio, Sant'Eustachio, San Lorenzo in Lucina, Sant'Ivo, or Santa Maria Maggiore, this is a lovely way to spend an afternoon or evening in Rome.

The **Associazione Internazionale Amici della Musica Sacra** (www.amici musicasacra.com, tel 06 6880 5816) offers a regular program of free concerts featuring choirs from all parts of the world. All you have to do is turn up. Every Friday young musicians hold chamber music concerts in the Borromini sacristy of **Sant'Agnese**

in Agone church (see p. 147) in Piazza Navona and, during the summer period, in the courtyard of **Sant'Ivo alla Sapienza** in Corso Rinascimento 40 (for the program consult the site www.santagneseinagone.org; for concerts with paid admission, tickets from 22€ can be purchased at the entrance, at the back, of Santa Maria dell'Anima 30, or on the site www.classictic.com).

Other concerts are held from November to May at the **Oratorio del Gonfalone** (Via del Gonfalone 32a); for reservations, call 06 6875 952 or email info@oratoriogonfalone. eu. The **Festival Internazionale di Musica e Arte Sacra** (www.festivalmusicaeartesacra. net) takes place every November in some of the city's most famous basilicas, including St. John's and St. Peter's.

FOUR CAMPO MARZIO CHURCHES

With works by some of Italy's most famous artists, four standout churches in Campo Marzio
are veritable treasures. San Luigi dei Francesi displays Caravaggio paintings, Sant'Agostino contains a magnificent Raphael fresco, Sant'Ivo alla Sapienza is an architectural play of fantasy and
mystery, and Sant'Andrea della Valle features artwork by rivals Lanfranco and Domenichino.

■ Sumptuously frescoed Sant'Andrea della Valle

**San Luigi dei
Francesi**

🅰 Map p. 145

✉ Piazza San Luigi
dei Francesi 5

☎ 06 688271

🕒 Closed 12:45–
2:30 p.m. Mon.
–Fri. & 12:15–
2:30 p.m. Sat.

🚌 Bus: C3, 30, 40,
46, 62, 64, 70,
81, 87, 130, 190,
492, 628, 916

San Luigi dei Francesi

Although the statuary dates to
the 18th century, the church,
bearing a Renaissance facade
attributed to Giacomo della
Porta, was completed in 1589.
It is dedicated to Louis IX, the
French king later made a saint;
the stone dragons that adorn the
facade bear the fleur-de-lis.

Inside you will find an overwhelming profusion of marble

decoration and monuments.
The Contarelli Chapel has three
Caravaggio paintings, all scenes
from the life of St. Matthew and
masterpieces of chiaroscuro and
realism. The dramatic content
of the "Vocation of St. Matthew," its use of indirect lighting,
and the incredulous expression
on the saint's face are enough
to rank Caravaggio among the
world's greatest artists. Look for
Domenichino's "Scenes From the
Life of St. Cecilia" in the second
chapel on the right.

Sant'Agostino

Sant'Agostino is located two
blocks north of San Luigi at the
top of a wide flight of stairs. Its
imposing Renaissance facade
is possibly one of the earliest
in Rome. Completed in 1483,
although the main altar was
refashioned in the 1600s, this
church features Raphael's magnificent fresco of the prophet
Isaiah. It decorates the third
pilaster on the left, against which
stands a lovely sculpture group,
"St. Anne, the Virgin and Child"
(1512), by Andrea Sansovino.

The first chapel on the left
houses Caravaggio's remarkable "Madonna dei Pellegrini"
(1605), highly controversial at
the time because of its realistic
depiction of pilgrims as old and
poor. To the right of the main
portal stands Jacopo Sansovino's

"Madonna del Parto" (*parto* means "childbirth"), with unusual Junoesque proportions.

Sant'Ivo alla Sapienza

Named for the patron saint of lawyers, this church is located on Corso del Rinascimento and inside the Palazzo della Sapienza (*sapienza* means "knowledge" in Latin), today the National Archives. Until 1935, this was the site of Rome's La Sapienza University (since moved), founded by Pope Boniface VIII in 1303.

A number of popes commissioned artists to work on the structure, as you can see from the papal insignias in the courtyard—eagles and dragons for the Borghese family, bees for the Barberini. Designed by Francesco Borromini, the 17th-century church mixes fantasy and mystery with Gothic overtones. Giacomo della Porta designed the courtyard and facade, of which the lower portion is concave. The convex curves of the cupola culminate in a spiral pinnacle. The all-white interior again alternates convex and concave forms.

Back outside, take the first right to see the small **fountain** of Sant'Eustachio, or Eustace, decorated with his symbols, books, a cross, and a deer's head. A Roman soldier who converted to Christianity after seeing a cross between the horns of a deer, Eustace was martyred and now gives his name to this neighborhood.

Sant'Andrea della Valle

The church of Sant'Andrea della Valle stands at the end of Corso del Rinascimento in Piazza Vidoni. Similar in style to Il Gesù (see p. 141), Sant'Andrea was designed by Giacomo della Porta, although the facade and the dome are fundamentally the work of Carlo Maderno. According to one story, there were supposed to be two angels, not just one, on the top of the facade, but the sculptor, irritated by criticism, told his episcopal patron to "go do it himself."

Inside, Lanfranco created the magnificent dome fresco, the "Glory of Paradise"; his archrival Domenichino painted the pendentives. Domenichino also painted scenes from the life of St. Andrew in the upper portion of the apse, where two popes are buried. The lovely Strozzi Chapel is in the Michelangelo style. The Barberini Chapel, the first on the left, corresponds to the chapel Puccini chose as the setting for the first act of *Tosca*. Here Tosca accused her lover of betrayal when she noticed that the Mary Magdalen he was painting resembled another woman. ∎

INSIDER TIP:
Opera buffs should not miss a visit to Sant'Andrea della Valle, Piazza Farnese, or Castel Sant'Angelo, three locations used by Puccini in *Tosca*.

—DENNIS CIGLER
Tour coordinator & guide, In Italy's Companions

Sant'Agostino
- Map p. 145
- Piazza di Sant'Agostino
- 06 6880 1962
- Closed noon–4 p.m.
- Bus: C3, 30, 40, 46, 62, 64, 70, 81, 87, 130, 190, 492, 628, 916

Sant'Ivo alla Sapienza
- Map p. 145
- Corso del Rinascimento 40
- 06 6864 987 or 328 4068 067
- Courtyard open daily. Interior only open Sun. 9 a.m.–noon
- Bus: C3, 30, 40, 46, 62, 64, 70, 81, 87, 130, 190, 492, 628, 916

Sant'Andrea della Valle
- Map p. 145
- Piazza Vidoni 6
- 06 6861 339
- Bus: C3, H, 30, 40, 46, 62, 63, 64, 70, 81, 87, 130, 190, 492, 628, 780, 916. Tram: 8

MEDIEVAL MYSTERY &
RENAISSANCE RICHES WALK

In Roman times, the vast area of the Campo Marzio was given over to army encampments, stadiums, and pleasure porticoes. It's mostly all gone or buried now, but many of the medieval and Renaissance buildings that came later remain, bearing witness to the intrigues and riches of a not-so-distant past.

St. Peter's and the Ponte Sant'Angelo

NOT TO BE MISSED:

San Salvatore in Lauro • View from Ponte Sant'Angelo • Chiesa Nuova • Oratorio dei Filippini

This walk starts just north of Piazza Navona at **Piazza di Tor Sanguigna,** where a chunk of the first-century foundation of **Domitian's Stadio** (see p. 51) still sits below the railing. The medieval tower behind you gave the piazza its name. **Via dei Coronari**—where vendors once sold *corone* (rosary beads) to Catholic pilgrims—begins on your left, near the lovely 17th-century wall aedicula (shrine) at No. 2. Today the street is filled with wonderful (and expensive) antiques stores.

Walk west on Via dei Coronari. Look down the alley Vicolo del Volpe, on the left side of the street, to see the colorful tiled spire of **Santa Maria dell'Anima.** Farther down Via dei Coronari you will find **Piazza di San Salvatore in Lauro ❶,** with the church of the same name. Here, be sure to see the church's beautiful double *chiostro* (cloister).

Continue west on Via dei Coronari; turn right on Via di Panico. At No. 40, note the small marble relief on the wall, a stonecutter's shingle. At the end of the street, carefully cross the Lungotevere river road (Lungotevere Tor di Nona) to **Ponte Sant'Angelo ❷,** where you can enjoy a breathtaking view of Castel Sant'Angelo and St. Peter's dome. The bridge is magnificently decorated with monumental Bernini-designed statues, each holding a symbol (a crown of thorns, a whip, a nail) of the Crucifixion.

Toward Piazza di Pasquino

Cross back over Lungotevere Tor di Nona, and take Via del Banco di Santo Spirito. It is the middle street—note the columns of a medieval portico embedded in the corner building—of the three that fan out from here. Look for a dark, medieval passage on the right side of the street, the **Arco dei Banchi;** an inscription here marks the height of the 1277 flood.

The road forks at the Banco di Santo Spirito (No. 3). Take the picturesque Via dei Banchi Nuovi on your left to **Piazza dell'Orologio ❸,** named for the large clock on the tower. On the left, take Vicolo degli Orsini, and at the end, sneak a peek at the lush, green inner courtyard of a baronial palace built by the Orsini.

Backtrack to the piazza and continue along the same street (now called Via del Governo Vecchio). Turn right on Via della Chiesa Nuova and right again at the end to find yourself in front of the late Renaissance church that Romans call **Chiesa Nuova** ❹ (officially, Santa Maria della Vallicella). Stand near the statue for a better view of the church and the interesting Borromini facade of the **Oratorio dei Filippini** on the left. It has a curious porticoed courtyard and a charming if somewhat musty library, the Biblioteca Vallicelliana, designed by Borromini in 1637. The church has three Rubens paintings over the main altar and a ceiling fresco by Pietro da Cortona.

Leave by the side door and return to Via del Governo Vecchio, then proceed to **Piazza**

di Pasquino ❺, with its "talking" statue (see p. 147). The statue stands against the back wall of Palazzo Braschi, seat of the **Museo di Roma.**

Follow the street on the left, Via di Santa Maria dell'Anima, to **Tor Millina,** a medieval tower. Turn left and walk a block until you reach Via della Pace and, facing you, Pietro da Cortona's spectacularly dramatic facade of the church of **Santa Maria della Pace.**

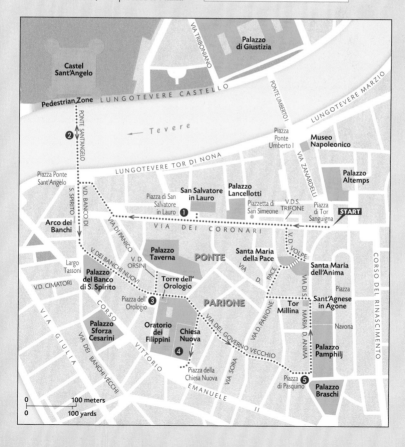

- See also area map p. 145
- ▶ Piazza di Tor Sanguigna
- 1 mile (1.5 km)
- 1.5–2 hours
- ▶ Santa Maria della Pace

PIAZZA CAMPO DE' FIORI

One of the liveliest spots in the city, Piazza Campo de' Fiori (its name means "field of flowers") has been an outdoor marketplace since 1869. On weekday and Saturday mornings you can buy fresh produce and fish. Come evening, young Italians and foreigners alike fill the square's inexpensive trattorias, while its bustling wine bars and pubs stay open late into the night.

■ The Campo dei Fiori market is one of Rome's most popular.

Piazza Campo de' Fiori

🗺 Map p. 145

🚌 Bus: 23, 40, 46, 62, 64, 190, 280, 916

Campo de' Fiori is one of the few important squares not linked to a particular patrician family or an important edifice. The only building of note is the **Palazzo Pio Righetti,** built over the ruins of the Teatro di Pompeo at its southeastern end. As is true of the rest of the Campo Marzio area, Campo de' Fiori became increasingly central after the Holy See's decision in the 14th century to set up residence in the Vatican. The square was, after all, directly on the now vanished Via Papalis and the Via del Pellegrino, the pedestrian routes for pilgrims arriving from the city's south side.

After Pope Sixtus IV built his bridge over the Tiber (Ponte Sisto) for the 1475 Holy Year, this piazza became a transit point for anyone coming from or going to Trastevere. Not surprisingly, until the 17th century, when most such activity moved to the Spanish Steps area, it was the center of a flourishing tourist trade. Indeed, the Albergo del Sole, just around the corner on Via del Biscione, is reputedly one the oldest hotels in Rome. Number 13, on the corner of the Via dei Cappellari and Vicolo del Gallo, was an inn, La Vacca, run by Vanozza Cattanei, a grande dame who for a time was the mistress of Rodrigo Borgia (the future Pope Alexander VI), and mother of the lovely, but infamous, Lucrezia.

INSIDER TIP:

The Campo de' Fiori market prompts a travel fantasy: Rent an apartment and add cooking to your Rome experience.

—SHEILA BUCKMASTER
National Geographic Traveler
magazine editor at large

The piazza's large, open space was once well suited to all sorts of games and processions as well as executions. The scholar Giordano Bruno, whose statue stands in the square, was burned at the stake as a heretic by the Inquisition in 1600. ■

EXPERIENCE: Outdoor Markets & Specialty Shops

In the past, before supermarkets and packaged food, a Roman housewife planned her family's meals around the seasonal products available in the nearest outdoor or *rionale* (neighborhood) food market. Although fewer in number today, those markets still exist. If you are staying in an apartment while in Rome and have decided to cook—or if you want simply to walk in the footsteps of generations of Roman *casalinghe* (housewives)—any morning except Sundays head straight to the Campo de' Fiori neighborhood (see opposite) and its famous market.

Campo de' Fiori is not the only area of old Rome where you can take an intriguing food-based walk. Alternatives include **Trastevere**, the ancient Jewish Ghetto area (see p. 206); **Testaccio**, under the shadow of the Aventine Hill; or **Piazza Vittorio Emanuele II**, where the huge new indoor market offers foods from all continents.

The Freshest Produce

As you make your way through the hodgepodge of vegetable and fruit stalls, the richness and abundance of available fruits and vegetables becomes apparent.

If it is spring you will find peas and *fave* (Roman lima beans), which Romans like to eat with the tangy local *pecorino romano* cheese. In fall or spring you'll see the amazingly bright green *broccolo romano*, a cross between cauliflower and broccoli. An old woman bent over a tub filled with curling pale green stalks is preparing *puntarelle*, made by peeling a type of raw chicory, served as a salad with olive oil and a garlicky anchovy sauce. Spring also brings piles of artichokes, the green-purple *romanesco* kind. In March, Sicily's bloodred oranges roll in, and in April or June you'll find tiny fragrant strawberries from nearby Lago di Nemi.

Meat & Fish

The **Macelleria Orelli** at Piazza del Biscione 97 (next to Piazza Campo de' Fiori) specializes in local products like milk-fed lamb (*abbacchio*) and offal (such as oxtail, tripe, liver, and heart). This area also boasts wonderful *norcinerie* (pork products stores): At the **Antica Norcerina Viola** (No. 43), you'll find, along with the classic prosciutto, typical Roman products like *coppiette*, two dried strips of pork eaten as a snack with drinks; *corallina* salami, made from lean pork; and lard, traditionally eaten at Easter with *torta pasqualina* (a local savory tart). For fresh fish and shellfish of every type, walk across the street to **Attanasio** in Via del Biscione 12 (a.m. only; closed Sun.–Mon.).

From the Oven

And of course you mustn't forget breads. **Il Forno**, which is located on the corner of Via dei Capellari and Campo de' Fiori, offers typically Roman breads such as *rosette*—hollow, rose-shaped rolls—and *pane casareccio*, either Lariano or Genzano, both ideal for *bruschetta*.

A few blocks away is another *forno*, **Roscioli** (*Via dei Chiavari 34*), one of Rome's oldest, with excellent pizza and bread, and specialties such as basic Lariano bread to which raisins, nuts, or olives have been added. You can also get *ciambelle al vino*, cookies made to dip in wine; *castagnaccio*, a flat cake made with chestnut flour, dried fruit, nuts, and rosemary; and *pangiallo*, a hard, spicy Christmas cake. During Lent there are the fried, sugar-sprinkled *frappe* and *castagnole*.

Food Walks

Do you need help? Several English-speaking residents of Rome offer food walks designed to give you an inside view of Roman cuisine and its ingredients.

Katie Parla (*www. katieparla.com/tours*) offers tours of Testaccio and the historic center, the latter with a focus on Rome's Jewish culinary tradition. **Kenny Dunn** (*www.eatingitalyfood tours.com*) does a four-hour walking tour with tastings in Testaccio. And also food writer **Maureen Fant** (*www. maureenbfant.com*) has a vast knowledge of Roman food and eateries.

PIAZZA FARNESE

Palazzo Farnese is widely considered to be the most beautiful Renaissance building in Rome, if not in Italy, and the imposing structure cannot be separated from the lovely piazza in which it stands. Commissioned in 1514 by Alessandro Farnese (the future Pope Paul III), the palazzo's magnificent proportions are the work of some of the major architects of the time, including Antonio Sangallo; Michelangelo, who designed the cornice and the loggia on the facade; and Giacomo della Porta.

Palazzo Farnese fresco (1553–1563) by Cecchino Salviati depicting the pontificate of Pope Paul III

Piazza Farnese

Map p. 145

Bus: 23, 40, 46, 62, 64, 190, 280, 916

Today the Palazzo Farnese houses the French Embassy and is only open to the public by prearranged visit *(www.inventer rome.com for bookings well before your trip)*. It is well worth visiting, as the interior was decorated by some of the best artists of the era, including Annibale and Agostino Caracci, Domenichino, and Lanfranco. The fleurs-de-lis on the palace's exterior and on the fountains have nothing to

do with France; these are the Farnese lilies, the symbol of that noble Roman family.

During the Renaissance a piazza was always considered an integral part of any aristocratic residence, and this one is adorned with **granite basins from the Baths of Caracalla.** It seems to be among the very few in the city not designed by Giacomo della Porta. Della Porta is instead credited with the rear facade

INSIDER TIP:

For a great glass of wine, stop in Il Goccetto, which has no sign except a dusty "Vino e Olio" (wine and oil) above the door. It's at Via dei Banchi Vecchi 14, a few hundred yards northwest of Piazza Farnese.

—PAUL BENNETT
*National Geographic writer &
founder of Context Travel*

of the palace, which faces the garden and the river. A project, attributed to Michelangelo, to link the palazzo to property on the Trastevere side of the river with an overhead bridge, was never completed. The lovely **arch** that romantically spans the Via Giulia is the only bit that was done. The church of **Santa Brigida,**

on the left side of the piazza, is the Swedish National Church. The adjacent convent is where St. Bridget died in 1373. Today it is also possible to stay overnight in the building (*www.brigidine.org*).

"Ecstasies"

The relatively small marble wall relief in the **Casa di Santa Brigida** showing St. Bridget's ecstatic face after a mystical communication with God was probably inspired by Gian Lorenzo Bernini. But, truth be told, it cannot be compared to the maestro's work. Bernini's marble rendering of the ecstasy of the "Blessed Ludovica Albertoni" in San Francesco a Ripa (see p. 198) is magnificent. As for the breathtaking and dramatically baroque "Ecstasy of St. Theresa" in Santa Maria della Vittoria (see p. 92), that work led one 19th-century traveler to quip, "If that's celestial ecstasy, then I've experienced it, too." ■

Casa di Santa Brigida

- Map p. 145
- Piazza Farnese 96
- 06 6889 2596 or 06 6889 2497
- Church: Open daily 6–8 a.m., Tues. 6–noon and 4–5:15 p.m. Closed Wed. & Sat. Casa: The rooms can be visited on request, 5:15–7 p.m.

Street Names

In medieval and Renaissance times, artisans typically set up shop in clusters, a practice often imposed by law as well as by convenience. Many of the streets in this central area of old Rome took, and kept, their names from the tradesmen who once worked there. Thus we have Via dei Cappellari, the street of the hatmakers, which starts at the northwest corner of Campo de' Fiori; Via dei Baullari, the street of the trunkmakers, which leads toward Piazza Navona; and Via dei Giubbonari, the street of jacket- or jerkinmakers, which runs toward Via Arenula and the Ghetto. Other examples are Via dei Chiavari, the street of the locksmiths; Via dei Sediari, the street of the chairmakers; and Via dei Balestrari, the street of the crossbowmakers. On Via dei Coronari, artisans specialized in the making of rosaries; the Cestari and the Canestrari made baskets; the Funari made ropes; the Staderari weighed things; and, on Vicolo del Bollo, jewelers brought gold or silver to be hallmarked. Piazza del Fico is named after its centuries-old fig tree, Via del Governo Vecchio after the large building that was once the seat of government, while Via dei Soldati, near Piazza Navona, was on a military patrol route. A small Italian-English dictionary will help you get a better idea of the historical context.

A WALK AROUND CAMPO MARZIO

On this walk, you'll feast on a wealth of Renaissance and baroque detail. Unlike other areas of Rome, the Campo Marzio is remarkably homogeneous: Most construction here took place only after the popes returned from exile in Avignon in 1377 and chose to set up in the Vatican, setting off a new period of urban development in the area.

Café life along Via di Monserrato

NOT TO BE MISSED:

San Girolamo della Carità
• Via Giulia • Galleria Spada
• Sant'Andrea della Valle

(painted building)—the L-shaped, 16th-century **Palazzo Ricci ②**. At the intersection of Monserrato and Via del Pellegrino, where **Via dei Banchi Vecchi ③** begins, don't miss the marble plaque, inscribed in Latin, on No. 145. Dating from the reign of Emperor Claudius (A.D. 41–54), it marks the perimeter of an ancient Roman neighborhood. Via dei Banchi Vecchi has charming little shops selling antiques and bric-a-brac. Take a peek into the old pharmacy at No. 24, then cross the street to look at its facade. You'll see why the building is called the **Palazzo dei Pupazzi** (puppets). At No. 118 you'll see the imposing *portone* to the **Palazzo Sforza Cesarini,** originally built by the infamous 15th-century Borgia pope, Alessandro VI.

Facing the Palazzo Farnese, take Via di Monserrato on your right. The first square you come to, tiny Piazza Santa Caterina della Rota, has three churches. The cream-colored **San Girolamo della Carità ①** (1650–1660) on your left is a must. The Spada Chapel, left of the entrance, has opulent polychromatic marble decor created by Francesco Borromini. The drapery between the two kneeling angels looks like cloth but is really marble.

Continue along Via di Monserrato until you reach Piazza dei Ricci with its *palazzo istoriato*

Via Giulia & Beyond

Continuing on, you will come to Via dei Cimatori, which leads to the most beautiful street in Rome—the Via Giulia—built by Pope Julius II in the early 16th century. To the right is the church of the Florentine residents of Rome, **San Giovanni dei Fiorentini.**

Turn left on **Via Giulia ④**. At No. 85, note the inscription "*Raf Sanzio*" (for Raphael, the painter) above the first-floor balcony. In Renaissance times many famous architects lived next door to their patrician clients. The travertine "sofas" on the building at No. 62 were part of the grandiose courthouse begun by Bramante for Julius II but never completed. Just past the ivy-clad overhead arch is the rear facade of **Palazzo Farnese.** After the arch is the striking Mascherone Fountain, which incorporates a giant marble mask of ancient Roman origin.

Turn left on Vicolo del Polverone. Walk to Piazza Capo di Ferro, where at No. 13 is the **Galleria Spada** ⑤ (tel 06 6832 409, closed Tues.), which has paintings by Rubens, Titian, Guido Reni, and others. The palazzo is equally interesting. Note the magnificent stucco decorations on its facade. From the central courtyard you can look at Borromini's famous optical illusion, which makes a tiny statue at the end of a short, 30-foot (9 m) corridor appear to be a colossus at the end of a long, imposing hallway.

From Piazza Capo di Ferro, walk down Via dei Balestrari, skirt the end of Piazza Campo de'

Fiori, and bear right to the Piazza del Biscione. Venture through the iron gate at the far end and down the covered passageway (Passetto del Biscione) to **Via di Grotta Pinta** ⑥. The buildings here were constructed over the stands of the Teatro di Pompeo (Pompey's Theater), the probable site of Julius Caesar's assassination. Heading left, cross the Largo del Pallaro and follow Via dei Chiavari to Corso Vittorio Emanuele II. The large church on your right is **Sant'Andrea della Valle** (see p. 151).

🅰 See also area map p. 145
➤ Piazza Farnese
↔ 1.5 miles (2.5 km)
🕐 2.5–3 hours
➤ Sant'Andrea della Valle

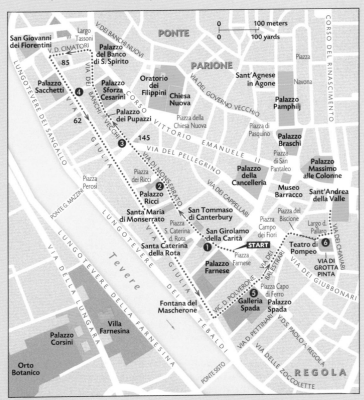

More Places to Visit

Museo Barracco

This little-known but delightful museum is often referred to as La Piccola Farnesina. It has no connection with the Palazzo Farnese, but confusion arose because the royal fleur-de-lis used by its noble French owners resembled the Farnese coat of arms. Built in 1523, probably by Antonio Sangallo the Younger, it has been altered several times. Now the property of the Rome city government, it houses the Barracco collection of ancient artwork, primarily sculptures. The collection, donated to the city in 1902, includes Egyptian, Greek, Assyrian, Etruscan, and Roman pieces. The late Roman ruins beneath the museum are often accessible to the public.

www.museobarracco.it 🗺 Map p. 145 ✉ Corso Vittorio Emanuele II 166a ☎ 060608 🕐 Closed Mon. 💲 $. Audio guide: $ 🚌 Bus: 40, 46, 62, 64, 190, 492, 916

Palazzo della Cancelleria

Completed in 1517, this palazzo ranks as one of the finest Renaissance buildings in the city, with a history intimately linked to the Roman nobility. It was paid for with the 60,000 scudi that Raffaele Riario, a nephew of Pope Sixtus IV, received from France-schetto Cibo, the nephew of Pope Innocent VIII, as payment for a gambling debt. The stone roses on the facade and in the court-yard were the heraldic symbol of the Riario family. Today, it is owned by the Vatican, which at one time used it as a chancellery, and it enjoys extraterritorial status. Bramante did some work on the palazzo. Don't miss the marvelous *cortile* (courtyard) with its impressive two-story double loggia.

Concerts are sometimes held upstairs in the **Sala dei 100 Giorni** *(tel 06 6989 3405),* the Hundred Days Room, which features frescoes by Giorgio Vasari depicting scenes from the life of Pope Paul III, a Farnese. Vasari claimed to have painted the room in a hun-dred days, leading Michelangelo reportedly to respond, *"Si vede bene"* ("You can tell"). On the right, incorporated into the palazzo, is the church of **San Lorenzo in Damaso.** Take note of the columns in the courtyard, some of which were taken from a preexisting fourth-century church.

San Lorenzo in Damaso: 🗺 Map p. 145 ✉ Piazza della Cancelleria 1 ☎ 06 6988 7566 🚌 Bus: 40, 46, 62, 64, 190, 492, 916

Caravaggio

Born Michelangelo Merisi in September 1571, Caravaggio was later known only by the name of the tiny northern town of his birth. He trained in Milan, far from the centers of classical Renaissance art, where he developed a style of painting that mixed realism and dramatic lighting.

Caravaggio arrived in Rome at the age of 17 and took the art world by storm. He was one of the first painters to contrast light and dark to maximum effect, a tech-nique known as chiaroscuro. His wealth of detail and his ability to depict humanity with all of its defects and frailty were also exceptional. However, not everyone loved his work. The priests of San Luigi dei Fran-cesi rejected his first version of "St. Mat-thew and the Angel," labeling its extreme realism "disrespectful."

Caravaggio's life in Rome was marked by drunkenness, scrapes with the law, murder (albeit unintentional), poverty, illness, and, finally, death at 39. Today his works can be found in Sant'Agostino and Santa Maria del Popolo, as well as in most of Rome's leading museums.

The world's smallest independent state, the historic seat of Roman Catholicism, and the repository of numerous major artistic treasures

VATICANO

■ Detail of a Raphael fresco in the Musei Vaticani

VATICANO

The Basilica di San Pietro—built over the tomb of the Apostle Peter—is the center of Roman Catholicism and the largest basilica of Christianity. It is also the external face of the Vatican, the world's smallest independent city-state. Despite its minuscule geographical dimensions, however, the Vatican wields immense power and influence.

Built to keep out marauding Saracens, the walls of the Vatican enclose a miniature urban tapestry. The Vatican has its own post office and stamps, judicial system, pharmacy, gas station, railway station, commissary, television station, and special police force, the Swiss Guards corps, that dates back to 1505. It publishes a daily newspaper, the influential *Osservatore Romano*, and sends out daily radio broadcasts in more than a dozen languages. The church once ruled much of Italy, but between 1860 and 1870, Piedmontese troops conquered the Papal States. As a result, the pope did not leave the Vatican until peace was made with Italy in 1929 through the signing of the Concordat.

The popes have lived in the Vatican since the end of the 14th century, when they returned from

exile in Avignon and found the Palazzo Lateranense (see p. 80) in ruins. Settlement of the Vatican plain (Ager Vaticanus) occurred slowly, but the papal move to the Vatican accelerated development. The 15th and 16th centuries saw a rash of construction on what was called the Mons Vaticanus. The result, a labyrinthine complex of interconnected palaces, grew up around St. Peter's in a largely disordered fashion.

In the mid-1400s, Nicholas V (1447–1455) enlarged and beautified earlier structures, and his successors followed suit. Sixtus IV built the chapel that bears his name (the Cappella

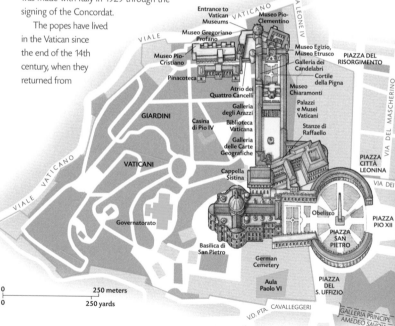

Sistina, or Sistine Chapel), Alexander VI (1492–
1503) built a nearby tower (Torre del Borgia),
and Julius II (1503–1513) arranged for Donato
Bramante to construct the new St. Peter's.

Near St. Peter's

Outside, the Borgo neighborhood is flanked
by the remains of the ninth-century Leonine Wall, a portion of which connects the
Vatican to Castel Sant'Angelo. Built as a
mausoleum for a Roman emperor, the castle
later operated as a fortress and a papal
refuge. In the 1930s, Mussolini gave Pope
Pius XI (1922–1939) permission to connect
the Vatican and the castle with the broad
Via della Conciliazione (reconciliation). This
made St. Peter's more visible but destroyed
a historic neighborhood in the process.

Much of the Vatican today is occupied
by the Musei Vaticani, or Vatican Museums,
which, along with the Sistine Chapel and the
Stanze di Raffaello (Rooms of Raphael), include
the Pinacoteca art gallery and the Musei Pio-
Clementino, Gregoriano Profano, Egizio, and
Etrusco. The entrance is well around the back
of Vatican City—beyond Piazza del Risorgimento—on winding Viale Vaticano. To the right
of St. Peter's, instead, is the Apostolic Palace
with Bernini's Portone di Bronzo, the Papal
Apartments (the pope appears in a window
every Sunday when he is in residence to bless
the faithful), and the offices of the Secre-
tariat of State (the foreign
ministry). It is from here
that the pontiff rules
his largely (but not
entirely) spiritual
empire. ∎

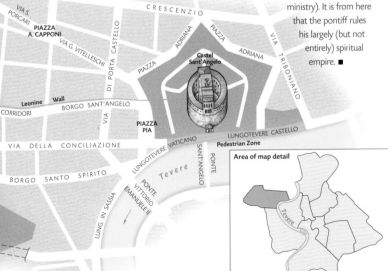

BASILICA DI SAN PIETRO

Nobody knows exactly in what year Peter came to Rome, other than that it was after A.D. 50. And no one knows the exact year of his martyrdom, only that he was crucified in an imperial circus near the Vatican during Nero's persecutions and therefore sometime between A.D. 64 and 67. What we do know is that from early on his grave site assumed a particular importance for the members of the then recently born Christian sect.

■ Michelangelo designed St. Peter's glorious dome.

**Basilica di
San Pietro**

🗺 Map p. 162

✉ Piazza San
Pietro

☎ 06 6988 1662

🚌 Bus: 32, 34, 40,
46, 62, 64, 81,
98, 190, 590,
881, 916, 982,
990. Tram: 19

www.vatican.va

Eager to help—and perhaps to be helped by—the growing Christian religion, Emperor Constantine laid the foundations for the first St. Peter's in the early fourth century. Consecrated by Pope Sylvester I in A.D. 326, the new church had a spacious atrium and elaborate decorations. When the popes returned from Avignon, they found that the old building had deteriorated

and risked collapse. Exactly 1,300 years later to the day (November 18, 1626), a new Basilica di San Pietro (St. Peter's Basilica) opened its doors, but its birth was slow and painful.

Shortly after his reign began, Julius II (1503–1513) commissioned Bramante to build a new church on top of Peter's tomb, and in 1506 the foundation stone was laid. However 120 years passed before this massive new structure was completed.

Construction of a Masterpiece

So just who did build St. Peter's? The answer is, just about everyone. And the fact that so many cooks did not spoil the broth is in itself a minor miracle. Nevertheless, the city's architects did argue over the basic plan.

Some, like Baldassare Peruzzi, wanted St. Peter's to be built in the shape of a Greek cross, with four arms of equal length. Bramante, for example, thought it should resemble Santa Sophia in Constantinople. Michelangelo, who joined the fray in 1546 but only had time to conceive the basilica's giant dome, was also in favor of the Greek cross plan. Others, including Raphael and Antonio Sangallo the Younger, preferred the shape of a Latin cross, which has a long vertical arm and a shorter crossbar toward one end, like a crucifix. In the end, Pope Paul V (1605–1621) finally decided in favor of the Latin cross, awarding the commission to architect Carlo Maderno in 1607.

INSIDER TIP:

Dress appropriately to visit St. Peter's. Ushers at the entrance do not allow the scantily clad to enter. And remember that getting into the basilica takes a while, due to the metal detectors.

—KRISTIN JARRATT
Founder of In Italy Online

At that time, the Catholic church was fully caught up in the Counter-Reformation, and Paul wanted the church to be at least as big as its predecessor. He also wanted it to have an even longer nave (615 feet/187 m), which would heighten the importance of ritual and make processions and other rites more dramatic.

The pope's plans for the new church meant that the dome would not be immediately visible to the entering faithful as originally planned. When completed, the dome designed by 71-year-old Michelangelo was also higher and more elaborately decorated than anyone had intended. Nevertheless, his mark on the church's structure, including the massive pilasters and the magnificent windows, is indelible.

Facade & Portico

Carlo Maderno also created the basilica's travertine facade—white and ocher, with red and green accents on the Loggia della Benedizione. Newly renovated, this internationally known landmark did not please everyone. French painter Henri Matisse once said that the wide (360 foot/110 m), two-story facade looked more like a train station than a church.

Piazza San Pietro

In contrast to the eponymous basilica, there is no doubt about who created Piazza San Pietro (St. Peter's Square). With its elliptical shape and its two semicircular colonnades, Gian Lorenzo Bernini's design, commissioned by Pope Alexander VII Chigi (1655–1667), has been universally acclaimed as an architectural masterpiece.

The square features 284 gigantic Doric columns in the colonnade, 88 other pilasters, and 140 statues. Statues of Jesus, John the Baptist, and 11 Apostles decorate the church facade. Three sets of steps, flanked by statues of St. Peter and St. Paul, lead to the entrance. In the middle of the piazza are two fountains, one by Carlo Maderno and a copy created in 1677 by Bernini, and an Egyptian obelisk (see p. 86), placed there before the creation of the colonnade. Halfway between the obelisk and each fountain is a plain stone disk reading "Centro del Colonnato." Stand on one and see the four rows of columns in the corresponding hemicycle miraculously line into one.

There are five entrances into the portico (and another five doors into the church). Inside—where you can see Maderno's stuccoed ceiling, now gloriously restored—note the two equestrian statues: "Constantine" by Bernini on the extreme right and "Charlemagne" (1725) on the extreme left. Together they represented the temporal power of the church.

Directly over the central doorway, but very difficult to see, is what is left of the famous "Navicella" mosaic by Giotto, which once graced the atrium of the old St. Peter's built by Constantine. This mosaic that depicts Jesus walking on water is best seen if you stand with your back to the church's central bronze doors. Also from Constantine's time, the doors were decorated in the 15th century by Florentine sculptor

Filarete (Antonio Averulino). Opened only during Holy Years, the **Holy Door,** or Porta Santa, is the one on the far right. The pope uses the central loggia when he delivers his *Urbi et Orbi* ("To the city and to the world") blessing on Christmas and Easter. It is also used for the "*Habemus Papam*" announcement after a papal election.

Inside the Basilica

Bernini must get much of the credit for the overwhelming baroque interior of St. Peter's. Enter through Filarete's doors, and stand briefly on the large porphyry circle just inside, the

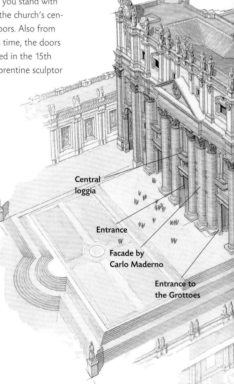

Central loggia

Entrance

Facade by Carlo Maderno

Entrance to the Grottoes

spot where Charlemagne and others after him knelt when crowned emperor. Walk straight up the nave to the transept. The bronze strips on the floor mark the lengths of other famous, but shorter, cathedrals.

Just as Bernini intended, your eyes go immediately to the enormous bronze **baldacchino** (canopy) over the

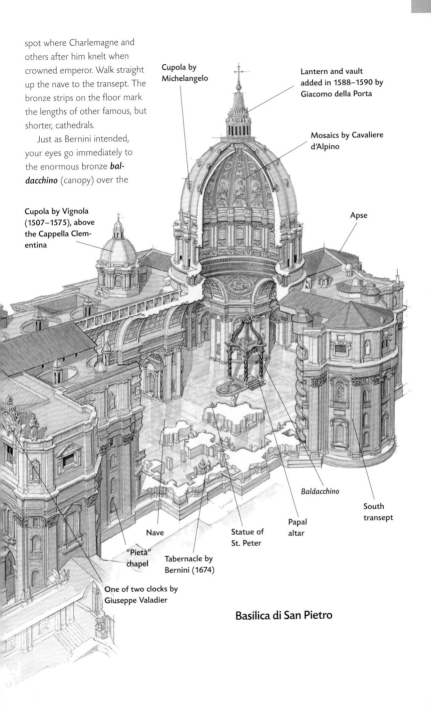

Cupola by Michelangelo

Lantern and vault added in 1588–1590 by Giacomo della Porta

Mosaics by Cavaliere d'Alpino

Cupola by Vignola (1507–1575), above the Cappella Clementina

Apse

Baldacchino

South transept

Nave

Statue of St. Peter

Papal altar

"Pietà" chapel

Tabernacle by Bernini (1674)

One of two clocks by Giuseppe Valadier

Basilica di San Pietro

papal altar, made with bronze stripped from the portico of the Pantheon. Don't miss the "Woman-in-Childbirth" sequence on the column bases; marble reliefs depict her changing expressions and end with a smiling *bambino* (baby). The sunken **confessio** in front of the canopy, designed by Maderno, is surrounded by a balustrade with 95 perennially lit lamps. It marks St. Peter's tomb several levels below.

Michelangelo's "Pietà"

You wouldn't want to travel all the way to St. Peter's and not see Michelangelo's famous "Pietà." It can be found in the first chapel of the right aisle. This is Michelangelo's only signed sculpture—see his signature on the sash across the Virgin's breast. The work has been protected by a transparent bulletproof panel ever since a deranged man attacked and damaged it with a hammer in 1972.

The *gloria* or sunburst in the apse is part of a magnificent baroque monument, the **"Cattedra Petri,"** into which Bernini incorporated an early ninth-century papal throne once thought to have been Peter's. An alabaster window with a dove, the symbol of the Holy Spirit, at its center is flanked by the tombs of Pope Paul III (left) and Pope Urban VIII (right).

The Dome & Its Decoration

Although completed well after his death in 1564, the basilica's dome is Michelangelo's architectural masterpiece. Warmly illuminated by the light from 16 windows and, in the upper portion, divided into 16 wedges by ribs that run up to the lantern at the top where God the Father is depicted, the dome is supported by four enormous pilasters. Note the mosaic decoration in the four **pendentives**, the triangular spaces where the pilasters reach the dome. Each represents one of the four Evangelists. Note the enormous proportions; St. Mark's pen is more than 49 feet (15 m) long. The Latin **inscription around the base of the dome** comes from the Gospel of St. Matthew (16:18) and affirms the importance of Peter and his successors: "You are Peter and on this rock I will build my church. I will entrust to you the keys to the kingdom of Heaven."

Pope Urban VIII requested that Bernini decorate the dome's four enormous supporting piers with large **aediculae (niches) holding oversize statues,** each more than 16 feet (4.8 m) tall: St. Longinus (created by Bernini), St. Andrew, St. Veronica, and St. Helen. Sometimes precious relics are exhibited on the balconies above the statues: the lance of St. Longinus (the Roman soldier who prodded the crucified Jesus with his spear), portions of the cross brought back from the Holy Land by St. Helen, and St. Veronica's veil, said to bear the image of Jesus' face. Against

EXPERIENCE: Papal Audience

If you have always wanted to receive a papal blessing, you will find it fairly easy to arrange one during your stay in Rome. You won't be alone, of course; thousands turn out week after week. In fact, during much of the year, the Wednesday general audiences are held in the Aula Paolo VI, an audience hall that can hold more than 10,000 people. But never mind. Once seated in the modern auditorium, you will be so caught up in the proceedings that you will feel as if it has all been arranged for your benefit.

People have been visiting Rome for nearly three millennia. After the onset of the Christian era, or rather since Rome became the center of the Christian faith, a huge number of those people have been pilgrims. While legions of ancient pilgrims may feel distant to us, they nevertheless had something in common with today's visitors, whether Roman Catholic or not. They wanted to visit the seat of Christianity and, if possible, see the pope and obtain a papal blessing.

Pope Francis, elected pontiff in March 2013

The Audience

Once you have applied for and received your free tickets (see below), you will file into the spacious Aula Paolo VI, also known as Sala Nervi, and take your seat among laypeople, clerics, and nuns from all over Italy and almost every country in the world. In summer, the general audiences are held in St. Peter's Square.

The ceremony takes place every Wednesday and begins approximately at 10:30 a.m. with the papal address, during which you may hope to hear at least parts in a language you understand. Afterward, representatives of groups from selected countries may be asked to stand and even perform, possibly a song, a little dance, a piece of music, or a reading. The pontiff will then thank them in their own language. And the two-hour meeting—a cross between a revival meeting and a pop concert—will end with a solemn blessing that will likely make you, and everyone else in the room, feel simply splendid.

Practical information

You can order tickets by mail or fax (06 6988 5863); you download the form from www.vatican.va. If you choose to order tickets by mail, the form should be addressed to the *Prefettura della Casa Pontificia, 00120 Città del Vaticano*. The tickets can be collected from the appropriate office in the atrio of Aula Paolo VI, in Piazza del Sant'Uffizio, from 3 to 7 p.m. on the previous day or the same morning as the audience from 7 to 10 a.m. For more information, you can contact the **Prefettura della Casa Pontificia** *(tel 06 6988 3114, Mon.–Fri., 8:30 a.m.–1:30 p.m.).*

Another Option

No tickets are necessary to see the pope, albeit from a great distance, at the Sunday midday Angelus in St. Peter's Square, when he appears in the library window to deliver his weekly homily and blessing.

the Longinus pier stands Arnolfo di Cambio's wonderful bronze **statue of St. Peter.** Once thought to be much older, it dates from the late 1200s.

Tombs & Monuments

At present, 148 popes are buried in St. Peter's. The **tomb of Alexander VII**, a Chigi, is in a corridor off the left transept. Rich in colored marbles and statuary, this magnificent late work (1678) of Bernini's shows the pope kneeling in prayer and surrounded by statues representing the virtues. Look closely and you will notice that from beneath the folds of patterned marble, Winged Death—with hourglass in hand—rears his ugly head.

INSIDER TIP:

The cupola atop St. Peter's basilica affords a wonderful view of the city, not to mention an eerie climb through the inside of the dome.

—RUTH ELLEN GRUBER
National Geographic author

The **tomb of Innocent VIII** stands against a pilaster in the left aisle. It was created by Antonio del Pollaiuolo and is the only papal tomb taken directly from the old St. Peter's, other than those in the Grottoes.

Only three monuments in the church are dedicated to women. Queen Christina of Sweden abdicated her throne in 1654 to convert to Catholicism. Countess Matilda of Tuscany sided with the papacy in the 11th-century conflict with the Holy Roman Emperor. And Maria Clementina Sobieski (1702–1735) was mother to the last two Stuart pretenders to the English throne, Bonnie Prince Charlie and Henry Stuart.

With only two exceptions (the ceiling fresco over the "Pietà" and the Pietro da Cortona oil in the Cappella del Santi Sacramento), all the "paintings" you see here are actual mosaic copies of famous paintings in other churches or in the Vatican Museums.

Other Attractions

Consider spending some time in the **Museo del Tesoro** (located off the left transept; $$), where you can see magnificent church vestments and crucifixes, a Bernini angel, and another Pollaiuolo tomb; and in the **Grottoes,** where many popes are buried—but not John Paul II, his tomb is in the basilica. A visit to the Tesoro museum will also allow you a glimpse of St. Peter's shrine.

Do not miss a visit to the dome's **cupola.** Take the elevator ($$) from the far end of the portico to get to the first level. A short climb from there will get you inside the dome, where you can really appreciate the church's immense proportions. Another narrow, seemingly endless circular staircase will take you to the balcony atop the cupola from which the view is superb. But be sure you're physically fit and not claustrophobic. This closed-in staircase is one-way, so you can't change your mind halfway up. ∎

MUSEI VATICANI

It is hard to think of any greater museums than those of the Vatican. Other galleries may match the broad span and myriad origins of its artifacts, but none also offer works of art that include entire rooms painted by Raphael and the ceiling frescoes of the Capella Sistina, or Sistine Chapel.

Visiting the Museums

The Musei Vaticani (Vatican Museums) are immense, and you cannot see everything in one visit. Select what interests you the most and head straight there; do not try to absorb or read everything along the way. And remember, there is a lot of walking: about 0.3 mile (0.5 km) from the museum entrance to the Sistine Chapel alone! Try scheduling your visit later in the morning, around 11:30, to avoid the long lines that form when the museum opens. Admittance stops at four in the afternoon.

Getting Your Bearings: Once through the spacious entrance on the Viale Vaticano, climb the few steps and take the escalators to the top. The **Pinacoteca** (Painting Gallery; see p. 178) is to the right. Most first-time visitors, however, will want to head straight for the Stanze di Raffaello (Rooms of Raphael) and the Sistine Chapel. To do this, proceed left to the **Atrio dei Quattro Cancelli** (Atrium of the Four Gates). Note the enormous bronze Roman *pigna*, or pinecone, in the courtyard **Cortile della Pigna,** through the door facing the other side of the *atrio*. Now turn left and walk up the stairs to the first landing and the **Sala a Croce Greca** (Greek Cross Room), part of the Museo Pio-Clementino (see pp. 177–178).

Galleria delle Carte Geografiche, the Gallery of Maps

Musei Vaticani

- Map p. 162
- Viale Vaticano
- 06 6988 4676 or 06 6988 3145 (guided tours)
- Open Mon.– Sat.: last entrance at 4 p.m. Last Sun. of month: last entrance at 12:30 p.m.
- $$. Free last Sun. of month. Audio guide: $. Guided tours with online booking ($$$) every day except Sun.
- Bus: 81, 98, 492, 990. Metro: Linea A (Ottaviano– Musei Vaticani)

www.museivaticani .va

Don't miss the stupendous fourth-century porphyry sarcophagi; St. Helena, Constantine's mother, was buried in the one on the right, decorated with battle scenes.

Take the stairs to the second floor and walk down a long corridor divided into three sections: the **Galleria dei Candelabri** (candelabras); the **Galleria degli Arazzi** (tapestries); and the **Galleria delle Carte Geografiche,** which features interesting map frescoes depicting Italy's and the church's possessions in the 1580s. The windows on the right look out on the **Casina di Pio IV** (a Renaissance villa) and the **Giardini Vaticani** (see p. 178). The Sala dell'Immacolata, at the end of the corridor, leads to the Stanze di Rafaello.

Stanze di Raffaello

The Stanze di Raffaello (Rooms of Raphael), of which there are four, were commissioned by Julius II in 1508, supposedly because the existing papal apartment reminded him too much of his hated predecessor, Alexander VI. The order of the visit described here is subject to change.

Used by Julius as a library, the **Stanza della Segnatura** (Signatura) is considered one of Raphael's greatest works. It contains two of his best known works, painted between 1508 and 1511. In the "Disputation of the Sacrament"—meant to glorify faith—Jesus, the Virgin, and St. John the Baptist are flanked by figures from the Old and New Testaments; those from the New Testament have halos. Below is an altar with the Host and, farther down, Doctors of

the Church, saints, and scholars. Dante appears on the right in the lower section.

A tribute to philosophy, the "School of Athens" depicts Plato and Aristotle in animated conversation inside a large classical building. Raphael, who clearly enjoyed painting his contemporaries into historical tableaus, painted himself second to last in the group of hatted gentle-

---

INSIDER TIP:

Bring a small pair of binoculars to Rome— not for birding, but for the close-up details of the ceiling paintings and mosaics in the vast churches and basilicas as well as the Cappella Sistina.

—TIM JEPSON
National Geographic author

---

men on the right. Just in front is Bramante, in the guise of Euclid, who is bending over, compass in hand, to explain a problem to his students. The pensive figure seated in the forefront, his head leaning on his left hand, is Michelangelo as Heraclitus, the pessimist.

Originally a bedroom, the **Stanza di Eliodoro** (Heliodorus), which was decorated between 1512 and 1514, is noted for its stunning use of color and the dramatic lighting in the "Liberation of St. Peter." The room also contains the "Expulsion of

Heliodorus" (from the temple in Jerusalem), and "Pope Leo Meets Attila the Hun," recounting how St. Leo the Great (Pope Leo I, 440–461) turned Attila and his Huns away during a fifth-century attack on Rome. After Julius II died, Raphael repainted the face of St. Leo with the features of the new pope, Leo X (1513–1521). However, Leo X already appeared in the painting as a cardinal, so now he appears twice.

Raphael's students painted the **Stanza dell'Incendio** (fire), formerly a dining room, between 1514 and 1517. Based on Raphael's designs, it depicts events from the lives of Leo III and Leo IV, the pope who built the Vatican walls in the ninth century. The most famous painting shows how, in 847, Leo IV quenched a fire in the surrounding Borgo neighborhood by making the sign of the cross. Nearby is the small **Cappella di Niccolo V** (Chapel of Pope Nicholas V), frescoed by the Florentine artist Fra Angelico.

The **Sala di Costantino** was finished in 1524, after Raphael's death, and he probably only did some preliminary sketches. The underlying theme of this room, attributed largely to Giulio Romano, Francesco Penni, and Raffaellino del Colle, and told through scenes from the life of Constantine, is the triumph of Christianity over paganism.

After the Rooms of Raphael, and before the Sistine Chapel, consider visiting the **Appartamento Borgia,** the rooms of the Borgia pope Alexander VI, decorated with lovely frescoes by Pinturicchio and his disciples.

■ **The Vatican Museums' immense spiral staircase, designed by Giuseppe Momo in 1932**

Cappella Sistina

Built by Giovanni de' Dolce during the reign of Sixtus IV (1471–1484), the Cappella Sistina—Sistine Chapel—has seen a lot of history. This rectangular hall was the private chapel of the pontiffs, and for centuries it has been the room where the conclaves, or papal elections, are held.

The floor is decorated in an exquisite *opus alexandrinum* pattern reminiscent of the cosmatesque pavements (see sidebar p. 208) from the 13th and 14th centuries. An elegant sculpted screen—by Mino da Fiesole, Andrea Bregno, and Giovanni Dalmata—divides the chapel into two sections. But the room is best known for the recently restored wall and ceiling frescoes, considered by many to be the supreme example of Renaissance, if not universal, art.

The decoration of the Sistine Chapel can be divided into three periods, each coinciding with an

Musei Vaticani

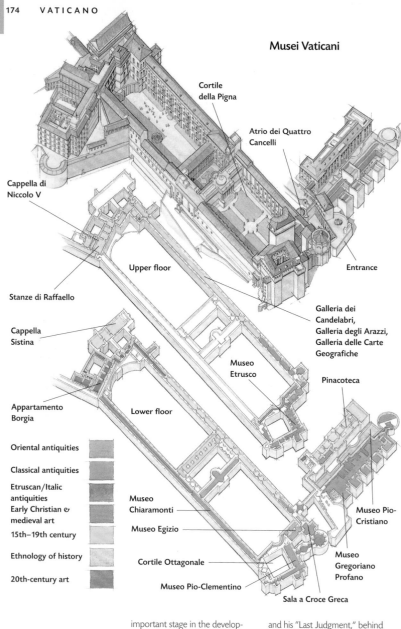

Cortile della Pigna

Atrio dei Quattro Cancelli

Cappella di Niccolo V

Upper floor

Entrance

Stanze di Raffaello

Galleria dei Candelabri, Galleria degli Arazzi, Galleria delle Carte Geografiche

Cappella Sistina

Museo Etrusco

Pinacoteca

Appartamento Borgia

Lower floor

Oriental antiquities

Classical antiquities

Etruscan/Italic antiquities

Early Christian & medieval art

15th–19th century

Ethnology of history

20th-century art

Museo Chiaramonti

Museo Egizio

Cortile Ottagonale

Museo Pio-Clementino

Museo Pio-Cristiano

Museo Gregoriano Profano

Sala a Croce Greca

important stage in the development of Renaissance art. The frescoes on the long walls were painted between 1481 and 1483; the ceiling was painted by Michelangelo between 1508 and 1512;

and his "Last Judgment," behind the altar, was executed between 1534 and 1541.

Long Walls: The long walls of the chapel were decorated

by some of the most important 15th-century Renaissance
painters (Pinturicchio, Botticelli,
Perugino, Ghirlandaio, Rosselli,
Signorelli), all of Tuscan or
Umbrian origin. During this
period, under the impetus of
a reinvigorated and dynamic
papacy, the cultural epicenter

"Calling of Peter and Andrew"
(Domenico Ghirlandaio),
and "Jesus Giving the Keys to
Peter" (Perugino).

On the end wall, opposite
the "Last Judgment," are the
"Resurrection" by Ghirlandaio
and Salviati's "St. Michael," both
later repainted.

■ **Many important religious ceremonies are still held in the Sistine Chapel.**

of the Renaissance was shifting
from Florence and its environs
to Rome.

On the left, starting from
the "Last Judgment," are **scenes
from the Old Testament**
including the "Burning Bush"
and "Moses Slaying Egyptians"
(Botticelli), the "Punishment
of Korah, Dathan, and Abiram"
(Botticelli), and the "Last Days
of Moses" by Signorelli.

On the right, **scenes from
the New Testament** include
the "Baptism of Jesus" (Pinturicchio or Perugino), the "Temptation of Christ" (Botticelli), the

Ceiling: Michelangelo's decoration of the ceiling (originally blue
with stars) coincided with the
mood of cultural and political
self-confidence that characterized the early Renaissance. Not
particularly keen on accepting
this commission, Michelangelo,
who considered himself a sculptor, not a painter, wanted to
keep working on the marble
tomb of Julius II. When he did
accept (possibly to foil his impla-
cable rival, Bramante), he turned
a simpler project (the "Twelve
Apostles") into the more ambitious "Creation."

to view the ceiling comfortably.
Remember, start your gazing from
the altar end of the room.

There are nine central scenes
on the ceiling. Alternating in
larger and smaller rectangles are
"Separation of Light and Dark-
ness"; "Creation of the Sun, the
Moon, and Planets"; "Separa-
tion of Land From the Sea" and
"Creation of Plants and Animals";
"Creation of Adam"; "Creation of
Eve From Adam's Rib"; "Expulsion
From the Garden of Paradise";
"Sacrifice of Noah"; "The Flood";
and "Noah Drunk."

Portraits of prophets form
a border around them (going
clockwise Jonah, Jeremiah, Ezekiel,
Joel, Zechariah, Isaiah, Daniel).
Alternating with these are sibyls,
the oracles of the ancient world
(clockwise the Persian, Erythraean,
Delphic, Cumaean, and Libyan
sibyls). The triangular lunettes
between the sibyls and prophets
contain images of the forerunners
and ancestors of Jesus Christ,
while the four larger corner
lunettes represent Old Testament
scenes. Between the prophets and
sibyls and above the triangular
lunettes are figures known as the
"Ignudi," athletic male nudes,
painted in various poses between
low, trompe l'oeil pedestals.

Statue of Venus Felix, ca A.D. 170, Museo Pio-Clementino

He spent four years "in the
utmost discomfort," as he
described it, to complete the
commission.

Michelangelo's choice of
subject matter was not acciden-
tal. The cosmology of the time
divided world history into various
epochs: the period before the
Law, the period of Law as given to
Moses, and finally the period of
Grace, which began with the coming of Jesus. The older decoration
on the side walls corresponded
to the eras of Law and Grace, so
Michelangelo decided to dedicate
the ceiling to the pre-Law era, that
is, to the Creation, the Garden
of Eden, and original sin. The
decoration is sublime. Ideally, you
will have brought your binoculars
or at least a decent-size mirror

"Last Judgment": By the
time Michelangelo got around
to painting the "Last Judgment,"
commissioned by Pope Paul III
(1534–1549), the mood in Rome
had changed drastically to one
of pessimism. The 1527 Sack of
Rome had created insecurity, and
the burgeoning Protestant movement was stimulating renewed

religious uncertainty and fervor. In the "Last Judgment" (which received far less favorable reviews than the "Creation," with many critics crying obscenity), you can read the drama, terror, and pathos of the era.

In the center of the composition is an athletic, beardless, and severe Christ in Judgment, flanked by Mary and a collection of saints. Below, on the left, are the blessed on their way to heaven; note the two figures suspended by a rosary, a clear anti-Lutheran statement.

In contrast, on the right the damned are being pushed down to hell while Charon, in his boat, watches. Michelangelo gave Minos, the judge of the damned, the face of one of his sharpest critics, Biagio da Cesena, a member of the papal court. He is the figure in the lower right-hand corner with the donkey's ears entwined in a serpent's coils. Below and right of the Redeemer, St. Bartholomew

holds his flayed skin, recalling the method of his martyrdom, but he has no beard. Why? Because his is the face of the beardless Michelangelo.

Museo Pio-Clementino

Access to the Pio-Clementine Museum is through the ground-floor Cortile della Pigna and up the stairs to the Palazzo del Belvedere, built during the reign of Innocent VIII. This museum's most impressive section may well be its vast display of classical statuary in the Cortile Ottagonale (Octagonal Court). You could say that the foundations of the entire Vatican museum complex were laid right here when, in 1503, Pope Julius II placed a statue of Apollo, ever since called the "**Belvedere Apollo,**" in the Belvedere's courtyard. Clement XIV significantly enlarged the collection in 1770, and the museum was opened shortly thereafter.

The list of sculptures is endless,

Skip the Lines

One way to skip waiting in line at the Vatican is to buy your tickets ahead of time online at *www.museivaticani.va* or sign up for a tour. Another is to buy tickets from an online agency that organizes a tour—though, once inside, some then leave you to visit the museums on your own (sometimes with an audio guide).

Naturally, agency services cost more than the Vatican's normal entrance fee, but you may well decide it is worth it. (If not, try going to the Vatican just after lunch, when the regular line is likely to be much shorter.)

You can also avoid the line at the Colosseum by signing up for a guided tour. You can book tickets to many Rome museums at *www.coopculture.it,* or by telephone at 06 3996 7700. You get immediate access with the Roma Pass (see sidebar p. 11) or by simply going first to the Palatine Hill or the Roman Forum, where the ticket you buy also is good for the Colosseum.

Online sites which offer skip-the-line tickets for the Vatican and/or the Colosseum include *www.rome-museum.com, www.viator.com, www.traveltoe.com,* and *www.prestotours.com*

but there are several pieces that are not to be missed, especially the **"Laocoön"** (see sidebar below). The Cabinet of Apoxyomenos, just beyond the round vestibule, houses a statue known as the **"Apoxyomenos Athlete,"** a first-century Roman marble copy of a bronze statue by Lysippus from about 320 B.C. Found in Trastevere in 1849, it shows an athlete in the process of scraping oil from his body. The street where it was found is now called the Vicolo dell'Atleta. The remaining rooms include the Animal Room, the Gallery of Statues, the Gallery of Busts, the Mask Room, and the Hall of the Muses. Near the exit is a domed room with a reconstructed *biga*, or two-horse chariot.

Pinacoteca & More

As you can imagine, over the centuries the popes have also built quite a collection of paintings. You can see them in the **Pinacoteca.** (Turn right at the top of the escalator on entering the museum complex instead of left.) Although not enormous, the collection is impressive and includes Raphael's "Transfiguration," his "Madonna di Foligno," and his "Coronation of the Virgin," all in the same room. There are also paintings by Giotto, Fra Angelico, Simone Martini, Perugino, Bellini, and Titian, to name only a few.

For more specialized interests, there are the **Museo Egizio** (Egyptian Museum), the **Museo Etrusco** (Etruscan Museum), and the **Museo Gregoriano Profano** (Gregorian Profane Museum), which displays several Greek and Roman collections, arranged either by era or thematically. It is in this museum that you can see the famous mosaics of athletes found in the Baths of Caracalla (see pp. 212–213).

The **Braccio Nuovo** of the **Museo Chiaramonti,** a smaller adjunct to the Pio-Clementino that was organized by the sculptor Canova in the early 19th century, also displays Roman floor mosaics. There you will also find the famous statue of Augustus from the villa of his wife, Livia, at Prima Porta. The **Museo Pio-Cristiano** (Pio-Christian Museum) displays early Christian antiquities.

It is also possible to visit the 16th-century **Giardini Vaticani** (Vatican Gardens). On guided tours that last about two hours, you get to see the medieval German cemetery attached to the Teutonic College, several major fountains, and the main buildings (mostly from outside) including the new (1971) Aula Paolo VI (Paul VI Audience Hall), the Governatorato (Governor's Palace), and the Casina di Pio IV, today seat of the Pontifical Science Academy. ∎

"Laocoön"

In the Cortile Ottagonale (Octagonal Court) you'll find the "Laocoön," possibly the most sublime classical marble group to have survived. Excavated in 1506 on the Esquiline Hill and possibly from the Domus Aurea, it is attributed to three first-century sculptors from Rhodes working from an older bronze original. It tells the story (related by Virgil in the *Aeneid*) of the Trojan priest, Laocoön, and his two sons whose warnings about the wooden horse angered Athena, who sent two huge serpents to kill them. Their facial expressions convey human suffering in an unparalleled fashion.

CASTEL SANT'ANGELO

Built as a mausoleum by Emperor Hadrian (but completed after his death), Castel Sant'Angelo has also been a fortress, a prison, a papal refuge, a barracks, and a pleasure palace. This circular structure was once topped with trees and, possibly, a large statue of the emperor.

■ Romans play in the shadow of the second-century Castel Sant'Angelo, initially built as a mausoleum.

At the end of the sixth century, with Rome decimated by plague, Pope Gregory the Great led a massive procession to St. Peter's to ask for divine intercession. Along the way, he saw the archangel Michael standing above the mausoleum and sheathing his sword as if to mark the end of the scourge. Subsequently, a statue of the archangel was placed atop the tomb, which was renamed Castel Sant'Angelo. Erected in 1753, the bronze statue you see today replaced an earlier stone one created by Raffaele da Montelupo.

Throughout the Middle Ages, the papacy and Rome's noble families frequently vied for

control of the castle, and thus the city itself. During the Sack of Rome in 1527, Clement VII took refuge here, probably using the secret corridor (passetto) that was built into the Leonine Wall in 1277; you can see it on a guided tour of the castle.

Because bits and pieces have been added on over the centuries, you'll need imagination and a discerning eye to separate the original Roman portions from the additions of later eras. The vestibule downstairs was the original entrance. A statue of Hadrian probably stood in the niche at the far end. Like the rooms directly above it, the vestibule is in the central Roman

Castel Sant'Angelo

Map p. 163

Lungotevere Castello 50

06 681 9111 or 06 32810. Online tickets: www.ticketone.it

$$. Audio guide: $. Guided tours in English on request: $$$

Bus: 30, 34, 40, 49, 62, 130, 280, 990

www.castelsantangelo.beniculturali.it

core of the building. Walk up the long ramp, which still has portions of the original mosaic floor. Go left and continue until you reach the **Cordonata di Alexander VI,** a shallow staircase that cuts diagonally across the structure and eventually ends at the **Cortile dell'Angelo.**

The Prison

For centuries parts of Castel Sant'Angelo were used as a prison. Benvenuto Cellini, a 16th-century Florentine goldsmith, tells in his autobiography of being imprisoned there, and Puccini made it the scene for Tosca's suicide. In the 1930s, it was restored and turned into a museum.

Along the way you will walk over a drawbridge, which, until 1822, could be pulled up to protect the upper stories of the castle from intruders. The bridge spans the funeral chamber, where Hadrian's remains were originally kept. Named after the cannonballs stored there, the Cortile delle Palle is also known as the Cortile dell'Angelo because it has housed da Montelupo's gigantic angel statue after its replacement.

The rooms on the left are named for the various popes who inhabited them or for the subject matter of their decoration. The **Sala di Apollo** has lovely "grotesque" decorations on the walls. When you come to the **Sala di Giustizia,** once a courtroom, you will be back in the Roman part

of the structure. Be sure to note the fresco of the Angel of Justice, over one of the doors, by Perin del Vaga.

A corridor from the Apollo Room leads to a courtyard, called either the **Cortile del Teatro,** because theatrical performances were given there during the Renaissance, or the Cortile del Pozzo dell'Olio, because of the wellhead. Just past the entrance, a short flight of stairs through the door on the right takes you to **Pope Clement VII's bathroom,** with frescoes by Giulio Romano. The courtyard's other rooms were used as **prison cells;** the ones on this floor were for VIPs; the ones downstairs, for ordinary prisoners.

Farther upstairs, the **Loggia of Julius II** overlooks the Ponte Sant'Angelo. Its walls were lengthened in the 19th century when the walls along the Tiber were built.

Up a short flight of stairs from the loggia are the **Papal Apartments** frescoed by Perin del Vaga for Paul III (1534–1549). Note another angel frescoed on the far wall and the amusing portrait of a gentleman peering out of a trompe l'oeil door. A curving corridor, decorated with more grotesques, leads to what was once the library; only the upper portion of the walls was frescoed because bookcases covered the lower part.

Through a door in the center of the wall is the **Camera del Tesoro** or dell'Archivio Segreto. Until 1870 the Vatican kept its secret archives here. A narrow winding staircase carved into the thick walls leads up to the terrace, where you will find a spectacular view of St. Peter's and the city. ■

In ancient times, it was inhabited by foreigners from the East. This fascinating tangle of alleys and little squares is today the right place to immerse yourself in the real Roman traditions.

TRASTEVERE TO GIANICOLO

A bust of Angelo Tittoni, one of many statues lining the Passeggiata del Gianicolo on the Janiculum Hill

TRASTEVERE TO GIANICOLO

To the Italians, Trastevere is a *popolare* neighborhood, one of the few still inhabited by "real" Romans. Until recently it was a working-class area, where typical Trasteverini were lower-income, extroverted, sharp-tongued—and possibly a bit arrogant, since they consider themselves to be the true descendants of the ancient Romans.

No one really knows why, but the Trasteverini tend to have loud, rather hoarse voices and to speak with a very heavy Roman accent. They drink lots of coffee, breakfast on *maritozzi* (a plain, sweet roll filled with fresh whipped cream), and favor heavy dinner dishes such as *spaghetti cacio e pepe* (spaghetti with grated cheese and pepper) and *coda alla vaccinara* (oxtail in tomato sauce). Over the past several decades their numbers have dwindled. Some have left the area by choice, others have been forced out by gentrification and spiraling rents. But enough Trasteverini remain to allow the neighborhood to keep much of its traditional color and character.

At the same time, Trastevere—which means trans-Tiberim (across the Tiber River)—also has a long history as a favorite residential area for foreigners and nonconformists. This was true even in ancient Roman times, when many outsiders settled here, including tens of thousands of Jews. According to local parish officials, there may once have been as many as ten synagogues in the neighborhood. The first Christians, for the most part converted Jews, settled here as well. And the area's international flavor was certainly heightened following World War II, when many foreigners settled here because of its traditions and because it was considerably cheaper than other central neighborhoods.

The Lay of the Land

Artisans abound, as do small shops, bars, and eateries. In fact, the trattorias of Trastevere have always drawn outsiders, especially on weekends and during July's Festa de' Noantri (Our Own Festival). These days, in the evenings the restaurants have been supplemented by scores of small *locali* (clubs), sometimes only a few tables or a bar counter, which appeal to young people. Many intellectuals—filmmakers, artists, and students—also live here. This, along with an abundance of street peddlers, art galleries, and boutiques, explains why Trastevere is often compared to Soho in London or New York's SoHo or Greenwich Village.

Trastevere stretches upriver from Viale di Trastevere almost to the Vatican and nestles on

GALLERIA PRINCIPE
AMEDEO SAVOIA AOSTA

PONTE
PR. AMEDEO
SAVOIA
AOSTA

VIA
LUNGOTEVERE DELLA

VIALE

Sant'
Onofrio

VIA DELLE

Passeggiata

Tasso's
Oak

Faro

Monumento ad
Anita Garibaldi

MONTE

MURA DEL

Villa
Lante

Monumento
a Giuseppe
Garibaldi

PIAZZALE
G. GARIBALDI

AURELIE

Porta San
Pancrazio

the lower slopes of Monte Gianicolo (Janiculum Hill). It also extends downriver beyond the Viale, running by Tiber Island and including lovely Piazza in Piscinula, the church of Santa Cecilia, and, at its outer limit, Porta Portese with its Sunday flea market. The heart of the neighborhood, however, is Piazza di Santa Maria in Trastevere, with the magnificent basilica of the same name and which, with its cafés and restaurants, newsstand, and pharmacy, is akin to a village square for the area's residents.

Many people still shop in the outdoor market at nearby Piazza di San Cosimato (weekday mornings) or buy bread on Sunday mornings at the *forno* in Via del Moro. Pass through the ancient Porta Settimiana on Via della Lungara, once the only road linking Trastevere to the Vatican, and you will find the Botanical Gardens, once part of the post-baroque Palazzo Corsini, and the Villa Farnesina, where archaeologists found the ruins of a splendid Roman villa. Above looms the Janiculum Hill, where San Pietro in Montorio and Sant'Onofrio compete for attention with the breathtaking Roman panorama. ■

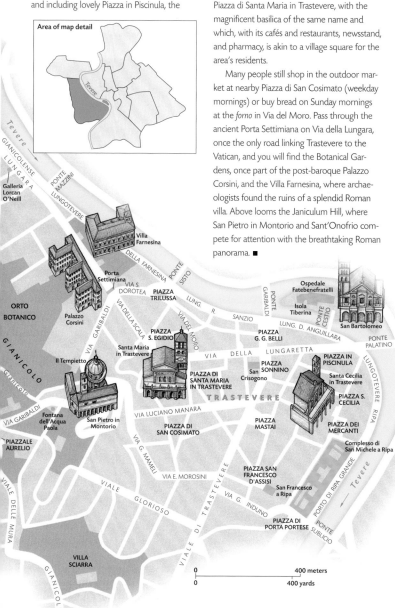

SANTA MARIA IN TRASTEVERE

According to St. Jerome, oil gushed from the ground in a veterans' hospital in Trastevere at the time of Jesus' birth, a clear sign of "the grace of Christ that would come to humanity." In the third century, a church was founded (probably by St. Calixtus) where the miracle supposedly took place. An inscription on the church floor, to the right of the altar, marks the spot.

■ Four columns made out of porphyry support Santa Maria in Trastevere's altar canopy.

Santa Maria in Trastevere

⬛ Map p. 183

✉ Piazza di Santa Maria in Trastevere

☎ 06 5814 802

🚌 Bus: 44, 115, 125, 780. Tram: 3, 8

Widely believed to be one of the first churches in Rome, Santa Maria in Trastevere was certainly the first to be dedicated to Mary. As we see it today, with its charming campanile (bell tower), the basilica—completed in the 1140s—is primarily medieval in style. Somehow the 12th-century aura has lingered, despite later additions such as Domenichino's gilded, coffered ceiling (1617) and Carlo Fontana's portico (1702) with its statues of four saints, including St. Calixtus.

The church is notable for its use of classical Roman architectural forms. The 22 columns in the nave, of various dimensions, types

of stone, textures, and colors, were looted from ancient ruins. The straight trabeation (or architrave) over the columns evokes classical Roman construction, a temporary rejection of the arches preferred by earlier and later architects.

Mosaics & More

What truly sets Santa Maria apart are its glowingly beautiful mosaics, which mark a return to a tradition that had been largely discontinued. For this we can probably thank Abbot Desiderius of Monte Cassino, who, toward the end of the 11th century, brought mosaic workers from Constantinople and used them to train local artisans. In this regard, note the cosmatesque pavement (see sidebar p. 208) that, though restored in the 19th century, dates to the 1100s.

The mosaics on the facade date from the 12th or 13th century and show a Madonna enthroned, flanked on either side by five women. They probably represent the Wise and Foolish Virgins from the Gospel, although some historians believe that the scene depicts a procession of eight virgins and two widows. The widows, they insist, are the women whose lamps have gone out. The two tiny figures at the Madonna's feet represent the donors who financed the piece.

The mosaics inside the church are even more exceptional. Those in the half-dome of the apse date from the 12th century and show Mary, enthroned, next to Jesus, who has his arm around his mother's shoulder. They are flanked by a collection of saints including, on the left and holding a model of the church, Pope Innocent II, the donor. The prophets Isaiah and Jeremiah are on the two sides of the apse. On the next row down is Pietro Cavallini's 13th-century mosaic of the "Life of the Virgin Mary" in six masterful scenes. Cavallini also created the mosaic showing the "Madonna and Child between St. Peter and St. Paul" on the apse's central lower segment.

The sumptuous **Altemps Chapel** on the church's left side (designed by Martino Longhi the Elder in the 1580s) has an ornate ceiling and numerous frescoes, including one that depicts the Council of Trent (1545–1563; see sidebar p. 23), a major event in Roman Catholicism's response to the Protestant challenge. Also interesting are the marble fragments embedded in the walls of the facade, bearing catacomb inscriptions from the third and fourth centuries. Between the gate and the facade are four magnificent medieval floor tombs. ■

EXPERIENCE: Cooking Classes

You know you are in love with Roman food when your mouth waters every time you think of those artichokes—*alla romana* or *alla giudia* (Jewish style)—the fried zucchini flowers, that luscious *saltimbocca*, the scrumptious *pollo con peperoni*, the tripe or oxtail in tomato sauce, the sauteed chicory, the fried mozzarella, and all those wonderful pasta dishes.

Sure, you can eat all these dishes, and scores more, in most Roman restaurants, but why not learn to cook them for yourself? If you do, you'll have more than just some photos and a few souvenirs to show your friends when you get home. This is

something you can do fairly easily, as long as you are willing to make arrangements in advance. Here are some suggested companies that offer cooking classes in Rome to make your search easier:

Daniela del Balzo (www.danielascooking school.com): Perfect to explore Rome's markets and learn how to cook traditional Italian dishes.

Rome Pizza and Pasta School (www.romepizzaschool.com): Cooking lessons starting from scratch.

InRome Cooking (www.inromecooking.com) Roman-style, Italian cooking classes, complete with market shopping.

A TASTE OF TRASTEVERE WALK

This two-part walk around Trastevere will give you a feeling for a neighborhood that boasts a vast spectrum of sights and sounds. Local artisans, young professionals, American college students, and transplanted foreigners congregate here to enjoy what many people say is one of the last remaining enclaves of the "real Rome."

Start at Piazza di Santa Maria in Trastevere, where you can enjoy a coffee at the Café de Marzio, in front of the glorious basilica, or at the more popular Bar San Callisto, in the square adjacent. Wear your bags or cameras across your chest. Or, better yet, don't carry a bag at all; a Roman purse-snatcher can spot a tourist a mile off. Exit the piazza by the newsstand and take Via della Lungaretta to Viale di Trastevere. On your right, the church of **San Crisogono ❶** (see p. 198) has an exceptional cosmatesque pavement (see sidebar p. 208).

INSIDER TIP:

Romans are fond of strolling through the Orto Botanico, a refreshing sanctuary boasting a variety of cacti and flora . . . as well as several inviting patches of grass, perfect for napping.

—NATASHA SCRIPTURE
National Geographic contributor

Cross the busy avenue, and continue along Via della Lungaretta, which takes you through a deliciously old neighborhood, to charming Piazza in Piscinula, where the Mattei family once had a palace. Before entering the piazza, turn right up the ramp Arco dei Tolomei, which brings you under a fascinating medieval archway. Turn left at Via dei Salumi and then right on Via dei Vascellari, which soon becomes Via di Santa Cecilia and takes you to the piazza and church of **Santa Cecilia in Trastevere ❷** (see pp. 194–195).

After visiting the church, check out lovely **Piazza dei Mercanti,** which is located between

> ### NOT TO BE MISSED:
>
> **San Crisogono • Santa Cecilia in Trastevere • San Francesco a Ripa • Villa Farnesina**

Piazza Santa Cecilia and the river, but avoid the restaurants; they are way too touristy. Continue along Via di Santa Cecilia toward Via Madonna dell'Orto. Note the long **Complesso di San Michele a Ripa** building on your left. A poorhouse in the 17th century, today it is used for governmental offices (see p. 198). **Santa Maria dell'Orto ❸,** the facade at the end of Via Madonna dell'Orto curiously decorated with obelisks, was once the headquarters for many guilds of the more humble occupations, such as fruit vendors and chicken keepers. If it's between 2 and 4 p.m. on a Tuesday or Thursday afternoon, make a brief detour right on Via Anicia and ring the bell at No. 12. The custodian will let you into the magnificent, hidden 15th-century cloister of **San Giovanni dei Genovesi ❹.**

After leaving the cloister, retrace your steps and continue along Via Anicia until you come to Piazza San Francesco d'Assisi and the church of **San Francesco a Ripa ❺** (see p. 198), where one of Bernini's "Ecstasies" is displayed. Via San Francesco a Ripa, which faces the church, will take you back to Viale di Trastevere. Cross over and, at the intersection with Via Luciano Manara, look left up the street at the lovely, moss-covered fountain set against the lower slope of the Janiculum Hill. Continuing along Via San Francesco a Ripa will bring you to Piazza di San Callisto and then to **Santa Maria in Trastevere,** where you began.

North of Piazza Sant'Egidio

The second part of this walk starts on Via della Paglia (the street flanking the basilica) and takes you to **Piazza Sant'Egidio** ❻ on the right, where there is a folk art museum (Museo di Roma in Trastevere). Here you have a choice. If you leave the piazza by Via della Scala (the street on the left) you will come to Piazza della Scala, where the Carmelite church of **Santa Maria della Scala** contains paintings by some of Caravaggio's pupils. The pharmacy outside is also very old. At the end of Via della Scala is the old stone **Porta Settimiana** gateway and Via della Lungara, which takes you to the **Orto Botanico** (Botanical Garden), **Palazzo Corsini**, and **Villa Farnesina** ❼ (see pp. 188–189).

If you take Vicolo del Cinque, the right-hand exit out of Piazza Sant'Egidio, you'll reach **Piazza Trilussa** and the wonderful fountain facing the Ponte Sisto pedestrian bridge spanning the Tevere, the Tiber River. Follow Via Santa Dorotea, on the other side of the fountain, to Porta Settimiana. The house to the right of the arch, **Casa della Fornarina** (today a restaurant), is said to have been the home of La Fornarina, Raphael's mistress.

- 🅰 See also area map pp. 182–183
- ▶ Santa Maria in Trastevere
- 🔁 1.5 miles (2.5 km)
- 🕑 2 hours
- ▶ Villa Farnesina

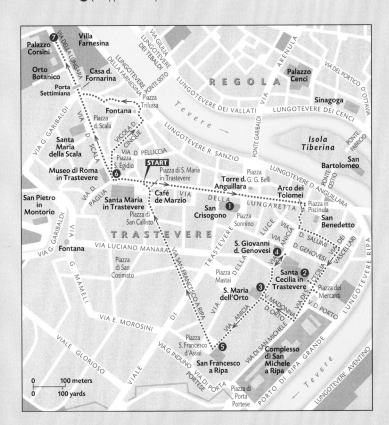

VILLA FARNESINA

Considered a gem of Renaissance architecture, Villa Farnesina—about a block from Porta Settimiana—was built in the early 1500s as a country villa for Sienese banker and businessman Agostino Chigi and later sold to the Farnese family. Chigi spared no expense in furnishing his new residence, decorating it with scenes from Greek and Roman mythology.

Raphael's frescoes in the Loggia of Cupid and Psyche depict incidents in the myth of these two lovers.

Ground Floor Magnificence

The first room on the ground floor is the **Galatea Room,** contiguous with the *loggia,* whose arches once opened onto the garden. Today it is known primarily for Raphael's **"Triumph of Galatea."** This wonderful fresco, dated around 1513, shows the sea nymph, wearing a red cloak, riding the ocean waves. Two straining dolphins, one of which is breakfasting on a small squid, pull her seashell carriage, which is surrounded by cupids. A triton appears to be molesting Galatea's handmaiden.

Created by Peruzzi, the sumptuous **ceiling** depicts the planets and constellations at the time of Chigi's birth. Some of the lunettes (by Sebastiano del Piombo) contain scenes from Ovid's *Metamorphoses.*

Next is the stunning **Loggia of Cupid and Psyche,** which Raphael designed to look like a summertime pergola with fruit and flowers, although most of the artwork was done by his pupils. Craning at the ceiling may give you a stiff neck, but the two large **ceiling frescoes**—the "Wedding of Cupid and Psyche" and the "Council of the Gods"—are breathtaking. Of the "Three Graces" in the fresco in the corner right of the door, the one with her back to you was probably Chigi's mistress and may have been painted by Raphael himself. The lunettes recount the various stages of Psyche's troubled relationship with the jealous Venus.

Upstairs

The upper floor is equally exciting. In the **Sala delle Prospettive,** the living room, Peruzzi repeated his indoor-outdoor theme, relying heavily on trompe l'oeil landscapes and urban scenes with real landmarks such as Porta Settimiana, an aqueduct, and the campanile of Santa Maria in Trastevere. Note the unfortunate graffiti, left by marauding soldiers during the Sack of Rome in 1527.

Next door you will find the villa's rather small **master bedroom.** Despite its size, however, the room is a magnificent riot of color, painted mostly by Giovan Antonio Bazzi, generally referred to as Il Sodoma (the Sodomite) because of his homosexuality. The central wall, the "Wedding of Roxanne and Alexander" (the Great), is considered Bazzi's masterpiece. The right-hand wall, "Alexander's Meeting With the Family of Darius of Persia," is less accomplished; the artist reportedly felt he was being underpaid. Whereas the central portion of the left-hand wall, the "Taming of Bucephalus" (Alexander's horse), was clearly painted by someone else. When Chigi's enormous gem-encrusted bed

was moved out of the house after his death, it left an empty space that had to be filled.

Chigi's Theatrics

Chigi was a very wealthy bon vivant with a keen sense of one-upmanship. A lavish reception organized in 1518

INSIDER TIP:

To complement Rome's rich artistic legacy and to get a feel for how Romans kick off the evening, check out exhibition openings at contemporary galleries.

—FILIPPO COSMELLI
National Geographic contributor & founder and director of IF Lifestyle Management

---

in honor of Pope Leo X was staged in the stables, which were appropriately decorated for the occasion. The idea was to embarrass the Riario family across the street by demonstrating that the Chigi stables were as elegant as the Riario's dining rooms. Later the same year another reception was held at a loggia on the riverbank. Guests were surely impressed (or perhaps horrified?) when, at the end of each course, the servants tossed the silver dishes into the Tiber. But not to worry—Chigi had strung nets below to retrieve them. ∎

Villa Farnesina

🗺 Map p. 183

✉ Via della Lungara 230

☎ 06 6802 7268 or farnesina@lincei .it for guided tours

🕐 Open 9 a.m.– 2 p.m. Mon.–Sat. & 9 a.m.–5 p.m. 2nd Sun. of month

💲 $

🚌 Bus: 23, 125, 280

www.villafarnesina.it

Galleria Lorcan O'Neill

🗺 Map p. 183

✉ Vicolo de' Catinari, 3

☎ 06 6889 2980

🕐 Closed Sun.

www.lorcan oneill.com

PALAZZO CORSINI

Across the street from Villa Farnesina is the Palazzo Corsini, an 18th-century reconstruction and amplification of the Renaissance palace owned by the Riario family in the 15th century. In the 17th century it became the home of Queen Christina of Sweden, a convert to Catholicism who had abdicated and moved to Rome in 1655. The Corsini, who were Florentines, moved to Rome after Lorenzo Corsini was elected to the papacy as Clement XII in 1736.

Palazzo Corsini

- 🅐 Map p. 183
- ✉️ Via della Lungara 10
- ☎️ 06 6880 2323
- 🕐 Closed Tues.
- 💲 $$
- 🚌 Bus: 23, 125, 280

www.barberini corsini.org

The 18th-century architect Ferdinando Fuga directed the restructuring, creating a new light-filled central body with an impressive and stately ceremonial double staircase leading up to the gallery and a monumental three-arched entryway. He also added another wing that was used to house the priceless Corsini library.

In 1883 the building and its art collection were bought by the Italian government, and today the building also houses the Accademia dei Lincei (1603), an academy of scholars founded to promote learning and said to be the oldest of its kind.

The **Galleria Corsini,** a suite of eight rooms that give off the atrium (one floor up), contains part of the collection of the Galleria Nazionale d'Arte Antica (see pp. 102–103). The paintings, from the 14th to the 18th century,

are somewhat haphazardly displayed but include one Caravaggio ("San Giovannino, the Young John the Baptist"), a "Trittico del Giudizio Universale" by Beato Angelico, and a bust of Pope Alexander VII, a Chigi, by Bernini. There are also works by Rubens, Van Dyck, Murillo, and Poussin, as well as sculptures, bronzes, and furniture from the 1700s.

Queen Christina of Sweden is one of only three women accorded monuments in St. Peter's (see p. 170). Despite several remodelings, the room in which she died on April 19, 1689, has remained as it was. Lavishly decorated, it has two yellow faux-marble columns as well as elaborate ceilings.

From the back rooms there is a lovely view of the Botanical Garden (formerly the gardens of the palazzo) and of the lower slopes of the Janiculum Hill. ∎

The Seven Hills of Rome

Many people think that the Janiculum was one of the original seven hills of Rome. But they are wrong. The seven hills of Rome are all on the other side of the Tiber. The Palatine, close to the river, was the site of the earliest settlements and later of the emperors' opulent residences. On the Capitoline were Rome's most

important temples, and in between the two hills was the magnificent Roman Forum. The remaining hills, which do not actually seem terribly high by today's standards, are the Caelian, the Esquiline, the Aventine, the Viminal, and the Quirinal, where the Italian president's residence is located.

SAN PIETRO IN MONTORIO & BRAMANTE'S TEMPIETTO

This magnificently placed Franciscan church is generally the first stop for visitors to the Janiculum Hill. The view of the city from the entrance steps is superb, and the church itself, with its fine travertine facade, is lovely. Dating from 1481, San Pietro in Montorio once enjoyed special significance in the erroneous belief that the lovely cloister next door was the site of St. Peter's crucifixion.

■ A series of steps starting in Trastevere lead up to San Pietro in Montorio.

San Pietro in Montorio & Bramante's Tempietto

🗺 Map p. 183

✉ Piazza di San Pietro in Montorio 2

☎ Church: 06 5813 940
Tempietto: 06 5812 806

🕐 Church: weekdays closed noon–3 p.m. & after 4 p.m.
Tempietto: closed Mon.

🚌 Bus: 115, 870

Inside, there is a beautiful "Flagellation" by Sebastiano del Piombo, and works by Peruzzi, Pomarancio, and Vasari. Bernini designed the second chapel on the left. Somewhere underneath is the grave of the young noblewoman Beatrice Cenci, whose 1599 execution at the age of 22 for patricide excited the popular imagination. She was the subject of poems, plays, and paintings, such as Guido Reni's portrait in the Barberini Museum.

In the courtyard of the adjacent monastery is the small, circular **Il Tempietto** (Little Temple) designed by Bramante and paid for by King Ferdinand and Queen Isabella of Spain to mark the birth of their son. The structure—a colonnade with Doric capitals topped by a balustrade and a cupola—is thought to embody the Renaissance ideal of classical harmony and proportion. Farther up the hill in a commanding position is the **Fontana dell'Acqua Paola** (otherwise known as the Fontanone, or Big Fountain). Like the Trevi Fountain, this is the *mostra terminale* of an aqueduct, the point where water first arrives from an extra-urban source (see pp. 98–99). Built of material plundered from the Roman Forum, it is composed of three large central niches flanked by two smaller ones. Water gushes from all five into the pool below. ■

GIANICOLO

The Gianicolo (Janiculum), the hill that runs from Trastevere to the Vatican more or less parallel to the Tiber, has little significance for ancient Roman history but was intimately associated with the Italian Risorgimento unification movement of the 19th century. The Porta San Pancrazio, at the top of the hill, and the surrounding area saw major battles between the French and the Romans and Italians. In the 1890s the entire area was turned into a public park.

Romans love to drive to the Janiculum Hill to enjoy the spectacular panoramic view of the city.

Gianicolo

Map pp. 182–183

Bus: 115, 870

Look for the main entrance to the Janiculum Park, the **Passeggiata del Gianicolo** (Janiculum Parade), on the right just past the Fontana dell'Acqua Paola, or Fontanone. This lovely tree-lined avenue has an equestrian statue of Garibaldi and busts of Italy's most important patriots. A favorite place for the *passeggiata domenicale* (Sunday walk), it also offers pony rides, puppet shows, and, in the evenings, ample space for couples to park.

The incomparable view of Rome, however, is the major attraction. This vantage point offers an unobstructed vista of all of the city's major landmarks and magnificent domes. On a clear day, you can see all the way to the Alban Hills. The view is also superb from the faro (light-house) beyond **Villa Lante,** donated to the city in 1911 by Argentinian Italians.

Little is left of **Tasso's Oak,** the tree under which the 16th-century poet liked to sit. Tasso died in 1595 in the convent of nearby **Sant'Onofrio,** a small, single-nave church. It boasts a lovely two-part "Annunciation" by Antoniazzo Romano and a 15th-century cloister with frescoes from the life of Sant'Onofrio. ■

EXPERIENCE: Appreciating the *Aperitivo*

It's late afternoon but too early for dinner. You have finished your shopping and touring and want to enjoy the afternoon sun or the sunset. What should you do? Everywhere you look, Romans are sitting at outdoor cafés with brightly colored drinks and nibbles in front of them and enjoying chit-chat, people-watching, and the view of some gorgeous ancient Roman monument or, if seated on a terrace or hill, the city below. You should join them.

The *aperitivo*—which has existed in Italy in some form or other for millennia—is an aromatic or alcoholic drink designed to encourage social contact and stimulate the appetite. Its first appearance in modern Italy may have been in Turin in 1796, when Antonio Benedetto Carpano invented his vermouth drink, later renamed "Punt e Mes" by Italian king Vittorio Emanuele II. Others say the tradition began in Milan, where the Ramazzotti brothers invented their "amaro," mixing 33 herbs and roots in an alcohol base. Also in Milan, the Martini family came up with their vermouth drinks, first Martini bianco and then Martini dry, and in 1862, Gaspare Campari created Campari bitter.

The Roman Take

Whatever its origins, the aperitivo tradition is now in full swing in Rome, too, with many cafés offering a lump-price "happy hour." At **Ombre Rosse** (*Piazza S. Egidio*) in Trastevere, the aperitivo of choice these days is a "spritz" made with white wine, the orange-colored nonalcoholic Aperol, and soda. Elsewhere people choose the more traditional drinks, like a negroni (vermouth, gin, and Campari

over ice) or a surprisingly yellow nonalcoholic Crodino. Drinks newer to Italy, like the Brazilian caipirinha or the Cuban mojito, also abound, as do old classics like the Bellini (champagne and peach juice) or—the choice of many—a simple glass of sparkling prosecco. But really, what's most important is your mood, that feeling of joie de vivre and expectation—that despite everything, all's right with the world.

INSIDER TIP:

Start a meal with an *aperitivo*: It doesn't need to be Campari and soda—the nonalcoholic Crodino is also very popular.

—TIM JEPSON
National Geographic author

Stellar Views

To heighten the aperitivo experience even further you should combine your predinner drink with nothing less than an astounding view. One way to do this is to head either for the cafés at **Piazza della Rotonda,** where the magnificent second-century Pantheon stares you in the face, or those at **Piazza**

Navona, where your eyes can feast on Bernini's glorious fountains. Or you can choose **Rosati** in Piazza del Popolo, where you can look up toward the Pincio and think about Daisy Miller riding in her carriage there.

You could also opt for the "high road." Several hotels have terraces from which you can feast on a wonderful view while sipping your Campari and orange juice: The **Raphael** (see p. 249) near Piazza Navona overlooks the rooftops of medieval Rome; the **Minerve** (see p. 249) has a splendid view of the back of the Pantheon; the **Forum** (see p. 244) looks out over the Forum; and the **Eden** (see p. 246) overlooks the Villa Medici and Trinità dei Monti. Two other deluxe hotels—the **Hassler** and the **De Russie** (for both, see p. 247)—don't have views, but they do have lovely gardens for a predinner drink.

If you have spent the morning or afternoon at the **Musei Capitolini,** another "high" is to sip something from the museum complex's terrace bar as you scan the city's rooftops. And then, of course, there is the **Janiculum Park** above Trastevere, from which, as you sip, you can see all of Rome unfold before your eyes.

SANTA CECILIA IN TRASTEVERE

An oasis of peace and quiet in a noisy neighborhood, this church was built to honor St. Cecilia, an important early Christian saint, martyred by the Romans, together with her husband. It is said that on her wedding night, the well-born Cecilia converted her husband and the two then lived together platonically. The remains of their house, containing some sarcophagi, mosaic floors, and other classical remnants, are below the church and can be visited when the church is open.

In an inscription accompanying his statue of the dead St. Cecilia, sculptor Stefano Maderno attests that the artwork is a true likeness of her body as seen by him when the tomb was opened in 1599.

Santa Cecilia in Trastevere

- Map p. 183
- Piazza Santa Cecilia 22
- 06 5899 289
- Basilica: closed 1–4 p.m. Cavallini fresco: open 10 a.m.–12:30 p.m. Mon.–Fri.
- Bus: H, 23, 44, 75, 125, 280. Tram: 8

Some say that Cecilia, the patron saint of music, invented the organ. Others claim that she sang hymns for three days while confined to the *calidarium* (hot room) of her house in a first, botched attempt by third-century Roman authorities to murder her. She was eventually stabbed in the neck, although decapitation proved, miraculously, impossible.

Pope Paschal I (817–824), who moved Cecilia's body here after seeing the location of her grave in a vision, built the first basilica on this site. Today's church is a hodgepodge of styles and colors. Ferdinando Fuga's monumental doorway opening

onto a garden with a fountain is from the early 18th century, as is the facade. The bell tower, however, and the portico, with its lovely mosaic decoration, are 12th century.

Inside, the church has a bland, 18th-century look, probably because of the decision to encase the Roman columns in concrete pilasters, but there are some marvelous remnants of the more distant past. The ninth-century **mosaic in the apse** showing Jesus flanked by St. Paul, St. Agatha, and St. Valerian on the right side and by St. Peter and St. Cecilia on the left is a more Byzantine version of the one visible in Santi

Cosma e Damiano (see p. 48). The figure farthest on the left, holding a model of the church, is Paschal, who cleverly had himself placed on equal footing with the saints and introduced to Christ by an affectionate St. Cecilia. The cosmatesque pavement (see sidebar p. 208) is, of course, medieval. The beautiful Gothic **altar canopy** by Arnolfo di Cambio dates from the late 13th century and is considered his masterpiece. Below is the heart-wrenching statue of Cecilia sculpted by Stefano Maderno, who viewed the supposedly intact body when the tomb was temporarily opened in 1599. In the chapel at the end of the right aisle, a damaged 12th-century fresco depicts the discovery of the saint's body.

Cavallini's "Last Judgment"

Unfortunately, church authorities have closed off the corridor where the calidarium was located and which also has a Guido Reni painting. And you can only look into the Ponziani Chapel. But don't despair. Every morning, for a small fee, the Benedictine nuns of the adjacent convent allow you to see the enthrallingly warm colors of Pietro Cavallini's fresco of the "Last Judgment." Rediscovered in 1900, but dating from 1293, the fresco is the only major Cavallini to survive. Christ is shown enthroned and surrounded by Apostles, saints, and angels whose multicolored wings run from cream to rose.

The nuns of Santa Cecilia have an extra behind-the-scenes job. Every year they are entrusted with two lambs blessed by the pope. They keep them until Easter, when they shear the wool—used to make the *pallia* (stoles) given to new patriarchs and archbishops. ■

Street Markets

A well-established tradition in Italy, street markets for used clothing, antiques, gifts, and bric-a-brac can be found throughout Rome. The Romans call them *mercatini* to distinguish them from the city's neighborhood food markets, or *mercati rionali*. For years, the giant flea market held Sunday mornings *(6 a.m.–2 p.m)* at **Porta Portese,** on the far side of Trastevere, was the sole option for bargain-hunters and browsers in Rome. But nowadays, if you want to spend your Sunday looking for a treasure, you have several options.

Every Sunday from 10 a.m. to 7 p.m. (but not in August) at the **Borghetto Flaminio** *(Piazza della Marina 32, metro: Linea A/ Flaminio)*, you can browse the 240-odd stands for everything from linens to old records. Or try the market at **Via Conca d'Oro,** where you can also taste specialties from the Italian south. And if antique prints are your thing, the **Mercato delle Stampe** in Largo della Fontanella Borghese (near the Spanish Steps) offers vintage prints, books, and magazines.

Other street markets operate only once a month from September to June, although some, like the open-air market in **Via Sannio** near San Giovanni, are open Mon.–Sat. all year, 8 a.m. to 2 p.m. (4 p.m. on Sat.). And since October 2009, a thriving farmers market near the Circo Massimo *(Via di San Teodoro 74)* has offered all types of local produce on weekends, 8 a.m. to 3 p.m. Nov.–Apr. and 8 a.m. to 7 p.m. May–Oct. (See p. 155 for more food markets.)

ISOLA TIBERINA & SAN BARTOLOMEO

A tiny gem of travertine and plane trees located in the middle of the Tiber River, Isola Tiberina (Tiber Island) has long been associated with both medicine and religion. Connected to both shores of the river by pedestrian bridges, it is the site of a major hospital, Fatebenefratelli (Do Good, Brothers); a 12th-century church; and the small Panzieri-Fatucci synagogue, reportedly the oldest surving one in Rome.

■ Ponte Quattro Capi connects Tiber Island to the east side of the Tiber and the Ghetto.

Isola Tiberina
🗺 Map p. 183

San Bartolomeo
✉ Piazza di San Bartolomeo all'Isola 22
☎ 06 6877 973
🕐 Closed 1:30–3:30 p.m. Mon.–Sat. & after 1 p.m. on Sun.
🚌 Bus: H, 23, 63, 280, 780. Tram: 8

Isola Tiberina

Legend has it that in the third century B.C. a delegation of Romans returned from a visit to the sibyl in Epidaurus (Greece) with instructions to build a temple to Aesculapius, the god of healing, if they wanted an outbreak of the plague to be quelled. As they sailed up the Tiber in 219 B.C., they saw a snake like the one wound around Aesculapius' staff (traditionally the doctor's symbol).

It supposedly slithered off the ship and swam to the island, indicating its choice of a temple site.

Over the centuries, the island became so closely associated with this ancient story that travertine blocks were used to give the island itself the appearance of a prow and a stern, and vestiges of this construction in the form of a trireme's keel—including a relief depiction of the sacred

Il Tevere

Although it runs right through the city, Il Tevere, or the Tiber, does not play much of a role in the lives of everyday Romans. It's there, it's picturesque, and it is spanned by a variety of bridges, including charming Ponte Sisto, from which there is a glorious view that includes St. Peter's Basilica. But ever since the end of the 19th century, when high embankments were built to put an end to frequent flooding, the Biondo Tevere (Blond Tiber, so called for its yellowish, muddy bottom) has pretty much played a minor role. And this despite new sightseeing boat trips and summer amusements along its shores.

But this was not always the case. Romulus and Remus, supposedly Rome's founders, were reportedly found on the riverbank by the she-wolf who adopted them. In the first century B.C. rich Romans had garden-parks, or *horti*, on its banks, and throughout ancient times, the Tiber was a major point of access for ships sailing the Mediterranean. The Ripa Grande, the large commercial river port in Trastevere, and the smaller Porto di Ripetta (which once boasted a monumental, tiered riverside staircase believed to have been the inspiration for the Spanish Steps) were both of vital economic importance to the city.

snake—can still be seen on the side of the island that faces the Great Synagogue of Rome.

Centuries later, the young Holy Roman Emperor Otto III chose the ruins of Aesculapius' temple as the site for a new church dedicated to his friend Adalbert, the first bishop of Prague, who had been martyred a year earlier in A.D. 997. Otto is said to have personally directed the construction, using Roman columns and other ancient remnants for the nave and the portico.

Somehow, however, poor Adalbert got lost in the shuffle. Otto had returned from a trip to Benevento in the Italian south with the remains of the Apostle Bartholomew (also known as Nathaniel), which he deposited, temporarily he thought, in the new church then under construction. But when he died in a skirmish with rebels, St. Adalbert was quickly forgotten and St. Bartholomew became the church's patron saint.

INSIDER TIP:

In 2003, the Tiber opened its waterways for tours of the Eternal City. Gain a different perspective of Rome by taking a boat tour—for information, go to *www.romeboatexperience.com*

—MAURO PELELLA
National Geographic researcher

San Bartolomeo

Rebuilt in 1113 and again in 1624, San Bartolomeo has a 12th-century campanile and baroque facade. Inside, a marble wellhead located on the steps leading up to the tribune bears four carved figures: Jesus, St. Bartholomew (holding the knife with which he was martyred), St. Adalbert with his bishop's staff, and Otto III with his crown and scepter. ∎

More Places to Visit

Complesso di San Michele a Ripa

Today the massive 1,099-foot-long (335 m) San Michele complex houses government offices, a branch of the Central Restoration Institute, and several exhibition spaces. Located on the bank of the Tiber, San Michele was founded in the late 17th century as a refuge for orphans and delinquents and later became a home for old folks and spinsters. Its upper end faces the Porta Portese gate, an entrance to the Sunday flea market.
🅰 Map p. 183 ✉ Via de San Michele 25 ☎ 06 6723 4400 🕐 Varies by exhibit 💲 Varies by exhibit 🚌 Bus: 23, 44, 75, 125, 280. Tram: 3

San Crisogono

Situated on busy Viale di Trastevere, this large church is sadly often passed over by tourists. Built in the style of a classical Roman basilica, its cosmatesque pavement (see sidebar p. 208) may be one of the most beautiful in Rome. The baroque facade and interior decoration give little clue to its medieval beginnings; only the Romanesque campanile (one of the few in Rome with a triangular top) and the right flank are a giveaway to the church's 12th-century origins.

The two porphyry columns supporting the triumphal arch are among the largest in Rome. The gilded and blue coffered ceiling is a masterpiece of the genre, but the 17th-century painting on the ceiling ("Triumph of St. Crisogono") is a copy of a Guercino. The original is now in London. The medieval altar has a cosmatesque finish, and the framed late 13th-century mosaic in the apse ("The Virgin Between Two Saints") has been attributed to Pietro Cavallini. The **underground ruins** of the original fifth-century paleo-Christian church are open to the public, although large groups should make a reservation.

During the July Festa de' Noantri the church becomes a Marian sanctuary. The "Virgin of Mount Carmel," an icon, is carried in procession through the streets and put on view in the church for eight days.
🅰 Map p. 183 ✉ Piazza Sonnino 44 (Viale Trastevere) ☎ 06 5810 076 or 06 5818 225 🕐 Upper church: closed 11:30 a.m.–4 p.m. Mon.–Sat. & 1–4 p.m. Sun. Underground church: closed 11:30 a.m.–4 p.m. Mon.–Sat. & 1–4 p.m. Sun. 💲 Underground church: $ 🚌 Bus: H, 23, 125, 280, 780. Tram: 8

San Francesco a Ripa

St. Francis took a vow of poverty, but at St. Francis on the Riverbank (named for the ancient riverport that once existed near here) someone may not have been paying attention. When this 13th-century church (erected on the site of a hospice where the saint had once stayed) was rebuilt in the 17th century, it was done in no-holds-barred baroque—the decor is deliciously dramatic with opulent paintings, gold leaf, and stucco everywhere.

The **Pallavicini Chapel** at the end of the right aisle nearest the altar is a triumph of multicolored marble; wall tombs sport garishly wicked winged skeletons. The **Altieri Chapel** across the aisle holds one of Bernini's majestic "Ecstasies," the magnificently dramatic statue of the "Blessed Ludovica Albertoni" (1674). Pay no attention to the stucco putto heads gazing down on the blessed Ludovica as she reclines in mystical ecstasy; they were added later. Bernini preferred natural and concealed lighting, but if the light from the side window is not enough for you, ask the sacristan to turn on the electric light for a moment. He'll also take you to visit St. Francis's cell with its stone pillow.
🅰 Map p. 183 ✉ Piazza di San Francesco d'Assisi 88 ☎ 06 5819 020 🕐 Church: closed 1–4 p.m.; St. Francis's cell: visits can be booked 🚌 Bus: 23, 44, 75, 125, 280, 780. Tram: 3, 8

The remains of ancient temples and monuments, Piazza Venezia, the 16th-century Jewish Ghetto, and the quieter Aventine Hill

FORUM BOARIUM TO AVENTINO

■ Forum Boarium's Tempio di Portunus, a second-century A.D. temple dedicated to the god of ports

FORUM BOARIUM TO AVENTINO

Some 2,000 years ago, the zone between the Campidoglio and the Tiber was the location for the Forum Boarium and the Forum Holitorium, two bustling outdoor markets for, respectively, cattle and vegetables. The Velabrium, as the area was then called, straddled a road that led straight to the city center, the Roman Forum.

The adjacent area, too, abounds in vestiges of Roman rule. The remains of the Teatro di Marcello, designed by Julius Caesar's architects but completed by Augustus, were incorporated into an elegant 16th-century palazzo. Three columns from the temple of Apollo Sosianus are dramatically outlined against a medieval urban background, and the remnants of the Portico d'Ottavia, which Octavius dedicated to his sister, lie within the area known as the Ghetto, to which the Jews of Rome were confined for centuries.

A large modern thoroughfare, opened in 1933 and now called Via Luigi Petroselli, takes car and bus traffic north past the central Registry Office (the Anagrafe) to Piazza Venezia. But some remarkable remnants of those earlier times remain; all you need to enjoy them is a vivid imagination. Picture the cattle traders as they crowded under the Arco di Giano to avoid the winter rain or the scorching summer sun. Imagine how they decided to build a second arch (Arco degli Argentari) to honor Emperor Septimius Severus. Surely you can appreciate why an anonymous wealthy cattleowner would be willing to spend many *sesterces* to build a circular temple in honor of Hercules Victor,

the god of merchants and traders. A second rectangular temple was built to provide offerings to Portunus, the god of ports. The church of San Nicola in Carcere incorporates the ruins of three other temples (note the columns embedded in its walls). Several of the other churches in the area, in particular San Giorgio in Velabro, San Teodoro, and the

---

NOT TO BE MISSED:

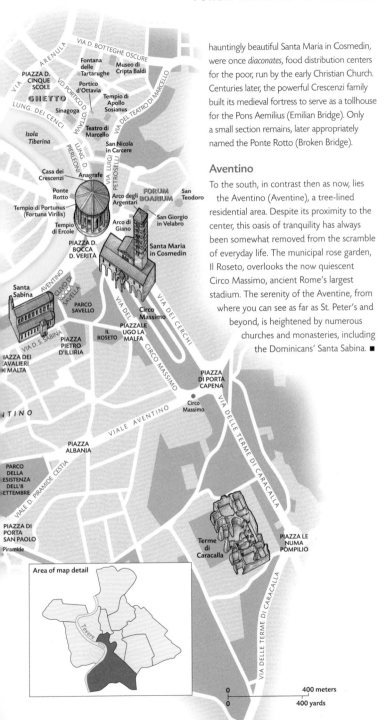

hauntingly beautiful Santa Maria in Cosmedin, were once *diaconates*, food distribution centers for the poor, run by the early Christian Church. Centuries later, the powerful Crescenzi family built its medieval fortress to serve as a tollhouse for the Pons Aemilius (Emilian Bridge). Only a small section remains, later appropriately named the Ponte Rotto (Broken Bridge).

Aventino

To the south, in contrast then as now, lies the Aventino (Aventine), a tree-lined residential area. Despite its proximity to the center, this oasis of tranquility has always been somewhat removed from the scramble of everyday life. The municipal rose garden, Il Roseto, overlooks the now quiescent Circo Massimo, ancient Rome's largest stadium. The serenity of the Aventine, from where you can see as far as St. Peter's and beyond, is heightened by numerous churches and monasteries, including the Dominicans' Santa Sabina. ■

FORUM BOARIUM'S TEMPLES, ARCHES, *& DIACONATES*

The massive fourth-century Arco di Giano, or Arch of Janus, hasn't much in common with the triumphal arches built by emperors such as Titus and Septimius Severus, but that's because its purpose was primarily practical. Despite its decorations (the niches on the facades held statues, and various deities are depicted above the archways), this was primarily a covered crossway, erected to protect the cattle traders of the Forum Boarium from inclement weather.

■ The second-century B.C. Tempio di Ercole is reportedly Rome's earliest extant marble building.

Forum Boarium

 Map p. 201

🚌 Bus: C3, H, 30, 44, 63, 81, 83, 118, 130, 160, 170, 628, 715, 716, 780, 781

Arco degli Argentari

The same is true of the tiny Arco degli Argentari (Arch of the Moneychangers), attached to the church of San Giorgio in Velabro. Erected in A.D. 204 by the cattle merchants and their financial backers, and dedicated to the Severans, the arch was basically the gateway to the cattle market. If it seems dwarfish, remember

that centuries of silt and debris accumulation have raised the ground level, thus hiding a good part of the bottom section, which was made of plain travertine to avoid the wear and tear caused by passing bovines. The upper portion, made of white marble, is decorated with reliefs showing members of the imperial family performing religious rituals. Septimius Severus and his wife are on the right and Caracalla, who erased his brother Geta's image after murdering him, is on the left.

Facing the arch, at Via del Velabro 3, is an iron gate and a lovely arched passageway, unfortunately now inaccessible, which leads to an entrance to the **Cloaca Massima,** the enormous sixth-century B.C. drainage system that ran from the Roman Forum to the Tiber.

San Giorgio in Velabro

This former *diaconate,* or food distribution center, is dedicated to St. George (of dragon-slaying fame), who, contrary to popular belief, was not British but rather an early Christian martyr from Palestine. Here you will find a 13th-century **Madonna and Saints fresco** attributed to Pietro Cavallini and a lovely 12th-century **portico and bell tower.** The saint's relics (including, they say, his head) were brought to this church in the middle of the eighth century, when Pope Zaccaria reportedly found them languishing in the Palazzo Lateranense.

Tempio di Portunus

Across Via Luigi Petroselli, a stone's throw from the river, stands this first-century B.C. temple dedicated to Portunus, the god of ports. Rectangular, with a colonnaded porch and remnants of the stucco used to create a marblelike effect, it is an excellent example of temple architecture and is remarkably intact. In the ninth century, this

building, like many others, was converted into a church.

The medieval **house of the Crescenzi family** across the narrow Via del Ponte Rotto has Roman columns embedded in

INSIDER TIP:
You will find useful information about what's going on in Rome and events around town at *www. turismoroma.it.*

—ANTONIO BARBIERI
National Geographic contributor & co-founder of Concierge in Rome

its walls and a classical architrave made from ancient fragments.

Tempio di Ercole

Just behind is the lovely round shrine that for centuries was mistakenly called the Tempio di Vesta because of its resemblance to the temple of that name in the Roman Forum. Instead, experts now say it was almost certainly dedicated to Hercules Victor, who slew the giant Cacus for stealing his cattle. Indeed, the god's image is on the upper left of the Arco degli Argentari. This temple, too, was converted into a church, but its original pieces, in white marble, are easy to spot. Many of the 20 Corinthian columns are also original. The interior of the cylindrical cell is formed of Pentelic marble. ■

ROMANS, JEWS, & CHRISTIANS WALK

This part of Rome encompasses the Jewish Ghetto and the few remains of an area that the ancient Romans dedicated to knowledge and entertainment as well as to commerce. Today it is home to many artisans and merchants, Jewish and not. It is also a desirable address for up-and-coming professionals.

Begin in front of the **Tempio di Portunus** (see p. 203) and proceed up to the Lungotevere. Traffic permitting, cross the street for a magnificent view of **Isola Tiberina** (Tiber Island). To the right, the restored Torre dei Caetani, or Pierleoni tower (recently renovated), stands like a sentinel over the oldest bridge in the city, the Ponte Fabricio (aka Ponte Quattro Capi), constructed in 62 B.C. At the stoplight by the bridge, cross back (in greater safety) and you will find yourself at the beginning of the **Via del Portico d'Ottavia ❶**, the main street of the Ghetto (see p. 206). The square-dome building on your left is Rome's main synagogue, built a

INSIDER TIP:

Even Pope Benedict XVI was said to be a fan of the cinnamon and almond biscotti, sweet "Jewish pizza," and other goodies at Boccione, the kosher pastry shop in the Ghetto.

—RUTH ELLEN GRUBER
National Geographic author

century ago in an odd, but not unpleasing, mock Assyro-Babylonian style. The temple and museum *(tel 06 6840 0661, www.museo ebraico.roma.it, closed Fri. p.m. & Sat., $$, www. museoebraico.roma.it)* are worth a visit.

The small church on your right is **San Gregorio della Divina Pietà,** one of the churches where Jews were forced to attend Christian services. They could avoid this only by paying a

NOT TO BE MISSED:

View of Tiber Island • Casa di Lorenzo Manilio • Fontana delle Tartarughe • Palazzo Caetani's courtyard

bribe or, as many did, using earplugs. Over the door there are Latin and Hebrew inscriptions.

Walk down the Via del Portico d'Ottavia to the large marble pediment supported by columns, all that's left of the **Portico d'Ottavia ❷**, the huge colonnade that Augustus built in 23 B.C. and dedicated to his sister, Octavia. In the Middle Ages, the church of **Sant'Angelo in Pescheria** (*pescheria* means "fish market") was built into its ruins. The marble plaque on the far right pilaster says that from any fish that was longer than the plaque itself, the head (then considered quite a delicacy) was to be handed over to city officials.

Where the street turns 90 degrees, go left; note that the buildings on the left are newer than those on the right. Because of poor sanitary conditions in the overcrowded Ghetto, a century ago everything from here to the river was razed and rebuilt. At Nos. 1 and 2 is the **Casa di Lorenzo Manilio ❸**, built in 1497. Classical inscriptions and beautiful Roman reliefs are embedded in the walls. **Boccione,** the pastry shop on the corner (at No. 1), makes delicious Jewish cakes and pastries.

Backtrack to the Via della Reginella, which leads to Piazza Mattei with its delightful **Fontana delle Tartarughe ❹** (Fountain of the

Tortoises, see p. 99), designed by Giacomo della Porta in the 1580s. Take Via dei Funari (Street of the Ropemakers) and peep into the courtyard of **Palazzo Caetani** at No. 31 to observe the fragments of classical sculpture covering the walls. **Santa Maria in Campitelli** ❺ (1662–1667), in nearby Piazza di Campitelli, is architect Carlo Rainaldi's masterpiece.

Exit the square from its farther end. On your right you'll see the remains of the **Teatro di Marcello** and the three surviving columns of the **Tempio di Apollo Sosianus.** The theater, erected between 13 and 11 B.C., was

dedicated to Marcellus, Augustus' nephew. A short distance on is **San Nicola in Carcere** ❻, the medieval church built into the remains of the Forum Holitorium's three temples. Proceed along Via Luigi Petroselli to **Santa Maria in Cosmedin** ❼ (see pp. 207–208).

- See also area map pp. 200–201
- Tempio di Portunus
- 1 mile (1.5 km)
- 1.5 hours
- Santa Maria in Cosmedin

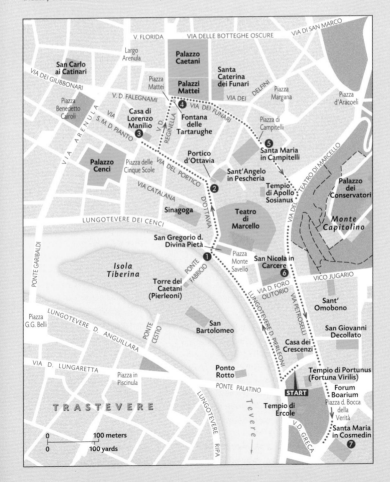

THE GHETTO

The papal bull issued by Pope Paul IV on July 12, 1555, confined the Jews of Rome to a walled-off area of less than 3 acres (1.3 ha), where they were forced to live for more than 300 years. He was motivated in part by simple anti-Semitism. But the Counter-Reformation zeal inspired by the Protestant schism probably also played a key role in the creation of the Ghetto, which was not formally abolished until 1883.

The Ghetto

 Map p. 201

Bus: 46, 60, 63, 80, 190, 280, 780, 781, 916. Tram: 8

Jews have lived in Rome since the second century B.C., settling first in areas favored by foreigners, such as the Aventine and Trastevere. By the 16th century, however, many Roman Jews, especially merchants, had moved to this thriving commercial riverport neighborhood. The bridge to the Tiber Island was often referred to as the Pons Judaeorum, and the **Piazza delle Cinque Scole** (off today's Via Arenula), with its five temples, was called Piazza Giudea.

The papal edict made it illegal for Jews to live anywhere else in the city, barred them from certain professions, and forced them to attend church services. Although enforcement was patchy, severe overcrowding was inevitable. In

A Unique Jewish Community

The Babylonian exile of the sixth century B.C. dispersed Jews throughout the known world. Rome's Jewish community first developed a few hundred years after the diaspora, making their descendants members of the oldest continuous Jewish community in the world today.

INSIDER TIP:

Rome's quietest and prettiest late-night stroll is through the old Ghetto district east of Via Arenula.

—TIM JEPSON
National Geographic author

the 1600s, some 6,000 people crammed into this tiny area when the gates closed at sunset.

Today the area is dominated by an imposing synagogue. Pope John Paul II made history with his unprecedented visit here in 1986.

Rome's Jews are neither Ashkenazi nor Sephardic and pride themselves on being part of a community that preexists the destruction of the Jerusalem temple in A.D. 70, a distinction that entitles them to certain privileges, such as eating lamb at Passover.

Jewish people have been in Rome so long that Jewish and Roman cuisines, pork dishes excluded, are now almost indistinguishable. Some favorites of Jewish origin are *carciofi alla giudia* (fried, whole artichokes), *filetti di baccalà fritti* (fried codfish fillets), and marinated zucchini. The Jewish bakery on **Via del Portico d'Ottavia** is known for its delicious ricotta cheesecakes (chocolate or berries). ■

SANTA MARIA IN COSMEDIN

Set in the heart of an area rich in ancient monuments and memories, Santa Maria in Cosmedin is unfortunately known primarily for the Bocca della Verità (Mouth of Truth). This stone disk adorned with the carved image of a sea god tempts hordes of tourists to see whether, as medieval legend had it, the mouth will bite off a liar's hand. It is also worth visiting the interior of the church.

A Diverse History

The two columns flanking the door inside, the three others embedded in the left wall, and the freestanding, shorter column in the bookshop are remnants of an earlier structure. In the fourth century, this building was the seat of the *statio annonae*, the city office for food distribution and market inspection. By the sixth century it had become a *diaconate*, a center set up by the church to provide food and other services to the poor.

An oratory was also added in the sixth century, but it was only in the eighth century that Pope Hadrian (772–795) turned the structure into a bona fide church, donating it to Greek Christian refugees from the religious turmoil in Byzantium. Thus it became Santa Maria in Cosmedin, or, as it was sometimes called, Santa Maria in Schola Graeca.

Whichever name you prefer, both testify to the Eastern origin of the new church's parishioners. Cosmedin is no doubt derived from Constantinople's famous Kosmidion Monastery and neighborhood whereas Schola Graeca (which means "Greek school") speaks for itself.

Damaged during the Norman invasion in the late 11th

The Romanesque bell tower of Santa Maria in Cosmedin

century, the church was restored in the early 12th century. The redbrick columned porch, the portico, and the lovely seven-story Romanesque bell tower also date from this period.

Church Porch & the Bocca della Verità

The Bocca della Verità was placed on the left-hand wall 370 years ago, but the porch shelters far more interesting treasures. The marble decoration around

Santa Maria in Cosmedin

🗺 Map p. 201

✉ Piazza della Bocca della Verità 18

☎ 06 6787 759

🚌 Bus: C3, H, 30, 44, 63, 81, 83, 118, 130, 160, 170, 628, 715, 716, 780, 781

INSIDER TIP:

Many churches in Rome sit on top of ancient ruins or incorporated much older buildings into their construction. Keep an eye out for these anachronisms.

—SARAH YEOMANS
Archaeologist & National Geographic contributor

the portal dates from the 11th century. The tomb to its right is that of Alfano, the papal chamberlain who supervised the 12th-century restoration. The inscriptions on the wall record ninth-century donations.

Inside the Church

In the hush of the church's penumbra it is easy to feel yourself transported back in time and possibly moved to spiritual contemplation. This church abounds in Eastern or Byzantine influences, primarily the *schola cantorum,* the walled-off area reserved for worshippers; *matronei*, the balconies reserved for women; and the iconostasis, the marble divider delimiting the priests' domain.

The magnificently patterned floor is pre-cosmatesque, whereas the decorated Gothic canopy over the main altar is dated 1294 and is signed by Deodato, a son of one of the Cosmas (see sidebar below). There is cosmatesque decoration on the paschal candlestick—note the stylized lion at its base—just behind the right pulpit. And don't miss the framed eighth-century mosaic in the sacristy with its fine gold background, which comes from the original St. Peter's. It may be a scene from the Adoration of the Three Kings. ■

The Cosmati Marble Workers

Many of Rome's greatest 12th- and 13th-century stonecutters bore the surname Cosma, perhaps because the name was common or perhaps for some other reason. We do know that these "Cosmati" reinvented mosaic art.

The cosmati technique or cosmatesque are the terms now used to describe their type of inlay decoration, which relied on the use of tiny pieces of colored marble—red, green, black, white— to create intricate patterns, at times resembling Islamic geometric motifs. Often, in a break from ancient Roman techniques, the Cosmati combined them with larger stone rounds and strips to make multicolored pavements such as

those in Santa Maria in Cosmedin, San Crisogono, and Santa Maria in Trastevere.

Cosmati work was also applied to church accessories such as paschal candlesticks (notable in San Lorenzo), tombs, episcopal chairs and pulpits, and the small columns often used in church cloisters. The most impressive columns in Rome can be found in the cloisters of San Giovanni in Laterano and San Paolo fuori le Mura, both of which are signed by Pietro Vassalletto and his son, masters of this kind of workmanship.

The production of cosmati work was interrupted in the 14th century, when the popes fled temporarily to Avignon, and it never again reached its former levels.

CIRCO MASSIMO

If you look down at the Circo Massimo (Circus Maximus) from the imperial residences on the Palatine Hill, you can almost hear the crowds cheering on the city's most popular charioteers as their two-wheeled chariots rounded the course for the seventh and last time.

Crowds still gather at the Circo Massimo, such as for a celebration marking Rome's founding.

Charioteers once raced here, their colors—white, red, green, or blue—signifying membership in one of the *factiones* or parties that paid for the outfitting of the equestrian teams.

Archaeologists say that the starting gates and the *spina*, or raised spine that ran down the middle of the race course, still exist. The new guided tours using augmented reality technologies are useful means for comprehending the archaeological area and its history, guaranteeing that the visit is an involving and innovative experience of one of the largest stadiums that humankind has known. A long rectangle about the size of a football field, it had a triple tier of stone and wood bleachers believed to have held more than 250,000 people.

Tucked into the valley between the Palatine and Aventine Hills, the Circus Maximus dates back to the fourth century B.C. and is the oldest of the known Roman circuses. During the frequent *ludi* (games), the circus was primarily for horse racing and chariot races, although gladiatorial exhibitions were sometimes held there, as were public executions. It was last used as a Roman circus in A.D. 549, during the reign of the Ostrogoth (barbarian) king, Totila, who had temporarily won control of Rome from the city's Byzantine rulers. It then gradually fell into disuse (at one point cabbages were grown here).

The small medieval tower at the eastern end has nothing to do with the original circus. It belonged to the Frangipane family, which during the Middle Ages controlled much of this area. ■

Circo Massimo

Map p. 201
C3, 75, 81, 118, 160, 628, 715. Tram: 3. Metro: Linea B (Circo Massimo)

AVENTINO

The most picturesque way to get up to the Aventino (Aventine Hill) and to Santa Sabina is to walk up the lovely cobblestone street called Clivo di Rocca Savella, which starts about 110 yards (100 m) from Santa Maria in Cosmedin (along Via Santa Maria in Cosmedin, the continuation of Via Luigi Petroselli).

■ The Giardino degli Aranci offers a wonderful view, with St. Peter's dome visible in the distance.

Aventino

🅐 Map pp. 200– 201

Santa Sabina

🅐 Map p. 201

✉ Piazza Pietro d'Illiria 1

☎ 06 579401

🕐 Closed during religious functions

🚌 Bus: 23, 30, 44, 83, 130, 170, 280, 716, 781

Parco Savello

Skirt the medieval wall—once part of the Savelli family's fortress, on your right at the top—to reach the entrance to the Parco Savello, also called the Giardino degli Aranci (Garden of Oranges) because of the orange trees brought from Spain in the 13th century by St. Dominic, founder of the Dominican order. An oasis of peace and quiet, this lovely spot affords an unbeliev- able panoramic view of the city.

The imposing rear view of the Dominican basilica of **Santa Sabina** makes it easy for you to grasp the essentials of

fifth-century church architecture in Rome. The apse is clearly outlined, and you can see how the center part of the church, over the nave, is higher than the sides, permitting greater illumination through the clerestory windows.

By the time this church was built, Christianity had become a mainstream religion and, as you can see from the 24 fluted Corinthian columns, the remain- ing mosaic decorations above the entrance door, and the beautiful Roman marble inlay ornamenta- tion above and between the arches, it was built to be seen.

The mosaic over the entrance

is particularly interesting. Two female figures, resembling classical Roman matrons, represent the major components of early Christianity, the pagans or gentiles *(Ecclesia ex gentibus)*, and the Jews *(Ecclesia ex circumscisione)*. The gold lettering on a deep blue background is striking. And don't miss the cypress door on the far left of the portico. Its 18 fifth-century paleo-Christian panels depict scenes from the Old and New Testaments, including one of the earliest surviving representations of Jesus' crucifixion.

On leaving the church, note the superb *mascherone* (mask) on the wall to the left of the park entrance, used in the fountain by Giacomo della Porta.

Piazza dei Cavalieri di Malta

Farther along Via di Santa Sabina you'll come to Piazza dei Cavalieri di Malta, a quaint space designed

INSIDER TIP:

Climb the Aventine Hill and find the *buco della serratura*, a keyhole through which you'll see Rome's most unique and memorable view of the dome of St. Peter's.

—CJ FAHEY
National Geographic contributor

by 18th-century graphic artist Giovanni Battista Piranesi. The monumental entrance leads to the residence of the Grand Master of the Knights of Malta, **Villa del'Ordine dei Cavalieri di Malta.** Piranesi (who is buried there) also designed the church, **Santa Maria del Priorato.** Peep through the keyhole to see the justifiably famous picture-postcard view of the dome of St. Peter's. ∎

EXPERIENCE: The Ancient & the Experimental

Next to the Bocca della Verità, you can admire Arco di Giano and, if it is evening, its permanent illumination by Vittorio Storaro. You will also note a gigantic life-size rhinoceros made of resin inside the railings. Appropriately named "Rhinoceros," the sculpture was curated by Raffaele Curi for the Fondazione Alda Fendi, which in 2011 purchased the adjacent small building at Via Velabro 9. Its appearance heralded the creation of a citadel of art in the heart of the Forum Boarium. The project was entrusted to French star architect Jean Nouvel and concluded in 2018. It envisages: three floors of exhibition rooms open to the public day and night, with the exception of the ground floor space, which closes at 7 p.m.; 24 luxury apartments integrated into the gallery, with haikus inscribed on every door frame together with the word *pensiero* (thought), translated into 24 languages; a restaurant of the French food and wine brand Caviar Kaspia on the top floors; and a terrace with a breathtaking view. The first exhibitions, absolutely free like access to all the other spaces managed by the Fondazione, proposed works by Michelangelo: Florentine and Roman architectural studies, and the work "L'adolescente" on loan from the Hermitage in Saint Petersburg. *(Via Velabro 9, tel 340 6430435, organized visits can be booked, free entrance)*

TERME DI CARACALLA

Begun in A.D. 206 and inaugurated in 217 by Caracalla, the mammoth Terme di Caracalla (Baths of Caracalla) went beyond simple hygiene and pleasure to satisfy the needs of the leisured class. Romans came here not just for a swim and a sauna but, as in any elitist club, to while away a lazy afternoon, to catch up on some reading, or even to make a business deal or two.

■ To build the third-century A.D. Baths of Caracalla, an average of 9,000 workers toiled daily over the four main years of construction, reaching an estimated high of 13,100 in 213.

The Baths of Caracalla have been "out of order" since the sixth century, when the invading Goths destroyed the aqueducts and cut off their water supply. The majestic ruins, which loom in the shadow of the second crest of the Aventine Hill, will give you only a partial idea of the baths' extravagant scale.

Along with the bathing rooms, there were libraries (Greek and Latin), art galleries, meeting halls, and a stadium. The buildings were surrounded by a shaded esplanade with fountains, playing fields, and a covered portico.

The materials used to decorate the baths were lavish, as can be seen from the mosaics now displayed in the Vatican Museums, such as the "athletes in training." Monumental sculptures included the granite basins since incorporated into the fountains of the Piazza Farnese, and the so-called Farnese Bull and Farnese Hercules, both in the Naples archaeological museum.

EXPERIENCE: Learn Your Local Snack Options

In the 1970s, eating on the street, except for gelato, was done only by Americans and was strongly frowned upon. But that's no longer the case, and today Romans, too, carry snack food around with them or eat standing up at a counter. When you don't want a full meal, or if you are feeling hungry between meals, you will find a wealth of snack options. Here's a primer.

In late morning, you might stop by the local *forno* (bakery) and ask for a slice of *pizza rossa* (pizza with some tomato conserve on it) or, better yet, *pizza bianca*, a slightly thicker, plain warm pizza that is delicious with prosciutto but even better, in the summer, with fresh figs. Local legend has it that Roman bakers invented pizza bianca when they rolled out some

extra dough to make sure their ovens were at the right temperature. Or it may just be another variety of Mediterranean flat bread, similar to pita.

But that's just the start of your snack discoveries. Other Roman nibbles started out in life as a way of using leftover risotto. These include *supplì al telefono*, egg-shaped rice croquettes with mozzarella and ragù, and *arancini di riso* (little oranges), fried rice balls with meat sauce and peas inside, originally a Sicilian recipe.

And then there are the various sandwiches you can buy at most cafés: *tramezzini*, which are white bread sandwich halves; *panini*, sandwiches on a roll; and *piadine*, sandwiches on flat bread that need to be toasted.

Plundered over the centuries, the baths' retain little of their original grandeur.

The main bathing rooms—which could reportedly seat 1,600 people at one time—formed an axis of the central quadrilateral. Secondary rooms were arranged around the apodyterium (dressing room), the palaestrae (open-air exercise rooms), the *calidarium* (hot room), tepidarium (warm room), and the frigidarium (cold room). Other structures, like the libraries, were outside the perimeter.

Your visit begins in one of the two palaestrae. This, like its twin on the far side of the complex, has segments of black-and-white, and patches of multicolor, mosaic flooring. One door out of the workout room leads to a dressing room with a black-and-white pavement, a vestibule, and then, a few steps down, a *natatio* (swimming pool). Another brings you to an atrium

and then into the frigidarium. If you walk straight through here and the transition room on the other side, you'll come to the other palaestra with its many mosaic panels. Next to nothing remains of the enormous and circular calidarium, with its seven plunge baths, except two brick pilasters. The dome was said to have been as big as the Pantheon's. ∎

INSIDER TIP:

What better place to enjoy a Puccini aria than at the imposing ruins of the Terme di Caracalla? Various Italian operas are staged at this ancient bathhouse in the summer.

—SOPHIE GORDON
Travel journalist

Terme di Caracalla

- Map p. 201
- Via delle Terme di Caracalla 52 (at the intersection with Via Antonina)
- 06 3996 7700. Online tickets: www.coopculture.it
- $. Audio guide: $
- Open 9 a.m.–4:30 p.m. or 9 a.m.–7:15 p.m. according to the season. Closed Mon. after 2 p.m.
- Bus: 118, 160, 628, 671, 714, 717. Tram: 3. Metro: Linea B (Circo Massimo)

www.soprintendenza specialeroma.it

More Places to Visit

Cimitero Acattolico

This burial place for non-Catholics was founded in 1738 to provide a final resting place for visiting foreigners who died in Rome. These include the famous—such as Keats and Shelley—and the ordinary, such as 16-year-old Rose Bathurst, who, in 1824, fell off her horse and drowned in the Tiber, and Devereux Plantagenet Cockburn, who died in 1850 at the age of 21 after vainly traveling through Europe in search of a suitable climate. Banked up against the Aurelian Wall, their final resting place is verdantly tranquil, a place of blossom and birdsong.

Maps and guides are available from the visitor center left of the entrance. Genuine mourners pay nothing; tourists are asked to make a small donation ($). If you're short of time, remember you can see Keats's grave from outside, through a small window in the cemetery wall at the start of Via Caio Cestio, a street named after the first well-known non-Catholic to be buried in the area: Caius Cestius, a senior Roman magistrate who died in 12 B.C. but not before building himself a pyramid for a tomb (**Piramide di Caio Cestio**). In the third century A.D., like other preexisting monuments, the tomb was incorporated into the walls built to protect the city from the growing threat of barbarian attack, which probably accounts for its survival over the centuries.

www.cemeteryrome.it 🗺 Map p. 200 ✉ Via Caio Cestio 6 ☎ 06 5741 900 🕐 Closed Sun. p.m. 💲 Tours in English on request for 10 to 20 people: $ per person suggested 🚌 Bus: 23, 30, 75,0130, 280, 716, 719. Tram: 3. Metro: Linea B (Piramide)

Museo Montemartini

This former power station on the Via Ostiense has been transformed into a small branch of the Musei Capitolini, a provocative setting for 400-odd Capitoline marbles. Pediment sculptures, friezes from temples and the Teatro di Pompeo, statuary from the *horti* (monumental gardens of ancient aristocratic residences), mosaics, and republican-era busts are dramatically displayed amid the equipment once in use in the likes of the Machine, Furnace, and Column Rooms.

en.centralemontemartini.org 🗺 Map p. 200 ✉ Via Ostiense 106 ☎ 060608 🕐 Closed Mon. 💲 $$. Tours in English on request: $$$ 🚌 Bus: 23, 769, 792. Metro: Linea B (Garbatella)

EXPERIENCE: *Granita,* or Rather *Grattachecca*

The name stems from the operation of grating the ice from a block with a special tool. The traditional name in Roman dialect is *checca.* Syrups, fresh-squeezed fruit, and pieces of fruit are added to the thin powdered ice. Thus the handmade, typically Roman *granita* is born: a street food ahead of its time from the end of the 19th century. The tradition has remained intact and been handed down to the present day. The scorching Roman summers are graced by *grattachecche* always prepared by hand in the historic kiosks on the Lungotevere or at Testaccio. However, grattachecca and granita are two different products: Let's not confuse them! First of all, the consistency of the ice is very different: In the former, it is worked into dense and compact flakes, while in the latter it is completely ground. Also, in the grattachecca the syrups and juices are added afterward and the resulting taste is heightened in a contrast of flavors taking place directly on your palate.

Early Christian catacombs, a contemporary world-class music venue, and the lovely Via Appia Antica

FUORI LE MURA (OUTSIDE THE WALLS)

■ Many consider San Paolo fuori le Mura's cloister Rome's most beautiful.

FUORI LE MURA

Rome, like most ancient settlements, was a walled city. Today the walls that once surrounded almost all of inhabited Rome no longer have the same function or import as in the past. Nevertheless, the words *fuori le mura*—outside the walls—continue to have particular significance even for modern Romans.

In the sixth century B.C., an early king named Servius Tullius built fortifications to protect the nascent city, the so-called Servian Walls, of which only a few small sections remain. In the third century A.D., Emperor Aurelian began construction on a 12-mile (19 km) wall around the city. Maxentius continued the wall, which eventually doubled in height under subsequent emperors. When it was finished, the Aurelian Wall, as it is called, enclosed all seven hills, the Campus Martius, and Trastevere.

The mammoth ring of brick wall had an obvious function and a corresponding significance. Aurelian, who in A.D. 271 had already repelled the Alemanni Germanic tribes, had built the wall to protect the city in the event of another barbarian onslaught. All remained quiet until A.D. 410, when the Goths sacked the city. Romans hunkered down inside the city, leaving everything fuori le mura—the catacombs, monasteries, vineyards, and farmlands—vulnerable to the foreign assault. The growing realization that the walls were necessary marked the decline of an empire that once had been invincible.

As built by Aurelian, the wall was interspersed by a series of 18 *porte* (gates), many of which are still in use today. The gates were often access points to the consular roads.

Consular Roads

The first consular road, leading out from the massive Porta San Sebastiano, was the Via Appia, or Appian Way, inaugurated in 312 B.C. and named for the city's ruler, Appius Claudius Caecus, who also built the first aqueduct (the Appia). The Via Appia, once the site of grandiose funeral processions, such as that of the emperor Augustus in A.D. 14, and of triumphal marches into the city by returning army legions, soon became a cemetery for the rich and powerful: underground cemeteries for the multiple burials of the Christian dead. Today it is possible to visit them by walking in the wonderful Parco Regionale dell'Appia Antica which extends south of the capital. We find the Studios of Cinecittà along Via Tuscolana, a medieval road intersecting at some points the Via Appia for Frascati.

Another important consular road, in this case heading north, toward Rimini, was the Via Flaminia. Today in the quartiere Flaminio we find the MAXXI, Museo Nazionale delle Arti del XXI Secolo, the Auditorium Parco della Musica, designed by Renzo Piano and, on the opposite bank of the Tiber, the Foro Italico multisport complex, also including the Stadio Olimpico.

Between the quartiere Salario and Nomentano, in the northeast quadrant–the starting point of Via Salaria, which linked Rome to the Adriatic Sea, and Via Nomentana, which leads to Nomentum (present-day Mentana)–we find Villa Ada, Villa Torlonia, the Basilica di Sant'Agnese fuori le Mura, and the Museo di Arte Contemporanea MACRO.

Via Tiburtina begins behind Termini Station, toward the east: It links Rome with Tibur (Tivoli), and the historic quartiere di San Lorenzo, with the Basilica fuori le Mura of the same name and Verano cemetery.

Along Via Ostiense, heading for Ostia, we see the Basilica di San Paolo fuori le Mura and in the southwest quadrant, the rationalist architecture of the quartiere EUR. ■

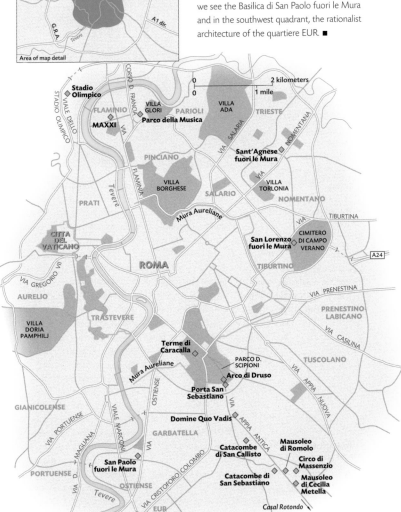

VIA APPIA ANTICA

Believe it or not, those large, irregular flagstones that still pave some sections of the Via Appia Antica—often rutted by the wheels of carts and chariots that passed here so very long ago—are original, hewn by hand from the basaltic lava cliffs. In many ways, thanks to unchanging nature, the scene here has not changed all that much over the centuries.

Via Appia Antica

🄰 Map p. 217

🚌 Bus: 118 (Basilica San Sebastiano), 218 (Ardeatina/ San Sebastiano), 660 (Cecilia Metella)

Parco dell'Appia Antica

✉ Via Appia Antica 58/60

☎ 06 5135 316

www.parcoappia antica.it

Museo delle Mura–Porta San Sebastiano

✉ Via di Porta San Sebastiano 18

☎ 060608

🕐 Closed Mon. & at 2 p.m. other days

www.museodelle muraroma.it

Catacombe di San Callisto

🄰 Map p. 217

✉ Via Appia Antica 110

☎ 06 5130 151

🕐 Closed noon– 2 p.m., Wed., & 4 weeks over Jan.–Feb.

💲 $$ (incl. guided tour in English)

www.catacombe .roma.it

Imperial roads are the most graphic evidence of Roman expansion.

The Via Appia Antica formally begins at **Porta San Sebastiano,** where there is a small, interesting **museum.** About 100 feet (30 m) on the right is the road's only extant original Roman milestone.

About half a mile (1 km) farther, on the left, is the **Domine Quo Vadis,** where Jesus is said to have appeared to Peter as he was fleeing Nero's persecutions and convinced him to return to Rome and certain martyrdom. This church faces a clearly marked entrance to the Catacombe di San Callisto; another entrance to the catacombs lies about half a mile (1 km) down the road.

Catacombe di San Callisto: The Catacombs of San Callisto are the best known of the Roman catacombs and the first official underground burial site for early Christians, including numerous second- and third-century martyrs. Excavations have revealed five different levels of *loculi,* niches where the bodies, wrapped in sheets, were placed in tiers. The openings to the loculi were closed with slabs of marble, but these have long since disappeared, as have any artifacts of value.

A major attraction of the 40-minute guided tour *(available in several languages)* is the **papal crypt,** which holds the remains of several martyred early popes. Nearby, with its Byzantine frescoes, is the **Cubiculum of St. Cecilia.** You won't find her body here, however; Pope Paschal I moved it to Santa Cecilia in

Trastevere (see pp. 194–195).

In the **Crypt of St. Eusebius** you will see a sarcophagus that contains two mummified bodies.

Catacombe di San Sebastiano:

Only a little farther along, in the church of San Sebastiano, are the catacombs of the same name. The church dates back to the early fourth century, when it was called the Basilica Apostolorum because the bodies of Peter and Paul were hidden here during one of the more violent periods of anti-Christian persecution.

Inside the Catacombs of San Sebastiano, archaeologists have excavated four levels. The tour of these catacombs, which have second-century **pagan tombs** along with Christian chapels, will take you down a staircase studded with pieces of sarcophagi with imperial seals.

For those of you with good legs, or a bicycle, the next several kilometers of the Via Appia become increasingly beautiful and evocative.

First, on the left, are the remains of the fortified **Villa di Massenzio** built by Emperor Maxentius (a.d. 306–312), whose siege mentality led him to avoid the Palatine Hill. The site includes the **Mausoleo di Romolo** (Mausoleum of Romulus), for his young son, and the **Circo di Massenzio,** a Roman circus that is smaller but better preserved than the Circo Massimo.

Next comes the massive, circular **Mausoleo di Cecilia Metella.** It's round shape clearly indicates that originally this was a tomb. The marble frieze has reliefs of flowers, ox skulls, and weapons.

Traveling on, you will find yourself increasingly in the open countryside, where umbrella pines alternate with funerary remains. Off to the left, you can see the ruins of the impressive second-century B.C. **Acqua Marcia** aqueduct, the longest of the aqueducts that supplied ancient Rome. ∎

Catacombe di San Sebastiano

- 🅼 Map p. 217
- ✉ Via Appia Antica 136
- ☎ 06 7850 350
- 🕐 Closed Sun. & Dec.
- 💲 $$ (incl. guided tour in English)

www.catacombe.org

Villa di Massenzio

- 🅼 Map p. 217
- ✉ Via Appia Antica 153
- ☎ 060608
- 🕐 Closed Mon. & at 4 p.m. other days
- 💲 $

Mausoleo di Cecilia Metella

- 🅼 Map p. 217
- ✉ Via Appia Antica 161
- ☎ 06 3996 7700 or www. coopculture.it (reservations)
- 🕐 Closed Mon.
- 💲 $

EXPERIENCE: Attending Sporting Events

The full Roman international sporting calendar begins in April with the Maratona di Roma: It starts and finishes at the Fori Imperiali. The route runs alongside the Tiber, then beneath the Vittoriano, in front of the Circo Massimo, and through Piazza Navona and Piazza di Spagna. The **Foro Italico,** a multi-sport complex built in the 1930s, has many events. In mid-May tennis enters the scene with the Internazionali d'Italia. At the beginning of June, attention moves to the Foro Italico athletics stadium for the Golden Gala Pietro Mennea, a regular meeting in the IAAF Diamond League, the athletics season rotating between 14 cities around the world. The Foro Italico also includes the **Stadio Olimpico,** the "home" of the two city soccer teams, AS Roma and SS Lazio, and venue of the Coppa Italia final, in May. In May and June, the Villa Borghese hosts the Piazza di Siena, one of the eight most prestigious equestrian events in the world. Italian participation in rugby is more recent: The Stadio Olimpico is the home venue for the Six Nations matches, but it is planned to convert the Stadio Flaminio for this.

QUARTIERE EUR

Designed in the 1930s for the 1942 Universal Exposition of Rome, from which the acronym stems, the quartiere EUR today has some examples of monumental architecture that coexist with the modern structures built in the following years. These include the Palazzo dell Civiltà Italiana, later known as the *Colosseo Quadrato* ("square Colosseum") because of the arches of the facades.

The convention center and Fuksas' Nuvola

A relaxing recreation area because of the amusement **Park Luneur** (*Via delle Tre Fontane 100, tel 345 1437 055, www.luneurpark.it*), the small lake, and the Palazzo dello Sport, where musical and sporting events take place, this elegant district southwest of the capital also houses an important museum complex.

Subdivided into four sections, the **Museo delle Civiltà** (*Piazza Guglielmo Marconi 14, tel 06 549521, museocivilta.beniculturali.it, closed Mon.*) comprises: the Museo Preistorico Etnografico Luigi Pigorini, the Museo delle Arti e Tradizioni Popolari Lamberto Loria, the Museo d'Arte Orientale Giuseppe Tucci, and the Museo dell'Alto Medioevo Alessandra Vaccaro. Unfortunately, the architectural reconstructions and scale models of the Museo della Civiltà Romana are not visible because the museum is currently closed for remodeling; it will reopen in the next few years.

The Parco Centrale del Lago, an artificial lake with an area as great as 914,932 square feet (85,000 sq m), also houses the **SEA LIFE Roma Aquarium** (*Piazza Umberto Elia Terracini, www.visitsealife.com/rome*); the rooms and sealed spaces are beneath the lake. Apart from the traditional aquarium, there is also an exhibition area, a reference point for the publicizing of scientific research on the marine activity in the Mediterranean. ∎

Roma Convention Center & the Nuvola

In 2016, a new convention center opened in the quartiere EUR (*Viale Asia snc, tel 06 5451 3710, romaconventiongroup.it, for opening times consult the online "calendario degli eventi," metro: Linea B/EUR Fermi*). Covering some 592,015 square feet (55,000 sq m), the center, which hosts conferences and exhibitions, is composed of three elements: the Nuvola (Cloud), Teca (Case), and Lama (Blade). The first element, the Nuvola, is the heart of the project. Created by Italian architect Massimiliano Fuksas, it comprises a load-bearing structure in steel—which supports the 1,800-seat auditorium and three levels of event rooms—as well as a secondary flexuous structure. Sheets of translucent fiberglass fixed to the beams of the secondary structure suggest the soft lines of a cloud. They cover a surface area of 161,459 square feet (15,000 sq m) and appear to be "floating" inside the Teca, the external "box" and second architectural element, the main site in the Corso delle Fiere. The third element is a hotel with more than 400 rooms beside the main structure.

THREE CHURCHES OUTSIDE THE WALLS

The Aurelian Wall encircled central Rome, but some important churches stand outside those fortifications: San Paolo, San Lorenzo, and Sant'Agnese, all of which have "fuori le mura" attached to their names to distinguish them from similarly named churches downtown.

The central nave of the Basilica di San Paolo fuori le Mura

San Paolo fuori le Mura

San Paolo fuori le Mura (St. Paul Outside the Walls) seems isolated today, but until the eighth century, the church was linked to the city by a long, covered portico that led to Porta San Paolo, the city's southernmost gate. It was built over the spot where St. Paul was buried after having been beheaded at the nearby Abbey of the Three Fountains.

A small basilica built here by Constantine was enlarged by subsequent emperors. By the ninth century, it was the largest church in Rome and reputedly the most beautiful. Unfortunately, it was destroyed in an 1823 fire. However, its 19th-century replacement is grandiose.

San Paolo's large central nave is flanked by two aisles separated by 80 columns. The **bronze doors,** which survived the fire, were made in Constantinople in 1070. Other pre-fire survivors include the fifth-century mosaics in the **Triumphal Arch,** a 13th-century mosaic in the apse, and more mosaic decoration on the inner side of the arch. Arnolfo di Cambio created the Gothic canopy over Paul's tomb in 1285. Don't miss the 18-foot (5.5 m) 13th-century cosmatesque **paschal candlestick,** decorated with scenes from the Passion of Christ. The Cosmati artisans who fashioned it also worked on the church's small **cloister,** with its fluted and spiraling colonnettes.

San Lorenzo fuori le Mura

San Lorenzo fuori le Mura (St. Lawrence Outside the Walls) is another of the seven pilgrim

San Paolo fuori le Mura

🅰 Map p. 217

✉ Piazzale San Paolo 1

☎ 06 698 0800

🚍 Bus: C6, 23, 128, 669, 769, 792. Metro: Linea B (Basilica San Paolo)

**San Lorenzo
fuori le Mura**

⚐ Map p. 217

✉ Piazzale del
Verano 3

☎ 06 491511

🕑 Closed 12:30–
4 p.m.

🚌 Bus: C2, C3, 71,
88, 163, 448,
492, 542, 545.
Tram: 3, 19

**Sant'Agnese
fuori le Mura**

⚐ Map p. 217

✉ Via Nomentana
349

☎ 06 8620 5456

🕑 Mausoleum
& catacombs:
closed 12 a.m.–3
p.m.; catacombs
also Sun. a.m.

💲 $ (incl. guided
tour of
catacombs)

🚌 Bus: 60, 66, 82,
89, 90, 168,
235, 310, 544.
Metro: Linea B
(Sant'Agnese)

churches. Unusually, it was formed from the fusion of two early churches, the Minor and Major Basilicas.

In A.D. 330, Emperor Constantine built a church to honor the martyr St. Lawrence. In the sixth century, Pope Pelagius rebuilt the minor basilica next door to a fifth-century place of worship honoring the Virgin Mary. In 1216, Honorius III knocked down their apses and joined the buildings together. The **chancel** and the ten superb Corinthian columns surrounding it are from Pelagius' church.

The **nave** and **aisles**, slightly lower in level, belonged to the second church. Its splendid 12th-century cosmatesque pavement was reconstructed after the war. In the portico, lovely frescoes dramatize the lives of the two saints. The remains of both are in the crypt. From the sacristy, in the right aisle, you exit into a charming 12th-century cloister.

Sant'Agnese fuori le Mura

About 2 miles (3 km) north of San Lorenzo lies the church of Sant'Agnese, who was martyred in A.D. 304 at age 13. Near the

burial place, a historical complex was built by Emperor Constantine's daughter Costantina (or Costantia). The Chiesa di Sant'Agnese, built in the seventh century by the wish of Pope Honorius I (A.D. 625–638), rose on the ruins of the cemetery basilica including the Catacombe di Sant'Agnese.

Enter the complex on ground level from Via Nomentana and then descend a broad staircase to reach the front entrance. Note the early Christian tombstones and inscriptions embedded in the walls.

The seventh-century **apse mosaic** has a gold background against which Sant'Agnese (with the sword of martyrdom at her feet) stands between two popes. The figures are totally Byzantine.

In contrast, the mosaic decoration in the ambulatory, or arcade, of **Santa Costanza** is an eloquent example of classical mosaic art. Note the absence of any explicit Christian symbolism or iconography, which had probably not yet developed. The ceiling is covered with a variety of distinctly pagan motifs—geometric, classical leafy scrolls, trees, and animals. ■

EXPERIENCE: Dream Factory

Has your biggest dream always been to live in ancient Rome or in 15th-century Florence? The famous Studios di Cinecittà (*Via Tuscolana 1055, tel 06 722861, cinecittasimostra.it, closed Tues., metro: Linea A/ Cinecittà*) will give you the chance. The studios are open to the public and it is possible to visit the great sets erected outside and the historical buildings with exhibition itineraries organized within them.

The scenes, the costumes, the props that tell the history and expertise of the Italian cinema will thrill all cinema fans. Among these: objects symbolizing the dream-like imagination of Fellini, placed in the scenographic reproduction of the *Colosseo Quadrato*, legendary costumes from films like *La Bisbetica domata* by Franco Zeffirelli, *Il Gattopardo* by Luchino Visconti, and *Per un pugno di dollari* by Sergio Leone.

MAXXI & PARCO DELLA MUSICA

Two inviting cultural sites beckon visitors beyond the city wall. The MAXXI, which opened in 2010, is developing into a premier museum of contemporary art and architecture, while the Parco della Musica, inaugurated in 2002, is one of the largest multifunctional music and events venues in the world.

MAXXI

MAXXI stands for Museum of the Arts of the 21st Century (Museo Nazionale delle Arti del XXI Secolo). But in Italian the name is particularly evocative since, in contemporary jargon, "maxi" means extremely large or important, be it a film screen or a building. This museum is the latest addition to Rome's "maxi" campaign. Conducted by Rome's municipal government, the campaign means to brush off some of the dust accumulated on the Eternal City's image in the world of contemporary art and architecture.

The museum also aspires to put Rome on the map for contemporary art and aims to be included on the short list of world-class museums such as the Tate Modern in London, MoMA in New York, the Reina Sofia in Madrid, and Beaubourg in Paris.

The 310,000-square-foot (29,000 sq m) museum complex is housed in a former military barracks in the Flaminio neighborhood, within walking distance of Renzo Piano's Parco della Musica. Of the 15 semifinalists in the 1999 international competition, the project presented by London-based superstar architect Zaha Hadid (and Patrik Schumacher) to create an

Works by Lucy + Jorge Orta in a 2012 exhibit at the MAXXI

urban campus dedicated to art and culture was judged to be the best. The 118,000-square-foot (11,000 sq m) display area is divided into two sections: **MAXXI Art** and **MAXXI Architecture.**

The art collection (which takes up roughly two-thirds of the museum's display space) already counts more than 400 works by artists like Boetti, Clemente, Kapoor, Kentridge, Merz, Penone, Pintaldi, Richter, and Warhol. The architecture section (occupying about a third of the museum) holds the archives of world-class architects and engineers of international repute, such as Carlo Scarpa, Aldo Rossi, and Pierluigi Nervi, as well as projects by contemporary architects like Toyo Ito, Italo Rota, and Giancarlo De Carlo.

MAXXI

Map p. 217

Via Guido Reni 4a

06 3201 954 (info line) or 892234 (reservations)

Closed Mon. Open 11 a.m.– 7 p.m. (till 10 p.m. on Sat.)

$$

www.maxxi.art

Parco della Musica

🗺 Map p. 217

✉ Viale Pietro de Coubertin 30

☎ 06 8024 1281 (info line), 060608 or 892101 (box office)

🚌 Bus: 53, 168, 217, 282, 910. Tram: 2. Metro: Linea A (Piazza Flaminio)

www.auditorium.com

In addition to display space, the MAXXI complex includes an auditorium, library, bookshop, cafeteria, and areas indoor and out for temporary exhibits.

Parco della Musica

Not all of the *fuori le mura* sites have been around for millennia. Inaugurated in 2002, the Parco della Musica is the biggest multifunction complex in Europe and one of the ten largest in the world. It already boasts one of the highest rates of attendance among similar structures, probably thanks to the wide variety of special events it hosts in addition to its regularly scheduled chamber music, symphonic, jazz, and rock concerts.

Designed by internationally acclaimed architect Renzo Piano, the main attractions are the three mushroom-shaped halls for indoor concerts, authentic resonance boxes, among them, the Sala di

Santa Cecilia, with cherrywood panels to make the listening experience unforgettable. They are clustered around an **open-air amphitheater** *(cavea)* that, in summer, constitutes a fourth venue. There are also conference rooms, spaces for temporary exhibits, a bookshop, library, bars, and even the remains of a Roman imperial villa.

Opened in early 2008, the **Museo degli Strumenti Musicali** (Museum of Musical Instruments; *open 11 a.m.–6 p.m., closed Wed.*) houses one of Italy's main collections of musical instruments. But it is best known as the home of Rome's Accademia Nazionale di Santa Cecilia *(www.santacecilia.it)*, a symphonic orchestra and choral group.

Do you prefer the cinema? In the fall, there is the **Festa del Cinema di Roma** *(www.romacinema fest.it)*, of which the first edition took place in 2006. ∎

EXPERIENCE: The Museum Becomes City

The main site of MACRO (*Via Nizza 138, tel. 06 696271, closed Mon., www.museomacro.it*) has been a reference point for contemporary art in the capital for about 20 years. It is located near Porta Pia, in the quartiere Salario-Nomentano. At the moment, an experimental project conceived by Giorgio de Finis is in progress: It is intended to transform the entire museum into a real hospitable living organism. The idea is to establish a lasting connection with the public, to open all the spaces of the museum, and to promote interaction between visitors and the world of art. Thus, not only are there artistic, theatrical, and musical performances in the auditorium, video projections in the foyer, and permanent exhibitions in the Sala Rome and the Sala Lettura, but it is also possible to be present at the creation of works of art at the very moment when artists are about to create them. The spaces "Atelier" and "Ambienti" on the second and third floors of the building have been designated for this purpose. They will be occupied by a rotation of different artists who will create their works every week or monthly. The Sala Rome (Romes) invites all the community and the institutions to propose ideas for the capital by participating in the work in the room around a *tavolo mappa* (map table) representing the city, and to place their proposals in the enormous set of drawers against the wall.

Bewitching scenery, seaside resorts, lakes, charming hill towns, and important historical monuments

EXCURSIONS

■ Detail of the Fontana della Natura in the Villa d'Este, Tivoli

EXCURSIONS

At its height, the influence of the Roman Empire extended as far north as Britain, as far south as North Africa, and over all of Asia Minor and much of the Middle East. But the first focus of Roman expansion was, as is natural, close to home.

According to legend, Ancus Marcius, the fourth king of Rome, founded Ostia, the seaport at the mouth of the Tiber River in the seventh century B.C. This is probably just a legend; the earliest remains found at Ostia date from the fourth century B.C., and the colony, in the form of a *castrum* (fortified city), was probably founded at that time.

Whatever the actual date, it was clear from the start that an outlet to the Mediterranean would be essential for Rome's growth and expansion, and indeed Ostia was to have immense strategic and commercial importance. It was, for example, the terminus for the massive grain imports from North Africa that allowed Rome to implement the policy of *panem et circensis* (bread and circuses) that proved successful in assuring the affections of the populace. Ostia was the headquarters for the Annona, which supplied Rome with

grain and distributed it (generally at no cost) to the people. The Annona's presence in Ostia gave impetus to the proliferation there of guilds and corporations involved in other

---

INSIDER TIP:

Rome is a big, bustling city— if you need to slow it down for a day, take a local train to one of the small, charming towns just outside the city. You'll be surprised at how dramatically the landscape changes from urban to pastoral in only 12 miles (20 km).

—SARAH YEOMANS
Archaeologist & National Geographic contributor

NOT TO BE MISSED:

kinds of trade. The mosaic remains of their storefronts in the Piazzale delle Corporazioni testify to their importance. So does the advanced level of decorative embellishment in the city in general, the proliferation of baths and temples, and of the *insulae* (multistory apartment houses) that give you a good idea of what life was like in ancient Rome as well.

Tivoli

Early expansion also looked eastward, and it wasn't long before the Romans set their sights on Tibur (modern-day Tivoli) in the Sabine Hills. Originally inhabited by tribes such as the Sabines and the Volsci, Tibur was conquered first by Tiburnus or Tiburtus, the son or grandson of a Greek hero named

Amphiaraos, and quickly became the target of Roman attentions because of its strategic location on the banks of the Aniene river. Not surprisingly, when conflict between the two finally broke out, Rome emerged as the victor and Tibur's fate was sealed.

By the first century B.C. Tibur's relatively cool climate and lush vegetation had made it a highly touted holiday resort for well-born, well-off Romans. It was here, in fact, that Augustus came to consult the Albunea Sibyl, who reportedly saw in one of the young emperor's dreams the onset of Christianity, thereby winning him an unusual special mention in the iconography of the Aracoeli church on Capitoline Hill in Rome.

Brutus and Cassius, Julius Caesar's assassins, had villas here, as did the poets Horace and Catullus. And it was to Tibur that emperors such as Trajan and his successor, Hadrian, repaired to wait out the hot and sultry summer months, far from the heat of Rome. Even Totila, the Ostragoth chieftain who briefly conquered Rome in the sixth century, made Tibur the capital of his short-lived reign.

It was, however, Hadrian (A.D. 117–138) who really put Tibur on the map. His magnificent imperial villa (Villa Adriana) may well be the major architectural achievement of the philosopher-emperor from Spain to whom one must already feel grateful for the Pantheon and Castel Sant'Angelo.

The town's traditional appeal to the Roman elite may have reached its apex during the Renaissance, most notably after 1550, when Cardinal Ippolito II, a scion of the wealthy d'Este family, became governor and settled here. The d'Estes' architects turned an old monastery into a sumptuous palace, embellishing it with magnificently elaborate terraced gardens and a Mannerist complex of secluded grottoes, classical statuary, waterfalls, and cascading fountains. ∎

OSTIA ANTICA

Follow the Tiber River out of Rome, down to its mouth on the Mediterranean, and see the fascinating ruins of the ancient settlement of Ostia. A Roman military installation and a major commercial port, the once thriving city's second-century B.C. population exceeded 100,000.

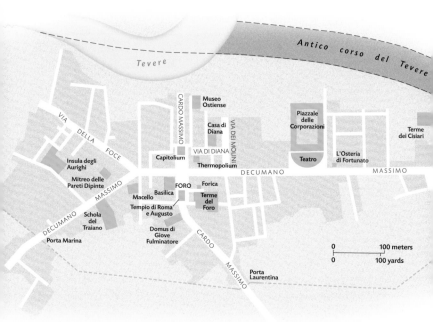

Located only 14 miles (23 km) from Rome, Ostia is easily reached by car or train, and its limited size makes navigation simple. Unlike Pompeii, this hauntingly lovely site was not a resort for the rich and powerful; it was an urban complex made up for the most part of ordinary people. It had baths, temples, a civic center, and *insulae* (multi-story apartment houses) similar to those in Rome.

History of Ostia

The name Ostia comes from *ostium*, the Latin word for "river

mouth." It was probably Rome's first colony, and the oldest remains found date from the fourth century B.C. By late republican times (the second century B.C.), it had become Rome's major port, as well as an important naval outpost.

Throughout the first two centuries of the imperial period, Ostia flourished and acquired all the trappings—forums, basilicas, porticoes—of an important urban center. It maintained its primacy until Constantine's reign in the fourth century, when it gradually became more residential.

Ostia was home to shippers and shipbuilders, merchants and traders, tanners, ropemakers, tavern keepers, prostitutes, and priests. The city's lower- and middle-class residents lived in rooms or apartment buildings that by law could climb as high as four stories (about 46 feet/14 m).

At its apex, Ostia had all the amenities of a leading Roman city, including a lovely theater (still used in summer), scores of bathhouses, shops, temples, and taverns, as well as commercial offices, which were concentrated in the Piazzale delle Corporazioni, a sort of ancient mall or port authority.

Decumano Massimo

To get the best possible sense of this ancient coastal town you'll need several hours. Start at the beginning of the Decumano Massimo, the main drag, lined with shops, baths, theaters, and warehouses. This street was a continuation of the Via Ostiense, which connected Ostia to Rome. It is crossed at midpoint by the Cardo Massimo.

Just inside the Porta Romana, the city's main gateway, is a large **statue of Minerva Vittoria** (Victory) from the first century A.D. To the right, a path leads to the **Terme dei Cisiari,** the Carter Guild's Bathhouse, with a black-and-white mosaic of a cart and driver that you shouldn't miss.

Continue along the Decumano to the **Osteria di Fortunato,** or Tavern of Fortunatus. The mosaic inscription on the floor (an early advertisement?) reads, "Fortunatus says: Drink from this bowl to quench your thirst." Farther on is the **teatro,** or theater, built by Agrippa. It held 2,000 to 3,000 people. Originally, there were three tiers of seats (the top one has not survived) and, like today, there were snack stands in the alcoves between the external arches on the ground floor.

The pulse of second-century Ostia may have beat hardest, however, in the **Piazzale delle Corporazioni,** a huge portico behind the theater, where some 70 local guilds and foreign corporations had their offices. Their trademarks, which have supplied historians with invaluable information, are immortalized in the arcade's mosaic floors.

Via di Diana

Continue along the Decumano to the Via dei Molini, turn right. then take the first left, Via di Diana. The **Casa di Diana,** a large *insula,* had shops on the ground floor, apartments with windows on the first floor, and balconies higher up.

INSIDER TIP:

In a beautiful location in the countryside, Ostia Antica is a perfect place to imagine life in the times of the Roman Empire.

—CJ FAHEY
National Geographic contributor

Ostia Antica
- Map p. 227
- Viale dei Romagnoli 717, Ostia
- 06 5635 8099
- Closed Mon.
- $$
- Metro: Linea B to the Piramide, Basilica San Paolo, or EUR Magliana stops; then take the train of the urban railroad Roma–Lido to the Ostia Antica stop

www.ostiaantica.beniculturali.it

Next is the **Thermopolium,** a restaurant or snack bar with stone seats near the door (for waiting customers, perhaps?), an L-shaped counter, and holes in the wall, probably for coat hooks. Faded frescoes depict the day's fare. You can just make out eggs, fruits, and vegetables.

If you turn right at the next crossroads, you'll come to the **Museo Ostiense,** which displays artworks found during excavations. A snack bar and bookshop are behind it. Otherwise, turn left on the Cardo Massimo.

Cardo Massimo

The Cardo and Decumano intersect at the **Foro,** or Forum. At one end of the square was the **Capitolium.** Ostia's major temple—dedicated to Jupiter, Juno, and Minerva—still has the broad staircase that leads up to the *cella.* Niches once held statues of the gods. At the opposite end of the Forum was a second temple, **Tempio di Roma e Augusto,** dedicated to Rome and Augustus. The *terme,* or baths, and the basilica, or law courts, flanked the area. Don't miss the *forica* (public latrine) near the baths.

"Newer" Ostia

If you continue along the Decumano, you will eventually leave the *castrum* (the earlier, fortified city) and enter the newer Ostia Antica. Take Via della Foce to the right, from which a pathway to the right leads to the **Domus di Amore e Psiche,** richly decorated with a polychrome marble pavement. Continue on to see the charioteer frescoes at the **Insula degli Aurighi.**

Find your way back to the Decumano, where there is a traders' guild, the **Schola del Traiano.** Back behind the Temple of Rome and Augustus, on the Cardo, are a number of elegant one-story houses. The **Domus di Giove Fulminatore** has an interesting welcome mat: a mosaic depicting a phallus. ∎

EXPERIENCE: Join Romans at the Beach

When in Rome, do as the Romans do and head for the closest beach. Located some 15.5 miles (25 km) west of Rome on the Tyrrhenian shore, **Lido di Ostia** is a major destination for those seeking sun and surf. On an average summer day, as many as 55,000 people descend on this satellite city of 250,000 inhabitants to frolic in the sand.

You may find totally free beaches, where bathers use their towels or bring their own beach chairs. But most Romans prefer to use *stabilimenti,* or beach clubs.

From Rome, you can drive to Ostia, or take the train from one of the stations of the urban railway line Roma–Lido (Piramide, San Paolo, EUR Magliana). Get off at Stella Polare, Castel Fusano, or Cristoforo Colombo.

If you are looking for less crowded beaches, continue south along the coast by taking the bus in the direction of Torvaianica/Campo Ascolano (Linea 07) from the terminus of the railroad line Roma–Lido (Cristoforo Colombo). You will reach the municipal bathing facilities known as the *cancelli* and the beaches of Castelporziano and Capocotta; the last is particularly suitable for those interested in nudism.

TIVOLI

Green hills, rivers, and cascading waterfalls—for centuries, ancient Tibur (later Tivoli) was a well-known summer resort. If contemporary Tivoli has unfortunately lost much of its charm under the onslaught of runaway postwar building construction, the historic center still retains much of the atmosphere of a medieval hill town.

■ The atmosphere of the Villa d'Este is conducive to study and reflection.

Throughout its history, Tivoli has been a favored resort destination among Romans, but its fame as a getaway was greatly heightened by Emperor Hadrian's decision to make it the site of his magnificent imperial villa. The inventiveness of his design enabled him to create a sprawling residence where intellectuals and friends could enjoy the pleasures of a contemplative life.

More than a thousand years later, a noble Renaissance churchman decided to make life in Tivoli bearable by turning a dilapidated Benedictine monastery into the lovely Villa d'Este. This was embellished by one of the most fascinating garden and fountain complexes in the world, listed by UNESCO as one of Italy's 54 World Heritage sites of historical/artistic import.

The **Rocca Pia,** a fortress built over the ruins of a Roman amphitheater, dates back to the 15th century. There are some lovely churches. **Santa Maria Maggiore,** a fifth-century church next door to Villa d'Este, was rebuilt in the 13th century and has a Gothic portal set in a Romanesque facade. The church

Tivoli
🅰 Map p. 227
Visitor Information
✉ Piazzale Nazioni Unite
☎ 07 7431 3536
🕐 Closed 1–4 p.m. & Mon.
🚇 Metro: Linea B to Ponte Mammolo, then CoTral bus to Tivoli. Trains depart regularly from Tiburtina Station (Roma-Pescara line) to Tivoli Station, then shuttle bus

Villa d'Este

- Map p. 227
- Piazza Trento 5
- 199 766 166 (suggestion: call to make sure fountains are working)
- Closed Mon. p.m.; hours vary seasonally
- $$ Audio guide: $. Guided tours in English on request: $$$
- Metro: Linea B to Ponte Mammolo, then CoTral bus to Tivoli. Trains depart regularly from Tibertina Station (Roma-Pescara line) to Tivoli Station, then shuttle bus

www.villadeste
tivoli.info

of **San Silvestro,** charmingly Romanesque except for a hideous, recently built glass front door and a couple of garish shrines, contains some extremely attractive 13th-century frescoes. Next door is an interesting fountainhead and nearby is the attractive Casa Gotica (Gothic House). **San Lorenzo,** the Duomo, unfortunately was rebuilt in the 17th century, but the 12th-century "Triptych of the Saviour," in wood with a 15th-century gold-and-silver cover, is definitely worth a look. The same goes for the disturbingly modern-looking 13th-century "Deposition" group.

Walk down Via Valerio and along Via della Sibilla to the Sibilla restaurant to see the remains of both the circular **Tempio di Vesta** and the rectangular **Tempio della Sibilla.** Not far from here, on Largo Sant'Angelo, is the entrance to the gardens of **Villa Gregoriana,** with its lovely waterfall.

Villa d'Este

Cardinal Ippolito II, a son of Lucrezia Borgia, wanted to be pope. But things didn't work out, so in around 1550 this scion of the wealthy d'Este family of Ferrara settled for the governorship of Tivoli and decided to make the best of it.

Money was not a problem for the cardinal, who wasted no time in engaging the services of major architects to transform an old monastery into a sumptuous palace, the Villa d'Este.

After dispossessing many small landowners, the architects embellished the new villa with magnificently extensive

terraced gardens and an elaborate Mannerist complex of secluded grottoes, classical statuary, and fountains. After the cardinal died, the villa fell into neglect. In the 1920s, it was restored and opened to the public.

Among the most bewitching of the villa's mossy **fountains** are the Fontana del Bicchierone (water pours out from a large shell-shaped basin), attributed by many art historians to Bernini; the

---

INSIDER TIP:

Many towns in Italy hosts an annual *sagra,* or town party. Visit the websites *www. romatoday.it* and *www. lazioinfesta.com* to find a local sagra taking place during your stay.

—CJ FAHEY
National Geographic contributor

Rometta Fountain, which is a miniature Rome complete with Tiber, Tiber Island, and a wolf-suckling Romulus and Remus; the Avenue of the Hundred Fountains, where animal heads, lilies, a small boat, basins, and so on all spurt water; the Fontana dell'Ovato, whose sibyl watches over naiads and river gods; the Fontana dell'Organo, which once played music; and the Owl and Bird Fountain that once made hooting and chirping sounds. You can also visit the rooms of the *appartamento nobile,* but make sure you don't miss the **Loggia dello Scalone,** the terrace, from which there is a lovely view.

Villa Adriana

Just a few miles outside of Tivoli lie the ruins of Emperor Hadrian's villa, or summer estate, undoubtedly the largest and most elaborate Roman imperial palace ever to have existed. As one can see from the plaster model in the kiosk near the entrance, it extends over a broad area and includes the remains of an enormous villa, with baths, theaters, libraries, and extensive gardens. Underground is a network of tunnels, some large enough for a horse and carriage. Choose a nice day and plan on spending several hours. It is best to buy a brochure in the bookstore adjacent to the café and follow the suggested itinerary.

After you enter, walk up the hill and pass through the high perimeter wall to find yourself at midpoint in the **Pecile,** a large square, said to have been modeled on the Stoa Pokile of Athens. The square was originally covered and surrounded by a portico. As you will see, it is also the upper story of a vast building with hundreds of rooms, probably for slaves and other palace staff.

Continuing on you come to the Small Baths and the Large Baths, much of which are still standing. Next is one of the complex's most mystical monuments, the **Canopus,** a 750-foot-long (228 m) reflecting pool. It is surrounded by columns and statues (don't miss the river god or the stone crocodile) and ends in a large nymphaeum that once held fountains and statues. The pool may have been inspired by the canal that linked Alexandria in Egypt to ancient Canopus. Along the west side stand six caryatids like those on the Erechtheum on the Acropolis in Athens.

Return via the Stadium and the Room With Three Exhedrae, or apses (probably a large outdoor dining room), to reach the remains of the **palace proper,** an enormous structure composed of pavilions built around peristyles, or courtyards. Don't miss the Fishpool Quadriportico; the Hall of the Doric Columns; the Heliocaminus Baths, which may have been heated by solar power; the circular Maritime Theater; and the Republican Villa, where you can see the remains of mosaic floors and vault decorations. ■

Villa Adriana

🅰 Map p. 227

✉ Largo Marguerite Yourcenar 1

☎ 07 7438 2733 or 06 3996 7900. Online tickets: www.coopculture .it

🕔 Closed at sunset

💲 $$. Audio guide: $. Guided tours in English on request: $$$

🚇 Metro: Linea B to Ponte Mammolo, then CoTral bus (direction Via Prenestina), which stops 330 yds/300 m from site. Or train from the Stazione Tiburtina to Tivoli, then CAT bus No. 4, which also stops 330 yds/300 m from site

www.villaadriana. beniculturali.it

Hadrian's Masterpiece

Hadrian ruled between A.D. 117 and 138. He began building Villa Adriana shortly after he ascended the throne and completed it in A.D. 133, although by that time he was ill and grief-stricken by the deaths of his wife and of Antinous, his young lover.

Much traveled and highly educated, Hadrian is known for other architectural achievements, such as the Pantheon and Castel Sant'Angelo in Rome, but the villa is his masterpiece. When he built the villa, Hadrian sought to re-create, or evoke, some of the world's architectural wonders. The vast sprawling site (almost 300 acres/121 ha) was designed both as a monument to man's achievements and as a place for study and reflection.

More Excursions from Rome

Italians love Sunday outings, and fortunately for Romans the regional bus company CoTral goes most places *(tel 800 174 471 or 06 7205 7205, www.cotralspa.it).* If you have a car, so much the better, as all roads leading out of Rome go someplace interesting. Here are some suggestions.

Castelli Romani

Situated among the chestnut trees, olive groves, and vineyards that cover the slopes of extinct volcanoes, the Castelli Romani (Roman Castles) are small towns in the Alban Hills southeast of Rome best known for their white wine, *porchetta* (roast pork), and restaurants.

Founded in the Middle Ages, **Frascati**—home of the once best-known Roman white wine—became a resort for the wealthy, who built luxurious villas (many of which, sadly, were damaged during World War II). The best preserved is Villa Aldobrandini, while the park attached to Villa Torlonia has wonderful fountains designed by Carlo Maderno. Nearby is the Etruscan settlement of **Tusculum.** The view from the ruins, which include a forum, a small theater, and an amphitheater, is wonderful.

Grottaferrata's beautiful fortified Greek-rite abbey was founded by St. Nilus in the tenth century and later incorporated into a castle. Don't miss the St. Nilus Chapel in the church of Santa Maria, with Domenichino's wonderful frescoes. **Marino,** on Lake Albano, is known for its October wine festival, when the town fountains spew forth wine rather than water. There's a Guido Reni painting in the Trinità church and a Mithraeum with interesting frescoes. Medieval **Rocca di Papa** is the highest of the Castelli, whereas the most charming town is **Nemi,** with a Renaissance castle that overlooks a miniscule lake in a crater. The remains of two of the emperor Caligula's pleasure boats (burned by the Germans in 1944) are housed in a small museum. Across Lake Nemi, **Genzano,** with its lovely lakeside restaurants and a 13th-century castle, is known for the June *"infiorata"* when

the streets are "paved" with pictures made out of flower petals.

Near Albano, once the Castra Albana, headquarters of Rome's Second Legion, is the Etruscan-style Roman tomb of the Horatii and Curiatii. And **Castel Gandolfo's** castle, the pope's summer residence, was built by Carlo Maderno over an earlier fortress. The fountain in the piazza is by Bernini.
www.visitcastelliromani.it 🅰 Map p. 227 **Visitor Information** ✉ Piazza Marconi 1, Frascati ☎ 06 9420 331 (Frascati), 06 4540 1679 (Grottaferrata), 06 9366 2386 (Marino) 🚇 Metro: Linea A to Anagnina then CoTral bus to all Castelli Romani towns. Train: Termini Station to Frascati

Palestrina

Some say ancient Praeneste was founded by Ulysses' son, Telegonus. In any case, this medieval town outside Rome is built over the remains of the **Sanctuary of Fortuna Primigenia,** a Roman shrine that dates back to the second century B.C. This may have been the largest Hellenistic construction in Italy, a series of climbing terraces culminating in a (now) partially reconstructed temple. Its foundations are incorporated into the Palazzo Colonna-Barberini, currently the site of the **Museo Archeologico Nazionale Prenestino,** *(Via Barberini 2, tel 06 9538 100),* which houses numerous statues, artifacts, and reliefs. But its prized possession is the remarkable **Nile Mosaic,** discovered in the city's ancient forum.

Don't miss the **Cathedral of St. Agapitus** *(tel 06 9534 428),* with a 12th-century campanile that was built over the remains of a pagan temple. A grill opens onto a small section of Roman road. The city was also home to Renaissance musician Giovanni Pierluigi da Palestrina, the creator of contrapuntal composition.
🅰 Map p. 227 🚇 Metro: Linea A to Anagnina then CoTral bus to Palestrina. Train: Termini Station to Zagarolo, then CoTral bus to Palestrina

TRAVELWISE

With parking hard to find, small cars make sense in Rome.

TRAVELWISE

Rome is a very rewarding city to visit and, on the whole, it's also very welcoming. However, some aspects of life here are difficult to understand for those used to a more streamlined (and less idiosyncratic) way of doing things. Although tales of Italian inefficiency may well be exaggerated, there is no doubt that some of your transactions may take far longer, or be much more complicated, than you would have expected.

PLANNING YOUR TRIP

When to Go

Rome has a typical Mediterranean climate, with moderate winters (average 50°–59°F/10°–15°C) and hot dry summers—sometimes oppressively so in July and August. Spring and autumn are mild with clear skies. November and December are the wettest months. From May through summer, Rome's social life takes place outdoors. Restaurants and bars move their tables onto the streets, and there is a plethora of open-air music and arts festivals. Many stores and restaurants close in August, but fewer than in previous years. Romans have learned that the city can be enjoyable in August, when traffic jams end and the thermometer normally drops a bit compared to July. In recent years hotel prices have risen significantly, but in the off-season (Oct.–Nov. & Jan.–Feb.) they are considerably lower.

What to Take

Unless you have a work meeting or a special occasion to attend, casual clothes prevail. In spring and fall it's a good idea to dress in layers as temperatures in the evenings sometimes drop sharply. If you plan on visiting churches, make sure you pack clothes that cover your knees and shoulders (this applies to both men and women). Rome is best seen on foot, so bring comfortable shoes as the cobblestoned streets can be tough on your feet. It is wise to pack a hat for protection from the hot summer sun, and an umbrella if you are planning a visit in winter. Binoculars are useful if you want a closer look at the lavishly decorated interiors. Other essentials are your passport, driver's license, credit cards, and insurance documentation.

Insurance

Take out enough travel insurance to cover emergency medical treatment, repatriation, and loss or theft of money and possessions.

HOW TO GET TO ROME

Visa Requirements & Passports

You can enter Italy on your passport which must be valid for at least three months after the date foreseen for leaving the Schengen Area. On entering Italy, immigration can ask you to show documentation supporting the reasons for and duration of your stay in Italy. Schengen citizens, EU citizens, and citizens of some non-Schengen countries, among which are the United States, Canada, and Australia, can remain in Italy and in the Schengen Area countries for 90 days without a tourist or work visa. Citizens of all other non-Schengen countries need a visa to visit Italy and other countries in the area, whatever the reason for their visit.

Arriving by Plane

Rome has two international airports, Leonardo da Vinci–Fiumicino, about 18.5 miles (30 km) west of Rome, and the smaller Ciampino, 9 miles (15 km) southeast of the city, which currently serves low-cost airlines and charters only; both are managed by Aeroporti di Roma (tel 06 65951). For information on airport facilities, its website (www.adr.it) has plenty of useful information for the traveler, including transportation to and from the airport and real-time arrival and departure times.

Getting to Rome From Leonardo da Vinci–Fiumicino Airport

Two railroad services link the airport to the center of Rome. The **Leonardo Express** leaves every day from Roma Termini from 5:35 a.m. onwards, leaving every 15 minutes in rush hours and every 30 minutes outside rush hours, and is direct; from the airport from 6:08 a.m. until 11:23 p.m.; the journey costs €14 and lasts about 30 minutes.

The **regional train FRL** leaves every 15 minutes, 30 minutes on Saturdays, Sundays, and public holidays, and links the airport with various city stations, among them Trastevere, Ostiense, and Tiburtina; the service from the airport to the city is from 5:57 a.m. until 11:37 p.m., and the one from the city to the airport from 5:01 a.m. until 10 p.m.; the journey lasts 40 minutes and costs €8.

For exact departure times, see www.trenitalia.com (tip: To search, enter "Fiumicino Aeroporto" and "Roma Termini" for the Leonardo Express or "Roma" for the FL1 service).

The following bus companies also link the airport to the

Termini Station: **Sitbus Shuttle** *(tel 06 5916826, www.sitbusshuttle. com, fare €6),* **Terravision** *(www. terravision.eu, fare €5,80),* **Rome Autobus-Schiaffini** *(tel 06 7130531, www.romeairportbus.com, fare €6,90).* Service starts early in the morning, with buses departing regularly throughout the day and into the evening. For departure times check each company's website. The trip takes about one hour, longer at peak traffic times. The **CoTral** bus company *(tel 800 174471, www. cotralspa.it)* runs a night service to and from the airport; it costs €5 (€7 if bought on the bus).

Getting to Rome From Ciampino Airport
There is no direct train from Ciampino Airport to central Rome. **Rome Autobus-Schiaffini** *(tel 06 7130531, www.romeairport bus.com, fare €6,90)* runs a bus shuttle to Anagnina Station on the metro's A line, where you can catch a train to Termini Station. The company also provides a service linking the airport to Termini Station *(fare €5.90).* Other companies providing the same service are **Sitbus Shuttle** *(www. sitbusshuttle.com, fare €4–€6)* and **Terravision** *(www.terravision.eu, fare €5).* Buses start early and run frequently throughout the day until late at night. The trip takes about 40 minutes, longer at peak traffic times.

Taxi & NCC
According to the new regulations, there are fixed fares for the taxi journey from Fiumicino to the center of Rome (within the Mura Aureliane), and vice versa, and for the taxi journey from Ciampino to the center of Rome, and vice versa. The cost is €48 to and from Fiumicino and €30 to and from Ciampino. For further information, consult the site of the Comune di Roma

(www.comune.roma.it). You can choose a white taxi managed by the municipal service or a private NCC taxi (car rental with driver), *(tel 06 89561862, www.ncc.roma.it)* for a personalized service.

Limousine & Shuttle Service
Airport Connection Service *(tel 338 9876465, www.airportconnec tion.it)* offers a shuttle and limousine service to Rome's airports and other cities in Italy. **Air Port Shuttle** *(tel 06 4201 3469, www. airportshuttle.it)* serves the airports at reasonable rates. **Shuttle Door to Door** *(tel 380 4989782, www.shuttlerome.it)* offers shared transfers from the airports to hotels and accommodation, with compulsory booking.

Arriving by Train
Roma Termini *(Piazza dei Cinquecento, www.romatermini. com)* is the historical train station in Rome and hub for city public transportation. Both metro lines intersect here and a major city bus depot is located out front. **Roma Tiburtina** *(Piazzale Della Stazione Tiburtina, www.stazioneroma tiburtina.it)* is now becoming the main railroad station in Rome, a high-speed hub with galleria shopping. Located in northeastern Rome, the station serves regional, national, and international trains. There are also several smaller stations, the most important being Trastevere and Ostiense, where you can get the regional train for Fiumicino Airport.

GETTING AROUND
By Car
A car in Rome is more of a hindrance than a help. For a good part of the day and night the historic center is a limited traffic area (ZTL) with cameras at entry points. If you enter when the ZTL sign says "Varco Attivo" and you are without a ZTL pass, you will be fined. Park-

ing is nearly impossible, the local driving style seems undisciplined, and gas is expensive. If you do have a car, it is best to park it and visit Rome using public transportation. Check out these websites for centrally located parking: *www. sabait.it/en/parking* (for Spanish Steps area) and *www.myparking. eu* (search for "Rome Vatican" or Rome Termini Station").

Car Rentals
Check for the most competitive prices before leaving home. Major rental companies include the following:
Avis, tel 06 452108391, www.avis.com
Budget, www.budget.it
Europcar, www.europcar.com
Hertz, www.hertz.com
Maggiore, tel 06 22456060, www.maggiore.com
Sixt, tel 02 58240502, www.sixt.com

Driving Regulations & Conventions
When driving in Italy you need to carry the vehicle registration, valid insurance, a valid national license, and, unless your license was issued by an EU member state, an international driving permit. Italian law makes seatbelts obligatory and also prohibits driving while using a cell phone without a headset.

Outside Rome, headlights should be on even in daytime. There are official speed limits; 30 miles an hour (50 kph) in built-up areas, 70 miles an hour (110 kph) on other roads, and 80 miles an hour (130 kph) on toll roads (Autostrade). The legal limits for drinking and driving have been toughened and now are about two (women) to three glasses of wine, less for hard liquor. For further information, consult the excellent site of the **Automobile Club d'Italia** *(tel 803116, www.aci.it).*

The police may tow away your car if you are parked illegally; if you think this has happened call the Polizia Municipale *(tel 06 67691)*.

Car Breakdowns

Rental car companies have an emergency number for breakdowns. Otherwise call the emergency number of the **Automobile Club d'Italia** *(tel 803116, then press "3" to get an English-speaking operator)*. Foreigners do not have to join; they pay a per-incident fee.

Public Transportation

Buses, trams, the metro, and local rail services in Rome are all integrated into one transportation system.To plan your route around the city check out the excellent websites *www.muoversiaroma.it* or *www.atac.roma.it*. A regular ticket (BIT) costs €1.50 and entitles you to 100 minutes of travel. The Roma 24H costs €7 and lasts 24 hours from the first validation. There are also Roma 48H and Roma 72H, which last 48 and 72 hours respectively from the first validation. A weekly pass (CIS) costs €24. All the above tickets allow unlimited bus, tram, and metro rides.

The tickets can be bought at most tobacconists, newsstands *(edicole)*, ATAC booths, and at machines placed in key locations. Some buses have ticket-dispensing machines that work with coins. Tickets of longer duration can be bought at authorized newsstands, tobacconists, and ATAC booths (see *www .muoversiaroma.it* for information on the closest location). Children up to age ten travel for free.

All tickets must be validated at the start of your first ride and again if your ticket is about to expire, or if you switch to the metro. Yellow-validating machines for doing this are on the buses and at the entrances to stations. Keep your ticket until the end of your journey; if you

cannot produce it when asked, you are liable for a fine of at least €50.

Metro

Rome has three subway lines, A, B, and C, which operate from 5:30 a.m. to 11:30 p.m. (Fri. *&* Sat. until 1:30 a.m.). Line A runs across the city from Battistini to Anagnina and intersects with Line B at Termini Station. Line B runs from Rebibbia to Laurentina in the EUR district. Line B1 from Laurentina to Jonio. Line C, the most recent, which is being extended, links San Giovanni (where it meets Line A) to Monte Compatri-Pantano.

Buses & Trams

ATAC *(www.atac.roma.it)* has a vast bus and tram system. On weekdays most lines run until midnight or 12:30 a.m; there are several nighttime *(notturni)* lines as well. Several small, electric buses navigate the historic center's narrow streets and are good for sightseers. Service 85 goes from San Giovanni to Barberini via Piazza Venezia; Service 81 from San Giovanni to San Pietro crosses the historic center; the 115 from Viale Trastevere to Gianicolo; the H from Monteverde crosses Trastevere to Termini Station. Watch out for pickpockets, especially on the tourist services like the 64 and the 40, which go from Termini to the Vaticano, and at the Barberini e Spagna stops on the metro Line A.

Buses to many towns in the Lazio region are operated by **CoTral** *(tel 800 174 471, www.cotralspa.it/ ENG)*. They depart from nine terminals, coinciding with railway and metro stations. National and international buses depart from the bus depot at Tiburtina Station.

Taxis

Official taxis are colored white, with a taxi sign on the roof and the license number clearly

displayed inside and outside the vehicle. Taxis wait at taxi stands, marked by a sign "Taxi." They can also be hailed in the street, although by law they are not allowed to pick you up within 100 meters (110 yds) of a stand. When a cab is free the taxi sign on the roof is lit up.

Taxis run on meters, which start at €3 and increase every km plus journey time. On Sundays and holidays, the beginning fare is €4.50, at night (10 p.m.–6 a.m.) €6.50. Once onboard check the taxi meter is turned on. The first piece of baggage is free; additional bags cost €1 each. For rides out of town (except for the airports which have fixed fares) a different fare system kicks in. Drivers prefer cash but some will take credit cards. Tipping is optional, and if you need a receipt ask for a *ricevuta*.

Radio-Dispatched Taxis

There are three companies: **Radio Taxi 3570** *(tel 063570)*, **Radio Taxi Tevere** *(tel. 06 4994, www.taxitevere.it)*, and **Samarcanda** *(tel 065551, 065551.it)*. When you call, wait until the recorded message finishes and a live operator comes on the line. Most speak English. Give your address; they may ask you to wait and then will provide the code number of the cab and the length of your wait. Be aware you start to pay when the driver accepts the call. Reservations in advance can be made only for trips to the airports or to Termini or Tiburtina train stations.

Trains

Rome is served by both a public train company, **Trenitalia** *(tel 892021 or 063000, www.trenitalia .com)*, and the private train company **Italo** *(tel 060708, www. italotreno .it)*. Trenitalia has an extensive network of regional, national, and international trains. Italo offers high-speed service between Milan and Salerno, with stops at Venice, Bologna, Florence, Naples, and Rome (Ostiense, Termini, and Tiburtina Stations).

Trenitalia train tickets can be bought at a station's ticket windows or automatic ticket kiosks. Tickets for national and international trains can be bought by phone and online, although they do not accept foreign credit cards. If you book online and choose the "ticketless" option you will receive a reservation code; you must give this to the conductor when you are on board and you will get a receipt in return. All tickets (except those bought online) must be validated before boarding: Punch your ticket in one of the yellow boxes scattered about the station. Tickets can also be bought from some, but not all, travel agencies.

Tickets for Italo can be bought online, by telephone, or at the Termini and Tiburtina Stations' Italo ticket window.

Internal Flights

Airitaly, tel 0789 52682, www.airitaly.com
Alitalia (tel 06 65649, www.alitalia .com) flies from Rome to most major Italian cities, as do several low-cost airlines:
Blue Panorama, www.blue-panorama.com
Easy Jet, www.easyjet.com
Ryanair, www.ryanair.com

Bicycle & Scooter Rental

Rome has about 100 miles (160 km) of cycle paths. The itinerary along the Tiber is perhaps the most picturesque and constitutes a support for the local mobility network within the city districts as an alternative to the car. Another unmissable destination for cyclists is the Parco Regionale dell'Appia Antica. On Sunday, you can use a cycle in the historic center when it

is closed to traffic, but be careful to avoid pedestrians.

If you do want to rent a bike or are interested in taking a bike tour of Rome, contact **Bici & Baci** (Via del Viminale 5, tel 06 482 8443, www.bicibaci.com).

If you wish to brave the city's traffic on a scooter, you can rent from the conveniently located **Scooter Rent** at Termini Station (to the right of Piazza dei Cinquecento, tel 06 4890 5823, www.trenoescooter .com). Other bike and scooter rental companies are listed on the Rome Tourist Information website (www.060608.it). If you are tempted to see Rome from the backseat of a classic Vespa scooter, or feel more comfortable touring in a Fiat 500 or golf buggy, check out **Roma Rent Bike** (Via dei Mille 8, tel. 380 6432278, www.romebyvespa.com).

PRACTICAL ADVICE
Communications
Post Offices
The Italian post, which has branch offices in every neighborhood, is far more functional than in the past. The central post office (Piazza San Silvestro 19, Mon.–Fri. 8:20 a.m.–7:20 p.m, Sat. 8:20 a.m.–12:35 p.m) has a multilingual information desk and offers a range of services. Most tourists' needs will involve mailings (padded envelopes can be bought here along with stamps), so head for the line for Prodotti postali. Most smaller post offices (Mon.–Fri. 8:30 a.m.–2 p.m., Sat. 8:30 a.m.–1 p.m.) have a number queuing system—but make sure you take a number for the proper sector (Prodotti postali for stamps). Tobacconists also sell stamps, but you will need to know the mailing cost. Most mail boxes have two slots, one for the city you are in (per la città) and one for everywhere else.

You can have mail sent to you at the post office by having it

addressed "Fermo Posta" followed by your name, the branch name, and its address.

Vatican Post
The Vatican has its own postal system with the main post office (winter: 8 a.m.–6:45 p.m. Mon.–Fri. & 8 a.m.–1:45 p.m. Sat.; summer: 8 a.m.–1:45 p.m. Mon.–Sat.) located in Piazza San Pietro on the right side of the church.

Telephones
To call Italy from the United States, dial 011 39 (international and Italian country code) followed by the local number, which always includes the city area code, for example, 06 for Rome. Toll free numbers start with 800; 199 numbers have a higher rate. To make an international call from Italy, dial 00 plus the country code (1 for the U.S. and Canada, 44 for the U.K.) followed by the local number.

With the increasing use of cell phones, public telephones have become somewhat of a rarity. They are operated by phone cards, which can be bought from tobacconists and post offices. Most have clearly displayed instructions in English. To make a call, lift the receiver, insert the card (after breaking off the perforated corner) in the slot, and dial the number. Inexpensive international phone cards are also available at most tobacconists.

If you are in Italy for any length of time you might consider buying a local SIM card when you arrive. You can find them at service provider stores such as WIND, TIM, or Vodafone, and they can be as cheap as €10. If unused for a year the SIM card expires. You will need some form of identification and a cell phone that is unlocked and dual, tri, or quad band (most U.S. phones are not). Cheap cell phones are available at most stores.

Internet Access

If you are traveling with a device that has Wi-Fi you will find many cafés offering free Internet access (generally you need to ask for a passcode). **Digit Roma** *(www. digitromawifi.it/en/index.html)* offers four hours of free access a day from many of the historical sites and parks of the city; you will need a valid mobile telephone number to register, but it is free of charge. A list of hot spots is on their website. You might also consider buying a local SIM card and signing up for a monthly Internet access deal for approximately €9. Ask at service provider stores such as WIND, TIM, or Vodafone for details.

Crime

See sidebar p. 105.

Electricity

Italian circuits use 220 volts; American appliances need adapter plugs and those that operate on 110 volts will also need a transformer. These can be bought at a hardware store *(ferramenta)* or before you leave home.

Etiquette

Say *"buongiorno"* (*"buonasera"* after lunch) and *"arrivederci"* when entering and leaving shops, restaurants, and bars. Although no one expects you to speak Italian, an attempt to utter a few words, no matter how basic, is appreciated. In general Italians use "please" and "thank you" *(per favore* and *grazie)* less than English-speakers do, so don't be offended if people seem brusque. If you are giving flowers, avoid chrysanthemums; here they are only put on graves.

Media

Newspapers

Most downtown newsstands *(edicole)* have a selection of English-language papers and magazines; *The New York Times* and *The Wall Street Journal* are widely available.

Television

The main national stations are the state-owned RAI 1, 2, and 3, Mediaset's Italia Uno, Rete Quattro, and Canale 5 and Cairo Communication's La7. English-language channels such as CNN, BBC, Al-Jazeera, France 24 English, Fox, Bloomberg, and CNBC are available via cable or satellite.

Radio

Vatican Radio (105 FM, *www.radio vaticana.va*) broadcasts news and other programs in a wide range of languages including English. For 24-hour classical music without breaks, try Rai Radio5 Classica (100.3 FM).

Money Matters

The euro is the official currency in Italy. There are 100 cents to the euro which is available in bills and coins. Bills come in denominations of 5, 10, 20, 50, 100, 200, and 500; coins are in denominations of 1 and 2 euros and 1, 2, 5, 10, 20, and 50 cents.

You can change money in banks *(approx. 8:30 a.m.–1:30 p.m. & 2:45 p.m.–4 p.m. Mon.–Fri.).* Private exchange offices (look for the *"cambio"* sign) also change money. They have longer hours and are usually open on the weekends. ATMs (Bancomat) are often the most convenient way of changing money. Check with your bank for charges and be aware that there may be a daily withdrawal limit. It is difficult to exchange traveler's checks in stores and hotels, but banks and exchange offices will accept them. The central post office (Piazza San Silvestro) will also change foreign currency into euros.

National Holidays

Jan. 1, Jan. 6, Easter Sun., Easter Mon., April 25, May 1, June 2, June 29 (Rome only), Aug. 15, Nov. 1, Dec. 8, Dec. 25, Dec. 26.

Opening Hours

Hours in Rome can be erratic, making sightseeing and shopping difficult. Many shops in central Rome now stay open all day, but they have no obligation to do so. Others close at lunchtime *(generally 1 or 1:30 p.m–3:30 or 4 p.m.).* Many clothing stores are closed Sundays. Hairdressers are closed Sundays and Mondays. Food shops often close on Sundays. Supermarkets (there are many in central Rome) are generally open nonstop Monday through Saturday, and often on Sunday.

Cafés open in the early morning and often stay open until late. Traditional restaurants generally serve between 12:30 p.m. and 3 p.m. and from 8 to 11 p.m. but nowadays in many downtown areas they serve nonstop from noon until midnight.

Many businesses close for summer holidays in August.

Sightseeing hours at major attractions are much longer than in the past. In general, archaeological sites are open the whole day, closing an hour before sunset. Museums sell their last tickets an hour before closing.

Churches generally close from noon to 3 or 4 p.m. and then in the evening at around 6 or 7 p.m.

Sightseeing Tours

Bus Tours

Several companies run all-day stop-and-go bus tours to the major sights of Rome. They are equipped with audio guides and allow you to hop on and off where you like.

City Sightseeing Roma *(tel. 06 69797554, www.city-sightseeing.it/ en/rome)* offers combined tickets including tours with guided visits to historic sites and principal attractions. They guarantee preferential access and allow you to avoid waiting a long time in line. It is possible to purchase the tickets at the visitor centers (there are two near Termini Station, one at the Colosseo and two others in the San Pietro area) or on board the Open Buses.

Opera Romana Pellegrinaggi *(Piazza Pio XII 9, tel 06 698961, www. operaromanapellegrinaggi.org)* runs the Open Bus Vatican&Rome, a stop-and-go tourist bus service that goes to the most important churches and holy places in Rome. The service runs every 20 minutes and departs from near St. Peter's (9:30 a.m.–6:20 p.m.). The trip lasts about two hours. Tickets can be bought directly on board, at tourist information points, and online at *www.terravision.eu* (small additional fee). The cost for the 48-hour ticket is €28, the 24-hour ticket costs €25, and a one-way ticket is €12. The same agency runs tours that include the Musei Vaticani, Basilica di S. Pietro, Giardini Vaticani, and San Giovanni in Laterano, among others. For these bus tours, there are discounts for Roma Pass holders.

Boat Tours

Rome now has its own *bateaux mouches* on the Tiber. **Roma Boat Experience** *(tel 06 89567745, www.romeboatexperience.com)* organizes cruises of 1 hour 20 minutes (10 a.m.–6:30 p.m.) with free embarkation and disembarkation. If you wish, you can have dinner or an aperitif on board, and enjoy the live music and the wine bar. The cruises run from April to October. It is also possible to buy a ticket including a bus tour.

Walking Tours in English

Context *(tel 06 967 2737, www .contexttravel.com/city/rome)* offers in-depth walking seminars (archaeology, art, and cuisine) for small groups of curious travelers.

Grand Tour *(tel 06 4549 3814, www.thegrandtour.it)* offers walks

and activities to enjoy Rome's cultural and historical heritage.

Alternative Tours

If you're the sporting type and want to combine a sprint around Rome with tourism, you might want to give sight jogging a try. A knowledgeable personal trainer will run you around the city's sights. Contact **Sight Jogging** *(tel 347 335 3185, www.sightjogging.it).*

If you are interested in seeing Rome by **horse carriage** and want to book in advance, see *www.romeguide.it/ROMATOUR/ albertos/index.htm.*

Renting or touring with a Segway offers a convenient and eco-friendly way to visit the city. Companies offering tours and rentals are **Rome by Segway** *(tel 800250077, www.romeby segway.com)* and **Segway Rome Tour** *(www.rome segwaytour.com)*

Time Differences

Italy is six hours ahead of New York and nine hours ahead of Los Angeles. Europe changes to daylight savings time on the last Sunday of March and returns to standard time on the last Sunday in October.

Tipping

Tipping is not obligatory in Italy, but it is appreciated. It is common to round off the fare in cabs. Theoretically service is included in restaurants, but it is usual to leave a small amount. Tipping hotel porters and maids is also appreciated.

Tourist Information

Use the official tourist information channels of Roma Capitale to discover the city. The site *www. turismoroma.it* proposes novelties and events in progress, and enables you to download brochures and follow proposed itineraries. The contact center and tourist and cul-

tural information site 060608 *(tel 06 0608, www.060608.it)* enables you to book visits to museums, gives museum services and opening times, and supplies information on hotels and non-hotel facilities, car parking and garages, restaurants, travel agencies, and cultural associations.

For information, bookings, and ticket purchase online regarding Rome city museums, consult *www. museiincomuneroma.it.*

The state museums are free for those under 18 years: They are given a special ticket that will allow them to enter together with an adult. You can book online for privately-managed museums and archaeological sites *(on www.coopculture.it)* or telephone *(tel 06 3996 7700, 9 a.m.–1 p.m./2 p.m.–5 p.m. Mon.–Fri., 9 a.m.–2 p.m. Sat.).*

Both **Angloinfo** *(rome.angloinfo. com)* and **In Rome Now** *(www. inromenow.com)* have extensive sections on events in Rome, as well as other useful information. The *Wanted in Rome* magazine, available at newsstands and online at *www. wantedinrome.com,* is highly useful.

Travelers With Disabilities

For information about guided visits and tours for people with disabilities, you can contact the tourist service company **Rome and Italy – Tourist Services** *(Via Giuseppe Veronese 50, tel 06 44258441, www.romeanditaly.com),* which offers dedicated trips and excursions using special equipment and specialist staff. They supply transportation, accommodations, and guided visits to all archaeological sites and museums. **Accessible Transportation** *(tel 06 503 6040, accessibletransportationrome.com)* has a service for transporting people with disabilities, and organizes tours in Rome and the surrounding area. Most of the museums in the capital guarantee accessibility for people with disabilities and supply dedicated services and equipment; the same is true for the Musei Vaticani (see services for people with disabilities on their website: *www.museivaticani. va/content/museivaticani/en/vis- ita-i-musei/servizi-per-i-visitatori/ accessibilita.html*).

Consult the website *www.060608.it* for information on accessibility in the metro (search for "Accessibility to Underground"), and to orient yourself regarding tourism opportunities in the city accessible to people with disabilities or particular needs.

EMERGENCIES
Embassies & Consulates

British Embassy and Consul- ate, Via XX Settembre 80a, tel 06 4220 0001

Canadian Consulate, Via Zara 30, tel 06 854441 (24-hour emergency service, *travel.gc.ca/ assistance/emergency-assistance*).

United States Embassy and Consulate, Palazzo Margherita, Via Vittorio Veneto 121, tel 06 46741.

Emergency Phone Numbers & Addresses

European emergency number 112
Italian Red Cross, tel 065510 (ambulance emergency)

For urgent medical treatment, head for the Pronto Soccorso (emergency room) of the nearest hospital. For children, go to the Ospedale Bambino Gesù *(Piazza di Sant'Onofrio 4, Gianicolo, tel 06 68591)*. For dental emergencies, the G. Eastman dental hospital *(Viale Regina Elena 287b, Policlini-*

co, tel 06 4997 5734) is the place to go. For less serious matters (or if you need a prescription) go the Touristic Medicine Service (Guardia Turistica: *Via Morosini 30, Trastevere, tel 06 7730 6650; Via Antonio Canova, 19, Piazza di Spagna, tel 06 7730 6112)*, which provides first aid and emergency medical treatment for tourists.

Pharmacies

By law every neighborhood must have one pharmacy that is open 24 hours a day. Visit *farmaturni. federfarmaroma.com/orario.aspx* to find the pharmacy open after hours in your neighborhood. There are also nighttime phar- macies; centrally located ones include **Piran** *(Via Nazionale 228, tel 06 488 4437)* and **Farmacia Internazionale** *(Piazza Barberini 49, tel 06 487 1195)*.

The Vatican Pharmacy *(Via della Posta, Vatican City, enter at the Porta Sant'Anna gate of the Vatican)* is open Monday through Friday 8:30 a.m.–6 p.m. (in summer, only until 3 p.m.) and Saturday 8:30 a.m.–1 p.m.; it has an English-speaking staff and a wide range of non-Italian pharmaceuti- cal products. Remember, as you are entering the Vatican City, you must be dressed appropriately (shoulders covered). Tourists must obtain a temporary pass from a special registry office at the Porta Sant'Anna gate, showing their ID and a medical prescription.

Lost Property

The Lost and Found office of the Rome city council is located in Circonvallazione Ostiense 191 *(tel 06 6769 3214, Mon.–Wed. & Fri.*

8.30–1 p.m., Thurs. 8:30 a.m.– 5 p.m.). Enquiries can also be made at *oggettismarriti@comune .roma.it*. To collect a possession from the office, you must have proof of identity, a police report of theft/loss, and pay €9–24. Details of lost objects belonging to foreigners are sent to the relevant embassies.

Lost or Stolen Credit Cards

American Express, tel 800 874333 (toll free), 06 7290 0347 or 06-722-801 (24 hrs)
Bank of America 001 757677 4701 (international collect)
Diners Club, tel 800 864 064 (24 hrs)
MasterCard, tel 800 870866 (24 hrs)
Visa International, tel 800 877232 (24 hrs)

FURTHER READING

If you're interested in ancient Rome, read Suetonius' *The Twelve Caesars,* Livy's *History of Rome,* and Tacitus' *The Histories.* Also try Robert Graves's *I, Claudius* and *Claudius the God,* Marguerite Yourcenar's *Memoirs of Hadrian,* or the works of Allan Massie— *Augustus, Caesar,* and *Tiberius*— which, although fiction, give a good idea of what life was once like. Robert Harris's novels *Impe- rium* and *Lustrum* about Cicero are also enlightening as well as fun.

Literary works set in later times include *The Marble Faun* by Nathaniel Hawthorne; *Daisy Miller* by Henry James; *Roman Fever* by Edith Wharton; *A Time in Rome* by Elizabeth Bowen; *History* by Elsa Morante; and the works of Roman author Alberto Moravia.

HOTELS & RESTAURANTS

While Rome is not particularly known for its accommodations, both luxurious and charming places do exist, if you know where to look. The cuisine is a different story. It's very difficult to eat badly in Rome—even the humblest of fare in the smallest trattoria is usually lovingly prepared and tasty.

HOTELS

Accommodations in Rome are expensive and, in the peak tourist months, scarce. If you are planning to come at this time you should book well in advance.

Here are some things you should keep in mind when booking accommodations:

Many areas of central Rome are noisy until 2 or 3 a.m. If you are a light sleeper ask for a quiet room—and consider earplugs. Remember, too, that many hotels have fairly small rooms.

If you have a car and plan to stay in the historic center, know that for a good part of the day and night this area is a limited traffic zone (ZTL), with cameras at entry points. You will be fined if you enter when the ZTL sign says "Varco Attivo" and you are without a ZTL pass. Parking can also be a big problem, so ask your hotel about their parking arrangements.

Few hotels have rooms that are specially adapted for disabled travelers, but many will do all they can to accommodate special needs, especially if you let them know in advance. See *www.accessibleitalian holiday.com* for hotels with facilities for disabled travelers.

Grading System

Italian hotels are rated from one to five stars by the government's Tourist Office according to the facilities they provide to the customers (such as the number of rooms with private bathrooms, rooms with TV, etc.), the style, and the comfort. Unless otherwise noted, all the hotels listed here have private bathrooms in all rooms. English is spoken at all the hotels listed; however, the amount spoken varies and may only be sufficient to take a booking and deal with the most basic visitor requests. Value-added tax and service are included in the prices, and so is breakfast, unless otherwise noted. Room price categories are given only for guidance and do not take account of seasonal variations.

Alternative Accommodations

Many Roman monasteries and convents have rooms to rent at reasonable prices. If you are staying for more than a few days, an economical alternative to a hotel is a short-term apartment rental. Check out the following websites for information and last-minute deals:

www.romerents.com
www.romesweethome.com
www.rentalinrome.com

Tourist Tax

As of 2011, nonresidents in Rome now pay a tourist tax for accommodation (per person, per night) and for entry into museums (€1). An extra €3.50 is charged in hotels up to a two-star rating, at B&B's, or at short-term rentals; for four- or five-star hotels, €3 to €7 is charged; and for campsites, €2. Youth hostels are exempt from the charge, as are visitors younger than ten. The tax is levied on the first ten nights of a hotel stay, or the first five nights for a campsite stay. The tax can be paid in cash or with a card, at the end of your stay, directly to the accommodation facilities, which issue a receipt of payment.

RESTAURANTS

Italians take eating seriously. A traditional meal consists of *antipasti* followed by a first course *(primo)* of pasta, soup, or risotto before hitting the main course *(secondo)*, accompanied by a side dish *(contorno)* of salad or vegetable, which is ordered separately. Desserts or fruit round off the meal, followed by an espresso. These days, however, most restaurants are used to people only having one or two courses. Be aware that when ordering fish the price quoted on the menu is usually by weight, so if you want to avoid any nasty surprises order by weight.

Dining Hours

Lunch is eaten between about 12:30 p.m. and 2:30 p.m. Dinner is seldom served before 8 p.m. and continues until about 10:30 p.m. or even later. In traditional restaurants, making reservations is often advisable, sometimes essential.

However, today there are more and more restaurants in areas like Trastevere and around Campo de' Fiori that adapt to the needs and timing of tourists, by staying open all day. The menu can often be consulted outside the restaurant.

In some restaurants you can try the specialties on a tasting menu.

Types of Establishments

Although the dividing lines are no longer clear cut, the traditional divisions are somewhat like this: *Ristorante*—more formal and in general more expensive. *Trattoria*—relatively simple restaurants that are often family run. *Osteria*—a modest place to get food and drink.

Pizzeria—a place for pizza. If you just want a slice of pizza any time of the day look for a *"pizza al taglio"* sign (choose how much you want and pay by weight). *Enoteca*—a wine bar, often serving delicious snacks.

Beware however that while the general rule holds, there are many exceptions; osterias and trattorias can be very expensive.

Smoking

Smoking is forbidden in all public indoor spaces, including bars, cafés, restaurants, and discos. However, special smoking rooms are allowed in those very, very few bars and restaurants that have installed the powerful ventilation equipment required by law. Fortunately for smokers, many restaurants and cafés have outside seating, where one is free to smoke.

The Bill

When you ask for the bill in Italy *(il conto)*, always check that it is a legal fiscal receipt *(ricevuta* or *scontrino fiscale)* and it is itemized.

There may or may not be a service charge on the bill (although if there is it should be written on the menu, if not you can ask them to take it off). If there is a service charge it is not necessary to add a tip on top (although a few coins on the table shows you have enjoyed your meal).

Organization & Abbreviations

All sites are listed first by price, then in alphabetical order. The abbreviations used are:

L = lunch
D = dinner
AE = American Express
DC = Diners Club
MC = MasterCard
V = Visa

► ANCIENT ROME

Until a few years ago, the Monti area (which straddles the lower end of Via Cavour) was busy during the day but relatively quiet in the evening. That has all changed. Monti, now full of bars, pubs, and restaurants, has become a nighttime destination. 🚌 Bus: 50, 75, 105, 150, 117. Metro: Linea B (Colosseo or Cavour)

🏨 FORUM
$$$$ ★★★★
VIA TOR DE' CONTI 25
TEL 06 679 2446
FAX 06 678 6479
www.hotelforum.com
Tucked in a comparatively quiet corner behind the Imperial Forums, the atmosphere and decor of this grand hotel are reminiscent of an English gentlemen's club. Rooms vary in size, but all are well furnished, and there's a wonderful roof garden restaurant with a view of the Imperial Forums.
🛏 80 P 🛗 🛎
🅰 All major cards

🏨 INN AT THE ROMAN FORUM
$$$$ ★★★★★
VIA DEGLI IBERNESI 30
TEL 06 6919 0970
FAX 06 4543 8802
www.theinnattheroman forum.com
Located just a few steps from the Forum, this luxury hotel actually houses Roman ruins. Three of the rooms offer terraces with delightful views of a little garden with palm and fig trees, which is also a lovely spot for a drink in the evening. Pet friendly.
🛏 12 🛗 🛎 🅰 All major cards

🏨 NERVA
$$ ★★★
VIA TOR DE' CONTI 3
TEL 06 679 3764
FAX 06 6992 2204

PRICES

HOTELS
An indication of the cost of a double room in the high season is given by **$** signs.

$$$$$	Over $450
$$$$	$350–$450
$$$	$250–$350
$$	$120–$250
$	Under $120

RESTAURANTS
An indication of the cost of a three-course meal without drinks is given by **$** signs.

$$$$$	Over $80
$$$$	$55–$80
$$$	$40–$55
$$	$25–$40
$	Under $25

www.hotelnerva.com
This modern and stylish hotel, situated just steps from the Roman Forum, underwent a recent renovation. The public areas are pleasingly decorated and the rooms comfortable and sound-proofed.
🛏 18 P 🛗 🛎 🅰 All major cards

🍽 OPEN COLONNA
$$$$$
VIA MILANO 9A
TEL 06 4782 2641
www.antonellocolonna.it
This Michelin-star restaurant is located in a large glass loft on the top floor of the Palazzo delle Esposizioni (not be confused with the lunches of Open Colonna one level down). It serves inventive cuisine inspired by traditional dishes.
🪑 40 🕐 Closed Aug. 🛎
🅰 All major cards

 Hotel   Restaurant   No. of Guest Rooms   No. of Seats   Parking    Public Transit   Closed

🍴 CAVOUR 313
$$
VIA CAVOUR 313
TEL 06 678 5496
www.cavour313.it
This wood-lined wine bar has more than a thousand different wines from all over the world and serves an interesting range of cheeses, salamis, and freshly prepared salads.
🔲 50 🕐 Closed Aug.
🏧 All major cards

🍴 L'ASINO D'ORO
$$
VIA DEL BOSCHETTO 73
TEL 06 4891 3832
A quiet little restaurant serving a cuisine typical of Rome and the surrounding area, with dishes often slightly modified, based on cheap cuts and offal. Fixed lunch menu for 12 euros.
🔲 35 🕐 Closed Sun. & Mon.
🔵 🏧 DC, MC, V

▶ COLOSSEO TO SAN CLEMENTE

The streets around the Colosseum, particularly Via Capo d'Africa, have undergone a renaissance. New hotels have opened, restaurants serving innovative food thrive, and bars stay open until the early hours of the morning. 🚌 Bus: 51, 75, 85, 87, 117, 118, 650. Tram: 3. Metro: Linea B (Colosseo)

🏨 CAPO D'AFRICA
$$$ ****
VIA CAPO D'AFRICA 54
TEL 06 772801
FAX 06 7728 0801
www.hotelcapodafrica.com
Located in the shadow of the Colosseum, this four-star hotel is a fusion of contemporary and classic styles. The rooms have been furnished with great attention to detail. There is a wonderful view of the Colosseum from the terrace.
🛏 64 🅿 (extra) 🔀 🔵 🔧
🏧 All major cards

🏨 CELIO
$$$ ***
VIA DEI SANTI QUATTRO 35C
TEL 06 7049 5333
FAX 06 709 6377
www.hotelcelio.com
Located on a quiet street near the Colosseum, this family-run hotel is one of Rome's most pleasant, and offers rooms of various types, a meeting room, small pool for children, wellness corner.
🛏 19 🅿 (extra) 🔀 🔵 🔧
🏧 All major cards

🍴 PAPAGIO'
$$$
VIA CAPO D'AFRICA 26
www.ristorantepapagio.it
TEL 06 700 9800
A blend of traditional and innovative cuisine plus efficient service makes this restaurant a popular choice. Fish is their specialty. Outdoor seating.
🔲 50 🕐 Closed 2 weeks in Aug. 🔵
🏧 All major cards

🍴 IL BOCCONCINO
$$
VIA OSTILIA 23
TEL 06 7707 9175
www.ilbocconcino.com
In this local trattoria you can find typical Roman dishes such as spaghetti alla carbonara, tripe, and roast lamb with potatoes. Outdoor seating.
🔲 60 🕐 Closed Wed. & Aug.
🔵 🏧 All major cards

▶ LATERANO TO TERME DI DIOCLEZIANO

Although the area immediately around Termini Station is probably best avoided at night, the atmosphere changes quickly as you move slightly farther out. Here you will find hotels and restaurants ranging from the simple to the most luxurious. For public transportation, see individual listings.

🏨 ST. REGIS
$$$$$ *****
VIA V.E. ORLANDO 3
TEL 06 47091
FAX 06 474 7307
st-regis.marriott.com
A traditional luxury hotel with public rooms that are awe-inspiringly decorated with marble columns and richly patterned Oriental carpets. The spacious and comfortable guest rooms are furnished with valuable antiques, and bathrooms are well equipped. Its highly recommended restaurant, LUMEN Cocktails & Cuisine, serves refined traditional dishes and drinks in an exclusive ambience.
🛏 184 🅿 Garage 🔀 🔵
🏧 All major cards 🚌 Bus: 60, 61, 62, 66, 82, 492, 910. Metro: Linea A (Repubblica)

🏨 HOTEL ALPI
$$$ ****
VIA CASTELFIDARDO 84A
TEL 06 444 1235
FAX 06 444 1257
www.hotelalpi.com
Comfortable, reasonably priced hotel in attractive Liberty building. Located close to Termini Station. Pet friendly.
🛏 48 🅿 (extra) 🔀 🔵 🏧 All major cards 🚌 Bus: 38, 97, 217, 360, 492

🏨 YELLOWSQUARE
$
VIA PALESTRO, 51
TEL. 06 446 3554
www.the-yellow.com
Multifunctional hostel near Termini Station where you can listen to live music, do yoga in the morning, and change your look in the hairdressing salon. The hotel also organizes guided tours (tel 388 371 1433) and rents out bicycles and scooters.
🛏 40 🚌 Metro: Linea B (Castro Pretorio) 🔀 🔵 🏧
All major cards

🔀 Elevator 🔵 Nonsmoking 🔵 Air-conditioning 🚠 Outdoor Pool 🔧 Health Club 🏧 Credit Cards

🍴 DA DANILO
$$

VIA PETRARCA 13
TEL 06 7720 0111
www.trattoriadadanilo.com
At this small, family-run
restaurant, Danilo serves the
tables while his mother looks
after the kitchen.
🍴 55 🕐 Closed Mon. L, Sun.,
& Aug. 🅿 🚇 V 🚇 Metro:
Linea A (Manzoni)

🍴 TRATTORIA MONTI
$$

VIA DI S. VITO 13A
TEL 06 446 6573
A warm welcome is guaran-
teed at this elegant yet cozy
trattoria serving traditional seasonal dishes from the Marche
region—lamb with artichokes,
mushrooms, and truffles or
thick winter soups.
🍴 45 🕐 Closed Sun. D, Mon.,
& Aug. 🚇 All major cards
🚌 Bus: 71, 590, 649 Metro:
Linea A (Vittorio Emanuele)

🍴 EST! EST! EST!
$

VIA GENOVA 32
TEL 06 488 1107
www.anticapizzeria
ricciroma.com
This well-loved pizzeria has
been here since 1905. It serves
both thin-crust (Roman) and
thick-crust (Neapolitan) pizza
and the usual range of fried
suppli (rice balls), cod fillets,
and zucchini flowers.
🍴 120 🕐 Closed Mon. & Aug.
🅿 🚇 MC, V 🚌 Bus: H, 40, 60,
64, 70, 170

▶ FONTANA DI TREVI TO VIA VENETO

Many of Rome's luxury hotels can
still be found on the Via Veneto,
made famous by Fellini's film *La
Dolce Vita.* 🚌 Bus: C3, 52, 53, 61,
63, 80, 83, 150, 160, 590. Metro:
Linea A (Barberini)

🏨 ALEPH
$$$$$ ★★★★★

VIA SAN BASILIO 15
TEL 06 4229001
FAX 06 4229 0000
alephrome.com
Luxury hotel recently acquired
by the Hilton chain, which
renewed it, seeking to enhance
to the utmost the original
1930s architecture. The guests
will enjoy really top service,
excellent restaurants, and an
exclusive area to smoke a cigar
and sip Cognac. The spa in the
basement restores you after a
day out in the city.
🛏 88 🅿 (extra) 🚇 🚇
🚇 All major cards

🏨 EDEN
$$$$$ ★★★★★

VIA LUDOVISI 49
TEL 06 478121
FAX 06 482 1584
www.dorchester
collection.com
This luxury hotel is a favorite
among international celebrities.
Every detail has been thought
of, from the antique furnishings
to the imaginative welcome
baskets when you arrive. Stunning views from the famous
roof terrace bar and restaurant.
Breakfast extra.
🛏 98, including some suites
🅿 Garage 🚇 🚇
🚇 All major cards

🏨 WESTERN EXCELSIOR
$$$$$ ★★★★★

VIA VITTORIO VENETO 125
TEL 06 47081
FAX 06 482 6205
www.westinrome.com
A dramatically grand hotel,
opulently decorated with
swaths of rich fabric and
antique and reproduction
furniture. All the more-or-less
uniformly decorated rooms are
luxurious, while the suites look
like stage sets. Breakfast extra.
🛏 316, including some suites
🅿 (extra) 🚇 🚇
🚇 All major cards

🏨 FONTANA
$$$ ★★★

PIAZZA DI TREVI 96
TEL 06 678 6113
FAX 06 679 0024
www.hotelfontane-trevi.com
The view over the Trevi
Fountain from this quirky little
hotel is breathtaking (also
sleep-depriving—in summer
the noise can go on all night).
Rooms come in all shapes
and sizes in this rambling old
building.
🛏 25 🚇 🚇 🚇 AE, MC, V

🏨 LA RESIDENZA
$$ ★★★★

VIA EMILIA 22/24
TEL 06 488 0789
FAX 06 485721
www.laresidenzaroma.com
At this converted town house
conveniently situated near
Via Veneto, the service is
attentive and the rooms comfortable. But the real charm
of this hotel is found in the
bar, terrace, and warmly
decorated lobbies.
🛏 29, including some junior
suites 🅿 Garage 🚇 🚇
🚇 All major cards

🍴 GIRARROSTO FIORENTINO
$$$

VIA SICILIA 46
TEL 06 4288 0660
www.girarrostofiorentino.it
This classic Roman restaurant
has been making clients
happy for the last 50 years.
Known for its open-fire
grilled beef, it also has excel-
lent appetizers that are piled
onto your table, a large selec-
tion of fish and other meat
dishes, and a good wine list.
🍴 75 🕐 Closed Dec. 24–26
🚇 🚇 All major cards

🍴 TRATTORIA TRITONE
$$$

VIA DEI MARONITI 1
TEL 06 679 8181
www.trattoriatritone.com
Here you're guaranteed

not just excellent Roman cuisine, but courteous, attentive (English-speaking) service and a warm welcome. Underneath the elegant extension are some carefully preserved ancient remains. Il Tritone's popularity with journalists from the nearby *Il Messaggero* newspaper proves its appeal with discerning locals.

🛏 180 🕐 Closed Dec. 25–26 🔆 🅾 All major cards

🍴 TULLIO
$$$

VIA SAN NICOLA DA TOLENTINO 26
TEL 06 474 5560
www.tullioristorante.it
A Tuscan restaurant particularly famous for its *bistecca alla fiorentina* (T-bone steak) and other grilled meats, Tullio also has an extensive selection of Tuscan wines.

🛏 120 🕐 Closed Sun. & Aug. 🔆 🅾 All major cards

🍴 PICCOLO ARANCIO
$$

VICOLO SCANDERBEG 112
TEL 06 678 6139
www.piccoloarancio.it
This popular little restaurant is located on a narrow side street near the Trevi Fountain. The food offers a good, rather than exceptional, range of Roman standards slightly adapted for international tastes.

🛏 50 🕐 Closed Mon. & 3 weeks in Aug. 🔆 🅾 All major cards

▶ PIAZZA DI SPAGNA TO VILLA BORGHESE

Rome's main glamour shopping district also boasts a variety of interesting and original hotels and restaurants. 🚌 Bus: 61, 89, 117, 150, 160, 495, 590. Metro: Linea A (Spagna)

SOMETHING SPECIAL

🏨 DE RUSSIE
🍴 $$$$$ *****

VIA DEL BABUINO 9
TEL 06 328881
FAX 06 3288 8888
www.roccofortehotels.com
In the heart of the city, between the Spanish Steps and Piazza del Popolo, this hotel is the ultimate in luxury. The guest rooms are spacious and exquisitely decorated. A stunning feature of the hotel is its extensive, terraced gardens, which provide a tranquil oasis amid the bustle of central Rome. Nestled in the garden, the hotel's restaurant, **Le Jardin du Russie,** is a perfect place for a drink or a meal. The menu is devoted to classic Italian cooking with an emphasis on Mediterranean flavors based on olive oil, tomatoes, and garlic.

🛏 121 🅿 (extra) 🛗 🔆 🅾 All major cards

SOMETHING SPECIAL

🏨 HASSLER ROMA
🍴 $$$$$ *****

PIAZZA TRINITÀ DEI MONTI 6
TEL 06 699340
FAX 06 678 9991
www.hotelhasslerroma.com
The hotel's enviable location at the top of the Spanish Steps is matched by elaborate interior design (marble columns and well-upholstered seating) and bustlingly attentive service. The good-size rooms are comfortably furnished and have traces of their more than 100-year history as a hotel. Breakfast extra. The hotel's panoramic Michelin-star restaurant, **Imàgo,** has a spectacular view over Rome and serves fine Italian cuisine in elegant surroundings.

🛏 92 🅿 🛗 🔆 🅾 All major cards

🏨 BABUINO 181 LUXURY SUITES
$$$$

VIA DEL BABUINO 181
TEL 06 3229 5295
FAX 06 3229 5299
www.romeluxurysuites.com
Boutique hotel located in a superbly renovated palazzo on the Via del Babuino between Piazza del Popolo and the Spanish Steps. The hotel offers superior-class double rooms and suites, excellent examples of Italian comfort and design even in the smallest detail. Roof garden on the top floor.

🛏 14 🔆 🅾 All major cards

🏨 D'INGHILTERRA
$$$$ *****

VIA BOCCA DI LEONE 14
TEL 06 69981
FAX 06 6992 2243
www.starhotelscollezione.com
Famous for well over a century as one of the best in Rome, this hotel can list Oscar Wilde among its VIP guests. Antique furnishings tend toward the lugubrious but make for an appropriately historic atmosphere. It's also perfectly placed to set off for a stroll around the city's most exclusive shopping streets. Breakfast extra.

🛏 98 🛗 🔆 🅾 All major cards

🏨 INN AT THE SPANISH STEPS
$$$$ *****

VIA DEI CONDOTTI 85
TEL 06 6992 5657
FAX 06 678 6470
www.atspanishsteps.com
This small, family-run luxury residence sits on Rome's famed shopping street, Via dei Condotti. Quality and style in a discreetly refined atmosphere, with a lovely rooftop terrace for breakfast and aperitifs. Pet friendly.

🛏 24 🛗 🔆 🅾 All major cards

LOCARNO
$$$ ★★★★
VIA DELLA PENNA 22
TEL 06 361 0841
FAX 06 321 5249
www.hotellocarno.com
This intriguing art deco hotel is just off Piazza del Popolo. Both the lobbies and guest rooms are tastefully decorated, and in winter there is an open fire in the bar area. It also boasts a lovely roof garden.
60 (extra) All major cards

PIRANESI
$$$ ★★★★
VIA DEL BABUINO 196
TEL 06 328041
www.hotelpiranesi.com
Boutique hotel situated in the heart of the glamour shopping area. Roof garden with charming view of the rooftops of Rome.
32 All major cards

PARLAMENTO
$$ ★★
VIA DELLE CONVERTITE 5
TEL/FAX 06 6992 1000
www.hotelparlamento.it
A simple, well-run, and spotlessly clean *pensione* where not all rooms have air-conditioning. Double-glazing reduces outside noise. Breakfast is served in the little roof garden in summer.
23 Extra fee All major cards

DAL BOLOGNESE
$$$$
PIAZZA DEL POPOLO 1/2
TEL 06 361 1426
www.dalbolognese.it
This chic restaurant is where the in-crowd gathers to enjoy the time-honored cuisine of Bologna. Try the *bollito* (boiled meats). Outdoor seating.
80 Closed Mon. All major cards

SOMETHING SPECIAL

OTELLO ALLA CONCORDIA
$$$
VIA DELLA CROCE 81
TEL. 06 679 1178
otelloallaconcordia.it
A small family trattoria with over 60 years of history. It offers the typical dishes of Roman cuisine. It is a short distance from Piazza di Spagna, with access through a courtyard with a pergola. The famous director Dino Risi used to dine here.
30 Closed D Sun. All major cards Metro: Linea A (Spagna)

'GUSTO
$$–$$$
PIAZZA AUGUSTO IMPERATORE 28
TEL 06 6813 4221
www.gusto.it
Occupying an entire block, this amazing gastronomic center contains three restaurants, an *enoteca*, a cheese shop, a deli, and a cocktail bar. The informal street-level pizzeria ($$) serves homemade pasta, salads, and grilled dishes. The upscale restaurant upstairs serves a fusion of Italian and Pacific Rim cuisine. The Osteria *(Via della Frezza 16, tel 06 3211 1482, $$)* around the corner serves traditional Mediterranean cuisine. Attached to the Osteria is the cheese shop.
250 All major cards

MATRICIANELLA
$$
VIA DEL LEONE 4
TEL 06 683 2100
www.matricianella.it
Located nearby Piazza di Spagna, this popular trattoria serves traditional Roman cuisine. Outdoor seating.
54 Closed Sun. & Aug. All major cards

PRICES

HOTELS
An indication of the cost of a double room in the high season is given by $ signs.

$$$$$	Over $450
$$$$	$350–$450
$$$	$250–$350
$$	$120–$250
$	Under $120

RESTAURANTS
An indication of the cost of a three-course meal without drinks is given by $ signs.

$$$$$	Over $80
$$$$	$55–$80
$$$	$40–$55
$$	$25–$40
$	Under $25

NINO
$$
VIA BORGOGNONA 11
TEL 06 679 5676
www.ristorantenino.it
A classic restaurant serving excellent Tuscan cuisine. Warm, cozy atmosphere, homemade pasta and meats seasoned with the family oil.
95 Closed Sun. & Aug. All major cards

VYTA ENOTECA REGIONALE DEL LAZIO
$$
VIA FRATTINA 94
TEL 06 8771 6018
A few steps from Piazza di Spagna, this wine bar/restaurant founded by the Region of Lazio (the area that surrounds Rome) specializes in showcasing the products of the region, including wines, olive oils, cheeses, and cured meats. After recent restyling, the ambience is more refined and

Hotel Restaurant No. of Guest Rooms No. of Seats Parking Public Transit Closed

elegant, but the substance certainly has not changed. Open from breakfast to dinner.

90 All major cards

▶ ## PANTHEON TO PIAZZA VENEZIA

The true heart of Rome includes the parliament and senate buildings, some of the city's oldest monuments, as well as a labyrinth of narrow streets and alleys. It is also home to some of the city's most established restaurants and hotels. 🚌 Bus: 30, 40, 46, 62, 64, 70, 81, 87, 130, 190, 492, 628, 916. Tram: 8

🏨 GRAND HOTEL DE LA MINERVE
$$$$$ ★★★★★
PIAZZA DELLA MINERVA 69
TEL 06 695201
FAX 06 679 4165
www.grandhotel
delaminerve.com
Renovated by postmodernist architect Paolo Portoghesi, this 17th-century building has all the comforts of a luxury hotel, including a beautiful roof garden (closed in winter), where you can enjoy a superb view of the Eternal City. Guest rooms are elegantly furnished and of varying size. Breakfast extra.

🛏 134 🅿 (extra) 🔁 🚭 📺
All major cards

🏨 SANTA CHIARA
$$$ ★★★
VIA DI SANTA CHIARA 21
TEL 06 687 2979
FAX 06 687 3144
www.albergosantachiara.com
Located behind the Pantheon, this hotel is known for its pleasant, calm atmosphere and efficient service. Bright rooms combine function with comfort.

🛏 100 🅿 (extra) 🔁 🚭
All major cards

🍴 MASSIMO RICCIOLI LA ROSETTA
$$$$$
VIA DELLA ROSETTA 8
TEL 06 686 1002
www.larosettaristorante.it
Fresh seafood delivered daily from Sicily and simply prepared makes the Michelin-starred La Rosetta one of the best seafood eateries in Rome. Good selection of wines and efficient service. Small outdoor garden for spring and summer dining.

🛏 40 🕐 Closed for 2 weeks in Aug. 🚭 All major cards

🍴 ARCHIMEDE SANT'EUSTACHIO
$$$
PIAZZA DEI CAPRETTARI 63
TEL 06 686 1616
www.archimedesanteustachio.it
Restrained, polite atmosphere with pleasant outdoor dining in summer. The menu features Roman and more elaborate dishes—*saltimbocca* (veal with ham), *fritto misto vegetariano* (lightly fried artichokes, cheese-and-rice croquettes, mozzarella, and zucchini strips), salmon *carpaccio*, and satisfying homemade tarts for dessert.

🛏 100 🕐 Closed Sun. & 2 weeks in Aug. All major cards

SOMETHING SPECIAL

🍴 CASA BLEVE
$$$
VIA DEL TEATRO VALLE 48/49
TEL 06 686 5970
www.casableve.com
A refined, elegant wine bar with stained-glass and stucco ceilings and marble columns. Offers an exceptional selection of wines, an excellent choice of cold dishes, and knowledgeable and efficient service.

🛏 100 🕐 Closed Sun. & Aug. 🚭 All major cards

🍴 ARMANDO AL PANTHEON
$$
SALITA DEI CRESCENZI 31
TEL 06 6880 3034
www.armandoalpantheon.it
Although located in one of the busiest tourist areas of Rome, this restaurant serves genuine classic Roman dishes.

🛏 40 🕐 Closed L Sat. & Sun. 🚭 DC, MC, V

🍴 ENOTECA CORSI
$$
VIA DEL GESÙ 87
TEL 06 679 0821
www.enotecacorsi.com
This trattoria has managed to maintain its original wine-and-olive-oil shop feel. Here you can order simple tasty Roman food. Order the house wine, or choose from a large selection of bottled wines.

🛏 100 🕐 Closed D Mon., Tue., & Sat.; closed Sun. & Aug. 🚭 All major cards

🍴 VINANDO
$$
PIAZZA MARGANA 23
TEL 06 6920 0741
www.vinando.eu
Situated on the pretty Piazza Margana, just steps from busy Piazza Venezia. This wine bar/restaurant offers delicious dishes and a large selection of wines in quiet surroundings. Outdoor seating.

🛏 50 inside, 20 outside 🚭 All major cards

▶ ## CAMPO MARZIO

This area, central Rome at its most charming and typical, is one of the city's busiest areas both day and night. The range of hotels and restaurants offers something to suit all pockets. For public transportation, see individual listings.

🏨 RAPHAEL
$$$$ ★★★★
LARGO FEBO 2

🔁 Elevator   🚭 Nonsmoking   🚬 Air-conditioning   🏊 Outdoor Pool   📺 Health Club   💳 Credit Cards

TEL 06 682831
FAX 06 687 8993
www.raphaelhotel.com
Just a step away from Piazza Navona, this hotel is known for its quiet, luxurious charm and stunning terrace (closed in winter) with bar and restaurant. Guest rooms, though small, are attractively decorated. Breakfast extra.

🛏 58 **P** (extra) 🔲 🔲 📺 ⧉ All major cards 🚌 Bus: C3, 30, 70, 81, 87, 130, 491, 628

🏨 DUE TORRI
$$$ ***
VICOLO DEL LEONETTO 23
TEL 06 6880 6956
www.hotelduetorriroma.com
Elegant furnishings and a warm welcome combine with a romantic atmosphere to make this one of the most attractive hotels in its price category. The 19th-century building, on a quiet street near Piazza Navona, used to be the home of bishops and cardinals.

🛏 26 **P** 🔲 🔲 ⧉ All major cards 🚌 Bus: C3, 70, 81, 87, 492

🏨 RELAIS GIULIA
$$$ ****
VIA GIULIA 93
TEL 06 9558 1300
FAX 06 9558 1313
relaisgiuliahotel.it
This charming boutique hotel is located in an ancient Roman palace decorated with stucco reliefs, close by Piazza Farnese.

🛏 13 🔲 ⧉ All major cards 🚌 Bus: 23, 40, 46, 62, 64, 98, 115, 870, 881

🏨 RESIDENZA IN FARNESE
$$$ ****
VIA DEL MASCHERONE 59
TEL 06 6821 0980
www.residenzafarneseroma.it
Housed in a converted 14th-century monastery near Campo de' Fiori, this quiet comfortable hotel has pleasant rooms, some with frescoed ceilings, overlooking either the gardens of Palazzo Farnese or Palazzo Spada.

🛏 31 🔲 🔲 ⧉ All major cards 🚌 Bus: 23, 280

🏨 TEATRO PACE
$$ ***
VIA DEL TEATRO PACE 33, 00186
TEL 06 687 9075
FAX 06 6819 2364
www.hotelteatropace.com
This 17th-century cardinal's former residence offers tastefully appointed bedrooms equipped with modern comforts. Conveniently located only 20 yards from Piazza Navona.

🛏 23 🔲 ⧉ All major cards 🚌 Bus: 30, 40, 46, 62, 64, 190, 916

🍴 IL CONVIVIO TROIANI
$$$$$
VICOLO DEI SOLDATI 31
TEL 06 686 9432
www.ilconviviotroiani.com
Three brothers run one of the best restaurants in Rome. Service is cordial and informative and the food is ambrosial—basically Italian with some touches of creative genius from the chef (one of the brothers). Every dish is a beautifully presented work of art but the desserts are masterpieces.

🪑 40 🕐 Closed L & Sun. 🔲 ⧉ All major cards 🚌 Bus: 30, 70, 87, 186, 492 (Corso del Rinascimento)

🍴 IL PAGLIACCIO
$$$$$
VIA DEI BANCHI VECCHI 129A
TEL 06 6880 9595
www.ristoranteilpagliaccio.it
If you are looking for upscale fine dining, check out Anthony Genovese's centrally located restaurant. The chef offers a varied menu of elaborate and ambitious dishes from around the world.

🪑 28 🕐 Closed Sun.–Mon., L Tues., & 2 weeks in Feb. 🔲 ⧉ All major cards 🚌 Bus: 23, 40, 46, 115, 280, 870

🍴 IL SAN LORENZO
$$$$
VIA DEI CHIAVARI 4/5
TEL 06 686 5097
www.ilsanlorenzo.it
Built over the foundations of the Teatro di Pompeo, this palazzo now houses a restaurant, which combines a sense of history with contemporary style. It serves modern cuisine and has excellent fish specialties.

🪑 60 🕐 Closed L Mon. & Sat, and all day Sun. 🔲 ⧉ All major cards 🚌 Bus: 40, 46, 62, 64, 81, 87, 492

🍴 DITIRAMBO
$$$
PIAZZA DELLA CANCELLERIA 75
TEL 06 687 1626
www.ristoranteditirambo.it
Charming staff and attractive decor make for a pleasantly busy atmosphere that is matched by the standard of the ever changing menu. Innovative versions of Italian regional dishes include a potato and broad bean soup and lamb with lentils. Good value for money. Reservations are essential.

🪑 50 🕐 Closed L Mon. & Aug. 🔲 ⧉ MC, V 🚌 Bus: 40, 46, 62, 64, 81, 87, 916

🍴 LA CAMPANA
$$$
VICOLO DELLA CAMPANA 18/20
TEL 06 687 5273
www.ristorantelacampana.com
This trattoria is one of the oldest in the city and is well known for its traditional Roman cooking. The menu offers a wide choice, but don't miss the *spaghetti alla carbonara*.

🪑 130 🕐 Closed Mon. & Aug. 🔲 ⧉ All major cards 🚌 Bus: 70, 81, 87, 116, 492, 628

▮ PIERLUIGI
$$$
PIAZZA DE'RICCI 144
TEL 06 686 8717
www.pierluigi.it
Located on a small attractive piazza in central Rome, this establishment specializes in fresh fish dishes.

🛏 120 🕐 Closed Mon. 🆒 🆑 All major cards 🚌 Bus: 23, 40, 62, 64, 116, 280

▮ RISTORANTE ROSCIOLI
$$$
VIA DEI GIUBBONARI 21
TEL 06 687 5287
www.salumeriaroscioli.com
The Roscioli brothers have transformed the family grocery into Ristorante Roscioli, a fashionable wine bar where you can eat high-quality food and buy specialized food products.

🛏 42 🕐 Closed Sun. 🆒 🆑 All major cards

▮ CUL DE SAC
$$
PIAZZA DI PASQUINO 73
TEL 06 6880 1094
www.enotecaculdesacroma.it
A lively wine bar with a good reputation for food. The Cul de Sac offers a variety of light dishes and has a vast selection of wines. Outside tables.

🛏 60 🆒 🆑 MC, V 🚌 Bus: 46, 62, 64, 70, 81, 87, 116, 492, 628

▮ TRATTORIA DA LUIGI
$$
PIAZZA SFORZA CESARINI 24
TEL 06 686 5946
www.trattoriadaluigi.com
This friendly, large trattoria offers an extensive menu that includes the best of Italian cuisine. The outdoor dining area in a lovely, tree-shaded square seems more Parisian than Roman.

🛏 240 🕐 Closed Mon. & Dec. 25–26 🆙 Upstairs only 🆑 All major cards 🚌 Bus: 40, 46, 62, 64, 116

▮ ANTICO FORNO ROSCIOLI
$
VIA DEI CHIAVARI 34
TEL 06 686 4045
www.anticofornoroscioli.it
The Roscioli brothers have opened a *tavola calda* (the Italian version of a fast-food counter) in their bakery, where you can get cheap delicious ready-made dishes to take away or eat on the premises. You can also buy a roll and have a sandwich made at the counter.

🛏 34 🕐 Closed D 🆒 🆑 All major cards

▮ INSALATA RICCA
$
LARGO DEI CHIAVARI 85
TEL 06 6880 3656
www.insalataricca.it
This establishment fills a real niche in the Roman dining scene, especially at lunchtime. *Insalata ricca* means "luscious salad" and that is exactly what it offers. If you are not hungry enough for a meal of pasta or meat but want something light, here you can choose from the long list of deliciously fresh, hearty lunch salads. Pasta dishes and meat courses are also available. Outdoor dining in good weather. Very inexpensive.

🛏 90 🆑 All major cards 🚌 Bus: C3, 30, 70, 81, 87, 492

▮ PIZZERIA DA BAFFETTO
$
VIA DEL GOVERNO VECCHIO 114
TEL 06 686 1617
www.pizzeriabaffetto.it
One of Rome's most popular and best pizzerias, lingering is not possible here. Unless you come early or late, you'll have to wait for a table and then possibly share it when you are seated.

🛏 100 🕐 Closed L & Aug. 🆑 Cash only 🚌 Bus: 40, 46, 62, 64, 116

▶ VATICANO

Much of the solidly respectable residential area around the Vatican dates from the late 19th and early 20th centuries. There are a few unflashy but high-quality hotels. With few exceptions, most of the touristy eating places close to the Vatican are best avoided. For public transportation, see individual listings.

🏨 COLUMBUS
$$$ ★★★★
VIA DELLA CONCILIAZIONE 33
TEL 06 686 5435
FAX 06 686 4874
www.hotelcolumbusrome.com
A 15th-century building right in front of St. Peter's is the setting for this aristocratically austere hotel. Guest rooms and bathrooms are functional, but public areas make up with a surfeit of carved stone and frescoed walls.

🛏 92 🅿 🛗 🆒 🆑 All major cards 🚌 Bus: 23, 34, 40, 62, 982

🏨 FARNESE
$$$ ★★★★
VIA A. FARNESE 30
TEL 06 321 2553
FAX 06 321 5129
www.hotelfarnese.com
A charming choice (and value for money) in the residential Prati area near St. Peter's, connected to the center by metro. Tranquil atmosphere with 17th-century decor and comfortable rooms.

🛏 23 🅿 🛗 🆒 🆑 All major cards 🚌 Bus: 30, 70, 87, 130, 280, 301. Metro: Linea A (Lepanto)

🏨 SANT'ANNA
$$$ ★★★
BORGO PIO 134
TEL 06 6880 1602
www.santannahotel.net
Located in the shadow of St. Peter's, this small family-run hotel offers tastefully

decorated, comfortable rooms and caring service. Breakfast is served in a pleasant, inside garden in the summer.

[i] 20 [P] (extra) 🔒 [C]
[cards] All major cards 🚌 Bus: 9, 23, 49, 32, 81, 590, 982

🍴 L'ARCANGELO
$$$
VIA G. G. BELLI 59
TEL 06 321 0992
www.larcangelo.com
A popular restaurant whose fame rests on its inventive cuisine, which uses the best regional products.

🪑 35 🕐 Closed L Sat., Sun., & Aug. 🔒 [cards] All major cards 🚌 Bus: 30, 70, 81, 87, 130

🍴 TAVERNA ANGELICA
$$$
PIAZZA A. CAPPONI 6
TEL 06 687 4514
www.tavernaangelica.com
Reservations are essential for this romantic little corner restaurant serving delicate, flavorful, and innovative Italian cuisine, like *tagliatelle* with nettles and curry, duck breast in balsamic vinegar, and chocolate crêpes. All are accompanied by a carefully selected wine list.

🪑 45 🕐 Closed L Mon., L Tue., & 2 weeks in Aug. 🔒 AE, MC, V 🚌 Bus: 23, 34, 49, 982

🍴 DAL TOSCANO
$$
VIA GERMANICO 58
TEL 06 3972 5717
www.ristorantedaltoscano.it
Located conveniently close to the Vatican Museums, this well-established restaurant specializes in traditional Tuscan cuisine. Outdoor seating.

🪑 120 🕐 Closed Mon. & Aug. 🔒 [cards] All major cards 🚌 Bus: 32, 81, 590, 982

🍴 IL MOZZICONE
$$
VIA BORGO PIO 180
TEL 06 686 1500

A simple family-style trattoria said to serve some of the best *spaghetti alla carbonara* in the city. In nice weather, you can eat lunch or dinner outside, resting up from your hours in the Vatican Museums and St. Peter's.

🪑 40 🕐 Closed Sun. & Aug. 🔒 Cash only 🚌 Bus: 19, 23, 32, 70, 180, 492, 990

▶ TRASTEVERE TO GIANICOLO

Visitors and Romans alike come nightly in search of a good time in this lively area "across the Tiber." It has always been packed with bars and restaurants, but recently a number of appealing hotels have also opened. 🚌 Bus: H, 23, 115, 125, 280, 710, 870. Tram: 3, 8

🏨 VOI DONNA CAMILLA SAVELLI HOTEL
$$$$ ★★★★
VIA GARIBALDI 27
TEL 06 588 8861
FAX 06 588 2101
www.voihotels.com
After a remarkable restoration, this 17th-century convent in the heart of Trastevere now operates as a refined hotel. Broadband access to the Internet is available.

[i] 78 [P] 🔒 [C]
[cards] All major cards

🏨 HOTEL SANTA MARIA
$$$ ★★★
VICOLO DEL PIEDE 2
TEL 06 589 4626
www.hotelsantamaria trastevere.it
A charming, ground-floor hotel set in the tranquil garden of a 16th-century cloister, only a few minutes' walk from Piazza Santa Maria in Trastevere.

[i] 18 [P] [C] [cards] All major cards

🏨 SAN FRANCESCO
$$$ ★★★
VIA JACOPA DE' SETTESOLI 7

PRICES

HOTELS
An indication of the cost of a double room in the high season is given by $ signs.

$$$$$	Over $450
$$$$	$350–$450
$$$	$250–$350
$$	$120–$250
$	Under $120

RESTAURANTS
An indication of the cost of a three-course meal without drinks is given by $ signs.

$$$$$	Over $80
$$$$	$55–$80
$$$	$40–$55
$$	$25–$40
$	Under $25

TEL 06 5830 0051
FAX 06 5833 3413
www.hotelsanfrancesco.net
San Francesco offers pleasant guest rooms, a breakfast area facing a 15th-century cloister, and a terrace with a 360-degree panoramic view over Rome.

[i] 24 [P] (extra) 🔒 [C]
[cards] All major cards

🏨 DOMUS TIBERINA
$$ ★★
VIA IN PISCINULA 37
TEL 06 5813648
www.hoteldomustiberina.it
This hotel is located in the heart of Trastevere, not far from both Santa Cecilia and Tiber Island. The rooms are small but comfortable and attractively decorated.

[i] 10 [C] [cards] All major cards

🏨 VILLA DELLA FONTE
$$
VIA DELLA FONTE D'OLIO 8
TEL 06 580 3797

FAX 06 580 3796
www.villafonte.com
This tiny, welcoming B&B is
just a few yards from Piazza
Santa Maria in Trastevere.
The guest rooms are com-
fortable and well equipped,
and after a busy day of
sightseeing guests enjoy
relaxing on the lovely terrace.
Breakfast extra.

🛏 5 🚭 🅰 All major cards

🏨 ORSA MAGGIORE WOMEN'S HOSTEL
$
VIA SAN FRANCESCO
DI SALES 1/A
TEL. 06 6893753
FAX 06 68401725
www.orsamaggioreroma.com
Housed in a 16th-century
former convent in Traste-
vere, the Orsa Maggiore
Women's Hostel, as its name
implies, offers accommo-
dations for women only.
Completely refurbished but
maintaining the building's
former style, the rooms
are simple and look onto
a peaceful courtyard. Both
singles and dormitory rooms
are available. Restaurant on
the premises (women only in
the evenings).

🛏 10 🚭 🅰
🅰 All major cards
🚌 Bus: H, 23, 75, 115, 125, 271,
280, 780

🍽 ENOTECA FERRARA
$$$$
VIA DEL MORO 1
TEL 06 5833 3920
enotecaferrara.com
This excellent and popular
wine bar has an impressive
list of wines and after-dinner
drinks to accompany a con-
stantly changing menu.
The soups are particularly
recommended. The decor is
original and pleasing; glass
panels in the floor allow you
to look down into the all-
important cellars.

🪑 120 🅰 All major cards

🍽 GLASS HOSTARIA
$$$$
VICOLO DE' CINQUE 58
TEL 06 5833 5903
glasshostaria.it
Highly rated restaurant serving innovative cuisine in the
heart of Trastevere. There is
an excellent chef: the star-
winning Cristina Bowerman,
among the most popular
in Italy.

🪑 55 🕐 Closed Mon. & L
🚭 🅰 DC, MC, V

🍽 SABATINI
$$$$
PIAZZA SANTA MARIA IN
TRASTEVERE 13
TEL 06 581 2026
www.ristorantisabatini.it
Tourists love the stunning
setting and archetypal Italian
restaurant ambience of this
Trastevere locale. The mainly
fish-based cuisine also draws
locals. Super-fresh ingredients.

🪑 120 🚭 🅰 All major cards

🍽 BIR & FUD
$$
VIA BENEDETTA 23
TEL 06 589 4016
birandfud.it
This pizzeria combines the
best ingredients in unusual but
delicious ways. It also offers
Italian artisanal beer, perfect
for hot summer nights.

🪑 60 🕐 Closed L., Mon.–Thu.
🚭 🅰 MC, V, AE

🍽 DA LUCIA
$$
VICOLO DEL MATTONATO 2B
TEL 06 580 3601
The same family has run this
no-frills trattoria for more
than 60 years. In summer
tables fill the alley outside.
The interior is lined with
wooden slats. The unchanging
menu includes some standard
primi followed by dishes such
as rabbit alla cacciatora and
cuttlefish with peas.

🪑 45 🕐 Closed Mon., 3 weeks

in Aug., & Christmas 🅰 Cash
and ATM card

🍽 LA SCALA IN TRASTEVERE
$$
PIAZZA DELLA SCALA 60
TEL 06 580 3763
www.ristorantelascala.it
A former, low-end birreria
(beer and food joint), this
warmly decorated restaurant
offers very friendly service,
good and abundant food, and
low to moderate prices. It also
has uninterrupted service to
the wee hours of the morning.
For those who just want a
drink, an adjacent entrance
leads to a cozy, wood-paneled
bar. Outdoor seating.

🪑 120 🅰 All major cards

🍽 LE MANI IN PASTA
$$
VIA DEI GENOVESI 37
TEL 06 581 6017
www.ristorantedipesce
trastevere.roma.it
This reasonably priced trattoria, small with a simple
interior and a view of the
kitchen, offers a wide selection
of delicious pastas, fish, and
grilled meats.

🪑 70 🕐 Closed Mon. & Aug.
🚭 🅰 All major cards

🍽 AI MARMI
$
VIALE TRASTEVERE 53/57
TEL 06 580 0919
Also known as the "mortuary"
(obitorio) because of its marble
tabletops, this place is an
institution for both its pizza
and the typical Trastevere
atmosphere. Outdoor seating.

🪑 70 🕐 Closed Wed.
🅰 MC, V

🍽 DAR POETA
$
VICOLO DEL BOLOGNA 45/46
TEL 06 588 0516
www.darpoeta.com

A lively Trastevere pizzeria offering a wide selection of pizzas and *bruschette* (toasted breads). Arrive very early to get a seat. A few outdoor tables.

 70 All major cards

▶ ## FORUM BOARIUM TO AVENTINO

The Forum Boarium was the site of ancient Rome's cattle market and sits between three of Rome's seven ancient hills: the Palatine, Capitoline, and Aventine. The area now contains some excellent, tranquil hotels. Many of the nearest restaurants are in the popular Testaccio area or the Ghetto. For public transportation, see individual listings.

AVENTINO SAN ANSELMO
$$$ ★★★★
PIAZZA DI SANT'ANSELMO 2
TEL 06 570057
FAX 06 578 3604
www.aventinohotels.com
Sant'Anselmo's lush garden shaded with orange trees on the Aventine Hill makes the perfect setting for relaxing after sightseeing. And you can wake to the singing of birds yet be at the Roman Forum in minutes. The lobbies and guest rooms are attractively decorated.

34 P All major cards Bus: 23, 30, 75, 130, 280, 716. Tram: 3

FORTY SEVEN
$$$ ★★★★
VIA LUIGI PETROSELLI 47
TEL 06 678 7816
FAX 06 6919 0726
www.fortysevenhotel.com
A jewel that holds works by 20th-century Italian artists: Mastroianni, Greco, Modigliani, Quagliata, and Guccione. The guest rooms are large and luminous, many overlooking the surrounding monuments. Breathtaking

views from the rooftop terrace bar/restaurant.

61 All major cards

PALAZZO AL VELABRO
$$$ ★★★★
VIA DEL VELABRO 16
TEL 06 679 2758
FAX 06 679 3790
www.velabro.it
If you are planing to stay a week or more this could be a good choice. Centrally located near the Palatine Hill, it offers quiet, comfortable studio apartments with kitchenettes for two to four people, some with wonderful views.

35 All major cards Bus: C3, H, 30, 44, 63, 81, 83, 130, 118, 160, 170, 628, 715, 780

GIGGETTO AL PORTICO D'OTTAVIA
$$$
VIA DEL PORTICO D'OTTAVIA 21A
TEL 06 686 1105
www.giggetto.it
The main street of the Jewish Ghetto is the perfect setting for sampling traditional Jewish-Roman cuisine—starting with fried cod, anchovies, zucchini flowers, and artichokes and finishing with cheesecake and blueberry sauce.

200 Closed Mon. & last 2 weeks in July All major cards Bus: H, 23, 46, 60, 63, 80, 280, 780. Tram: 8

PIPERNO
$$$
VIA MONTE DE' CENCI 9
TEL 06 6880 6629
www.ristorantepiperno.it
In the heart of the Jewish Ghetto, this longtime favorite has changed little over the years. Here *carciofi alla giudia* (fried Jerusalem artichokes) are at their best, or try the *fritto misto vegetariano* (lightly fried artichokes, cheese-and-rice croquettes, mozzarella, and stuffed zucchini

blossoms). Outdoor seating available.

70 Closed D Sun., Mon., & Aug. All major cards Bus: H, 23, 46, 60, 63, 80, 280, 780. Tram: 8

FLAVIO AL VELAVEVODETTO
$$
VIA DI MONTE TESTACCIO 97
TEL 06 574 4194
www.ristorantevelavevodetto.it
This popular restaurant in the Testaccio area is home to the *cucina romana* (Roman cuisine), based on the "fifth quarter" or the cheaper cuts of meat and innards that were once partial payment for the workers at the nearby slaughterhouse. Ancient potshards *(testae)*, fragments of broken amphorae which created the Monte Testaccio that gives its name to the neighborhood, are visible through the glass-paneled back walls of the dining rooms. Outdoor dining in summer.

100 All major cards Bus: 23, 83, 280, 716, 719. Tram: 3

LA TORRICELLA
$$
VIA EVANGELISTA TORRICELLI 2
TEL 06 574 6311
www.la-torricella.com
This family-run business popular with neighborhood residents specializes in the freshest seafood in its pastas and main courses. Outdoor dining in summer.

130 Closed L MC, V Bus: 83, 170, 719, 781

PIZZERIA DA REMO
$
PIAZZA SANTA MARIA LIBERATRICE 44
TEL 06 574 6270
Here you can find the traditional Roman pizza—thin and crusty. Arrive early if you don't want to wait for a table.

85 Closed L & Sun. Cash only Bus: 23,

30, 75, 83, 130, 170, 716, 781.
Tram: 3

🍴 VOLPETTI
$
VIA ALESSANDRO VOLTA 8
TEL 06 574 4306
www.tavernavolpetti.it
Around the corner from the
famous Volpetti deli (see
Taste Treats p. 260) the Volpetti brothers have opened
a *tavola calda* (the Italian
equivalent of fast food). The
selection includes both cold
cuts as well as freshly baked
pizza, excellent breads, and
prepared dishes.
🔲 35 🕐 Closed D Sun.–Mon.
🆑 All major cards

▶ FUORI LE MURA (OUTSIDE THE WALLS)

Italians love a day trip outside
the city, which usually includes
a visit to a historical site and
always lunch. Popular, close by
destinations are the Castelli
Romani, Tivoli, Ostia Antica, and
Palestrina. All have enjoyable
eating spots. Outside the Roman
walls, but still in the vicinity of
the city, you can also find a variety of hotels and restaurants.
For public transportation, see
individual listings.

🏨 ROME CAVALIERI
$$$$$ *****
VIA A. CADLOLO 101
TEL 06 35091
FAX 06 3509 2241

romecavalieri.com
A shuttle service transports
guests to and from central
Rome, leaving you free to
enjoy the peaceful location
on the Monte Mario hill
overlooking the city. The
well-equipped rooms have balconies, many with fine views
over Rome. Tennis courts, a
swimming pool, and a jogging
track are among the many features of this top-of-the-market
chain. Breakfast extra.
ℹ️ 345 rooms, 25 suites 🅿️ ⬆️
🆑 🏊 📺 🆑 All major cards
🚌 Bus: 913

🏨 HILTON ROME AIRPORT
$$$ ****
VIA ARTURO FERRARIN 2,
FIUMICINO
TEL 06 65258
www.hiltonhotels.it
Finally, Rome has an airport
hotel. Just 200 yards (200 m)
from Fiumicino Airport termi-
nals, the Hilton's bedrooms are
functional and fully equipped.
There is a restaurant and snack
bar, plus a complimentary
shuttle service into central
Rome eight times a day.
ℹ️ 517 🅿️ ⬆️ 🆑 🏊 📺
🆑 All major cards 📺 See
page 236 Fiumicino Airport

SOMETHING SPECIAL

🍴 LA PERGOLA
$$$$$
ROME CAVALIERI
VIA A. CADLOLO 101
TEL 06 3509 2152
romecavalieri.com
Recognized as Rome's best

and most innovative restau-
rant, La Pergola's reputation
has rocketed since the arrival
of Heinz Beck, as of 2005 the
only chef in the city awarded
three Michelin stars. His dishes
show strong Italian influ-
ences. The attentive service is
superb, the wine list extensive,
and the view of Rome near
unmatched.
🔲 55 🕐 Closed Sun., Jan., &
2 weeks in Aug. 🅿️ 🆑 🆑 All
major cards 🚌 Bus: 913

🍴 ANTICO ARCO
$$$$
PIAZZALE AURELIO 7
TEL 06 581 5274
www.anticoarco.it
Located just outside the wall
on the Janiculum Hill, this
popular restaurant offers a
gastronomic experience that
will not disappoint. Efficient,
friendly service and a good
wine list.
🔲 120 🆑 🆑 All major cards
🚌 Bus: 115, 125

🍴 ARCHEOLOGICA
$$$
VIA APPIA ANTICA 139
TEL 06 788 0494
www.larcheologia.it
A perfect lunch stop when
sightseeing along the Via
Appia Antica. In winter, the
dining areas have open fires,
and in summer there is a lovely
outdoor seating area.
🔲 300 (inside and out)
🕐 Closed Tues. 🅿️ 🆑
🆑 All major cards
🚌 Bus: 118, 218

SHOPPING

Combining shopping and sightseeing is one of the delights of Rome. Each shopping district has its own particular shopping characteristics, but generally speaking most shops are small and specialized, department stores are few and far between, and large shopping malls are situated outside the city.

Main Shopping Areas

Piazza di Spagna/Pantheon: In the streets around Piazza di Spagna and the Pantheon you will find the top names in Italian fashion and design. More reasonably priced clothes, and those for the younger generation, can be found on nearby Via del Corso.

Piazza Navona/Campo de' Fiori/Ghetto: The narrow, bustling streets here are home to many independent designers as well as to classy secondhand garment stores and accessory shops. Via Giubbonari offers reasonably priced clothes, shoes, and accessories—mostly for the younger generation. Look for top-quality antiques or prints on Via dei Coronari.

Trastevere: In this labyrinth of narrow streets you will find any number of small shops and street vendors selling unique pieces.

Via Cola di Rienzo: Close to the Vatican Museums, this area boasts stores selling mid-range clothes, leather goods, and accessories similar to those in Via del Corso and Via Nazionale (see below). For religious souvenirs, head for the shops around St. Peter's.

Via Nazionale: Starting near the Termini train station and running to Piazza Venezia, this street is the place to go for affordable fashion.

Monti: Squeezed in between Via Nazionale and the Roman Forum, this area is a gold mine for vintage and one-of-a-kind stylish clothing and accessories.

Opening Hours

See p. 240.

Tax-Free Shopping

Non-EU residents who make purchases amounting to more than €154.94 on the same day, in a store participating in the Tax Refund network, can ask for a sales tax refund. When you pay, ask for a tax refund form (you will need your passport). You can claim your tax refund on departure from the airport. You will need your yellow tax refund form, passport, and credit card. To complete the process the form must be stamped by the last customs office in the country of departure from the European Union. Once the form is stamped, mail it to Tax Refund. There are time limits for claiming and the merchandise you have purchased must be unused when leaving the European Union. For more information, see www.taxrefund.it.

Sales (Saldi)

Winter sales start after January 6 and go through the end of the month; summer sales start in early July. These are the best times to pick up a bargain: Prices are discounted by 50 percent or more. Make sure the original price is on the tag, along with the discounted sale price.

Malls & Department Stores

Malls

Although not nearly of the size and scope of their North American cousins, some malls do exist in central Rome. The **Galleria Alberto Sordi** (www.galleria albertosordi.it) at Piazza Colonna, is a small art nouveau mall near Piazza di Spagna. The **Forum Termini** (www.gandistazioni .it) with its 50-plus shops is located at the Termini train station, Piazza dei Cinquecento. It is Rome's handiest shopping mall for one-stop, last-minute shopping needs. Shops are open daily 7 a.m. to 10 p.m.; there's even a supermarket.

Department Stores

Rome has two department stores, both selling clothing, leather goods, accessories, cosmetics, and housewares: **Rinascente** (Via del Tritone 61/ Via dei Due Macelli 23, tel. 06 879161 & Piazza Fiume, tel. 06 8841231) and **Coin** (Via Cola di Rienzo 173, tel 06 3600 4298; Piazzale Appio 7, tel 06 708 0020; Forum Termini, Via Giolitti 10, tel 06 4782 5909).

Discount Outlets & Malls

Central Rome

Discount outlets are rare in central Rome and their stock is often limited. However, it is possible to pick up a designer item at a bargain price if you look hard.

   Galassia, Via Frattina 21 (Spagna), tel 06 679 7896. Take a look at its bargain basement for marked-down designer labels.

   Gente Roma Outlet, Via Cola de Rienzo 246, tel 06 6892672 (Vatican). It offers discounts on Prada, Miu Miu, Burberry, made in Italy accessories, shoes, and bags.

   Spazioespanso guardaroba, Piazza della Pigne 7 (Pantheon), tel 06 679 2879. Take advantage of the discounts on end-of-collection items in the boutique in Via Bergamaschi (see Clothing below).

Outskirts of Rome

Several major outlet malls are found outside central Rome (for each, a 30- to 40-minute trip).

MacArthur Glen Outlet, Via Ponte di Piscina Cupa, Castel Romano, www.mcarthurglen.com. It features more than 150 of the most famous designer labels in the world. A shuttle service leaves from Via Marsala 15 (Termini Station) and from Via Ludovisi 48 (Via Veneto). Buy the ticket *(€15 round-trip)* on the bus. For further information, see the website above or call 06 6979 7554. There is also a pick-up service from your hotel *(tel 333 190 4337 or 329 431 7686, fare €29).*

Parco Leonardo, Via Portuense 2000, tel 06 4542 2448, parcoleonardo.it. This major Roman mall has some 150 stores under one roof. To reach it, take the metropolitan train to Fiumicino from the Piramide or Trastevere metro station and get off at the Parco Leonardo stop.

Valmonte Outlet, www.valmontoneoutlet.com. This outlet is south of Rome. A shuttle bus runs Thursday to Sunday, leaving from Via Marsala 71 (Termini Station). For more information, see *www.terravision.eu.*

Clothing

Italy leads the world when it comes to designer fashion. All the major houses have branches in Rome. Tip: Always try on clothing and measure gifts, as sizes in Italy are not always uniform. Remember Italian shops rarely make refunds and the smaller shops are often reluctant even to exchange items.

Piazza di Spagna/ Pantheon Area

Armani Boutique, Via dei Condotti 77/79, tel 06 699 1460.

The king of understated elegance for men and women. **Armani Emporio** *(Via del Babuino 140, tel 06 3221 581)* carries more affordable clothes.

Armani Jeans, within the Rinascente stores. Sells the casual collection.

Aspesi, Via del Babuino 144/A, tel 06 323 0376. Elegant clothes for men and women.

Brioni, Via Condotti 21/A, tel. 06 6783428 & Via del Babuino 38/40, tel. 06 484517. The tailor of choice for Italian celebrities. A fine line of both off-the-rack and tailor-made men's suits. There is also a small women's collection.

Campo Marzio9, Via Campo Marzio 9, tel 06 6830 0131. Men's shirts in all colors and styles.

Capua, Via Campo Marzio 32, tel 06 6880 1441. Colorful, quality cashmere at more affordable prices than elsewhere.

Davide Cenci, Via Campo Marzio 1/7, tel 06 699 0681. Top-quality men and women's wear.

De Clerq e De Clerq, Via dei Prefetti 10, tel 06 6813 6826. Exquisitely styled knitwear in cotton, silk, and wool.

Degli Effetti, Piazza Capranica 73 (men)/93 (women)/75 (Neo Millennium), tel 06 679 1650. Clothes from major Italian, Japanese, and French designers.

Dolce e Gabbana, Via dei Condotti 51, tel 06 6992 4999. "In" clothes for men and women.

Ermenegildo Zegna, Via dei Condotti 58, tel 06 6994 0678. The place for classic men's fashion.

Fendi, Largo Goldoni 420, tel 06 3345 0890. This impressive store sells everything from furs to gifts.

FG-Albertelli, Piazza del Parlamento 9b, tel 06 687 3793. Beautifully styled menswear and irresistible accessories.

Gianni Versace, Piazza di Spagna 12, tel 06 678 0521. Flamboyant clothes for the glamour set.

Malo, Via Borgognona 4, tel 06 679 1331. Three floors of clothing

for men, women, and children, plus accessories and housewares.

Max Mara, Via dei Condotti 17/18/A, tel 06 6992 21045. Wearable, classic styles for women. The sporty more affordable line of Max Mara is sold at **Sportmax** *(Via Borgognona 7a/b, tel 06 6994 0967).*

Missoni, Piazza di Spagna 78, tel 06 679 2555. Well-known colorful, stripy knitwear and more.

La Perla, Via Bocca di Leone 28, tel 06 6994 1934. Luxury lingerie and swimsuits for women.

Prada, Via dei Condotti 88/92, tel 06 679 0897. Cutting-edge clothes and accessories.

Spazioespanso, Via dei Bergamaschi 59/60, tel 06 9784 3793. Located in the Pantheon area. For their discount shop, see "Outlets" above.

Trussardi, Via Frattina 130, tel 06 6938 0939. Beautifully tailored clothes for men and women.

Valentino, Via dei Condotti 13, tel 06 679 5862. Rome's most famous fashion house.

Piazza Navona/ Campo de' Fiori Area

Loulou, Via dei Banchi Vecchi 116, tel 06 6880 1968. A collection of unique clothing, bags, shoes, and accessories for women.

Pandemonium, Piazza Euclide 8/9, tel. 06 807 7538. This is the place for the latest look in young, casual wear.

Patrizia Pieroni-Arsenale Gallery, Via del Pellegrino 172, tel 06 6880 2424. Captivating clothes for women.

Regola 71, Via dei Cappellari 71, tel 06 683 2169. Stylish shop catering to women who are looking for something modern but not overly trendy.

SBU, Via di San Pantaleo 68, tel 06 6880 2547. Hipster casual menswear.

L'una & L'altra, Piazza di Pasquino 76, tel 06 6880 4995. Clothes for feminine sophisticates. Exclusive franchise for Issey Miyake and Yohji Yamamoto.

Uno Boutique, Piazza Mattei 1, tel 06 6830 1897. Well-researched selection of casual wear from off-the-radar designers.

Monti Area

Via del Boschetto, running through the heart of Monti, is one of the best shopping streets in Rome for original clothes, vintage clothes, and accessories: **Tina Sondergaard** (1d), **Creje** (5a), **Pulp** (140). Check out nearby streets for more choices: Sip a glass of wine while trying on shoes at **Smalto** (*Via Urbana 12, tel 06 484 766*) or eye the clothes at **Le Gallinelle** (*Via Panisperna 61, tel 06 488 1017*). Also visit **LOL** (*Via Urbana 92*) or see the interesting housewares at **Nora P** (*Via Panisperna 220, tel 06 4547 3738, open by appointment*).

Shoes, Bags, & Leather Goods

The Italian leather industry's worldwide reputation is well-deserved. Don't leave Rome without a bag, a pair of shoes, or another of the leather accessories available for all tastes and pockets. As with designer clothes, most of the top labels are found in the area around Piazza di Spagna. For more affordable leather goods, look in the streets around the Pantheon, Via del Corso, Via Cola di Rienzo, Via Nazionale, and in Monti.

Piazza di Spagna/ Pantheon Area

Bottega Veneta, Piazza San Lorenzo in Lucina 9, tel 06 6821 0024. The line's traditional leather goods as well as a more contemporary line of accessories, handbags, and shoes.

Dal Co', Via Vittoria 65, tel 06 678 6536. Highest quality made-to-measure shoes for women.

Di San Giacomo Sandals, Via di Tor Millina 10/11 (Navona), tel 06 9684 7938. Made-to-measure sandals in 30 minutes.

Fausto Santini, Via Frattina 120, tel 06 678 4114. Trend-setting styles ranging from everyday to eccentric.

Ferragamo, Via dei Condotti 65 & 73, tel 06 678 1130. World-famous designer shoes and apparel.

Furla, Piazza di Spagna 22, tel. 06 679 7159. Smart bags and accessories at accessible prices.

Gucci, Via dei Condotti 6/8, tel 06 679 0405. Also Via Borgognona 7d. The ultimate in elegance, top-quality shoes and accessories.

Hogan, Via del Babuino 110, tel 06 678 6828. Famous brand shoes for men and women.

Louis Vuitton, Piazza San Lorenzo in Lucina 41, tel 06 6880 9520. An impressive concept store for the entire LV range inside a former movie theater. Second shop at Via dei Condotti 13.

Mancini, Via della Palombella 28, tel 06 686 1485. In existence since 1918, the shop offers a wide range of artisan-made bags and leather accessories.

RE(f)USE, Via Fontanella Borghese 40, tel 06 6813 6975. Bags, accessories, furniture, and design objects using old materials or reusing existing ones and working them, by expert Italian hands, into new, beautiful objects.

Saddlers Union, Via Margutta 11, tel 06 3212 0237. Classic quality bags, luggage, and leather accessories, also customizable.

Tod's, Via Fontanella di Borghese 56/57, tel 06 6821 0066; Via dei Condotti 53, tel 06 699 1089. Attractive shoes and bags for men and women.

Jewelry

Bulgari, Via dei Condotti 10 (Spagna), tel 06 696 261. The ultimate in jewelry design.

Cillabijoux, Via Francesco Crispi 72 (Spagna), tel 06 484594. Original and elegant bijoux jewelry.

Delfina Delettrez, Via del Governo Vecchio 67 (Navona), tel 06 6813 4105. If you're looking for above-average jewelry, don't miss this hole-in-the-wall shop.

Fabio Piccioni, Via del Boschetto 77 (Monti), tel 06 472 837. A real find for costume or vintage jewelry.

Massimo Maria Melis, Via dell'Orso 73 (Navona), tel 06 9292 6933. Beautifully crafted gold jewelry.

Materie, Via del Gesù 29 (Pantheon), tel 06 679 3199. Unique jewelry made from a wide variety of materials. The store also carries scarves, handbags, and other accessories.

Old & New, Via Monserrato 99 (Campo de' Fiori), tel 06 6830 8885. Original bags, jewelry, and Bakelite brooches.

Other Accessories

Eyeglasses: Mondello Ottica, Via del Pellegrino 98 (Campo de' Fiori), tel 06 686 1955. Your best bet if you are looking for a very special pair of frames or sunglasses.

Gloves: Sermoneta, Piazza di Spagna 61, tel 06 679 1960. Gloves in all colors and styles.

Hats: Borsalino, Via Campo Marzio 72 (Spagna), tel 06 678 3945; Piazza del Popolo 20; Piazza Fiume; Via Sistina 58/A. Home of the fedora first produced by Giuseppe Borsalino in 1857. Today the company makes a variety of hats for both sexes.

Scarves: L'Accessorio–Faliero Sarti, Via Vittoria 62 (Spagna), tel 06 6994 2501. Stylish shawls, scarves for men and women, and cashmere pashminas.

Ties: La Cravatta, Via di Santa Cecilia 12 (Trastevere), tel 06 6901 6941. Off-the-rack and made-to-measure ties.

Umbrellas & Rain Gear: H.Due.O, Via Sant'Eustachio 20 (Pantheon), tel 06 6880 4612. An umbrella store with charming and whimsical rain gear items, including a dog's umbrella. Also in the Termini Station shopping mall.

Kids

Children's clothes don't come cheap in Italy, but they do have that inimitable touch of style.

Il Gufo, Via del Babuino 65, (Spagna), tel 06 321 7661. The collection follows the kids dressed like kids concept, with young, age-appropriate styles.

Neck and Neck, Via Vittoria 56 (Spagna), tel 06 6992 2363. Stylish casual clothes.

Prenatal, Via Nazionale 45, tel 06 488 1403. Stroller lost or damaged in transit? Prenatal has almost anything you might need for children, including clothing.

Toys

Città del Sole, Via della Scrofa 65 (Navona), tel 06 6880 3805. Educational and environment-friendly toys, books, games, and puzzles.

Al Sogno, Piazza Navona 53, tel 06 686 4198. Gorgeous, cuddly toys, some of them life-size. Collectors models, miniature Ferraris, and dolls.

Gift & Souvenirs Shops

Many such shops can be found in and around Piazza Navona and Campo de' Fiori. Along Corso del Rinascimento you will find Murano glass, ceramics, Roman reproductions, and stationery. Stores selling religious items cluster in Via dei Cestari (Pantheon) and around St. Peter's. Tip: Most Roman museums, galleries, and archaeological sites have excellent gift shops offering a broad range of souvenirs at reasonable prices.

Banchi141, Via dei Banchi Vecchi 141 (Campo de' Fiori), tel 06 6889 1812. Traditional, handmade ceramics from Puglia.

Campo Marzio Design, Via Campo Marzio 41 (Spagna), tel

06 6880 7877. Beautiful bright, leather-bound journals and writing accessories.

Campomarzio70-The Essential Culture, Via Vittoria 52 (Spagna), tel 06 6979 7739. Dedicated to the art of perfume, the expert assistants at this boutique will help you find the perfect scent.

Casali, Via dei Coronari 115 (Navona); Piazza della Rotonda 82 (Pantheon), tel 06 678 3515. A wide range of beautiful prints.

Emporium Roma, Via Zanardelli 3/4 (Navona), tel 06 6476 1160. Souvenirs, games, and books on Rome.

Fabriano, Via del Babuino 173 (Spagna), tel 06 3260 0361. Stylish store selling luxury stationery, photo albums, guest or address books, and fountain pens.

Ferrari Shop, Via Tomacelli 147/152 (Spagna), tel 06 8375 8510. Offers everything a Ferrari fan could want (except the car).

Limentani, Via del Portico d'Ottavia 47 (Ghetto), tel 06 6830 7000. A cavernous treasure trove of crockery and kitchenware. Many brand names are reduced by up to 20 percent.

Maurizio Grossi, Via Margutta 109 (Spagna), tel 06 3600 1935. Marble and stone statues and busts, as well as marble fruit, vases, and bowls. Also try the nearby **La Bottega del Marmoraro,** Via Margutta 53b, tel 06 320 7660. This marble-working shop will make you a "classical" statue or (far easier to carry) a lapidary inscription to order.

Officina Profumo Farmaceutica di Santa Maria Novella, Corso del Rinascimento 47 (Navona), tel 06 687 9608. The medieval Florentine pharmacy's products, made with natural ingredients and the monks' traditional methods.

Polvere di Tempo, Via del Moro 59 (Trastevere), tel 06 588 0704. Everything for measuring time and space.

Studio Forme-Arte da Usare, Via di Santa Cecilia 15 (Trastevere), tel 06 581 2927. Unique glass lamps, dishes, vases, and sculptures.

Specialty Shops

Il Fotoamatore, Via Piave 8/A, tel. 06 42014243. Cameras, video cameras and accessories.

Icon Store, Via Sforza Pallavicini 5/7 (Prati), tel 06 9727 1435. The place for your Apple needs.

Taste Treats

Antica Norcineria Viola, Piazza Campo de' Fiori 42, tel 06 6880 6114. An impressive selection of salamis, hams, and other pork products, many vacuum-packed for easy transportation.

Beppe e i Suoi Formaggi, Via Santa Maria del Pianto 9a/11 (Ghetto), tel 06 6819 2210. A "don't miss" if you are a cheese lover. Buy top-quality cheeses over the counter or order a cheese platter in the restaurant.

Boccione, Via del Portico d'Ottavia 1 (Ghetto), tel 06 687 8637. This bakery is known for its traditional Roman-Jewish cakes, particularly the *torta di ricotta* (cheesecake) with berries *(visciole)* or chocolate.

La Cannoleria Siciliana, Corso Trieste 100, tel. 06 9484 4621 (zona Trieste, Nomentano). Delicious freshly made Sicilian cannoli.

Eataly, Air Terminal Ostiense, Piazzale XII Ottobre 1492 (Piramide), tel 06 9027 9201, www.eataly.net. This Italian food megastore combines all elements of the national food industry, including, wine, oil, and beer, as well as restaurants, kitchenware, and a bookshop. Great place to find food gifts.

Giuliani Marron Glacés, Via P. Emilio 67 (Prati), tel 06 324 3548. Giovanni Giuliani's store has been making them for the last 50 years. The specialty is the chocolate-covered variety.

Moriondo e Gariglio, Via del Piè di Marmo 21 (Pantheon), tel 06 699 0856. Fantastic, homemade and custom-made chocolates.

Bar Pompi, Via Cola di Rienzo 313 (Musei Vaticani and other locations), tel. 06 6880 2048. The king of tiramisu. Eat a portion of the classic chocolate dessert (or their other flavors) on the spot or take it home.

Sant'Eustachio, Piazza di Sant'Eustachio 82 (Pantheon). This café, serving what legend says is the best coffee in Rome, also sells beans or ready-ground in a variety of gift packs.

Trimani, Via Goito 20 (Nazionale), tel 06 446 9661. Considered the best stocked wine cellar in Rome. Worldwide shipping.

Volpetti, Via Marmorata 47 (Testaccio), tel 06 574 2352. A must for any foodie. Specializing in aged cheeses, it sells and ships wherever.

Ice Cream
In Italy ice cream, better known as gelato, isn't just for kids. See sidebar p. 97 for several excellent options. Tip: Avoid flashy *gelaterie* such as Blue Ice or others with gelato that is improbably colorful or rippled. Nowadays every *gelateria* claims its ice cream is *artigianale* or made on the premises but often this is not true. Looking for natural colors is a good strategy.

Books, Music, & Film
There are some excellent English-language bookshops in Rome, as well as several Italian ones with a selection of English books.

The Almost Corner Bookshop, Via del Moro 45 (Trastevere), tel 06 583 6942. A welcoming treasure trove of English-language fiction, poetry, history, and more.

Altroquando, Via del Governo Vecchio 82 / 83, 06 68892200. Alternative "very open" bookstore. It offers "artisanal" books and "independent" beers.

Anglo American Bookshop, Via delle Vite 102 (Spagna), tel 06 679 5222. Particularly good for nonfiction catering to a wide range of special interests. At No. 27, a second branch *(tel 06 678 9657)* specializes in science and technology.

Borribooks, Termini Station, tel. 06 4828422. A good selection of foreign-language fiction and guidebooks.

Fahrenheit 451, Campo de' Fiori 44, tel. 06 6875 930. Historic bookshop in Campo de' Fiori.

Feltrinelli International, Via V.E. Orlando 84 (Nazionale), tel 06 199151173. Wide range of books in English and other languages

Libreria del Viaggiatore, Via del Pellegrino 78 (Campo de' Fiori), tel 06 8350 3490. Good selection of English-language travel books, guides, and maps.

Markets
Fruits & Vegetables:
See p. 155.
Flea Markets & Antiques:
See sidebar p. 195.

ENTERTAINMENT

Cultural life in Rome has become increasingly active and varied. The Parco della Musica represents an invaluable performance space; the Casa del Jazz is a focal point for jazz enthusiasts; and the Casa del Cinema is a must for film buffs. Temporary venues host world-class exhibitions and MAXXI is just one of many contemporary art spaces now scattered around the city.

Rome now also hosts a number of culture festivals. Rome's very popular film festival, **Rome Film Festival** (*www.romacinemafest .it*), inaugurated in 2006, is held in October at the Parco della Musica. **Estate Romana** (*estateromana. comune.roma.it*) runs from June through September at venues throughout the city with an array of outdoor cinema, theater, opera, music, and dance performances. **Romaeuropa Festival** (*romaeuropa.net*), a fall international cultural event, features a program of dance, theater, and music. **Più Libri Più Liberi** (*plpl.it*), Fiera Nazionale della Piccola e Media Editoria, with a full cultural program, initiatives to promote reading, music, and live performances. It is held in the new quartiere EUR conference center, south of the capital. The building is famous for a particular architectural element, La Nuvola, designed by the archistar Massimiliano Fuksas.

Entertainment listings are available at *www.turismoroma.it* and at *www.romeguide.it*. Phone 060608, which also has a booking service. **In Rome Now** (*www. inromenow.com*), **Angloinfo** (*rome. angloinfo.com*), and **Wanted in Rome** (available at newsstands and online at *www.wantedinrome.com*) all provide weekly information on English language theater and cinema as well as other cultural events. For films in English (and Italian) see also the website **Rome Review** (*www.romereview.com*). The Thursday edition of the Italian daily *La Repubblica* carries the *TrovaRoma* insert with information on cultural events for the following week.

Bookings for many cultural

events can be made through the **Vivaticket** (*www.vivaticket.it*) or **Ticket one** (tel. 892101, *www.ticketone.it*) agency's call center or online. Other centrally located ticket offices are **Orbis** (*Piazza dell'Esquilino 37, tel 06 482 7403*), which also sells tickets for sports events), and **Feltrinelli** (*Largo di Torre Argentina 5a, tel 199 151 173*). A commission is charged.

Cinema

Most films shown in Italy are dubbed into Italian. But several centrally located cinemas regularly screen films in English, while others show films in original language occasionally (usually one day a week). For a complete list of cinemas showing original language films see **Rome Review** (*www. romereview.com*).

The following cinemas regularly screen films in English:

Casa del Cinema, Largo Marcello Mastroianni (Villa Borghese, Via Veneto), tel 06 423601, www.casadelcinema.it. Screenings in Italian and original language. Cine Caffè, in the Villa Borghese park, serves drinks and light meals.
Cinema Farnese, Campo de' Fiori 56, tel. 06 686 4395. Foreign language films in the original language on Mondays and Thursdays.
Greenwich, Via G. Bodoni 59 (Testaccio), tel 06 574 5825.
Lux, Via Massaciuccoli 31.
Multisala Barberini, Piazza Barberini 24/25/26 (Spagna), tel 06 4201 0392.
Nuovo Olimpia, Via in Lucina 16 (Spagna), tel 06 8880 1283.
Quattro Fontane, Via Quattro Fontane 23 (Spagna), tel 06 8880 1283.

Exhibition & Art Galleries

Scuderie del Quirinale (*Via XXIV Maggio 16, tel 06 3996 7500, www. scuderiequirinale.it*), **Palazzo delle Esposizioni** (*Via Nazionale 194, tel 06 696271, www.palazzo esposizioni.it*), and the **Complesso dello Vittoriano** (*Via di San Pietro, Carcere, www.ilvittoriano.com*) all host temporary art exhibitions of international importance.
MACRO (*Via Nizza 138, tel 06 696271, www.museomacro.org*), **Mattatoio di Roma** (*Piazza Orazio Giustiniani 4, tel 06 3996 7500, www.mattatoioroma.it*), and **MAXXI** (*Via Guido Reni 4, tel 06 320 1954, www.maxxi.art*) are all dedicated to contemporary art.

Nightlife

Rome may not be the hippest of capitals, but it is possible to party all night if you know where to go. Discos and clubs start around midnight and go to the early hours of the morning. Wine bars tend to close around 1 a.m. In summer, clubs usually close or transfer to outside areas in Rome or to the nearby beaches of Ostia or Fregene. The greatest concentration of nightclubs and *risto-bars* (places where you can eat, drink, and dance) are in the Testaccio (Via di Monte Testaccio) and Ostiense (Via G. Libetta) districts. Cocktail and wine bars are mainly to be found in Trastevere and around Piazza Navona, the Pantheon, and Campo de' Fiori.

Clubbing

Alibi, Via Monte Testaccio 40 (Testaccio), tel 320 3541185. One of Rome's earliest gay bars/disco, and also one of its most popular regardless of sexual preference. There are several others in the vicinity.

Art Café, Viale Galoppatoio 33, Villa Borghese (Spagna), tel 340 620 7432, www.art-cafe.it. Located in the subterranean Villa Borghese parking structure (finding the entrance can be tricky). Take the tunnel at the Piazza di Spagna metro stop. The place is alive with movement: spacious dance floors surrounded by private lounges.

Goa, Via G. Libetta 13 (Ostiense), tel 06 574 8277, goaclub. com. The music at this chic, one-room club tends to be avant-garde, with some of the best DJs in town.

Neo Club, Via Argonauti 18 (Ostiense), tel 338 949 2526, www. piovra.it. Cocktail bar, disco-bar, DJ set, and sometimes also live music.

Shari Vari, Via De' Nari 14 (Pantheon), tel. 06 68806936. The place for Rome's chic young set. Offers predinner drinks, dinner, and very popular after-dinner cocktail and music of the "chill-out" variety, jazz, house, and disco.

Bars

Bars range from the classic *enoteca,* serving wine by the glass or bottle, to cool cocktail venues open until late and often serving light meals. In summer, many spill onto the street, particularly in and around Campo de' Fiori which, a fruit-and-vegetable market during the day, becomes a lively bar and meeting spot at night.

Bars/Cocktail Bars/Gay Bars

Charity Café, Via Painsperna 68 (Monti), tel 06 4782 5881, www.charitycafe.it. Small attractive club with a cocktail/wine bar, and buffet. Thursday to Sunday live jazz and blues.

Coming Out, Via di San Giovanni in Laterano 8 (Colosseum), tel 06 009871, www. comingout.it. One of the oldest of a cluster of bars and restaurants with

outside seating behind the Colosseum that in the evenings attracts a gay crowd.

Anfiteatro My Bar, tel 06 700 4425. Located next door, gets mostly tourists during the day but a largely gay clientele in the evening. Together they help organize Gay Street Roma events on summer nights when the street is closed to traffic.

Freni e Frizoni, Via del Politeama 4/6 (Trastevere), 06 4549 7499, www.freniefrizioni.com. A former car workshop, this fun place is perfect for brunch-lunch, cocktails, and nightcaps.

Mons, Via della Fossa 16 (Navona), tel 06 689 3426, www. monscrew.com. This chaotic, packed cocktail bar is not the place for shrinking violets: You may be pulled into one of the semi-impromptu evening floor shows that sometimes take place. The decorations—wall paintings, and statuettes—must be seen to be believed, especially the gorgeous bathroom.

Salotto 42, Piazza di Pietra 42, tel 06 678 5804. Trendy bar located in front of the Tempio di Adriano. Open from morning until 2 a.m. A great place to savor a coffee or an aperitif.

Stravinskij Bar, Hotel De Russie, Via del Babuino 9 (Spagna). One of the city's best for classy cocktails and the classical Italian *aperitivo.*

Bars/Wine Bars

Buccone, Via di Ripetta 19 (Spagna), tel 06 361 2154. Established in 1870, this traditional wine bar showcases an excellent selection of wines. Also offers lunch and dinner. Closed Sun.

Costantini, Piazza Cavour 16 (Prati), tel 06 320 3575, enotecacostantinipiero.it. Well-known cellar of Rome with a vast selection of wines. Closed Sun.

Enoteca Ferrara, Piazza Trilussa 41 (Trastevere), tel 06 5833 3920. Wine tasting (more than 600 varieties of wine are available)

begins at 6 p.m. every day—snacks are available.

Il Goccetto, Via dei Banchi Vecchi 14 (Campo de' Fiori). This cozy wine cellar specializes in wines from small Italian vineyards. The English-speaking owner can guide you in your choice. Closed Sun.

L'Angolo Divino, Via dei Balestrari 12/14 (Campo de' Fiori), tel 06 686 4413. Originally a wine shop, now transformed into a well-stocked wine bar. Small and friendly meeting place for wine buffs. Closed Sun. & Mon. L.

Open Baladin, Via degli Specchi 6 (Campo de' Fiori), tel 06 683 8989, www.openbaladinroma.it. If beer is your passion don't miss this retro bar that serves a vast number of artisan beers; it also serves light meals.

Trimani Wine Bar, Via Cernaia 37b (Termini Station), tel 06 446 9630, www.trimani.com. This elegant wine bar is an excellent place for enjoying good wine and food in a casual, fun atmosphere. Closed Sun.

Vinoteca Novecento, Piazza della Copelle 47 (Pantheon), tel 06 683 3078. Small, cozy wine bar with outdoor seating and romantic lighting. Head inside for salami and cheese tastings. Closed Mon.–Wed. L.

Opera, Music, & Dance

As well as the venues listed below, look for posters or check *www.in romenow.com* for details of free classical concerts held in historic churches (see sidebar p. 149).

Auditorium Conciliazione, Via della Conciliazione 4 (Vatican), tel 06 68439200, www.auditoriumconciliazione.it. Programs feature classical and contemporary music.

Auditorium Parco della Musica, Viale Pietro de Coubertin 15/30, tel 06 8024 1281, www .auditorium.com. This complex includes three concert halls offering a wide-ranging program of classical, jazz, and contemporary music, dance, an outdoor amphitheater, restaurants, art gallery, bookstore, and an archaeological area and museum. Home to the Santa Cecilia orchestra, the Parco della Musica offers a rich program of classical music and much more.

Il Tempietto, www.tempietto .it. This classical music association holds concerts throughout the winter at Sala Baldini (Piazza di Campitelli 9) and Villa Torlonia (Via Nomentana 7). In summer, it stages nightly outdoor concerts, each in the atmospheric Teatro di Marcello (Via Luigi Petroselli 8) and at Villa Torlonia.

Oratorio del Gonfalone, Via del Gonfalone 32/a (Campo de' Fiori), tel 06 6875952, www. oratoriogonfalone.eu. This glorious 16th-century setting is perfect for programs of chamber and choral music, with emphasis on the baroque.

Teatro dell'Opera, Piazza B. Gigli 8, tel. 06 4816 0255 or 06 4817 003, www.operaroma.it. The home of Rome's Opera and Ballet Company, this theater is host to classical productions as well as some more contemporary ones. In summer, opera and ballet are performed outdoors in the impressive surroundings of the Terme di Caracalla.

Teatro Nazionale, Via del Viminale 51 (Nazionale), tel 06 4816 0255, www.operaroma.it. A prime venue for ballet company performances and other productions of the Teatro dell'Opera.

Teatro Olimpico, Piazza Gentile da Fabriano 17, tel 06 326 5991, www.teatroolimpico.it. Home of the Accademia Filarmonica Romana, the program includes music, theater, and dance, with many visiting international artists.

Contemporary Live Music

Rome has a dynamic live-music scene, with a number of venues

offering jazz, soul, rock, and ethnic music. The Auditorium Parco della Musica, the soccer stadium, the Capannelle race track on Via Appia Nuova and other unusual locations are often settings for concerts and festivals, particularly in summer.

The jazz scene in Rome is one of the most active in Europe, with regular performances at the following venues:

AlexanderPlatz, Via Ostia 9, tel 06 8377 5604, alexander-platzjazzclub.com. Plastered with photos and signatures of visiting performers, AlexanderPlatz is one of Italy's most important and well-known jazz clubs. Reservations advised. In summer, the club moves to the outdoor setting of Villa Celimontana, where one can also enjoy light meals and/or a drink.

Arena Monk Club, Via Giuseppe Mirri 35, tel. 06 6485 0987, www.monkroma.it. Interesting creative center which has recently risen from the ashes of the Palma Club. The program includes excellent independent music, art exhibitions, dance, theater, literature, and food experience.

BeBop Jazz Club, Via Giuseppe Giulietti 14 (Testaccio), tel 06 575 5582, new.bebopjazzclub.net. BeBop is the smallest jazz venue in Rome, but it has its own special appeal, including the projection of black-and-white video footage of jazz masters such as Wes Montgomery and John Coltrane during performance breaks.

Big Mama, Vicolo San Francesco a Ripa 18 (Trastevere), tel. 06 581 2551, www.bigmama.it. Taking up the tradition from what was one of the most important creative centers in the capital, Folk Studio, Big Mama has become the home of blues in Rome. Legends from the Mississippi Delta like Louisiana Red and great Italian guitarists like Roberto Ciotti have performed here. We should not

forget, among the other resident bands, the Riding Sixties, a tribute band playing classics of 1960s Italian Beat and British rock music.

Casa del Jazz, Viale di Porta Ardeatina 55, tel 06 80241 281, www .casajazz.it. Villa Osio and its large park are the site of this center hosting top names in jazz. Facilities include a multimedia library, a book- and record store, bar, and restaurant.

Gregory's Jazz Club, Via Gregoriana 54d (Via Veneto), tel 06 678 6386, www.gregorysjazz .com. A meeting place for Rome's musicians, Gregory's is an Irish pub with a jazz club on the second floor. Downstairs, Guinness is served, along with an astonishing selection of malt whiskeys, and a kitchen serving Irish cuisine.

Soccer

See sidebar p. 219.

Theater

Nearly all theater companies based in Rome perform only in Italian, unless specifically noted.

Teatro di Roma, Largo di Torre Argentina 52 , 06 684000311 /14, www.teatrodiroma.net. This is the new name of the Teatro Stabile since it moved to its historic site of the **Teatro Argentina** in 1972. The repertory presented in this restored eighteenth-century theater includes the Italian classics, international contemporary works, dance, and festivals. The director, Franco Enriquez, has begun collaboration with two other creative centers in the city: the **Teatro India** (*Lungotevere Vittorio Gassman 1, zona Marconi, tel. 06 87752210*) and the **Teatro Torlonia** (*Via Lazzaro Spallanzani 1A, Villa Torlonia*).

Sistina, Via Sistina 129, tel 06 420 0711, www.ilsistina.it. A large theater specializing in theatrical and musical productions.

World-class theater, often in English, sometimes is programmed by the festivals listed above.

LANGUAGE GUIDE

Yes *Si*
No *No*
Excuse me (in a crowd or asking for permission) *Permesso*
Excuse me (asking for attention) *Mi scusi*
Hello (before lunch) *Buon giorno*, (after lunch) *Buona sera*
Hi or Bye *Ciao*
Please *Per favore*
Thank you *Grazie*
You're welcome *Prego*
Have a good day! *Buona giornata!*
OK *Va bene*
Goodbye *Arrivederci*
Good night *Buona notte*
Sorry *Mi dispiace*
here *qui*
there *lì*
today *oggi*
yesterday *ieri*
tomorrow *domani*
now *adesso/ora*
later *più tardi/dopo*
right away *subito*
this morning *stamattina*
this afternoon *questo pomeriggio*
this evening *stasera*
open *aperto*
closed *chiuso*
Do you have? *Avrebbe?*
Do you speak English? *Parla inglese?*
I'm American (man) *Sono americano*, (woman) *Sono americana*
I don't understand *Non capisco*
Please speak more slowly *Potrebbe parlare più lentamente*
Where is...? *Dov'è...?*
I don't know *Non so*
No problem *Niente*
That's it *Ecco*
Here/there it is (masculine) *Eccolo*, (feminine) *Eccola*
What is your name? *Come si chiama?*
My name is... *Mi chiamo...*
Let's go *Andiamo*
At what time? *A che ora?*
When? *Quando?*
What time is it? *Che ora è?*
Can you help me? *Mi può aiutare?*
I'd like... *Vorrei...*
How much is it? *Quanto costa?*

MENU READER

breakfast *la (prima) colazione*
lunch *il pranzo*
dinner *la cena*
appetizer *l'antipasto*
first course *il primo*
main course *il secondo*
vegetable, side dish *il contorno*
dessert *il dessert*
wine list *la carta dei vini*
the bill *il conto*
I'd like to order *Vorrei ordinare*
Is service included? *Il servizio è incluso?*

Pasta sauces
See Food, p. 36

Meat
l'abbacchio lamb
l'anatra duck
la bistecca beefsteak
ben cotta well-done
non troppo cotta medium
al sangue very rare
il filetto filet steak
il carpaccio finely sliced raw cured beef
il cinghiale wild boar
il coniglio rabbit
il fegato liver
le lumache snails
il maiale pork
il manzo beef
misto di carne mixed grill
il pollo chicken
le polpette meatballs
la porchetta cold roast pork with herbs
il prosciutto ham, *crudo* raw, *cotto* cooked
i rognoni kidneys
la salsiccia fresh, spicy (usually pork) sausage
saltimbocca alla romana veal and ham in a wine and sage sauce
straccetti pan-fried strips of beef or veal
lo stufato stew or casserole
il tacchino turkey
la trippa tripe
il vitello veal

Fish
L'alici/acciughe anchovies
l'aragosta/astice lobster
il calamaro squid
le cozze mussels
i gamberi prawns
i gamberetti shrimp
il granchio crab
le ostriche oysters
il polipo octopus
il salmone salmon
le sarde sardines
la sogliola sole
la spigola bass
il tonno tuna
la trota trout

Vegetables
l'aglio garlic
gli asparagi asparagus
il carciofo artichoke
la carota carrot
il cavolfiore cauliflower
la cipolla onion
i fagioli dried beans, usually haricot or borlotti
i fagiolini fresh green beans
i funghi (porcini) mushrooms
l'insalata mista/verde mixed/green salad
le melanzane eggplant
le patate potatoes
le patate fritte french fries
le patatine potato chips
il peperone bell pepper
i piselli peas
i pomodori tomatoes
il radicchio bitter reddish lettuce
il riso rice
gli spinaci spinach
il tartufo truffle
le zucchine zucchini

Fruit
l'albicocca apricot
l'ananas pineapple
l'arancia orange
le ciliegie cherries
le fragole strawberries
la mela apple
la pera pear
la pesca peach
la pescanoce nectarine
il pompelmo grapefruit
l'uva grapes

INDEX

ILLUSTRATIONS CREDITS

All photographs by Tino Soriano unless otherwise noted:

21, H. M. Herget/National Geographic Stock; 22, Rakesh Chandode/National Geographic My Shot; 25, Archive/AFP/Getty Images; 52, Fernando G. Baptista/National Geographic Stock; 107, Reproduced with the permission of Ministero per i Beni e le Attività Culturali/Alinari Archives/Alinari via Getty Images; 120, Rene Mattes/Hemis/Corbis; 122, Massimo Listri/Corbis; 132, Suchart Boonyavech/Shutterstock.com; 138, AlexAnton/Shutterstock.com; 156, De Agostini/Getty Images; 161, elen_studio/Shutterstock.com; 164, Janis Lacis/Shutterstock; 169, Dan Kitwood/Getty Images; 175, Franco S. Origlia/Getty Images; 192, Andreas Solaro/AFP/Getty Images; 209, Tiziana Fabi/AFP/Getty Images; 212, Giorgio Cosulich/Getty Images; 220, ValerioMei/Shutterstock.com; 225, PerseoMedusa/Shutterstock; 231, Gianluca Figliola Fantini/Shutterstock.